THE SPIRITUAL TOURIST

THE SPIRITUAL TOURIST

A PERSONAL ODYSSEY THROUGH THE OUTER REACHES OF BELIEF

MICK BROWN

BLOOMSBURY

ACKNOWLEDGEMENTS

Firstly, I owe thanks to all those who agreed to be interviewed, and who helped, sometimes unknowingly, in the course of the numerous journeys undertaken to write this book.

I am particularly indebted to the following, for their help, encouragement and friendship: Joan Anderson, Rosie Boycott, Martin Buckley, Tony Budell, Mike Bygrave, Robert Chalmers, Will Ellsworth-Jones, Mary Finnegan, Simon Freeman, Stephen Harris, Peter Heehs, Nigel Horne, Peter Kedge, Peggy Mason, Patricia Pitchon, Sarah Stewart-Smith, Claire Scobie, Jaslie and Jetty Singh, Andrew Stalbow, Alex Swindell, Steve Turner and Michael Watts. A large, cold beer to Peter Bialobrzeski for being such a good friend on the road in India.

Lillian Storey of the Theosophical Society in London kindly smoothed my path to the TS headquarters in Madras, and I am grateful to Leslie Price, founder of the Theosophical History Society in London, and Jean Overton-Fuller for their invaluable advice, and correction, on the subject of Madame Blavatsky. Stephen Batchelor's book, *The Awakening of the West*, was particularly helpful in tracing the introduction of Tibetan Buddhist teachings to the West.

I am deeply indebted to Emma Soames, the editor of the *Telegraph* magazine, for all her support, to my agent Caroline Dawnay, and to Mary Tomlinson for her patient and meticulous copy-editing. I owe special thanks to my editor Liz Calder, and to Ruth Logan, for their belief and encouragement.

Finally, I owe everything to my wife Patricia, and my children Celeste, Dominic and Clementine.

Published by Bloomsbury Publishing, New York and London.

A CIP catalogue record for this book is available from the Library of Congress

ISBN 1-58234-001-3

First published in Great Britain 1998 by Bloomsbury Publishing Plc.

First U.S. Edition
10 9 8 7 6 5 4 3 2 1

Typeset by Hewer Text Ltd, Edinburgh, Scotland
Printed in the United States of America

To Patricia and Celeste, Dominic and Clementine

'In wise love each divines the high secret self of the other, and, refusing to believe in mere daily self, creates a mirror where the lover or the beloved sees an image to copy in daily life.'

W.B. Yeats

CONTENTS

INTRODUCTION

Matthew Fox the theologian once observed that the generation that came of age in the Sixties is not interested in religion, but in spirituality. The agenda of the third millennium, as Fox has it, is to 'strip down religions to their spiritual experience', developing 'worship that awakens people instead of bores them; that empowers them; that brings out the gifts of the community'.

Spirituality. It has become a kind of buzz-word of the age. Musicians, writers, painters, even fashion designers, talk of evoking 'spiritual' qualities in their work. 'I'm trying to cultivate my spiritual side,' people say; or, 'I'm learning to connect with my spirituality.' You hear that a lot. Spirituality has become an all-purpose word, but one that describes what is felt to be missing rather than specifying what it is hoped will be found. The spiritual search, whatever that may mean – and it means myriad things to different people – has become a dominant feature of late twentieth-century life: a symptom of collective uncertainty, in an age when there are no longer jobs for life and the traditional institutions of church, family and community appear to be breaking down. It is a symptom of a disenchantment with the values of materialism, and a weariness of science, which has stripped all mystery out of existence, reducing man, as the biologist and evangelical atheist Richard Dawkins has it in *The Selfish Gene*, to nothing more than 'a survival machine', a robot blindly programmed to preserve the selfish molecule in his genes. As Peggy Lee sang, Is that all there is? There is a yearning for a sense of the sacred, for what the Benedictine monk Bede Griffith described as 'a myth that will give meaning to our lives now that the myth of Western science has betrayed us'.

Within Christianity, it has manifested in the rise of fundamentalism, whose rigid architecture of doctrine is clung to like a life-raft in a sea of moral uncertainty, and in the rise of the evangelical movement, with its claims for a direct experience of God through charismatic gifts.

It is manifest in the whole gaudy panoply of the New Age movement; in the fads of rolfing, rebirthing, past-life regression, channelling and angelology, and, at its furthest margins, the extremist cults and instant religions – the Solar Temple, the Aum movement of Japan, the Heaven's Gate cult of California, 'flickering and fading like off-peak commercials', as the novelist J.G. Ballard puts it. It is evident too in the flowering in the West over the past thirty years of Eastern philosophies; in the rising interest in Buddhism, Sufi-ism, the way of the Tao, the teachings of yogis and masters – even in such things as yoga classes in parish church halls and transcendental meditation courses for harassed business executives.

All of these things are a response to the spiritual vacuum at the heart of modern life, a symptom of the hunger to invest meaning in our lives, a yearning for mystery and transcendence.

The extraordinarily feverish public outpouring of emotion over the death of Diana, Princess of Wales in 1997, and her subsequent sanctification as a kind of patron saint of charity and compassion, was a potent symbol of this. Diana's status as the most famous woman in the world – a chimeric creation of global telecommunications – lent her a unique and curious glow of familiarity. In life, people had discussed her marriage, her divorce, her love affairs, her eating problems, her acts of charity, as if she was a member of their own family. And they mourned her death accordingly. She was the patron saint of every divorcee, every single mother, every bulimia sufferer, every compulsive shopper and health-club addict. But more than that, there was a sense in which her death was a catalyst for some deeper and unspecified collective sorrow, and the mourning a cathartic lamentation for the loss of innocence and the very pain of existence. This had everything and nothing to do with her status as a media icon. It was her unique celebrity, compounded of position and wealth, which made Diana a focus for attention in life, but it was the myth of her goodness and compassion that made her, in death, the object of such a peculiarly powerful and all–encompassing veneration. This myth of Diana gave people a glimpse of their higher selves, expressed in an outpouring of grief of religious intensity.

For as long as I can remember I wanted to be a journalist. To explain the world to myself, and to try to explain it to others. A hopeless ambition, but an interesting life. I sit down with people; I ask them questions; they tell me things. I am often enlightened by these conversations; sometimes uplifted, sometimes confused, but almost never bored. In my experience, people talking about themselves are seldom boring.

The nice thing about this transaction is that I seldom have to talk about myself. Sometimes, in conversation with a novelist, an actor, a musician, a philosopher, I feel the inclination to interrupt, to say, Hey! let me tell you about me! But I never do, and they usually don't ask. Which is just as well, for I could answer few of the questions I ask them. How do you do what you do? Why? What brings you fulfilment, what brings you pain? Are you happy? The more I ask these questions of myself, the more illusory and provisional my self seems – an aggregate of conditioned responses, received or manufactured opinions, memories, experiences, quirks, foibles, the opinions – good, bad and indifferent – of others; sometimes in command of my fate, sometimes at the mercy of it.

Sometimes, I have this feeling of keeping fate at bay. I give money to buskers, pan-handlers, scabbed drunks at railway stations, as if buying credit against the whims of fate. I have never received any evidence to suggest that this ploy is working, no stroke of good fortune clicking up black on the balance sheet of my life. But then again, who knows how much worse my life might have been without the payment of the penance?

'The secret of happiness,' Cyril Connolly wrote, 'is the avoidance of *Angst*. It is a mistake to consider happiness a positive state. By removing *Angst*, the condition of all unhappiness, we are then prepared to receive such blessings as may come our way.'

Happiness cannot be pursued. You do not find happiness; happiness finds you. It is not an end in itself, but a by-product of other activities, often arriving when it is least expected. You can be sitting in the best restaurant, wearing the finest clothes, surrounded by the most dazzling company, safe in the knowledge all your bills are paid, and you may still not be happy. And you can be standing at the kitchen sink, hands in washing-up water, with nowhere to go, and suddenly realise that you feel as happy as you've ever felt in your life. What Connolly calls *Angst* are the small, incremental uncertainties about our place in the scheme of things, the nagging sense that life could somehow be better, if only, if only ... what? It is the restlessness of self. And yet the very word – happiness – suggests something ephemeral, caught on the wing, no sooner ensnared than it slips from our grasp. To try to make happiness our property, to own it, is to lose it.

So what, then, is permanent?

I am at a funeral of a good man, a Roman Catholic, loved by his family and friends, who has lived a life of demonstrable kindness and virtue, who has lived by the tenets of his faith. Amid the displays of grief around me, one person alone is not crying. It is the man's wife, whose face is graced with a look of perfect serenity, of acceptance of the fact of her husband's death, and of a certainty that he has taken his place in heaven and that, in the fullness of time, she will be reunited with him there. Blessed assurance. I am in awe of her trust in the beneficence of God, in awe of her faith. How do you explain such faith; how do you find it?

I have received no epiphany to give me faith. I know of people who have heard the voice of God, or been brushed by the wings of angels. I am not among them. But I have come to believe that the world is more of spirit than of matter: that what is unseen is more important than what is seen. The things we most value are felt with the heart rather than viewed with the naked eye.

Transcendence is a natural human condition which we may all experience from time to time. A rhapsodic piece of music, a beautiful painting, a glorious sunset or some peculiar communion with nature – all may offer us moments of a particular clarity, in which our vision seems to grow larger, and we are no longer looking at the world through the muddy glass of our preconceptions but seeing it as it truly *is*; where we become momentarily aware of some pattern or order greater than ourselves, and of which we are an intrinsic part.

These moments cannot be legislated for: I am sitting in the domestic terminal of Chicago airport at eleven at night, waiting for a delayed connection to carry me to New Orleans. Suddenly, inexplicably, it is as if the weary chatter of my thoughts has subsided into a quiet still centre. A feeling of immeasurable peace descends, the certainty that everything is as it should be, that the world is infinite in its wonder, absolute in its harmony, and that I am cradled safely in its embrace.

I felt – and I hesitate to put it thus, but no other words seem adequate – as if God was within me. The porter, wheeling a trolley laden with baggage across the empty concourse who paused, caught my absent-minded grin and threw it back to me – God was in him too. And in the trolley, the luggage, the hum of the neon lights, the faint whisper of the public-address system, and the aircraft that carried me safely to New Orleans.

The great spiritual guide books suggest that, once embarked on the path, the seeker should never turn back – that it may be actively perilous to do so. Perhaps this means that once you have started asking certain questions it is impossible to stop asking them. That once you change, and begin to see the world in a certain way, it is impossible to go back to seeing it how you used to. I wish to know myself better, to live in more harmony with the people, the world, around me. I wish to rid myself of *Angst*. Perhaps I wish for some sort of revelation.

Change can be a daunting proposition. The familiarity of our weaknesses and shortcomings – the failings which in our moments of greatest self-delusion we may regard as charming idiosyncrasies – just *me* – can seem more comfortable than the uncertainties of change. But I wanted to know. What did I want to know? I wanted to know everything.

I wanted an adventure of the spirit.

1

GOOD EVENING, MR CREME

I suppose it was the autumn of 1984 when I got the call from Van asking whether I wanted to meet a man who claimed to know the whereabouts of Christ. I had known Van for only a few months, although for years I had admired his work from a distance. His records were as much a part of my life as they obviously were of his. And it was a measure of their candour, their immediacy and their beauty that I felt I knew him well even before meeting him.

Van had gone through his confessional period: excavating his childhood, his love affairs, the broken marriage, and now was making records about meditation, mysticism, the spiritual search. Nobody else was making records about that, and it seemed a further mark of his uniqueness and his honesty as an artist. I had come to interview him about a new recording, and the meeting started awkwardly – Van's reputation for being an obdurate interviewee, for not suffering fools, was legendary – but by the end of it we were deep in conversation, about the works of Rudolf Steiner, Kerouac, the Eastern mystics, the meaning of life.

And so we became acquainted – the occasional lunch, friendly telephone calls. Sometimes the telephone would ring in the middle of the night – it might be 2 or 3 a.m., and it would be Van, wanting to talk about a particular esoteric book he was reading, or a thought that had just occurred to him. There was never the slightest tone of apology in his voice about the lateness of the hour. I think he simply assumed that everyone kept the same hours he did. Sometimes, I would arrive on the doorstep of his small mews house as arranged, and ring the bell. There was always a lengthy wait, and then he would appear at the door, coat already buttoned, scarf around his neck, and step quickly outside, shutting the door firmly behind him, obviously reluctant to let me inside, as if he had something to hide.

One day when I rang the doorbell, he seemed to forget himself.

To my surprise, rather than stepping outside and shutting the door behind him, he held it open, stood to one side and ushered me in. The door led straight into a small sitting room, sparsely furnished with a battered sofa, a table and two wooden chairs. The shelves were groaning with records and books. He offered me coffee. I reached in the fridge. It was empty, but for a single carton of milk, which had long since curdled to cream, days, possibly weeks, past its sell-by date. The barely furnished room, the empty refrigerator lent a poignancy to those 2 a.m. calls; I could see him now, unable to sleep, bent over his books, the Dylan records, the acoustic guitar.

Music, Van would always say, was just a job of work. He was interested in developing himself. I was interested in developing myself too, but I wasn't sure how to go about it. And Van seemed to have no clearer idea. Our conversations followed a meandering path around the subject of philosophy, the existence of God, the various teachings of this guru, that swami. Van seemed to have read everything, and he had not yet made the record on which he would make his declaration: no guru, no method, no teacher. Then one day he phoned and invited me to a meeting; there was a man, he said, who knew the whereabouts of Christ.

We drove to a Quaker meeting house on the Euston Road. It was as austere and gloomy as a Victorian Sunday school. Perhaps a hundred people had crammed into a back room, seated on metal chairs – a curious assortment: people one would have taken for students or social workers; middle-aged women buttoned up in overcoats; a handful of elderly men who seemed to have strayed in to the meeting in search of a place to shelter from the autumnal drizzle outside. A solitary Asian man, dressed improbably in a jellaba and overcoat, with a woollen hat pulled down to his eyes, sat in the front row.

A hush descended as a man came to the stage. He was small and wiry, perhaps sixty years of age, dressed in a white rollneck pullover. His chubby face was framed by an aureole of snow-white hair, giving him the mischievous appearance of a battered cherub.

This was my first sight of Benjamin Creme.

He paused, smiled and waited for silence. Then he told his story.

We are entering the age of Aquarius, and of a new spiritual teacher, who will usher in an era of world harmony and peace, said Mr Creme. For millennia, man's development has been watched over by a hierarchy of spiritual masters, human beings who have transcended the cycle of life, death and rebirth, and who have guided the evolution of man's consciousness, releasing ideas sequentially into the world to bring about advances in science, politics, medicine. Every great religion anticipates the coming of a great redeemer. Christians await the return of Christ; Muslims await the Mahdi; Jews, the Messiah; and Hindus Krishna. But now, said Mr Creme, this redeemer is among us, and his name is Lord Maitreya, holder of the highest office in the Spiritual Hierarchy, the office of the Cosmic Christ.

Two thousand years ago, Maitreya manifested himself on earth through his disciple Jesus. Since then he has been living in a remote community in the Himalayas. But in 1977, Maitreya decided that he could no longer stand aside and watch wars and destruction, 'the massacre of the innocents' taking place among mankind. Thus, on 8 July 1977, Lord Maitreya came down from his mountain retreat, and on 19 July he boarded a Jumbo jet in Pakistan and flew to Heathrow airport.

Benjamin Creme paused to sip from a glass containing some amber-coloured liquid. I looked around me. Faces were staring earnestly at him, as if none of this were the least bit unusual. I glanced at Van. His face was an impassive mask. It was impossible to know if he thought all of this as fanciful and absurd as I did. Mr Creme placed his glass on the table and continued. Since arriving from Pakistan, Maitreya had been living and working in the Asian community in the East End of London, awaiting the appropriate moment to reveal himself. This moment – 'the day of declaration' – would soon be upon us. On this day of reckoning, Maitreya would appear on television across the world, and everyone would hear his voice, speaking telepathically in their own language.

Maitreya, he went on, has come to teach humanity the art of self-realisation – a three-fold path, consisting of honesty of mind, sincerity of spirit and detachment. He brings a message of peace and of sharing; a new world order based on co-operation and man's awakening to his own potential. 'We shall shortly find,' said Mr Creme, 'that each one of us is divine.'

All of this struck me as somewhat fantastic; but I found myself warming to Mr Creme enormously. He was a wonderful speaker, addressing the audience in a relaxed, affable Scottish lilt, peppering his monologue with jokes and the occasional self-deprecating aside.

He spoke of all this – of Maitreya and hierarchies and the day of declaration – as if it was the most natural thing in the world; extraordinary, certainly; of the utmost importance, no doubt. But implausible? Ludicrous? Fanciful and far-fetched? Not in the least. It was clear that Mr Creme believed every word that he was saying. And at that moment, my curiosity was hooked.

At the end of the evening, Mr Creme announced that he would now be 'overshadowed' by the spirit of Maitreya. 'You may feel or see something unusual,' he warned in a sonorous voice. 'If you do, don't be alarmed.'

The lights dimmed. Mr Creme settled into a position of meditation and appeared to go into a trance. An unnatural hush fell on the room. For perhaps five minutes we sat in the half-darkness, Mr Creme slowly turning his head from side to side, to bring everyone in the room under his gaze, as if he was strafing them with some sort of cosmic energy. Shifting in my seat in the stifling heat of the room, I could feel only discomfort.

Mr Creme brought the meeting to a close, and the audience shuffled into the night.

'Did you see anything? Feel anything?' said Van as we drove away. 'It's all a load of baloney, isn't it?'

Van's response to such things often seemed to fall into a pattern of interest followed by an equally intense suspicion which could border on hostility. The encounter with the Sri Lankan swami, which occurred shortly after we had attended Mr Creme's meeting, was another case in point.

In his native Sri Lanka the Swami was regarded as divine, and I had heard much of his miraculous powers. Like Sai Baba, the famous saint of Puttaparthi in India, the Swami was said to produce *vibhuti*, or holy ash, at will from thin air; to conjure rings and medallions as keepsakes for his devotees.

He was on a tour of ashrams, temples and the homes of devotees around Britain. We were given an address of a private house in a bleak suburb of North London, and arrived to find it crowded with people, overflowing from the lounge, sitting in the hall and up the stairs. A G-plan dais had been erected in the front room, and women moved among the throng, offering delicacies from plastic airline trays. Shortly before midnight, a whisper passed among the crowd: the Swami was arriving. A white car pulled up on the darkened street outside. Devotees swarmed on to the front lawn, banging finger-bells and cymbals and throwing rose petals at the Swami's feet as he walked up the garden path.

The Swami was a young man, dressed in saffron robes, two thick wodges of hair rising from his head like exclamation marks. Inside, songs were sung, as the Swami's feet were washed in rose water. He then offered a short discourse on 'right livelihood'. Afterwards, I was shown upstairs, to where the Swami was resting in a bedroom before continuing on his journey. Van sat on the stairs, awaiting his turn. The meeting was short, and when the Swami signalled that it was over I reached out my hand to shake his. Firmly, he took hold of my wrist, and turned my palm upwards. His own hand hovered above it. A quantity of *vibhuti* suddenly poured from his fingertips on to my outstretched palm. It did not come, so far as I could tell, from his sleeve, from under his fingernails, from pouches secreted between his fingers (all options which were later suggested to me), or, come to that, from anywhere else. It appeared to come from nowhere.

I backed out of the room, and Van was ushered in. I still had the *vibhuti* clasped in my hand. Somebody said, 'Eat it!' The minutes ticked past as I waited for Van. His audience seemed to be taking much longer. Eventually, he emerged from the bedroom. He looked pale and flustered, as if he had been shown his own worst nature. His palm was clenched tight. What is it? I asked. He pushed past me without a word.

We drove home through the dark London streets in silence, Van brooding beside me.

'What a fookin' joker,' he said at last. It was all he said of it then, and he never mentioned it again.

It was some months since I had first encountered Benjamin Creme, but the meeting continued to prey on my mind. I was working on a Sunday newspaper at the time, and one evening over a drink I mentioned Mr Creme and his outlandish claims to my news editor. He didn't believe it for one second, of course. And I could hardly blame him. After all, neither did I. But then again, he said, supposing it was true? Suppose Christ the Redeemer was living in the East End of London, ministering to the poor, the needy, the mini-cab drivers and sweatshop workers? What a revelation this would be for mankind; what a deliverance; what a *story* . . . We swallowed our beers in silent contemplation.

I wrote a brief account of Mr Creme for the paper. When it was published, I received a large postbag. Some of the letters were from people who wished to learn more about Benjamin Creme, to contact him and go to his meetings. A few were from people who were quite specific that Christ was not living in the East End, but was to be found in Bradford or Southampton. A couple claimed to be from Christ Himself, but I felt safe in discarding them. And so it was that I first made my way to Mr Creme's North London home, to listen to his stories.

He told me of Madame Helena Blavatsky, the Russian occultist – 'one of the most extraordinary women in history' – who in the nineteenth century had been contacted by members of the Hierarchy of Masters, the cosmic brotherhood, written *The Secret Doctrine*, and founded the Theosophical Society. And of her predictions of the coming Maitreya, the fifth Buddha. He told me of the English occultist Alice Bailey – 'a wonderful woman, a truly *wonderful* woman' – who, beginning in the 1920s, had written a series of books, supposedly under the guidance of one of the Hierarchy known pseudonymously as 'the Tibetan', prophesying the imminent return of the Cosmic Christ. This, said Mr Creme, was Maitreya. This, he explained, was the Esoteric Teaching. Bailey wrote that the teaching planned by the Hierarchy to precede and condition the coming 'Aquarian age' – the coming of the new Christ – fell into three categories: The Preparatory, given between 1875 and 1890, and written down by Madame Blavatsky; the Intermediate, given between 1919 and 1949, and written down by Bailey herself; and the Revelatory, which would emerge after 1975. That, said Mr Creme, was the stage we were at now.

All of this, and more, was explained in a book – one of several – that Mr Creme had written: *The Reappearance of Christ and the Masters of Wisdom*. In this, Mr Creme describes what appear to be exemplary credentials for his life as an occultist:

As a child of four or five, one of my favourite pastimes was to sit at a window and watch the wind; not the effect of the wind on the trees and leaves, but the wind itself . . . When I went to school I learned that air was invisible, the wind likewise, and forgot, I do not remember whether gradually or suddenly, my

ability to see what, of course, was some level of the etheric planes
of matter.

An interest in mysticism and the paranormal took hold. He studied
the writings of Wilhelm Reich on the orgone accumulator, and became
consciously aware of, and sensitive to, energy currents, 'So much so,'
he writes, 'that eventually I could tell when an atomic bomb had
been exploded in the Pacific or wherever. Across these thousands
of miles, I registered a shift in the etheric currents caused by the
explosions.'

He devoured the writings of Gurdjieff, Ouspensky, the Swamis
Vivekananda, Sivananda and Yoganada; and, of course, Blavatsky
and Bailey. He studied meditation techniques, and came to the
conclusion that he had mediumistic and healing powers. He quietly
pursued a life as a painter. And then, it seemed, something rather
odd happened.

One day in 1959, while sitting in his bath, Mr Creme received
his first telepathic communication from one of the Hierarchy of
Masters. By 1974, the communications were coming on a daily
basis, instructing him to pave the way for the coming of Maitreya,
the Christ. Mr Creme put advertisements in the newspapers, hired
halls and began to lecture. He circulated his own newsletter; a group
of interested people began to grow around him.

In 1977, he said, 'I was taken out of my body' actually to meet
Maitreya personally for the first time. Maitreya asked Mr Creme to
act as the emissary for a series of transmitted teachings. Over the
next five years, Mr Creme was the medium for 140 messages from
Maitreya, which were conveyed at Mr Creme's public meetings. 'It
was the most *difficult* thing I've ever done,' Mr Creme explained
one afternoon as we sat in his living room, drinking cups of tea.
'The first message was given experimentally, to see how I stood up
to doing this in public. You need enormous concentration, you see.
When I'm overshadowed, Maitreya activates a certain centre in my
brain; then I hear his voice, and I just say the words. My breath is
controlled by him so I can't say anything else, and I can't say it any
differently. It was,' he gave his musical laugh, '*terribly* difficult.'

Mr Creme's meetings, I discovered, traditionally began with
the replaying of one or two of these messages, rumbling from a
cumbersome, old-fashioned tape-recorder, operated by a bespectacled
woman in a blue cardigan. I found it an oddly disconcerting experience

to hear these messages, for the voice was clearly Mr Creme's, yet at the same time, not his at all – a groaning *basso profundo*, enunciated with agonising deliberation. The messages urged the listener to look to his conscience, to share, to 'take your brother's need as the measure of your action'. They promised that Maitreya would soon be revealed. They commanded the audience to 'know that you are gods'.

In May 1982, under the instructions from his Master, with whom he was now in more or less constant telepathic contact, Mr Creme took out a series of full-page advertisements in newspapers in America, Britain, France and Germany, announcing that 'the Christ' was now in the world. At a press conference in Los Angeles he made his momentous announcement that Maitreya was actually living in London, awaiting discovery.

There was a flurry of media interest but when the Christ somehow failed to appear, newspapers quickly lost interest in Mr Creme, and then forgot about him altogether. However, the non-appearance of Maitreya had done nothing to deter or discourage Mr Creme from his calling, or to diminish the apparent attraction of his message. He continued to hold public meetings, and people continued to flock to them. The organisation that had grown up around his teachings published a quarterly magazine, *Share International* – a curious publication which included articles by Mr Creme's Master (via Mr Creme) about Maitreya's teachings and his imminent arrival; esoteric lore about astral planes and the 'ray structures' of enlightened beings; and interviews with officials of various United Nations organisations about education and development programmes in the Third World. Its tone was resolutely upbeat, optimistic, beating a drum for the coming age of enlightenment. There were outposts of the organisation in America, Holland, Germany, France, Japan and half a dozen other countries. Mr Creme trotted around the world, lecturing, talking on the radio, establishing 'transmission groups' – small groups of meditators who had taken it upon themselves to channel the positive energy being beamed out from Maitreya into the world.

There always seemed to be an audience for Mr Creme some-where, and the tearing down of the Iron Curtain opened hitherto unexplored vistas. 'I've just come back from Romania!' he announced one evening when I called. 'It's fantastic over there. They're all claiming to be getting transmissions from Maitreya and the Masters and so on. It's total astral imagination! But the spiritual humility and the determination to get the message out is just overwhelming.'

The passing years had given Mr Creme a refreshingly matter-of-fact attitude to his calling. There was no eyeball-rolling, lollygagging, holy-roller evangelism about him. His rubicund countenance, twinkling eyes and snowdrift of hair lent him something of the caricature jollity of a Christmas-card Santa Claus. He did not appear to meet any of the criteria for the swindler or the charlatan. No money was collected at his meetings (although visitors were invited to buy his magazines, books and tapes); there were no appeals for funds; no promises of 'good works' in faraway places, no copper-bottom guarantees of salvation at a price. He lived extremely modestly, in a semi-detached house with his wife Phyllis, a polytechnic lecturer. He was anything but messianic. Indeed, on occasions, one could sense almost a note of regret in his voice as he contemplated his strange vocation. What he *really* wanted to do, he confessed one day, was to carry on painting. It was an 'embarrassing' claim to have to make, 'that Christ is giving messages through oneself', he said with a sigh. But he had given up apologising for it, and simply accepted it.

Why, I wondered, did he think he had been chosen?

'They were scraping the bottom of the barrel,' he replied, bursting into laughter.

'I have very little of Mr Blake's company,' Catherine Boucher, the wife of William Blake, complained. 'He is always in paradise.' And one fancied that Mr Creme's wife Phyllis must sometimes have felt much the same. But whatever strains his peculiar calling had put on their marriage, she had come to accommodate it. She had grown accustomed to his absences abroad, to his regular nocturnal sessions with his own 'transmission group' in the shed that had been specially built at the bottom of the garden; she had even grown accustomed – and this, I imagined, must have caused the greatest difficulty – to the ubiquitous psychic presence of Mr Creme's Master.

Mr Creme would not divulge the identity of his Master. I supposed he was talking to Mr Creme from another plane. But Mr Creme said that, in a sense, the Master was always there. 'He can hear this conversation,' he explained one day as we talked. 'Everything I hear, everything I see, he hears and sees. Everything I experience, he experiences. It must be terrible for him! He calls me his karma!'

Mr Creme chuckled. 'He doesn't take it all on, of course. But he makes a mental note.'

I came to enjoy my talks with Mr Creme. His stories of the Hierarchy, of hidden retreats in Tibet, of strange assignations, voices, instructions – the cogs of predestination smoothly shifting gear, guiding the planet towards an age of harmony and enlightenment . . . all of this had the wondrous, fantastical and uplifting quality of Hans Christian Andersen fairy stories. Mr Creme said there were other Masters of the Hierarchy already in the world, preparing the ground for Maitreya. The Master Jesus himself, he said, was to be found in Italy; another Master was living somewhere in Britain.

Devotees of the esoteric teachings evidently followed the progress of their own favourite Master with the eagerness of spiritual trainspotters. Once at one of Mr Creme's meetings an elderly man stood up to ask a question. What, he wished to know, would be the role of the Master St Germain in the forthcoming new world order? As a sixth-level Master, Mr Creme explained, the Master St Germain's present role was as 'a sort of general manager' of the Spiritual Hierarchy; his role in the new order would be Lord of Civilisation. Evidently satisfied with this answer, the elderly gentleman gathered up his belongings and shuffled out of the meeting.

But what are these Masters doing now? I asked one evening, as we sat in Mr Creme's living room.

'Good works,' said Mr Creme. 'They're among us all the time.'

Mr Creme told me a story: a group of Spanish visitors had come to his transmission group. It was sometime after midnight when they left, and they walked to the local underground station only to discover it was closed. There were no taxis to be seen. As their concern about getting home began to turn to real anxiety, a taxi suddenly appeared from nowhere. 'They were,' said Mr Creme, 'outside time.

'A young man was standing beside the taxi. He opened the door for them and gave the taxi-driver instructions. He shut the door and then he vanished. The driver set off, on the wrong side of the road, driving at breakneck speed. They were terrified! But they arrived quite safely, of course. Now, the young man who opened the door and saw them into the cab was the Master Jesus. And the driver of the cab was Maitreya.'

How, I asked, did Mr Creme *know* it was Jesus and Maitreya.

'My Master told me.'

I wondered, if Jesus and Maitreya were among us, wouldn't they perhaps be better employed ministering to the sick and the needy than running a taxi service in North London?

'They're doing that,' said Mr Creme, not the least put off by my question. 'Probably at the same time. Maitreya can be in many places at once, and I'm sure the Master Jesus likewise.'

Since first encountering Mr Creme I had continued to receive the occasional news-release from his organisation. These tended towards the repetitious, stressing Maitreya's message of sharing and love, and the imminence of his appearance. But in June 1988, the tenor of the releases suddenly changed. Along with the sharing and love came what were coyly termed 'forecasts of events'. These seemed more perceptive than the run-of-the-mill predictions of tabloid fortune-tellers or Old Moore's Almanack. America, it was stated, would gradually withdraw its military involvement in Central America; the bitter war waging between Iran and Iraq would soon end in compromise. (Some six weeks later, Ayatollah Khomeini announced that he was 'swallowing poison' to end the war with his neighbour.)

In August 1988, the releases were prophesying that Nelson Mandela would soon be released, and Margaret Thatcher would leave office as a result of popular feeling against the poll tax. By October it was being stated with some certainty that 'Drug taking will decrease.' 'Prince Charles will be a true king,' and, 'There is no hole in the ozone layer.'

These messages, I was told, came from Maitreya, via 'an associate', and were sent out by an acquaintance of Mr Creme, Patricia Pitchon. Patricia was a Colombian woman, living in London, who worked variously as a teacher, a translator and a financial journalist. She was married to a psychiatrist. From the moment I first met her, Patricia struck me as a highly intelligent and level-headed woman who was incapable of telling a lie.

Patricia had first become interested in the works of Helena Blavatsky and Alice Bailey while living in Colombia. Arriving in London, she had seen an advertisement for one of Mr Creme's meetings, and attended in a spirit of journalistic enquiry. But a curious thing had happened. At the moment when Mr Creme underwent the process of 'overshadowing', Patricia saw superimposed on his face the image of an Asian man. Patricia was so disconcerted by this that she went to Brick Lane in London's East End to make her own enquiries. There, seated in an Indian restaurant, she felt a sudden and compelling impulse to look towards the window. Gazing back at her was the Asian face she had seen superimposed on Benjamin Creme's. Patricia knew this sounded fanciful, far-fetched, not to say absurd. But she also knew that she had experienced it. For the past eight years she had been going to Mr Creme's meetings, she said, 'To keep an eye on things.'

Patricia told me how one day, out of the blue, she had received a telephone call from a young Asian boy, asking her to contact his employer, a North London pharmacist named Mr Patel. Patricia had duly contacted Mr Patel, who told her he was a disciple of Maitreya, and that she had 'work to do'. This work, it seemed, was to make public the prophecies that Mr Patel received from Maitreya. Which is precisely what Patricia had been doing.

Could I meet Mr Patel? Patricia made enquiries, then gave me his telephone number, and I made an appointment to see him. I took the underground to the end of the line in North London. The house was at the end of a small close, semi-detached and pebble-dashed, identical to all its neighbours. An Austin Allegro was parked in the drive.

As I rang the bell and waited, I fancied I saw a net-curtain twitch. The door was opened by an Asian woman in a sari, who waved me inside without a word and showed me into the lounge. On the sofa sat a slightly built Indian man, dressed in silk pyjamas, his grey hair pulled into a pony-tail. He could have been any age between thirty-five and seventy. This was Mr Patel. It was mid-morning, and he was watching Robert Kilroy-Silk on the television. He flicked down the volume with the remote-control, beckoned me to sit beside him, and embarked on a long and complicated discourse on the nature of self, his eyes drifting every so often to the silently flickering television screen. I wanted to ask Mr Patel about Maitreya and the prophecies, but his conversation meandered around abstruse philosophical points. I couldn't make up my mind whether he was being wise or evasive, or whether this was some sort of joke. He had shown not the slightest bit of interest or curiosity in what I was doing there.

I had been listening to Mr Patel speak for perhaps half an hour when the doorbell rang, and a tall African man came into the room. He introduced himself as Job Mutungi, a journalist for the *Kenya*

Times. Mutungi sat down and started talking about an incident that had occurred in a village near Nairobi, at a mission where a nun named Mary Akatsa conducts services of healing. Job said he had been sent by his newspaper to write an article about the mission. He produced a copy from his briefcase. Under the headline 'Did Jesus Christ Come to the City?' his account described how Mary Akatsa had addressed the crowd of 6,000 worshippers and announced that God had spoken to her and told her to expect a miracle, because, as Job Mutungi's article had it, 'A very important guest would be coming to give her a very vital message.'

Shortly afterwards a tall, bearded man, bare-footed and dressed in a flowing white robe, had walked from the crowd to stand beside her. The crowd, Job Mutungi wrote, had immediately acknowledged the figure as Jesus Christ. 'For many, it was the last prayer. It appeared to them that the Son of Man had at last fulfilled his promise of coming back to earth. They knelt down in emotional prayers in a frantic effort to save their souls at the eleventh hour.' The man then addressed the crowd in fluent Swahili, blessing them, urging them to respect Mary and reminding them to live by the teachings of the Bible.

> It took the crowd nearly twenty minutes to recover after the man left the meeting in a car belonging to a Mr Gurnam Singh, who offered to give him a lift [Mutungi's account continued]. But it will probably take Mr Singh a lifetime to recover from the shock he got two minutes later. On reaching the bus terminus for KBS Route No. 56 the man informed Mr Singh to stop the car as he wanted to alight and head for heaven. On getting out, he did not ascend. He walked a few paces beside the road and simply vanished into thin air. Several people who witnessed this were astonished by his mysterious disappearance.

Accompanying the story was a photograph of 'the Christ' standing beside Mary Akatsa, arms folded, an expression of bottomless gravity on his face. The description of Mr Singh's car ride and the strange disappearance of the mysterious visitor showed a certain imaginative flourish, I thought. But Job Mutungi insisted that the account of Christ's appearance was true in every particular. He had witnessed it himself.

Some weeks after the account had been published, Job had been contacted by a journalist in Holland, who had suggested that he should come to England and see Benjamin Creme. This, said Job, was easier than it sounded. The budget of the *Kenya Times* did not usually stretch to foreign travel, and he had no money himself; but extraordinarily, he said, his newspaper had agreed to pay. Arriving in London, he had gone directly to one of Mr Creme's meetings. There he had met P, who had looked at Job Mutungi's photograph of the mysterious visitor at Mary Akatsa's meeting and recognised the man as the one she had seen in her 'vision', and later in Brick Lane.

I did not know what to say to this. Was it mere coincidence that Job Mutungi had arrived at Mr Patel's house while I was there? Had Mr Patel deliberately arranged it? Was all this simply an enormous put-on? Job Mutungi said he did not know what to think, but he was keeping an open mind about everything, which seemed advisable under the circumstances. And what did Mr Patel make of this? He had been listening silently to Job Mutungi's story, his eye occasionally straying to the silently flickering images of morning television. Now he simply smiled and said God works in mysterious ways. Or words to that effect.

It was some months before I returned to see Mr Patel. The prophecies had continued to arrive in the post, veering from the wildly unspecific ('In China the people's will will prevail,' September 1989) to the beguiling ('Tory skeletons will soon emerge from cupboards,' June 1990). Terry Waite had not, after all, been released 'soon' (a prediction of June 1988 that would prove to be some three and a half years premature), but there had been sufficient earthquakes and political upheavals accurately foretold to warrant further enquiry.

Once more I rode the underground train to the end of the line, and trudged through the dreary suburban streets. Once more the woman in the sari answered the door, and wordlessly ushered me into the lounge. It was a few days before Christmas, and Mr Patel's television was tuned to the afternoon film – *King of Kings*. Men in jellabas were running across the screen shouting, 'The Messiah is come,' to the swelling strains of the 'Hallelujah Chorus'. When I remarked on this, Mr Patel brushed the coincidence aside with an impatient wave of his hand.

I pressed Mr Patel on the subject of the prophecies, but he was not a man to be hurried. He assembled his conversation like building blocks, resolutely ignoring interruptions or supplementary questions.

It was important, he said, that one should not misunderstand these matters. These prophecies, he explained, were given to him by the Master, to give to the world by way of a calling card, to make his presence felt.

And how, I asked, did he receive them?

'When your eyes are closed, you see nothing,' said Mr Patel. 'Open them, you see the chair, table, telephone. But when your eyes are open by the grace of the Lord then you can see what is happening in Kuwait, India, in all places. Master has ways to teach you, to break away from conditioning, beliefs, ideologies. On the physical plane we are prisoners of time, but in the spiritual plane there is no time. You get glimpses of eternity; and when you come back in your time, you explain it.'

Was he talking about telepathy? Clairvoyance? It was hard to stem Mr Patel in full flow and demand a cogent answer.

'Master does not make big statements,' he continued. 'He teaches only three things which you can remember all your life – be honest, sincere and detached.' He said these so quickly, as if ticking off items on a shopping list, that it was a moment before I realised that Benjamin Creme recited the identical list at his meetings.

'Master's teaching is such that you don't have to be a yogi or practising meditation and all that. The karmas – daily life – is the highest form of devotion to the Lord. When you are sitting on a nice beach, looking at the sky, you feel Oneness around you. That is the highest form of devotion. You think people who are going to Blackpool are wasting their time?' He scrutinised me intently, as if expecting an answer. But the question had taken me by surprise. 'No! The Lord says that when you are going there, you are experiencing me.'

Is the Master living in London? I asked.

Yes, said Mr Patel. But then again, he added, the Master could be everywhere.

Did Mr Patel know him personally?

Of course, he said. He met him often.

Why then was the Master so elusive?

'People must be ready for him,' said Mr Patel. 'If he comes in a form in which you recognise him, what will happen? People will run after him. Balance will be disturbed.'

Was Mr Patel talking about the same Master as Benjamin Creme?

'There is only one Master,' said Mr Patel. Personally, he had never met Mr Creme, although he had been told of his work, of course. 'Mr Creme has faith, and he has trust. These are very important in life. He has experienced something unique.'

Mr Patel's monologue moved on, brooking no interruption. At one point his wife moved through the room, shooting me a quizzical glance. Then the doorbell rang, and an Asian man entered, gave a cursory nod, sat down silently on the sofa beside Mr Patel and scrutinised the flickering television, apparently indifferent to our conversation. I was beginning to experience a curious sense of weightlessness. I had noticed something on the mantelpiece I had not remembered from my previous visit: a photograph of the Indian guru, Sai Baba.

'Is Sai Baba the Master?' I asked Mr Patel.

'Yes, Sai Baba is a Master,' he replied.

'But is Sai Baba *the* Master?'

Mr Patel was watching the television intently. 'The Master is everywhere,' he said.

If Maitreya was in London, and the day of reckoning was upon us, why didn't he just reveal himself, and get on with saving the world? Every time I put this question to Benjamin Creme the answer would be the same. For Maitreya to reveal himself would be a contravention of man's free will. Mankind must find him, and invite him to declare himself.

And how would mankind do that?

Through a body of representatives – politicians, the media, said Mr Creme. All of his efforts of the last ten years had been turned to precisely that purpose.

And yet, somehow, it had never happened. The handful of journalists who descended on Brick Lane in 1982, in the wake of Mr Creme's first announcement, had not, it seemed, been sufficiently representative to persuade Maitreya to come forward. Nor were the fourteen journalists whom Patricia Pitchon had persuaded to gather in a Brick Lane restaurant two years later. What were required, it seemed, were editors, proprietors, major network representatives, leading politicians, diplomats, heads of state. The ante was forever being raised.

Mr Creme spoke of a constant bustle of activity involving Maitreya, the details of which were transmitted to him by his telepathic Master. There had been meetings between Maitreya and sundry representatives of government, said Mr Creme. Maitreya had been present at a conference in South London, attended by some 200 people, including representatives of the media, the Vatican, and the Church of England. I made enquiries, but could find no evidence of counsels of swamis, diplomats and papal representatives. But then South London is a big and complicated place. I know because I live there.

Things were moving forward, Mr Creme said. In preparation for his imminent emergence, Maitreya had largely forsaken his duties in East London and was now engaged in global work. He had talked to President Bush, in the guise of a bodyguard, and to the Amir of Kuwait in the guise of his brother. At the time of the Gulf War he had appeared to Saddam Hussein in the vision that had been reported in newspapers around the world as Saddam dreaming of the Prophet Muhammad. He was addressing meetings in Germany, Mexico and Italy. Wells of miraculous healing water were springing up at his behest.

'He doesn't eat anything,' said Mr Creme. 'He doesn't sleep. He's on the go twenty-four hours a day.'

I felt curiously cheered by this news, even though I didn't, for one minute, believe it. One could understand the indefatigable optimism that buoyed Mr Creme in his mission. I even felt buoyed by it myself. He was a harbinger of hope! One could understand the rapt expressions on the faces of those at his meetings. The hour was almost nigh! Christ was a Mr Fixit, working overtime to put the world to rights. From the moment of his appearance, the community of spiritual Masters would take charge of government, international agencies, administrative and technical departments. The Hierarchy, Mr Creme said, had trained economists already in place, ready to implement a series of blueprints that would solve the fundamental problems of redistribution – of food, wealth, resources – that lay at the heart of the world's myriad crises. Mr Creme estimated that within fifteen years man would have mastered the art of sharing.

I wondered whether I was not beginning to take this all too literally. It was clear that none of this could be true (could it?). Yet how then could the possibility of its truth have gained such purchase? There were hundreds, thousands, of people around the world who attended Benjamin Creme's meetings, who subscribed to his magazine, who believed. There were fundamentalist Christian groups who actually believed something else entirely – that Benjamin

Creme was an agent for the Antichrist. I had come across a pamphlet published by an organisation called the Christian Research Institute, declaring its belief that Mr Creme was indeed 'deriving his inspiration from a spiritual realm, albeit a malevolent one'. Perhaps, the Institute concluded, through Creme, 'Satanic forces were testing the waters to see how much acceptance and support the Western world is ready to give to a scenario which so blatantly accords with the Bible's most dreadful prophecies.'

I became aware that there was a sort of war being waged at a level of which most people, including myself, were completely ignorant. A sort of bizarre world of claim and counter-claim over matters that most people would have regarded as fanciful, if not altogether insane.

But I did not believe that Mr Creme was the Antichrist. I believed that he believed that what he said was true. But then truth works on many levels – on as many levels, perhaps, as there are levels of consciousness. The literal truth is not always the same as the poetic truth; and the spiritual truth may be something else entirely. Even if you did not accept the idea that Christ was in the East End of London, it was hard not to accept the notion of humanity poised on the brink of change. Those who heeded Mr Creme's message were united in their optimism. The growth of democracy in Eastern Europe! The end of the arms race! The growth of eco-consciousness, of holism, of One-Worldism – revolutionary ideas that are transforming the way we think and live. Perhaps all of this was evidence of the Christ principle in action, and if the Christ principle was actually in action, could the Christ figure be far behind? If he had walked on earth 2,000 years ago, didn't we need him now?

One day, Mr Creme told me that I could talk to his Master through him, if I wished. The prospect was disconcerting. How could I talk to someone when I had neither evidence, nor faith, that they even existed? I sat on Mr Creme's sofa, feeling foolish and wondering what to say. Who, I asked at length, is Maitreya?

There was a moment's silence as Mr Creme set his face in an impassive mask. He appeared to be listening to something. 'The Master says that the Christ that people expect doesn't exist,' said Mr Creme. 'He is the son of man, not the son of God. The marvel of Maitreya is that as an ordinary man he has become a God; he has achieved by dint of his own efforts what all humanity could achieve. The Master says that Maitreya is here to show humanity how to become gods. Not God, but gods – that is, expressing all the potential for divinity as far as this planet is concerned.'

And what circumstances, I asked, would be necessary for Maitreya to make himself known?

'The Master says the time is almost with us when Maitreya will speak openly,' replied the voice of Mr Creme. 'World events, he says, are moving to a point where he will appear more often to more people.'

Does it require him to be found by man?

'Not found. Simply invited. His presence has to be taken sufficiently seriously to be invited.'

This was an odd feeling; to be conversing with an entity one could not be sure existed. Mr Creme was sitting quite peacefully in his chair, his face composed, awaiting my next question. Let me ask the Master, I said, what could any journalist do to hasten that process?

Mr Creme remained silent, attending his Master's voice. At length he said, 'Present a hypothesis which if true would be the beginning of a new civilisation for the world. Describe a world in which people are living in harmony, manifesting brotherhood; in which there has been an end to wars, starvation, divisions and separations. Everybody has this inner need; this expectation of a great and beautiful future; something in which their own higher aspirations are going to be fulfilled. And they will turn to whatever gives them this sense, this encouragement; this hope; this purpose and meaning in their life. You do that, even as a hypothesis, and you will present them with the truth about Maitreya. If it's true, this is what it will mean to the world.' There was a moment's silence. 'In other words,' said Mr Creme, back to his old self, 'act as if. . .'.

2

THE MIRACLE
IN NORTH LONDON

I did not see Benjamin Creme again for some time. Perhaps he was travelling; perhaps my interest had moved on. I continued to receive copies of *Share International* through the post. Mr Creme had now taken to publishing details of Maitreya's appearances around the world. 1994: 16 January, Port of Spain, Trinidad; 27 March, St Petersburg, Russia; 29 May, the Philippines; 1995: 23 April, Ulan Bator. (The week before that, apparently, he had been in Aberdeen.) Wells of healing water were being 'charged' in some of these areas, Mr Creme wrote, and were attracting growing numbers of visitors. But these miraculous appearances were never, it seemed, recorded anywhere else. The coming of Maitreya was an intriguing story, but its contradictions and confusions baffled and disheartened me. It was like trying to hold on to a handful of sand.

Then one day I received a telephone call from Patricia Pitchon. I had not seen her since our lunch in the Indian restaurant in Brick Lane where she had seen the man she believed to be Maitreya. Now she had news of another miraculous occurrence. At a house in North London portraits of Sai Baba, the legendary Indian swami, were 'producing' *vibhuti*. Patricia had seen it with her own eyes: the 'holy ash' produced by Baba as a token of his miraculous powers and a gift for devotees was forming on the outside of the frames and on the pictures themselves, apparently of its own accord. I thought of the portrait of Sai Baba hanging in the sitting room of Mr Patel's home and his talk of 'the Master'.

I had known of Sai Baba for more than twenty years. In 1973, Stephen, a close friend, had set off on the 'hippie-trail' across Asia, bound eventually for Australia. In the Indian city of Bangalore he had heard tales of a miracle-working saint named Sai Baba. He made his way to the ashram, where he had been granted an audience. When Sai Baba looked into his eyes, Stephen told me, it was as if he could see into Stephen's very soul, as if nothing was hidden from him, and everything forgiven. It was the look, Stephen said, of pure and unconditional love.

To call Sai Baba a man was not correct, Stephen said; he was a manifestation of God in the body of a man; an avatar – one of a rare body of divine beings, like Krishna and Christ, who take human form at specific times in history to aid man's spiritual evolution, and awaken him to the fact of his innate divinity. Stephen became a devotee. He gave me books, and a small packet of *vibhuti* which, he said, Sai Baba had materialised from thin air with a mere wave of the hand. I browsed through the books, then put them to one side; the *vibhuti* I sometimes showed to friends – my exotic souvenir of an Indian holy man, whose teachings I was too lazy or preoccupied even to read. After that, I hardly thought of Sai Baba at all until the day I received the telephone call from Patricia, telling me of the miracle in North London.

Two days later, I took the underground train to Wealdstone, a dreary North London suburb, its main street lined with cut-price clothing and furniture stores and slot-machine arcades where the unemployed were encouraged to fritter away their limited social security payments.

As I was walking along the road I was surprised to chance upon Austin, an old friend. Austin was in his early sixties. Years ago, in his native Ireland, he had been a Catholic priest, but he had suffered a crisis of faith which had led to a prolonged love affair with the bottle. He had left the priesthood, given up drinking and moved to England, where he now earned a living on the margins of the literary world, reviewing paperbacks for a Sunday newspaper. We greeted each other warmly and when I explained my mission he agreed to join me. I felt glad to have the presence of an independent witness – and a doubting Catholic at that.

The *vibhuti*, I had been told by Patricia, was materialising in the house of a Mr Patel, a mini-cab driver (and no relation to the Mr Patel I had visited some months earlier). The house was a between-the-wars semi-detached, set on a street of identically nondescript houses. It seemed an utterly, deadeningly parochial setting for a miracle.

The door was opened by a small man, dressed in a white dhoti, who nodded us inside. I was immediately struck by a powerful scent, like jasmine, perfuming the air. 'This way, please.' Mr Patel led the way through a lounge that had been transformed into something like a waiting room, with chairs ranged around its four walls, and then into an adjoining room. The scent became more overpowering, and I could hear sitar music percolating gently around the room from a small hi-fi system.

'There,' said Mr Patel. Hanging on the wall was a large head-and-shoulders portrait of Sai Baba, which appeared to be covered in a fine grey powder. The powder had been brushed off the face, giving the impression that the smiling countenance had sprouted a full grey head of hair and beard. 'Yes,' Mr Patel whispered. '*Vibhuti!*' Surrounding it were more pictures of Sai Baba; vividly coloured representations of the Hindu gods and goddesses, Shiva, Krishna, Ganesh; images of Christ. Some of these were merely spotted with the ash. On others it almost totally covered the glass, obscuring the image beneath. On some, I noticed, the ash had actually appeared *between* the image and the glass.

'It grows,' said Mr Patel with a smile.

Grows?

'Yes, yes. It comes of its own accord. All the time. One day a picture is clean, then the *vibhuti* comes, then we brush it off, and more comes.'

'Where does it come from?' I asked, although I already knew what the answer would be.

'Baba,' said Mr Patel in a tone of sombre reverence. 'It comes from Sai Baba.'

'And how does it come here?' I asked.

'It is a long story,' said Mr Patel.

He and I settled ourselves on a sofa, while Austin wandered off to examine the miracle at his leisure.

Mr Patel explained that he and his family had lived in this house for some years, as council tenants. And then they had decided to buy the house. Mr Patel was an avid snooker-player, and he had an extension built to house a table. He was not at the time, he said, a devotee of Sai Baba, but he was a devout Hindu, and in accordance with tradition, he arranged a small religious ceremony to bless the new extension. He constructed a small shrine in a corner of the room, on which he placed the traditional offering of coconuts. On the day of the ceremony, some fifty friends turned up, including some devotees of Sai Baba, who sang *bhajans*, or devotional songs.

It was during this singing, said Mr Patel, that the first mysterious thing occurred; the coconuts suddenly split open. Shortly afterwards a highly fragrant nectar began to pour from one of them. It continued to flow for seven days, in such quantities, said Mr Patel, that he had been obliged to put the coconut in a bowl to catch the nectar. Then an image appeared on a second coconut of an old man. He now recognised this old man as Sri Shirdi Sai Baba, a venerable Indian saint, and the previous incarnation, it is believed, of the present Sai Baba. Shortly afterwards, *vibhuti* appeared on the side of the coconut, spelling out the holy word Om.

'To be frank with you,' said Mr Patel, 'I thought the coconuts cracked because of the heat, but the picture and the *vibhuti* . . . my children were jumping up and down saying it's a miracle.' Mr Patel himself wasn't so sure. 'I wanted to put in my snooker-table. But a priest came and told me it was a sign from Sai Baba and that devotees will want to come and pray here. Give it a few days. But then one week became two weeks and that became three weeks . . .'

Devotees brought pictures of Sai Baba, to place around the shrine. *Vibhuti* began to appear on the pictures. The shrine grew in size. It was around this time, said Mr Patel, that his young daughter Jashree had a dream of people from different religions praying in a temple. Mr Patel took it as a sign. He added pictures of Christ, statues of the Buddha and symbols of the Muslim faith to the shrine. *Vibhuti* began appearing on all these too.

'Baba says that Christ, Buddha, Muhammad . . . all the religions of the world lead to the same God,' said Mr Patel. 'He does not want to start a new religion, but to turn people back to their own faith.'

The miracle in his snooker room had made a devotee of Mr Patel. The snooker room had become the temple which Jashree had dreamed of, where devotees gathered to worship and sing devotional songs. At one time, the shrine had been permanently open to whomever wished to come, but Mr Patel had now limited it to one evening a week. This was a family home, after all, and Mr Patel had a living to earn as a mini-cab driver.

Mr Patel did not require a scientific explanation. The phenomenon had occurred in his own home; he could see the evidence of a miracle every time he walked downstairs; that was all the evidence he required. 'Sometimes,' he said, 'Baba comes here himself.'

'Comes here?'

'Yes, in a trance or something, perhaps.' Mr Patel had installed a red velvet chair in the snooker room, 'for Baba to rest,' and Mrs Patel placed food at the shrine for him.

'Biscuits?' I asked.

Mr Patel looked offended. 'No! Proper dinner. Sometimes we collect the plate and some has been eaten!'

Mr Patel smiled at my incredulous expression, as if he was used to people not quite believing him, as if he couldn't actually care less. I looked around for Austin. He had stopped examining the pictures and was now sitting on a chair in the ante-room, listening to the sitar music; his eyes closed, a smile on his face.

I had no idea what to make of the pictures. To have applied the *vibhuti* to the glass would have been possible, perhaps, although I could not imagine how. The *vibhuti* was too evenly distributed to have been applied with a brush or sponge. The pictures did not seem to me to have been tampered with in any way. Rather, the *vibhuti* seemed to have grown from the surface of the glass, just as Mr Patel said it had. Even if placing *vibhuti* on the glass might have just about been possible, to have placed it *between* the picture and the frame, as was the case with some of the portraits, seemed to me to be too complicated and troublesome. It seemed preposterous to imagine Mr Patel and his family bent over frames and sheets of glass, fiddling with ash and screwdrivers. Anyway, why would anyone contrive such a spectacle? There was no apparent profit or gain to be had from it for Mr Patel. A large sign near the pictures urged visitors not to give money, but to 'leave only your troubles'.

What other motive could he have had? It had, if anything, caused him considerable personal inconvenience. His house was no longer his own. He entertained a constant stream of visitors and enquiries; he was required to maintain the shrine in proper order. He had long ago abandoned any thoughts of installing a snooker-table as he had originally planned. Besides, Mr Patel did not strike me as a man capable of deceit. His manner was humble, self-effacing, patently sincere. 'I am deeply blessed,' he said. Even questioning his account of the miracle I felt mean-spirited, a prisoner of rationalist thought. Perhaps it was better simply to accept it for what Mr Patel said it was, for what it seemed to be – the sparkle of holy ash enlivening the dreary suburb of Wealdstone. I walked away from Mr Patel's house with my head reeling, Austin at my side. His face still wore the same absorbed half-smile I had noticed when he was sitting in the ante-room.

'So what do you think?' I asked.

He walked along in silence for some moments, mulling it over. 'Well, if it's *not* a miracle,' he said at last, 'it's a wonderful fairy-tale.'

I told friends about the *vibhuti*-covered portraits; they looked at me in a bemused, eyebrow-arching sort of way. It couldn't be true, because such things simply don't happen, do they? But then they hadn't seen it, and I had. Nobody seemed inclined to go to Wealdstone to see it for themselves, and I could hardly blame them. Wealdstone was a bothersome place to get to.

I decided to write about the miracle in Mr Patel's house. Unlike the sundry gurus and swamis who have made their way to the West throughout the twentieth century, Sai Baba has left India only once, to visit Kenya and Uganda, in 1968. Estimates of the size of his following around the world vary between three and ten million. Scores of books have been written about him, yet in Britain, other than among his devotees, he remains almost completely unknown. His file in the *Daily Telegraph* library contained only a handful of small cuttings, and just one serious profile, written by a *Sunday Times* journalist who had visited Sai Baba in India in 1972. He recounted the familiar stories of Sai Baba's miracle-working – his materialisations, not only of *vibhuti*, but of lockets, medallions, wrist-watches; his powers of healing, the story that he had once raised a man from the dead. The journalist had travelled with the photographer David Bailey. Sai Baba had not, it seemed, granted the journalist a personal interview, but Bailey had asked if he could take photographs. You may take one exposure, Sai Baba told him. Bailey apparently protested that it was not enough. It will be perfect, said Sai Baba. Of course, it was – but then one would expect nothing less from a photographer of Bailey's calibre.

The features editor smiled indulgently when I delivered my copy and said nothing, clearly thinking I was deluded, the victim of an elaborate hoax. A photographer visited the shrine and returned with photographs of the *vibhuti*-covered portraits; he seemed awestruck. The photograph was dropped for reasons of space.

The day the article appeared I received a telephone call from a researcher at the University of London, named Caroline Thomas. She had seen similar manifestations of *vibhuti* on portraits at a Sai Baba temple in London. She had analysed those, and *vibhuti* produced in person by the Sri Lankan guru Swami Premananda, on a visit to England. It was Premananda who had 'materialised' *vibhuti* for Van and myself.

Thomas had published her findings in the *Journal of the Society for Psychical Research*. According to Hindu mythology, she reported, *vibhuti* (and *kum-kum* – a red, paste-like substance – and nectar) are 'symbols of the inner, noumenal kalas, produced by occult and mystical methods of yoga, which confer physical and/or spiritual immortality'. *Vibhuti* is an integral part of Hindu worship. It is the ash of burnt cow dung, which itself symbolises a noumenal psycho-sexual process; the mother of creation in the Hindu myths is symbolised as a cow. The *vibhuti* produced by Sai Baba is said to have therapeutic qualities. It is daubed on the forehead, placed on the tongue, or mixed with water and drunk as a specific against illness. It is carried as a talisman.

Materialisation of *vibhuti* is a demonstration of the myth of Siva-Sakti, which provides an explanation of the relationship between consciousness and matter. 'Siva is pure consciousness and Sakti is the active power to create. This unity is the initial expansion of consciousness in matter and the final contraction of matter into consciousness.' In short, the materialisation of *vibhuti* is a demonstration of mind over matter.

In its chemical constituents, the *vibhuti* that materialised on a portrait of Sai Baba was virtually identical, Thomas reported, to *vibhuti* taken from a Hindu temple in Archway, North London – a silica-glass, containing a few per cent of magnesium, sodium, potassium and calcium. The phosphorous and remnant structures indicated that it was of plant origin, such as would be expected when cow dung is burnt. It was impossible to determine, she reported, what had caused the *vibhuti* to appear on the photograph. And despite eye-witness accounts and the evidence of video film, it was also impossible to determine whether the *vibhuti* was fraudulently produced by Swami Premananda.

The phenomenon of *vibhuti* appearing on photographs was not confined to Mr Patel's house. I began to hear accounts of similar manifestations at houses and temples in Leicester, in New York, Canada, Australia and, of course, in India. Shortly after the article appeared I received another telephone call, from someone I had never met, inviting me to another house, also in North London, where *vibhuti* was said to be manifesting in even greater quantities than at Mr Patel's.

The Shahs were Kenyan-Asians, who lived in a large semi-detached house in a comfortable middle-class suburb near Harrow. As soon as I stepped inside I was assailed by the familiar sweet smell of *vibhuti*. The family were followers of the Aga Khan, Mr Shah explained, but his teenage son had been introduced to Sai Baba through schoolfriends. He had been given a photograph, which he placed in his bedroom, and shortly afterwards the photograph had started producing *vibhuti*. More photographs had been placed in the room, more *vibhuti* appeared. Mr Shah's son, a serious-faced boy of seventeen or eighteen, showed me to his room. It was the bedroom of a perfectly normal teenage boy, cluttered with homework and decorated with pictures of pop stars, save for the portraits of Sai Baba and several religious statues, all covered with a light coating of *vibhuti*. A mound of *vibhuti* lay on his dressing table, like a brick of grey sand, into which had been etched the letters SB.

'Sai Baba did this too?' I asked.

The boy smiled and nodded.

Had he ever been to visit Sai Baba, I wondered.

No, he said, but Sai Baba came to the house. He had seen him three times, in his bedroom and in the lounge.

Nobody else in the family had seen him, but nobody doubted the boy's word. The *vibhuti* was everywhere as material evidence. Its profusion was staggering; its sweet smell penetrated every corner of the house. It lay over pieces of furniture like dust; an Om sign had been carefully inscribed on a table. A shelf in the lounge was coated in the fine powder. The shelf had been cleared, Mr Shah explained, to make way for a new stereo-system. The family had gone out one Saturday to buy it; they returned to find that Baba had been in the house.

Just like Mrs Patel, Mrs Shah prepared a breakfast each evening for the nocturnal visitor. She fetched an exhibit from the kitchen for my inspection. It was a piece of toast, dusted with *vibhuti* spelling out her own initials. That had happened on her birthday, she explained, four months ago, 'But, look, the toast is still fresh,' and so it was.

Like Mr Patel's house – only a few miles away around the North Circular – the Shahs' home had become a temple. A velvet chair had been placed on the upstairs landing, garlanded with flowers and surrounded by pictures of Sai Baba and Hindu gods and saints. The Om symbol was sprinkled on the chair in *vibhuti*.

Tonight there would be *puja* – worship – at the shrine, prayers and the singing of devotional songs, and visitors had begun to arrive. A prosperous-looking businessman had just returned from visiting Sai Baba in India. He pulled back the cuff of his shirt to display a gold watch which, he said, Baba had made for him. 'Yes, in front of my very eyes. And it keeps perfect time.' Devotees filled the house, squatting cross-legged on the floor of the lounge and the bedrooms, up the stairs and on the landing, in front of the shrine. We sang devotional songs. Mr Shah distributed *vibhuti* that had been scraped from the pictures; people daubed it on their foreheads, licked their hands and fingers, then ran them through their hair, so none of the holy ash would be wasted.

As the visitors left, Mrs Shah distributed pieces of coconut and packets of *vibhuti* for those who wanted it. 'Yes, come again,' said Mr Shah, as I stepped into the night. 'Come whenever you like.'

Everyone is familiar with the phenomenon of coming across a name or a word for the first time, and that name or word seeming to recur thereafter, as if it has been implanted in the mind, to flower in the most unexpected of places.

I knew of Sai Baba, of course, yet after visiting the *vibhuti* houses his name began to pop up in my life with bemusing frequency. A stranger at a dinner party had just returned from visiting his ashram in India. Somebody else happened to be reading a book about him.

Shortly after visiting the house of Mr Shah, I was sent by the newspaper to write a story about a former long-distance lorry-driver named Tony Budell, who was organising and leading 'convoys of mercy', to deliver medicines and supplies to refugee camps and orphanages in Bosnia. I drove to Canterbury to meet him. The Volvo estate-wagon that he drove backwards and forwards across Europe was parked outside his house, marked by a large red cross – and, on the door, the multi-faith symbol which I recognised as Sai Baba's.

Tony Budell's story was an extraordinary one. Working as a long-distance lorry-driver, he had been in a state of constant depression. He was drinking heavily, enmeshed in an unhappy marriage, the sort of man, by his own description, who would punch someone as soon as look at them. When his marriage eventually broke up, he found himself living in the cab of his truck. So desperate had his life become that he decided to kill himself. Driving along an autoroute in France he tried to steer his lorry towards the concrete buttress of a flyover. At the last second his nerve failed him, and he swerved to avoid it. Shaken, confused and in the depths of depression, he made his way back to England. It was whilst waiting at the harbour at Dover, he said, that he had heard a voice, telling him not to give up; that there was work for him to do.

Tony Budell did not strike me as the sort of man who, under normal circumstances, would place much credence in disembodied voices. But, he said, he 'knew' the voice was God's. He gave up lorry-driving, and took a job as a hospital porter. He found a girlfriend who was associated with a local church, and became a church-goer himself. His girlfriend became his wife. He heard no more voices, but he never doubted his moment of epiphany at the Dover docks, or the abiding sense that something was in store for him.

Then one evening, watching a news programme about orphanages in Romania, he suddenly realised what he had to do. Going from door to door, writing to local companies and advertising in the newspaper, he began collecting toys, clothes and blankets for Romanian orphans. He bought his Volvo estate and a trailer and drove the provisions to Romania himself. Others joined him and before long, Tony was leading mercy convoys of up to a dozen trucks and vans.

When the civil war broke out in Yugoslavia, he decided to concentrate his efforts there. He began to raise a collection of supplies, but had no specific destination in mind, until one day he and his wife paid a visit to Glastonbury. As he was browsing in a bookshop, a book fell off the shelf above him and struck him on the head. It was a book about Sai Baba. Tony had never heard of Sai Baba, but some impulse made him buy the book. He took it home and read it that evening in a mood of mounting bemusement. The next morning the telephone rang. It was somebody who had seen Tony's advertisement in the local newspaper, soliciting for goods – a member of a local Sai Baba group. If he was leading a convoy to Bosnia, the caller asked, would he consider delivering goods to an orphanage that they had been supporting? Tony Budell told this story in a quiet, matter-of-fact way. The conjunction of the book falling on his head and the telephone call that had followed it were not a coincidence, he said. Sai Baba now came to him in dreams, and in meditation – guiding and encouraging him. He now realised that the voice he had heard at Dover docks was pointing him towards this moment; he believed that Sai Baba was divine.

It would not be correct to say that these incidents and these stories made me a devotee, but they convinced me that there must be something extraordinary about Sai Baba.

I continued to hear stories everywhere. On a business trip to Germany I fell into conversation with an Indian woman from London. She was a Sai Baba devotee. Her group, she told me, held summer retreats each year in a school outside London. On the most recent retreat, the school caretaker had asked whether the Indian gentleman in the red robe who had been with the group last year would be with them again. 'This Indian gentleman?' asked the secretary of the group, showing the caretaker a photograph of Sai Baba. 'That's the one,' the caretaker replied. But Sai Baba, of course, had not been at the college the previous year. He has never been to Britain.

I telephoned the secretary of a Sai Baba group in the Midlands. Dominic Prince, a hairdresser, told me he had never heard of Sai Baba until he found a copy of a book about him which had been left – improbably enough – in his own lavatory. 'I assumed it had been left by the friend who I was sharing the house with,' Dominic told me. 'But some days later he remarked on the interesting book that *I'd* left in the lavatory. Neither of us had put the book there, or had any idea how it had got there.' Shortly afterwards, Dominic said, Sai Baba had come to him in a dream. 'I dreamt that I was in India, at an ashram, going forward to see him. I'd never been to India before, and certainly never been to an ashram.' The combination of the book and the dream convinced him to visit Sai Baba at his ashram in India. 'And when I eventually got there, of course, I recognised it from my dream.'

The book that Dominic Prince had discovered in his lavatory was *Sai Baba, Man of Miracles*, by an Australian named Howard Murphet. I found it on my bookshelf at home. It was one of the books that Stephen had given me all those years ago.

Murphet was a journalist (he had been part of the press contingent covering the Nuremberg Trials immediately after the Second World War) and a theosophist, who was to become an ardent devotee of Sai Baba's after living in close proximity to him at his ashram in Puttaparthi. *Man of Miracles* is an extraordinary catalogue of Baba's supposed powers. Murphet recounts stories of countless materialisations – of *vibhuti*, wrist-watches, necklaces and pendants; he tells of Sai Baba materialising food for crowds of devotees, of healing the sick and, on at least one occasion, of raising a man from the dead. Many of these stories are almost identical to the biblical accounts of the miracles of Jesus – a similarity which Sai Baba's devotees have been quick to notice and develop in support of their contention that he is the Incarnate Christ of the age.

Some of these 'miracles', perhaps, could be explained as sleight-of-hand and prestidigitation, of the kind practised by street-magicians throughout India. But if Sai Baba were simply a magician, it seemed he must be an extraordinarily good one to have fooled so many people for so long.

Howard Murphet was clearly not a fool. He approached his subject with the journalist's criteria of proof and verification; testimonies were checked and counter-checked. 'The wealth of miraculous things that my own eyes have witnessed assure my acceptance of things of similar nature about which I have heard,' he writes, concluding that, 'The miracles of Christ and Krishna must be taken on trust or through faith, those of Sai Baba you can see for yourself.'

Sai Baba is believed by his devotees to be a reincarnation of Sai Baba of Shirdi, a swami and miracle-worker who was born in India sometime in the middle of the last century (his exact birthdate is unknown), and who died in 1918. 'Shirdi' Sai is one of India's most popular saints. Wherever you go in the south of the country you see his image in shop-windows, on car dashboards, on postcards and posters. Little is known of 'Shirdi' Sai's birth and parentage. He is believed to have been born in the state of Hyderabad of Hindu Brahmin parents, but at an early age the boy came under the care and guidance of a Moslem fakir, who became his first guru. After four or five years, the fakir died, and Sai came into the charge of a government official in Selu named Gopal Rao. Rao was a deeply religious man, and when he first saw the young Sai Baba it is said that he recognised him as the reincarnation of the Indian saint, Kabir. Sai Baba spent some years with Gopal Rao being educated and looked after. When Rao died, it is said, he pointed to the west and bade Sai Baba to travel in that direction in search of his new home. Following his guru's instructions, Sai Baba travelled westwards, coming at last to a small village called Shirdi in what was then the Bombay presidency. He set up home in a dilapidated Moslem mosque, where he kept oil lamps burning throughout the night as a sign of devotion. It was here that he is said to have performed his first public miracle.

While some villagers recognised Sai Baba's holy qualities, and came to pay homage, the majority thought him a madman. In the tradition of holy men in India he depended on alms for his needs, including oil for his lamps. One night, mocking the holy man, the local shopkeeper told Baba that his supplies of oil had been exhausted. Some villagers followed Sai Baba back to his dilapidated mosque, to see what he would do without his religious light. As dusk fell, it is said, they were astonished to see him pour water into the lamps instead – and light them. Word quickly spread throughout the region of the 'miracle' at Shirdi, and people flocked to pay homage to Sai Baba.

As his fame spread, so too did word of his miraculous powers. It was claimed that he was clairvoyant, and able to know what his devotees were thinking and saying when they were hundreds of miles from him; that he would appear whenever he was needed in moments of crisis, disguised as a beggar, a workman, a hermit, even a dog or a cat; that he could, in short, take any material form he chose and project himself through space. There are numerous accounts of him healing blindness, palsy and leprosy and casting out evil spirits. He kept a fire burning at all times at his mosque, to produce a ready supply of ash, which he called *udhi*, and used for healing.

Devotees continued to flock to him in their thousands. On one occasion he was processed through the streets in a silver chariot – a display of ostentatiousness to which he agreed, it is said, only to please his followers. He continued to live the life of a poor ascetic, and to beg for food as he had always done. He died with only enough money to pay for his funeral.

The present Sai Baba was born eight years later, on 23 November 1926, in the small village of Puttaparthi in the state of Andhra Pradesh. He was born into a modest, but not especially poor family. His grandfather had limited farm-holdings; his father, Pedda Raju, worked in the fields.

The most comprehensive account of Sai Baba's life and work is to be found in a four-volume biography, *Sathyam Sivam Sundaram*, written by his long-time companion and secretary, Professor N. Kasturi. According to Professor Kasturi, Sai Baba's birth had been presaged by extraordinary signs in the household. His father was a keen amateur musician and a tamboura and drum were kept in

the house. As the time of the child's birth drew nearer, the parents
were frequently awoken in the middle of the night by the sound of
the instruments playing of their own accord.

The child was named Sathyanarayan. From an early age he is
said to have been charming and unusual, the 'pet' of the village of
Puttaparthi, so often held up by other parents in the village as an
ideal that the children began to call him 'guru'. He avoided places
where animals were slaughtered, or fish caught, and avoided pots
used for cooking meat. He would bring beggars home to be fed, or
forgo his own food to give it to those less favoured. Sometimes, he
would go without any food at all for long periods, claiming that a
mysterious visitor, an old man, fed him with balls of rice.

His elementary teacher described him as 'a simple, unostentatious,
honest and well-behaved boy', the life and soul of school dramatics, a
pillar of the school athletic team, 'the best among the school scouts'.
At the age of ten, Sathya formed a 'Pandhari Bhajan' group, to perform
folk dances and religious songs. Among the group's repertoire were
traditional songs of pilgrimage, to which, it was noticed, the young
boy added his own compositions, about pilgrimage to the shrine
of a saint of whom most villagers had never heard – Sai Baba
of Shirdi.

It was three years later that Sathya began to undergo some
sort of mysterious transformation that would lead eventually to
his declaration that he was Sai Baba returned. One day, playing
near some rocks outside the village, known for the presence of
scorpions and snakes, the boy sprang backwards screaming, as if
he had been stung. But no scorpion was to be found, and that
night he slept peacefully, with no sign of pain. The next day,
however, the boy fell unconscious for twenty-four hours. When
finally he came round, he appeared to have undergone some sort
of personal change, bursting into song and prayer and then falling
into protracted, trance-like bouts of silence.

Doctors were called, and then a local exorcist. The boy's head was
shaved, and three X's scored into his scalp; the juice of garlic, lime and
other acidic fruits was poured into the wounds. When the exorcist was
still not satisfied, 108 pots of cold water were poured on the markings
and the boy was beaten with a heavy stick. Finally, some compound
was applied to his eyes which made his head and face swell beyond
recognition and caused tears to flood from his eyes. According to his
biographer, the young Sathya 'never spoke a word or moved a finger'

throughout these barbarities. Not surprisingly perhaps, the exorcist's treatments failed to restore the boy to his usual self. He continued to recite poems and prayers beyond the normal understanding of a thirteen-year-old boy, and to alternate between displays of unusual physical strength and death-like fragility.

On 23 May, writes Professor Kasturi, Sathya rose from his bed as usual, but after some time called the members of his family around him and began to give them sweets and flowers produced from 'nowhere'. Word spread quickly. The neighbours too rushed in and were each given a ball of rice cooked in milk, 'concretised by a mere wave of the hand'. At length Sathya's father arrived from the fields. Angry at the trouble his son had been causing him, he approached him with a stick, demanding, 'Are you a god, or a ghost or a madcap? Tell me.' His son replied, 'I am Sai Baba.' When his father asked, 'What are we to do with you?' his son replied, 'Worship me.' From that point on, the 'miracles' came in abundance. Challenged by someone to prove his identity, the young boy took some jasmine flowers and threw them on the floor. In falling, the flowers arranged themselves to spell out in Telegu letters, 'Sai Baba'. He now produced *vibhuti*, sweets and flowers seemingly at will, and is said to have cured a man of chronic tuberculosis with one touch.

On the morning of 20 October 1940, the boy set out for school as usual, but turned at the school gates and returned home. Standing on his doorstep he threw aside the books he was carrying and declared to his family, 'I am no longer your Sathya. I am Sai.' According to Professor Kasturi, a halo glowed around his head as he renounced life with his family, saying, 'Maya' (worldly illusion) 'has left; I am going; my work is waiting.' He was thirteen years old.

I began to make plans to visit India. I wanted to see Sai Baba for myself. 'Of course,' Dominic Prince said to me, 'you know that Sai Baba knows we are having this conversation, and he knows that you want to write about him. If he wants to see you, he will see you; but if he doesn't want to see you, there is no way you will get to see him. If he doesn't want you to get to Puttaparthi then something will happen to stop you.'

I had no evidence that any of this was true, of course; but I found the thought unsettling nonetheless. At Christmas, unexpectedly and delightfully, a card arrived from Australia. It was from my friend Stephen, who had first told me about Sai Baba so many years ago.

We had lost contact with each other for almost two years. Tucked inside the Christmas card was a small laminated photograph of Sai Baba. This, surely, was some sort of omen. I decided I would put the photograph in my wallet, to take with me to India, as a talisman. I put the photograph back inside the card, and the envelope in which it had arrived, and placed it on the mantelpiece. The next morning, I looked in the envelope. The Christmas card was still there, but the photograph had gone. I searched high and low, but there was no sign of it. It was as if it had vanished into thin air. For a moment I actually found myself wondering if it had somehow been 'dematerialised', 'retrieved' perhaps, and was now in an ashram in India. I found myself wondering if I would find it there.

Ten days later I left for India, still wondering.

3

THE TRAIN
TO DHARMAVARAM

The prolonged lesson in patience and forbearance which is India begins the moment the visitor sets foot in the country. At Bombay airport I queued for two hours to pass through immigration control. When at last I took my place at the desk of a brown-uniformed official he demanded to see my boarding-card. Of course, I had left it on the plane. He ranted and gesticulated for a further fifteen minutes before eventually waving me through in frustration. By the time I had collected my bags and found a taxi, dawn was breaking.

From London I had booked a hotel at Juhu Beach, close to the airport – one of the international chain hotels which line the road to the beach, catering to businessmen and travellers passing through. It quickly became apparent that no one would come to Juhu Beach and wish to stay for long. The morning sun blazed through a fine haze of air pollution. I walked to the beach through a maze of stalls selling food and trinkets. Bombay's sewers, I was told, empty into the bay, but the fetid water was crowded with swimmers, young children splashing in the shallows. Boys offered horse and camel rides, and pulled pitiful-looking performing monkeys on leads of string. Below the veranda of a beachside café, a family staged a performance, tumbling, juggling and forming pyramids. The youngest daughter, no more than seven, perched precariously on a pole, balanced on her father's head, then floated to the sand like a feather, dusted herself off and scampered among the onlookers, shaking a tin can for offerings.

As I sat watching this a steady stream of vendors beat a path across the beach to offer me bags of nuts, nougat, scraps of coconut, plastic toys and knick-knacks. Two *saddhus*, dressed in yellow robes, their faces daubed in white powder, came walking along the beach, changing direction when they saw me. I thought for a moment that they wanted conversation, but they simply stood in front of me demanding cigarettes. I gestured that I had none, and they walked off in a huff. Everybody else, I noticed, had pointedly ignored them.

I retreated to the hotel dining room, air-conditioned almost to the point of freezing and crowded with businessmen loudly making deals over their mobile phones, to the droning accompaniment of Madonna records. It hardly felt like India at all. That night I dreamed of Sai Baba – or rather I sensed the shadow of his presence somewhere in my dream. I came awake, remembering what I had been told by his devotees – that it is impossible to dream of Sai Baba without him willing it; and I wondered if I had really dreamed of him at all.

This belief propagated by his devotees, that Sai Baba knows exactly who each and every one of us is, knows what we are thinking, inhabits our minds, observes our actions, directs our dreams, suddenly struck me as less a belief founded in faith than a grave delusion, or a symptom of a profound need for reassurance. In my dream, somebody – I could not tell who – was telling me that Baba is the three aspects of the Guru, or perhaps it was the Guru in three aspects, simultaneous in time and space. But I had no recollection of what those three aspects might be, and I had not seen his face. But I would see it that morning, framed in tinsel like a Christmas decoration, hanging on the wall of the taxi-stand in Bangalore airport; and again on a medallion, dangling from the rear-view mirror in the motorised rickshaw that carried me from the airport into town.

Bangalore makes much of its status as India's 'garden city'. It is also the centre of the country's computer industry, and the scent of fast money was in the air; new Japanese cars and motor cycles jostled on its streets; huge billboards advertising every imaginable consumer product loomed over its pavements, and young Indians in smart Western clothes thronged its bars and discothèques. Belatedly, perhaps, the yuppie ethic had arrived in India with a vengeance.

In a restaurant I fell into conversation with an American girl named Ingrid. She was returning from Puttaparthi, where she had seen Sai Baba. 'I mean, I'd never heard of him before I came to India, but then I met someone on a train who told me about him, so I was obviously meant to go there, right? And when I got to the ashram, there were no rooms available, and I'm about to leave when out of the blue an Australian woman just offers me her room, and I'd have had to sleep in a dormitory otherwise, and I don't think

I'd have done that. So I have a room to myself, and I think: Wow!
A gift from Sai Baba! How nice! Because this woman had said to
me, if you're here, it's because he's *brought* you here knowingly,
like for a purpose, right?'

'And did you discover it?' I asked.

She pulled a face. 'I have to tell you, I hated it. It was like a
spiritual Disneyworld. I felt it was pretty close to a cult, and I'm
sensitive to that kind of thing. I could just feel my back tensing. I
had to get out.'

I walked back to my hotel through the crowded streets, thinking
of Ingrid's story. You did not have to travel far in India before
hearing such stories of predestination, *kismet*, *karma* – the slips
and slides of chance and synchronicity which bump us through life,
like the flippers and springs of a pinball machine. This seemed to
operate on two distinct levels. There was *karma*, the first kind –
the great, infinitely subtle and mysterious law of cause and effect
which shaped everyone's lives in ways that could never be properly
understood. And then there was *karma*, the second kind – working
its endless influence over backpackers and those on the path, and
which operated in such matters as railway timetables, hotel and
ashram vacancies and chance encounters on public transport.

A stirring of movement in a darkened doorway caught my eye; a
young girl, bandaged in rags and no more than twelve years old,
was asleep on the hard stone floor, cradling her younger sister in
her arms. People stepped past them paying no attention. I pushed
some rupees into the folds of her clothes, hoping the money would
still be there when she awoke, then returned to my hotel, eventually
to fall asleep, feeling angry and impotent.

The train to Dharmavaram left at eight the next morning. A group
of Tamil women had spread themselves on the station platform, their
vividly coloured saris lending them the appearance of a scattering
of wild flowers, their pots and pans and bundles stacked beside
them, silent children turning dark eyes towards me as I humped
my rucksack towards the train, their hands outstretched less in a
gesture of hope than of habit.

The train slipped out of Bangalore, past a roadside temple decorated with gaudily coloured gods, a resident swami superintending
offerings. A slum encampment had been thrown up beside a busy
roundabout, sheets of tarpaulin and rags draped carelessly over
rough frames. Ragged children played in the dust and fumes, under

a billboard advertising a dietary supplement: 'Build Your Child With Bonus'.

I consulted the handbook, 'Pilgrimage Notes and Suggestions for Those Visiting India for the First Time to See Bhagavan Sri Sathya Sai Baba', which had been sent to me by a devotee in England. It read:

> Reduce the luggage you carry about when on the journey of life. Remember, all that is not 'you' is luggage. The mind, the senses, the intelligence, the imagination, the desires, the plans, the prejudices, the discontents, the distress – all are items of luggage. Jettison them soon to make your travel lighter, safer and more comfortable. Less luggage, more comfort.

The imprecation seemed ironic. My bag was weighed down with books about Sai Baba – a library compounded of a tortuous and labyrinthine mixture of historical fact, philosophical speculation, pious faith and blind devotion. As the countryside slipped by outside the window, I immersed myself in the continuing mythology of his life-story.

Following his renunciation of all worldly ties at the age of thirteen, Sai Baba left his parents and set up encampment in Puttaparthi, in the garden of the village accountant, who built him a shed to use as a prayer hall. Pilgrims began to gather around him, and the stories of his miraculous powers grew. As Jesus fed the multitudes with loaves and fishes, so Sai Baba is said to have fed scores of devotees with just two coconuts. He began to travel further afield, around Southern India. At Masulipatam, he walked into the sea, and was seen by devotees to transform into a vision of Sesha-Sayee, the Lord of the Serpent Sesha, reclining on the waves. Shortly afterwards, he threw a silver cup on to the sea, and it returned to him filled with nectar. Flower-petals were transformed into medallions bearing his image and that of Shirdi Sai; *vibhuti* materialised on his forehead. He plucked apples, mangoes, figs and grapes from the branches of a tamarind tree. In his late teens he is said to have performed his first medical operation, in Bangalore, on a duodenal ulcer, materialising the instruments out of thin air. He also operated on the son of the Maharaja of Venkatagiri, for appendicitis, using *vibhuti* as an anaesthetic. The boy felt no pain, and the wound healed immediately.

Pilgrims began to flock to Puttaparthi in their thousands. In 1950, on his twenty-fourth birthday, he inaugurated his ashram on the outskirts of the village, naming it Prasanthi Nilayam – the Abode of the Highest Peace. The prayer hall took two years to build. Girders and bricks were transported to the remote village by train, and then lorry. A broken crane was repaired with the judicious application of *vibhuti*. 'If someone asks you in earnestness where the Lord is to be found,' Sai Baba once said, 'don't dodge; give them the answer that rises on to your tongue from your heart. Direct them to Puttaparthi and invite them to share your joy.'

The word avatar comes from the Sanskrit *ava*, down, and *tri*, to pass. In the Vedic scriptures it means the descent of the Divine into flesh; a living demonstration of the fact that man himself is potentially divine, that God is within man, but obscured by *maya* – the veil of our ego and intellect. An avatar, it is said, is one who has acknowledged and lives in the constant awareness of this divinity within. The powers, or *sidhis*, of the yogi are acquired through hours of meditation, training, practice. But the powers of the avatar are in his nature. He is born with them.

'The *Upanishads*,' Swami Paramahansa Yogananda writes in his spiritual classic *Autobiography of a Yogi*, 'have minutely classified every stage of spiritual advancement.' A *siddha* ('perfected being') has progressed from the state of a *jivanmukta* ('freed while living') to that of *paramukta* ('supremely free' – full power over death); the latter has completely escaped from the mayic thralldom and its reincarnational round. The *paramukta* therefore seldom returns to a physical body; if he does return he is an avatar, a divinely appointed medium of supernal blessings on the world.

Paramahansa Yogananda was one of the great emissaries of Vedic philosophy to the West. Sent by his guru, Sri Yukteswar, to America in 1920, as a delegate to the International Congress of Religious Liberals, he became the first Indian swami ever to be entertained at the White House (by President Calvin Coolidge), and eventually established the Self-Realization Fellowship in California, which was to introduce tens of thousands of students to the science of yoga for the first time.

Whether read as philosophy, history, an exposition of the spiritual traditions and teachings of India, an adventure yarn, or a metaphysical fairy-tale, *Autobiography of a Yogi* – which was first published in 1950 – is a simply extraordinary book, with its account of Yogananda's own path to enlightenment, his meetings with such figures as Mahatma Gandhi and Rabindranath Tagore, and its stories of Himalayan saints and miracle-working yogis and yoginis, utilising the power of consciousness over matter. Reading it for the first time I felt much as I had when confronted by the miracle in Mr Patel's snooker room – a sense of exhilaration and wonder, like a child seeing his first firework display.

Yogananda has much to say on the subject of avatars. He reminds us that *The Upanishads* teaches that an avatar is a being who has power over death, and who is free from any debt to nature.

> The casual glance may see nothing extraordinary in an avatar's form [Yogananda writes], but on occasion, it casts no shadow nor makes any footprint on the ground. These are outward symbolic proofs of an inward freedom from darkness and material bondage. Such a God-man alone knows the Truth behind the relativities of life and death.

'God,' Thomas Aquinas wrote, 'became human in order that human beings might become divine.' And just as Christianity prophesies the second coming of Christ at the time of the Apocalypse, and Islam the coming of the Mahdi, so Hindu scripture and mythology is filled with prophecies of avatars and great teachers who will come in the age of Kali Yuga -- the age of moral and spiritual decline, corruption, oppression and violence – to remind man of his innate divinity.

In the *Bhagavadgita*, Krishna reveals his identity and mission to Arjuna:

> O descendant of Bharata, each time that in some place in the universe religion declines and irreligion advances, I come in person. I incarnate from age to age in order to rescue the pious, to destroy unbelievers, and to re-establish the principles of religion.

In the *Mahabharata*, Vishnu, the Lord of Creation, says:

> When evil is upon the earth, I will take birth in the family of a virtuous man and assume a human body to restore tranquillity. This avatar will possess great energy, great intelligence and great powers. He will restore order and peace in the world, he will inaugurate a new era of truth and will be adored by spiritual people.

Krishna, Rama and Patanjali were ancient avatars. Many Hindus recognise Christ as an avatar. Swami Narayan, the founder of one of the largest Hindu sects in India (and to whom the largest Hindu temple in England – in the unlikely setting of Neasden – is dedicated), and who died in 1820, is believed by his followers to have been the last avatar manifest on earth.

Meher Baba, the mystic who maintained voluntary silence for forty-four years until his death on 31 January 1969, and who numbered the rock musician Pete Townshend among his followers, was adamant in his declaration that he was the avatar of the age, claiming to be 'God personified'.

'I am the Christ,' he said. 'I assert unequivocally that I am infinite consciousness. I am everything and I am beyond everything. Before me was Zoroaster, Krishna, Rama, Buddha, Jesus and Muhammad . . . My present Avataric Form is the last Incarnation of this cycle of time, hence my Manifestation will be the greatest.'

Mother Meera, the young Indian woman who now lives in Germany, is said to be an avatar – a manifestation of the divine feminine principle.

It had been claimed of Sri Aurobindo, the sage of Pondicherry, that he was an avatar; and too his French companion, Mirra Alfassa, known as 'Sweet Mother'. Great prophets like Christ and Krishna, Yogananda suggested, come at a particular time for a particular purpose: they depart as soon as it is accomplished. But other avatars arrive unannounced, unheralded; their works, 'concerned with the slow evolutionary progress of man during the centuries rather than with any one outstanding event of history', go largely unrecognised.

The greatest of these in Yogananda's view was Shiva Mahavatar Babaji – known simply as Babaji – 'the great Yogi-Christ of modern India – the deathless guru'. Babaji was said to be a *mahavatar* – the highest form of a human manifestation of God, not born of a human mother but simply materialising. Yogananda described Babaji's appearance as being that of a youth, no more than twenty-five years old, whose 'beautiful, strong body radiates a perceptible glow'. He lived a migratory life in the Himalayas, able to move instantly from place to place by astral travel.

Yogananda credits Babaji with being the founder of *Kriya Yoga* – 'union (*yoga*) with the Infinite through a certain action or rite (*kriya*)' – having rediscovered and clarified the technique after it had been lost in the Dark Ages. This technique was passed on by Babaji to his disciple Lahiri Mahasaya, who passed it in turn to his disciple Sri Yukteswar and thus to Yogananda, who taught it under the auspices of his Self-Realization Fellowship. According to Yogananda, Babaji was said to have lived through the centuries and to have vowed never to leave his physical body: 'It will always remain visible to at least a small number of people on this earth. The Lord has spoken His own wish through your lips.'

Yogananda encountered Babaji sometime towards the end of the last century. In 1970, Babaji is alleged to have 'reappeared', apparently miraculously unaged, in a sacred cave at the foot of the Kumaon Mount Kailah, close to the river Ganges in a remote village called Hairakhan in Uttar Pradesh. He was discovered in a state of *samadhi* – or meditative trance. He had no known parents or family. Some villagers, it is said, saw him as an old man with a long white beard; others as a young man with no beard. He was seen in different places at the same time. He knew the scriptures, could quote them in Sanskrit as well as Hindi, and was said to be gifted with great wisdom and divine powers.

The mythology that grew up around this particular Babaji added something to Yogananda's account. It was claimed that he had appeared around 1800 to villagers out of a ball of light, and in 1922, before a handful of followers, *disappeared* into a ball of light. He is said to have eaten nothing for two years on end, yet demonstrated boundless energy, and to have performed miracles of healing, feeding multitudes from small portions of food, and sustaining a sacred fire with water when oil was not available. (One is reminded of Shirdi Sai Baba's similar 'miracle'; the works of Indian saints tend to be repetitious.)

In the Seventies, a guru alleged to be the most recent incarnation of Babaji began to gather Western followers around him, and Hairakhan became a point of pilgrimage on the spiritual trail through India. This message was a familiarly eschatological one: that in the age of Kali Yuga mankind was on the brink of destruction; only those that truly worship God would be saved, and a new humanitarian society would arise.

For the first two or three years after his appearance, he hardly spoke at all in public. But some speeches were taped in 1983, a year before his death, in which he made quite specific predictions of a forthcoming Apocalypse. 'In the aftermath of the revolution,' he told

followers, 'which will be total; no country will be spared, big or small –
some countries will be totally erased, leaving no sign of their existence.
In some places 3 to 5 per cent and up to a maximum of 25 per cent of
the population will be spared and will survive. The destruction will
be brought about by earthquakes, floods, accidents, collisions and
wars.' The 'revolution', he claimed, had started on 26 July 1979.

Devotees at his ashram in Hairakhan were encouraged to work,
digging holes and erecting buildings. 'Action is the source of all
joy. Go on working!' he exhorted his followers. 'Go ahead making
progress. Work until your last breath.' Followers, he said, should train
themselves to be like members of a security force, 'Like Scotland Yard
or the CIA. Everybody should be advanced and attentive and should
stand out and be recognised by others.'

When asked once whether it was necessary for everyone who was
open to him and his message to come to Hairakhan he replied, 'No,
but world leaders will have to come here. It is compulsory. When
Krishna went into battle, all the leaders of the time came too, to
join Him on the battlefield of Kurukshetra.' There is no record of
any world leader heeding the call.

Reading the accounts by Babaji's devotees of his miracles, signs and
wonders, I felt uneasily stranded between bemusement, astonishment
and outright disbelief. Were avatars sequential? Was it possible for
there to be more than one on earth at any time? Did they recognise each
other? Meher Baba had said nothing of Babaji. Babaji apparently said
nothing of Sai Baba. There was no formal procedure of recognition
of avatars; no court of appeal. By their acts, it seemed, shall ye
know them.

Sai Baba's claim that he is the new messiah, the avatar of the
age, has been a constant theme of his teaching. He has frequently
identified himself as a *purna* avatar, that is to say, a fully divine
incarnation. Legend decrees that there have been only two *purna*
avatars in history – Rama, who lived 11,000 years ago, and Krishna
who lived some 5,000 years ago. Buddha, Muhammad and Jesus
of Nazareth, Sai Baba has claimed, all had some degree of divine
vision, but they did not come into incarnation, as he did, with their
divine powers intact.

Professor N. Kasturi suggests in *Sathyam Sivam Sundaram* that
Sai was born of immaculate conception. Kasturi tells of a certain
pundit, Mr Rama Sarma, 'well versed in the holy *Puranas*' asking

Sai Baba himself whether he incarnated by entering the world directly (*Pravesa*) or through human conception (*Prasava*).

> Baba turned to His mother, so that she could answer the question. And His mother said, 'I had a dream in which an angel of God (Satyanarayana Deva) told me not to be afraid if something should happen to me through the Will of God. That morning when I was at the well to draw water, a great sphere of blue light came rolling towards me. I lost consciousness and fell to the ground, I felt it slip inside me.' Baba turned to Rama Sarma with a smile. 'There's your answer! I was not born through conception. It was *Pravesa*, not *Prasava*. I was born through a descent, not from human contact.

Professor Kasturi describes Sai Baba as 'a multi-faced avatar' – that is, Rama, Krishna, Christ, Buddha, Zoroaster and others in one; as *Purna Brahman*, 'the Universal Absolute', and as *Sanathana Sarathi*, 'the Eternal Charioteer, who is the inner motivator in all ever since time was'.

Baba has described himself as a sort of divine policeman, come to quell the riotous and lawless human spirit. 'When there is a small local disturbance a police constable is enough to put it down. When the trouble is threatening to develop into sizeable proportions a police inspector is sent; when it grows into a riot, the Superintendent of Police himself has to quell it; but when, as now, all mankind is threatened with moral ruin the Inspector General comes down, that is the Lord.'

On 6 July 1963, Sai Baba announced that he would die in the year 2020, and that eight years later his third incarnation, Prema Sai, would be born in the village of Gunaparthy, in Karnataka state. 'Prema Sai, the Third Avatar,' Sai Baba has said, 'shall promote his evangelic news that not only does God reside in every body, but every one himself is God. That will be the final wisdom which will enable man and woman to rise to be God . . . He will work for the good and welfare of the world, and with his efforts love, goodwill, brotherhood and peace will abound throughout the world. He will receive universal recognition from mankind.'

In 1968, speaking at a world conference of Sai devotees in Bombay, in front of 25,000 people, he announced, 'In this human form of Sai, every divine entity, every divine principle, that is to say, all the names and forms ascribed to God by man are manifest.'

Sai Baba has frequently reiterated that he has not come to make a new religion, but to revive the old ones, 'To make a Christian a better Christian, a Moslem a better Moslem, and a Hindu a better Hindu.'

When one of his numerous biographers, Dr John Hislop, asked whether he was God, Baba is said to have replied, 'Let us say, I am the switch.'

He has often referred to the life of Jesus. At a discourse on Christmas Day in 1979, he announced that the celebrations were somewhat premature. Christ, he claimed, was actually born at 3.15 a.m. on 28 December. A Sunday, apparently. Seven years earlier, again speaking on Christmas Day, he invoked Christ's statement, 'He who has sent me will come again.' Jesus, he claimed, was referring to him, Sai Baba, and that Christ's actual words had been expunged from the Bible. 'His name will be Truth. He will wear a red robe. He will be short with a crown of hair.'

In *My Baba and I*, Dr John Hislop recounts how, out walking one day with Sai Baba, he witnessed the Swami take two twigs from a tree, shape them into a cross and blow on it three times, transforming it into a crucifix, complete with a silver statue of Christ. There was a small hole at the top of the cross. Baba explained that this was because the cross on which Christ was crucified was not hammered into the ground, but hung from a pole.

In 1984 Sai Baba is said to have materialised a photograph, purporting to be a portrait of Christ at the age of twenty-nine, for an Argentinian devotee. This photograph, faded in the manner of a Victorian sepia print, shows a bearded man with deep-set eyes, bearing some resemblance to the popular image of Christ rendered by Renaissance painters. Another story is told of how, in *darshan*, a woman once handed him a black-and-white photograph of the face imprinted on the Shroud of Turin for Baba to bless. As he placed his hand above it, the image immediately disappeared. Baba then made a pass over the blank piece of paper and the image reappeared in colour.

This photograph is circulated widely among Sai Baba devotees, and is reproduced on the cover of *A Gospel for the Golden Age*, by Peter Phipps. Phipps is a Christian and a Salvationist who became a devotee of Sai Baba after counselling survivors of the Armoana massacre in New Zealand, when a crazed gunman killed twelve people. In his book, he makes a detailed list of the correspondences between ancient scriptures and contemporary fact to argue his case for Sai Baba as 'the avatar of the age'.

Citing the Prophecies of Muhammad as recorded in the Hadis, and quoted in the Bihar-of-Anwar, Phipps writes that Muhammad told of 'the Guided One' to come, and gave a list of 300 identifying features, including a physical description of him as being 'short in stature' and 'highly intelligent'. He will have 'profuse hair, wear red robes, have a mole on the cheek, will give gifts that are light in weight, will tread the path of righteousness and gather the seekers of God around him'.

According to Phipps, Muhammad prophesied that this man will live for ninety-six years (the age at which Sai Baba has said that he will die), but that Moslems will only recognise Him nine years before his passing from the Earth. 'You could have stretched out your hand and been with Him, but you missed Him.' (This prophecy is often quoted in Sai Baba literature, but I could find no reference to it in standard Islamic texts.)

> Here is a Being [Phipps writes] who knows literally whenever the wind blows through a blade of grass, who knows our every thought, word and action, who is constantly involved in keeping the whole Universe functioning at every level from the smallest atomic particle to the most vast constellation of stars.

The ardour and devotion of these books made me feel both humbled and slightly uneasy. Like so much writing about the spiritual they had the perverse effect of deflating the spirits rather than raising them; I distrusted the naive simplicity of their faith, and yet, at the same time, found myself almost envying it. I had not had their revelations, their proof, and I did not have their faith. I did not disbelieve the accounts of the experiences, but nor could I wholeheartedly believe them either. I had only the small, nagging voice of doubt.

> It is only a matter of time [Phipps writes] before the churches will have to accept that the Lord has come again. By the end of this decade I expect the churches, beginning perhaps with the Church of Rome . . . to announce that they acknowledge that the Christ is with us now.

I thought this seemed overly optimistic, although one small step had been taken by an Italian priest and academic named Don Mario Mazzoleni, the author of probably the most remarkable of all the books written about Sai Baba. Mazzoleni's *A Catholic Priest Meets Sai Baba* is a methodical study of Christian and Vedic texts in which the author refutes the doctrine of his own church that Christ is the only son of God, and arrives at the conclusion that Christ and Sai Baba are one and the same manifestation of God on earth.

> No human being [Mazzoleni writes] has the authority to declare that God can only incarnate in a certain way, or that He cannot choose to spread His message as he wills, not only through prophets, but also by incarnating as the Christ, that is, as avatars. It would be an unforgivable theological and philosophical absurdity to deny the Divine Power the right of taking human forms in other epochs, among other nations, and in other human forms . . . God cannot be limited by anything, much less by a human mind.

Sai Baba, Mazzoleni concludes, declares his divinity with a forth-rightness 'which only a being of pure divine consciousness or a madman could use'.

Mazzoleni's book was published in Italy in 1990. In May 1992 he was invited by the Vicariate of Rome to 'retreat from his heretical doctrinal positions, to cease causing scandal, and explicitly to retract his errors'. In reply, Mazzoleni wrote that he had not forsaken his Catholic faith. 'On the contrary, after my encounter with the great "Indian Master" Sri Sathya Sai Baba, I feel that I live it with greater intensity, in a spirit of real communion with other religions. These all share the one goal of reaching the same and only God, who transcends all changing names and forms.' Mazzoleni was excommunicated in September 1992.

'Excuse me, sir – you are a follower of Sai Baba?'

I had been so engrossed in my reading that I had not noticed the young man who had joined me in the compartment.

'Not a follower, no . . .' But how should I describe myself? 'An interested observer,' I said.

His name was Niras, and he was Nepalese, a student, on his way from Bangalore, where he studied bio-technology, to his home in Kathmandu.

'Sai Baba is supposed to work miracles, yes?'

'That's what they say,' I replied.

'I'm not believing in miracles myself. The miracle of the milk, you know about this?'

Of course. The newspapers in Britain had been filled with stories of the curious phenomenon of the statues of Ganesh, the elephant god, which were said to drink milk from spoons. First identified in a temple in Delhi, the phenomenon had spread like wildfire through India and, within hours, to Britain (in itself, a miracle of the technological age, it seemed). There had been queues at Hindu temples of devotees, force-feeding statues with milk; shortfalls of the precious fluid reported at supermarkets and corner stores.

According to Hindu mythology, such miracles are said to mark a particularly propitious birth, and this too had been connected to Sai Baba. A devotee had told me that the day on which the statues had been taking milk, the girl who would become the mother of Sai Baba's next incarnation, Prem Sai, had been born. At a temple in Wembley, it was said, even as the statue of Ganesh was taking milk, a photograph of Sai Baba was producing *vibhuti* and nectar in sympathetic celebration. It was one of those stories.

The young boy smiled politely. 'Is surface tension, I think. The stone absorbs the milk, and people believe . . .' He shrugged.

'But this question of reincarnation, yes – I am believing in this. I have heard that Sai Baba is a good man, but I don't think I believe in God. Because I am studying science, you see.' He laughed again and we fell silent, our thoughts stilled by the sound of the train rattling over the tracks.

'We have a living goddess in Nepal, you know. Her name is Kumari, and she is three and a half years old.'

'Have you seen her?' I asked.

'No, not me. She stays in her house. Sometimes she comes to the window and looks down, but I have never seen her. When she is older, when she becomes a woman, you know?' He smiled sheepishly and gestured towards his groin. 'The blood . . .'

When she menstruates?

'Yes, when she menstruates, then another goddess must be found.'

'But you,' I teased him, 'don't believe in God, or in goddesses . . .'

At Dharmavaram, I took a bus to Puttaparthi. It shook and rattled across a countryside of baking browns and yellows, swerving to avoid oncoming vehicles, the driver with his hand jammed on the horn. I loved passing through these small villages, the rough, squat plaster houses in browns and oranges, the sudden splash of colour on a roadside stall or in a doorway, signalling some provisional and haphazard commercial enterprise; the somnambulistic oxen, pulling carts behind them, their horns painted or wrapped in tinsel, like Christmas decorations.

In the middle of open countryside, we passed under an elaborate alabaster arch, decorated with the symbol of ecumenicalism which is the motif of Baba's organisation – the first evidence that we were nearing Puttaparthi. A sign by the road announcing a water project provided by Sai Baba was followed by another, for a residential project, 'Divine Valley – a Spiritual Paradise', then 'Sai Mansions – deluxe apartments available' and 'Welcome to Sai Devotees! Sri Sathya Sai Spiritual Resorts Pvt. Ltd'. Whatever blessings Sai Baba may have brought to the world, there could be no doubting the blessings he had brought to the region's landowners and property developers.

Outside Puttaparthi, an improbable vision came into view: a huge building, looking for all the world like a Mogul palace, surmounted by onion domes and set in immaculately tended gardens. This was the Sathya Sai Super Speciality Hospital, designed by an English architect, Dr Keith Critchlow, of the Prince of Wales College of Architecture, and largely paid for by an American devotee named Isaac Tigrett, one of the founders of the Hard Rock Café chain, with the proceeds from the sale of his share of the business. (Curiously, Sai Baba's presence continues to haunt the Hard Rock in London. His photograph is on the wall behind the bar, in curious juxtaposition to the collection of guitars, gold records and stage costumes on the walls, smiling benignly over the crowds guzzling beers and hamburgers. I carried in my wallet a 'gold card' from the Hard Rock, a talisman of some media mail-out, which bore one of Baba's dictums: 'Love All, Serve All'. It entitled me to jump the queue at the door. The paradoxes in all this hardly bore thinking about.)

A short distance from the hospital, the bus passed a new air-strip, constructed both to serve the hospital and receive pilgrims from all over India. Then, at last, we were in Puttaparthi itself.

In two days' time it would be the Festival of Makara Sankranthi – a festival dedicated to the god of the sun, a period of energising and invigorating all life, and a propitious time for *sadhana*, or spiritual discipline – and the bus station was crowded with coaches, groaning under the weight of pilgrims and their baggage. A sign on the wall announced that the bus station too had been donated to Puttaparthi by Sai Baba.

Prasanthi Nilayam – the ashram of Sai Baba – stands in the very centre of Puttaparthi, behind high stone walls: a castle, it seemed, around which flooded a stream of commerce and mayhem, as if a caravanserai of pedlars, merchants, entrepreneurs, beggars, mendicants and chancers of every age and hue had pitched camp at its gates.

It was early evening; the afternoon *darshan* – or audience – with the guru had evidently come to an end and people were flooding out of the ashram gates into the street. A security guard nodded me through the gate. The babble from the other side of the wall receded to a barely perceptible hum, and then to something which almost resembled silence, save for the faint sound of music humming over the public address system.

The ashram was enormous. The drab, uniform dormitory blocks that lined the outside wall gave way to the most extraordinary structures; the *mandir* – or temple; an auditorium; and Baba's residence, Byzantine confections, sculpted in vivid pink and blue stone, like marzipan, decorated with deities as vivid as cartoons. I thought of Ingrid's description of the ashram as 'a spiritual Disneyland'.

The paths and walkways were crowded with people, perhaps one third of whom were Westerners. Of these, the women wore saris and scarves, while most of the men were observing the ashram's preferred dress code of white trousers and crisp white shirts – a uniform which occasioned a curious sinking feeling in my stomach. The Indians in the crowd seemed less hidebound; many of them wore brightly coloured shirts, and they chatted happily among themselves. By comparison, the Westerners seemed to be shrouded in an air of self-absorption. Nobody, I noticed, seemed to be laughing, or even smiling. I suddenly felt acutely conscious of my travel-soiled clothes, my dishevelled appearance and the rucksack flung over my shoulder.

I found my way to the admissions office and queued to register, then queued again for accommodation. There were no rooms left, I was told, only a bunk in a dormitory. I was tired and dirty and the thought of sleeping in a dormitory was suddenly intolerable. I would find a hotel. I walked back out of the ashram. Night had fallen, and the streets of the village were crowded with people.

There was a hotel directly opposite the ashram gates, a four-storey building, wedged between a jumble of shops. It looked newly built. I was shown to a room that was barely furnished and filthy; the price exorbitant. Only in India, I thought, could they conspire to make a new hotel seem so squalid. But I was too tired to look for anywhere else. The houseboy handed me the key-ring, inevitably bearing the image of Sai Baba. 'Sai Ram,' he said, backing out of the door with a smile.

You're ripping me off and laughing at me, I thought. The mood of anticipation that had sustained me on the journey was quickly evaporating into sourness and cynicism. I washed off the dust of the journey under a sparse trickle of cold water from the shower, then took a walk through the village, examining the detritus and tat that spilled out of the shops. Every shop was a jangling bazaar of Sai Baba merchandise – posters, ball-point pens, books, tapes, T-shirts, saris. His photograph was in every restaurant, every guest-house; his voice blared from shop doorways on beatboxes and ghetto-blasters, wafting his discourses on to the streets. My mind went back to the picture I had received all those weeks ago from Stephen in Australia. Whatever mystery or significance I had invested in its disappearance had evaporated. What did a picture mean or matter, after all? Here were literally thousands just like it, for a few rupees apiece.

At every step, I was dogged by shopkeepers attempting to wave me inside their premises, or people asking for money. I had never encountered so many beggars in such a confined space. A fragment of a verse from childhood – I could not remember what exactly – echoed in my mind: the rich man in his castle, the poor man at the gate . . .

In my room, I lay in bed, under a naked light bulb, thumbing through Professor Kasturi's book, and came across a pronouncement by Sai Baba on the burdens of divinity.

Some of you may feel that it is glorious for the Lord to come in human form. If you were in My place, you would not feel so glorious. For, I am aware of the past, present and future of every one of you. Therefore, I am not moved by mercy. I know why a person suffers in this birth, what it is the consequence of. So I react differently to you; you may call Me either cold-hearted or soft-hearted. I do not cause joy or grief; you design the chains that bind you, both gold and iron.

I turned off the light, and drifted into a half-sleep. I awoke in the darkness, the high-pitched whine of a mosquito in my ear, my arms and legs stinging from bites. Unable now to sleep, I cast my *karma* to the winds, and spent the rest of the night vengefully thrashing at the mosquitoes with my shoe, experiencing a feeling of crazed exultation with every minute black shape that I splattered against the whitewashed walls.

4

IN THE HOUSE OF GOD

In the ashram notes, I read a message from Sai Baba.

> Never underestimate what is being accomplished by the act of *darshan*. My walking amongst you is a gift yearned for by the Gods of the Highest Heaven and here you are receiving this grace. Be thankful. But also remember that to whom much is given – from him much will be demanded.

When in Prasanthi Nilayam, Sai Baba gives *darshan* at seven each morning in the *mandir* – a huge, rectangular marble-floored hall, the size of a football pitch, open on three sides, and built to accommodate upwards of 3,000 people. I arrived at five-thirty, to find that the courtyard outside the *mandir* had already begun to fill with devotees, preparing for the long wait for *darshan* to begin. Men and women are encouraged to remain separate within the ashram. They eat in different dining rooms, and enter the *mandir* from separate entrances at either end of the courtyard. I joined the men, milling around on the path, and in the dust of the courtyard. It is forbidden to wear shoes in the *mandir*, and piles of sandals and trainers had begun to accumulate along the walls and around the base of a huge tree which gave shelter to one corner of the courtyard.

Many of the Westerners, I noticed, had come in organised 'Sai' groups, and in addition to their white shirts and trousers wore scarves tied around their necks, like Boy Scouts, embroidered with the name of their country – Italy, Australia, Poland, Canada, Britain – lending the occasion the air of an international spiritual jamboree. This uniform seemed to be modelled on that worn by the ashram volunteers, universally known as the 'Seva guards' (*seva* means service), and identifiable by their blue neckerchiefs and the bossy, imperious manner they adopted to steer people off the paths and into the courtyard.

Devotees had arranged themselves in a series of ragged lines, waiting to be ushered into the *mandir*. I chose a line, sat down and waited, then waited some more. Some people bowed their heads in prayer, some studied books; nobody spoke. Some had brought pillows and blankets to sit on, and many of the Westerners carried what appeared to be large nylon shoulder bags, stamped with a logo saying 'Sai Ram'; these unfolded to make a hinged cushion and back-rest, which tied around the waist – a novel solution to the excruciating austerities of sitting cross-legged on a hard marble floor. For some reason, a part of me felt scornful of this soft compromise. But soon I wished I had one myself, to relieve my aching back.

At length, one of the volunteers passed along the front of the lines, holding a bag from which the first person in each line took a piece of paper, stamped with a number. Now the system of queuing became clear. Every devotee wants to be as close as possible to Sai Baba as he processes through the *mandir*. The lines which had drawn the lowest numbers would enter the *mandir* first; and thus be closest. Arriving early was no guarantee after all: providence would decide. 'What number? What number?' The information passed back along the line like a Chinese whisper. 35. Not so close. People shrugged and tried to conceal their disappointment.

At six, the Seva guards began to wave the first lines into the *mandir*, up a flight of steps and through a metal-detector, of the sort one finds at airports, its high-pitched, mechanical bleep fracturing the silence. It took almost forty-five minutes for all the lines to file inside, shuffling closer together at the urgings of the Seva guards. The *mandir* was spacious and airy, perfumed with the sweet smell of incense. On one side was an elaborate altar, with an idol of Shirdi Sai Baba at its centre, flanked on either side by life-size portraits of Shirdi Sai and Sri Sathya Sai Baba. Pictures of saints and teachers – Ramakrishna, Vivekananda, Buddha and Christ among them – decorated the walls.

A regiment of young Indian men, all dressed in white, had gathered at the *mandir* entrance, and now jogged to their places like a praetorian guard: students from the Sai university located in the ashram. Seats on the stage close to the altar were occupied by ranks of men, also dressed in white: teachers, dignitaries, bureaucrats of the organisation. A red-velvet swivel armchair had been placed centre-stage. This was Sai Baba's.

At seven, music suddenly filled the air, a gently undulating rhythm, filtering from loudspeakers in the roof of the *mandir*. A tangible ripple of expectation, like a keening sigh, passed across the crowd. He is coming! He is coming! Necks craned. At an entrance on the far side of the hall, beyond where the women sat, a figure had appeared. He was wearing a flame-coloured robe, fitted closely to his body and falling to the floor, almost covering his bare feet. There was the frizzy halo of black hair, there the plump, fleshy face.

He walked slowly through the crowd, almost gliding, it seemed, gazing this way and that at the sea of upturned faces, occasionally pausing to offer a word, a gesture. As he passed, people clasped their hands together in the *namaste*; those in the front rows touched their foreheads to the ground where he had walked, and hands reached out tentatively to touch his feet. He wound his way thus through the *mandir*, mounted the stage and exchanged a few words with the seated dignitaries, then walked to the red armchair and sat down. Now the music changed, to a lilting, almost jaunty air. Sai Baba settled into the chair, and waved his hand gently in time to the music, as if stirring the air. People who craned forward, or rose from their feet, the better to enjoy this spectacle, were pulled down by their neighbours. He sat for some moments, apparently indifferent to the people around him, for all the world as if he was alone in his private room.

Now he gestured towards the ranks of students seated to his right, and they sprinted from the hall, returning moments later with large metal bowls, filled with small cakes, wrapped in tissue paper. As the boys moved among the crowd, distributing the paper parcels, hands reaching up with desperation to grab them, Sai Baba reclined on his throne, an indulgent smile on his face. Finally, the tumult subsided. The crowd settled back on to the hard marble floor. There were a few moments' silence. Then Sai Baba rose from his chair, and with the briefest of waves, left the *mandir*.

That was *darshan*. Sai Baba did not demand anything of his devotees, it seemed, except devotion. There were no techniques, no special meditations. His message was simplicity itself, emblazoned on the posters that one saw everywhere in the ashram: 'Love All, Serve All.'

I spent that morning exploring the ashram. Sai Baba's residence was adjacent to the *mandir*, a large building, in the architectural style of a temple, sculpted in pink sandstone. From his balcony, the

Swami could look down on a towering plinth, surmounted by an open lotus, with the symbols of the world's great faith, set around its base. Directly opposite – the first thing Sai Baba would see each morning as he threw open his shutters – stood a shop selling ice-creams and milk-shakes: The Milky Way, 'the cream of ice-cream parlours'. A broad path led to the door of the residence, but when I stepped on to it I was immediately stopped by a Seva guard, gesticulating in an agitated fashion and shouting, 'Not allowed, not allowed.' Sai Baba has said that one day Prasanthi Nilayam will be 'bigger and more significant' than Delhi. It is certainly cleaner. I had never been anywhere so meticulously tended. The paths were swept endlessly. The very atmosphere seemed purged of any imperfection.

There were huge numbers of people milling around the paths, seated in groups, talking quietly among themselves or reading, and queuing at the canteens for breakfast, and at the store where one could buy food, provisions and soft drinks. (The prices, I noticed, were somewhat less than in the shops outside the ashram gates.) I sat on a wall, sharing my breakfast of bread and cheese with a morose-looking dog that had trailed me from the food stall.

Everywhere I walked there were pictures of Sai; imprecations to virtue. Outside a lecture hall, a notice drew the attention of devotees to an apartment development outside the ashram walls which, the notice explained, the developers were wrongly claiming had been blessed by Sai Baba. Devotees were cautioned not to become 'entangled in such dubious transactions'. Neither in the ashram itself, nor in any of its literature, could I could see any direct evidence of solicitations for money, other than the modest fees for accommodation and food. But clearly, money came from somewhere, and lots of it. The Sai Baba organisation includes colleges, schools, hospitals. The ashram itself is enormous. Something had paid for this. Only later did I notice somebody in the administration offices filling out a banker's order, available on request.

Next to the offices was a bookshop – more a warehouse – its shelves filled with transcriptions of Sai Baba's discourses and teachings, and biographies and personal memoirs by the score. Many writers had come in search of Sai Baba, it seemed, looking for some sort of affirmation, and they had left as devotees. I had read a few of these books, and wondered as I read them whether the pilgrimage I was making, the book I planned to write, would make me a devotee too.

My handbook offered a lengthy list of rules to be observed in the ashram, pertaining to dress, diet, washing, queuing, transistor radios, lights out (9 p.m.) and laundry. A code of conduct included the following advice:

> Do not get friendly with persons not known to you and encourage them to develop business relations with you; do not pay attention to those who claim to have close associations with Bhagavan, or to have 'inner' messages, or special Blessings from Bhagavan; do not rely on rumours, stories and personal impressions of other individuals. For information about Bhagavan and His teachings, read the books available from the ashram bookstall.

Visitors were encouraged not to leave the ashram, nor to engage in 'unnecessary talk', but to spend the day reading, attending lectures or in silent contemplation. Meals, it was suggested, should be taken in the ashram canteen; toiletries and essentials bought from the ashram shop. If leaving the ashram, my guide book advised, visitors should do their business and return quickly – as if the heaving tumult beyond the ashram walls, the trinkets glittering in the shops and stalls, were a source of moral pollution. One guide book warned explicitly, 'It is dangerous to eat in the village,' which I thought was taking a search for purity too far.

These words of advice did not seem to discourage people. The shopkeepers of Puttaparthi had no shortage of business. 'Sai Ram, Sai Ram,' they chanted as you walked past, as if the name itself were a charm to lure you inside; 'Sai Ram,' chanted the waiters in the cafés and restaurants, and the men who ran the STD phone booths which lined the village street. 'Sai Ram,' said the beggars, the street urchins, the cripples dragging themselves miserably through the dust, the mothers with babes in arms who tugged at your sleeve as you walked past, and tugged again when you sat down at a pavement café to drink coffee. 'Sai Ram,' said the devotees in their 125-dollar Reeboks, scrabbling in their pockets for change, or shooing the beggars away and scurrying back to the safety of the ashram.

There was a reason for the metal-detectors at the entrance to the *mandir*. On the night of Sunday 6 June 1991 four armed men broke into Sai Baba's private chambers, apparently intent on assassinating him, and murdered his chauffeur and his cook. The men lived in the ashram and were all devotees of Sai Baba. They were found by police in his living room, supposedly wearing bloodstained clothes and brandishing daggers. Sai Baba was said to have actually witnessed the attack on his two servants and 'chided the assailants', then slipped out of the living room and locked the door behind him before raising the alarm. This much could be discerned from Indian newspaper reports; everything else was speculation, gossip, rumour.

According to ashram officials, the assassination attempt was the result of a struggle between rival factions of devotees who had been denied positions of influence in the ashram. There were rumours of a conspiracy by 'foreign powers', or by political factions in India, fearful of Sai Baba's influence. (The ashram's board of trustees at the time included a former Chief Justice Minister, a former Supreme Court Judge, a former Chief of Air Staff, as well as the usual quota of prominent businessmen and public officials.)

At a public meeting, Sai Baba subsequently said that 'jealousy' was the cause of the attack, and criticised the press for false reporting and allegations that the attack was intended to 'destabilise' his spiritual empire. 'No power,' he said, 'can control or destabilise it.' He was never called to give evidence in the case, and has not commented on it since.

The Indian newspapers raised the obvious questions. Shouldn't a man who is omniscient have been able to anticipate the attack and avert it? And why did an incarnation of God need burglar alarms?

'I stayed in a small ashram in Gujarat with a swami. I couldn't understand a word he was saying, but his voice was so sweet it danced in my head. Then I went to Poona, y'know, to the Osho place? God, it was so horrible. It makes this place seem holy.' The man from California stubbed out his cigarette and ordered another coffee. We were sitting in a café, a short walk from the ashram gates, where people gathered to swap stories, to grumble, to compare notes and miracles. At an adjacent stall, a man produced wrist-watches bearing Sai Baba's image, using nothing more miraculous than a screwdriver and magnifying glass.

'What I really like about this place,' said Erica, 'is the people. I love a motley crew – and this is a motley crew.' Erica was from Oxford – a bright, cheerful, straightforward woman, travelling with her teenage daughter. And she was right. It was a motley crew. Australian back-packers; recidivist American hippies; austere-looking devotees in Sai Ram T-shirts, reading books or scribbling postcards, middle-aged European women in saris, sneaking out from the ashram for a furtive cigarette, like naughty schoolchildren behind the bicycle sheds.

Erica was an academic who, in the summer of her life, had decided to launch England's first bicycle-rickshaw service, an ecologically sound form of public transport. Erica knew more about the alloys used in bicycle frames and methods of gearing than anyone I had ever met. She had been told to come and see Sai Baba, she said, by a clairvoyant in London. I must have looked surprised – Erica did not seem the type to place much credence in clairvoyants. 'I *know* it sounds weird. I'm certainly not what you'd call a guru person. But we were coming to India anyway, so I thought: Why not? What I like about him is that he's saying we should dedicate our energies and talents to public service. That can't be bad, can it?' Erica had resolved to tithe 10 per cent of the pre-tax profits from her new business to clean-air campaigns.

'But you wouldn't describe yourself as a devotee?' I said.

'Most of the Westerners I speak to here, I ask them the same question,' said Erica with a laugh. 'And they all say no, then *but* . . . like underlined three times.'

I was familiar with this uncertainty. To commit yourself to the divinity of a guru was a big step; but, then again, nobody wanted to rule it out altogether, just in case. Is Sai Baba an avatar? Is he God? Does he really perform miracles? You could have a dozen conversations about this in the course of a morning. You could hear *vibhuti* tales, wrist-watch tales, healing tales. Tales about voices, messages, dreams, strange currents, weird drifts and twists of fate, dances of synchronicity, flips of providence, doors opening, opportunities suddenly presenting themselves.

'But, listen, you'll never believe this . . .' I had heard that before. Jackie was a handsome, rangy-looking woman in her mid-fifties. She wore a white sari and a flower behind her ear, and she carried an umbrella to protect herself from the sun. Twice married, twice divorced, she was an artist working in stained-glass. 'So I was in France and somebody had given me a book on Sai Baba, which I read. I'd parted from my second husband the year before and I'd had quite a struggle to survive the emotional trauma and the debt incurred. I was on my way back to England, and I went into a cathedral to pray, and I smelled sandalwood. I thought then: That's a bit strange – sandalwood in a cathedral. Then I remembered that the book mentioned that if you smelled sandalwood or jasmine and there was no obvious source, then Baba was present.

'And when I got back home to England, I smelled it again in my cottage, so strongly I found it hard to concentrate on my work. A friend came and giving me a hug caught the scent and said it was coming off my hair and hands. I was embarrassed; I thought: Why me? But I knew that I had to come here, and I did. When I first went to *darshan* I sat in the front row, and when Swami came he looked me straight in the eye and I *knew* him. When something knocks you back, that's when you're ready for him. Doors open; you have dreams; something is said in your hearing and it moves you. Everything you're guided to do seems easy, and if it doesn't seem easy then you're on the wrong path.'

I found such stories mystifying and enthralling but at the same time strangely unsettling. They reminded me of the film *Close Encounters of the Third Kind*, in which ordinary people suddenly find themselves in the thrall of some inexplicable compulsion, 'chosen', for reasons that are never made clear, by a force greater than themselves to fulfil their destiny. But *Close Encounters of the Third Kind*, of course, was fiction. I had no sense of being 'chosen'. The circumstances that had led me here seemed all too explicable.

I liked Jackie, with her unapologetic candour, her wide open smile and her umbrella, the flower she wore behind her ear, and her boundless optimism and faith. I felt impoverished and curiously heavy beside her, as if I carried the entire weight of scepticism on my shoulders. By comparison, Jackie seemed as light as a feather.

'This is what happens,' said Jackie. 'I believe that as soon as you start working for something greater than yourself then things *do* start to happen.' At *darshan* yesterday, Jackie said, she had seen white light flashing around Baba's head. I had seen nothing.

I left my first hotel, and found myself a cleaner, cheaper room, above a café, a short walk from the ashram gates. It was a small room, with blue shutters and cream walls and a cooling stream of air from a circling fan; I could hear the clatter from the kitchen, and a soft murmur of voices rising from the street below. I would rise each morning at four and walk through the village stirring in the darkness, the sound of a cock crowing, the rising chorus of birdsong, to take my place in the courtyard.

The ritual is always the same. The sitting down, the lining up, the filing in, the sing-song electric chirrup of the metal-detector. A man rises from his line, to walk away, and immediately another man senses unfair advantage. 'Hey, *siddown*. Stay in your place.' The disabled on sticks and in wheelchairs; the sufferers from Aids, cerebral palsy. All of humanity's sorrow and all of its yearning could be felt keenly here: faith, hope and desperation – all were palpable. The Sai students jogging into the *mandir* in their white uniforms, with name tags, some holding hands like schoolchildren. Baba moving through the crowd, heads bowing, hands reaching out to him. For some people, he pauses, exchanges a word or two, then reaches out to bless them. Perhaps in these moments, in the graceful, deliberate movement of his hands, he produces *vibhuti*. I am never close enough to tell. His expression is ever impassive; even his smile seems to reveal nothing; his appearance is fastidiously maintained (is he wearing powder, perhaps?), the face fleshy, the lips full, almost sensual. Devotees talked of his beautiful countenance, his heavenly gaze, his divine smile. But nothing can will me to see it. I had expected to be awed by the mood of reverence and adoration, to feel its contagion dissolving my bemusement and uncertainty. But if, like others I have spoken to, I have been called I can feel no sense of it.

Has Sai taken your letter? people asked. Have you had an interview? How do you get to be chosen? Everybody wanted to be chosen. You could see the people clutching their letters in their hands as they waited in the courtyard for *darshan* to begin. What were they asking for? A meeting? A blessing? Healing? All these and more, perhaps. As he passed among the crowd, the hands would reach out to him, clutching notes and envelopes, and you could see the look of eagerness and desperation flashing in people's eyes. Some he would take, passing them back over his shoulder to the young men walking behind him. By the end of *darshan* they would be holding a hundred, perhaps two hundred letters in all. Some he ignored altogether. It was never clear what determined his choice. What caught his eye? A certain gesture? A look of boldness or of chastened humility? Was it faith that was rewarded, need, or persistence? 'He sees into people's hearts,' I was told. It was during this procession among the faithful that he would choose those for interview. Again, it was never clear why particular people were chosen, or even how this was done; a gesture or a word would pass between Baba and his attendants, and at the end of the ceremony, a handful of people would rise and be led to a room at the back of the *mandir*.

I was never chosen. The constant recurrence of Sai Baba in my life began to seem less like design than the mere play of coincidence – if there is such a thing. It was a search for conviction rather than conviction itself that had drawn me here, and I could find none in myself. A saying of Sai Baba came to mind, referring to those who are not immediately and deeply touched by his presence. 'Old souls need a gentle touch with a hammer, young souls need twenty blows with a sledge-hammer.' So perhaps I was young, then. In this atmosphere of surrender and fervent devotion I began to feel curiously inadequate, wanting.

I had made friends with a Dutch woman, Anneka, who was in her early forties and who had suffered from multiple sclerosis. 'I was blind in one eye,' she told me. 'Now I am one of the fortunate people who are cured. My mother gave my picture to someone, who came here and gave it to Baba. And I started to improve.'

'And you think Sai Baba was responsible?' I asked.

'To be honest, I don't know. But I started to realise then that by changing my thinking, my attitude, I could make myself better. If you learn to listen to the body and develop bodily awareness, you can stop fighting it and come to an agreement with your body. Maybe Sai Baba was teaching me this.'

She shrugged. 'I'm not sure I'm believing in him myself. But if you get healing in your body, and it works, then you don't care how it works; you're just grateful. My parents were scientists, you know. I was schooled in logic. Once, I too used to believe only in scientific proof; now I believe in the truth of personal experience.'

The hard and fast laws of empiricism tended to evaporate in the heat of such conversations. What Western orthodoxy regarded as superstitious, wishful thinking – impossible – was here taken for granted. The apparently miraculous was commonplace. Why do you have to question it? people said. Accept it. Experience is its own proof. Through faith some connection is made. Is Sai Baba healing, or is faith in Sai Baba allowing people to heal themselves? What difference does it make either way? Even those who professed no faith talked of having been healed. As many as those who professed faith but had experienced no healing at all.

The books that I had read about Sai Baba contained countless examples of his powers of healing; testimonies from doctors, professors, civil servants, directors of the railways and postal services. He is said to have 'taken on' heart attacks, strokes, mumps, typhoid, and the pains of childbirth on behalf of his devotees. In one of these stories, a Dr Bannerjee recounts how he once touched the hem of Baba's robe at *darshan*, and his damaged finger, which was causing him great pain, immediately healed – a story which echoes the biblical account of a woman being healed by touching the hem of Christ's garment.

There are at least two claims that he has resurrected patients believed to be dead, although in both cases clinical death has not been proved. These accounts of Sai Baba's healings are thoroughly chronicled; too numerous to be dismissed as fantasy, wishful thinking or conspiracy. Yet the books seldom contained the accounts of those who had come in hope of healing and been disappointed. In England, a friend told me how she had come to see Sai Baba twenty years before, with a young man who was dying of cancer. Each day the sick man made his way to *darshan*, and each day Sai Baba conspicuously ignored him. After two months, he died, without a visit, or so much as a word from the Holy Man.

I had read this in Don Mario Mazzoleni's *A Catholic Priest Meets Sai Baba:*

> Some people who have seen Sai Baba pass in front of so many sick people, often without even looking at them, think they detect a mark of cruel insensitivity in this behaviour. The truth is that His apparent indifference to illness, which is nothing but a tiny episode among so many existences, contains a deeper message; it is not your bodies which move Me to pity – the great Master would tell us – but only your mental state. Heal your minds and then your bodies too will no longer undergo suffering. First remove all the causes which have brought you pain, and you will have perfect health.

> Then there is the profound and complex question of *karma* [Howard Murphet writes in *Sai Baba: Man of Miracles*]. To what extent is the specific ailment or the approach of death *karmic*, and how far should the God-man interfere with the patient's *karma*?

A question, perhaps, which only the God-man himself could answer.

It would be interesting, I thought, to know how many people die at Sai Baba's ashram; and how many are saved. But if there were such statistics I could never find them. The stories of his miraculous powers grew daily. When the River Chitravati, which flows near Puttaparthi, threatened to burst its banks and flood the village, he is said to have 'ordered' the floods to subside, although the rain continued to fall. 'If Swami wanted to,' I was told, 'he could have built the hospital, the school, with a wave of his hand. But he wants people to do these things for themselves.'

People said he never read books, yet he was able to quote from the Bible, the Koran, Marx, Kant and Socrates, as well as Hindu scriptures. They said he never slept. There were accounts of him travelling in the 'etheric form' and materialising in several places simultaneously. Like his predecessor, Shirdi Sai, he is said to have appeared before devotees in animal form – as a beggar, a *sadhu*, a workman. I thought back to the house I had visited in North London, the young Indian boy who 'saw' Sai Baba there; the meals that were left out for him, and eaten.

Among the most spectacular and famous of his phenomena was the production in his stomach of *lingams* – ellipsoids, about an inch and a half in length and made either from quartz, crystal, gold or silver – which he would regurgitate and take from his mouth. This extraordinary feat would take place each year at the Shivarati Festival, in front of spellbound crowds. The *lingam* symbolises the primary polarity principle of positive and negative forces on which the universe is founded – the basic principle and power of creation. Sai Baba has described it as a symbol of:

> . . . beginninglessness and endlessness, or the Infinite . . . That in which all names and forms merge . . . and that towards which all forms proceed. It is the fittest symbol of the omnipotent, omniscient and omnipresent Lord. Everything starts from it and everything is subsumed in it.

Some of these stories of healings, of divine intervention, were truly extraordinary and moving. But others seemed merely silly. Why would Sai Baba bother to help a Mrs Venkatamuri find her lost travellers' cheques on a shopping trip to Paris, when children were starving to death, and people dying? The stories of materialisations were countless. In 1970, Professor Kasturi estimated that Sai Baba had already produced in excess of five tons of *vibhuti* in his lifetime (I wondered, how did he arrive at this figure?). Then there were the wrist-watches, rings, amulets, icons, pendants, rosaries, lockets, figurines. More wrist-watches. 'I like this story,' said Anneka. 'A young man devotee went for an interview and Baba just said to him, without any reproach or judgement, you must stop wasting time. And then he materialised a wrist-watch for him, and of course it was showing exactly the right time. And I heard if he is wasting time, the watch stops.'

That *was* a good story, although it struck me less as an act of kindness than a recipe for a nervous breakdown.

Among the most remarkable of these stories of materialisations is one concerning a ring given to Dr John Hislop, the author of several books on Sai Baba. Hislop recounts that in discussing his next incarnation, Prema Sai, Sai Baba produced a ring, studded with a large brownish stone, imprinted with what appeared to be a face, in fuzzy profile. That, said Sai Baba, was Prema Sai. Stephen, the friend who had first told me of Sai Baba more than twenty years ago, had seen the ring in Puttaparthi, on John Hislop's finger, shortly after it had been made. Ten years later he met Hislop again. The face on the ring had now turned from profile to full-face and clarified to show a man with straight hair, a beard and a vaguely Western appearance. John Hislop is now dead. He never allowed the ring to be photographed in his lifetime.

In *Autobiography of a Yogi*, Paramahansa Yogananda describes his meeting with Gandha Baba, a swami able to conjure the smell of whatever perfume he chooses in the outstretched hand of the supplicant. Yogananda is unimpressed. 'Perfume fades with death,' he reflects. 'Why should I desire that which only pleases my body?' 'But many members of the Calcutta intelligentsia are among his followers,' a disciple tells him. 'I inwardly resolved not to add myself to their number,' Yogananda retorts. 'A guru too literally "marvellous" was not to my liking.'

Yogananda offers a helpful explanation of Gandha Baba's powers:

The different sensory stimuli to which man reacts – tactual, visual, gustatory, auditory and olfactory – are produced by vibratory variations in electrons and protons. The vibrations in turn are regulated by *prana*, 'lifetrons', subtle life forces or finer-than-atomic energies intelligently charged with the five distinct sensory idea-substances. Gandha Baba, attuning himself with the pranic forces by certain yoga practices, was able to guide the lifetrons to rearrange their vibratory structure and to objectify the desired result. His perfume, fruit and other miracles were actual materialisations of mundane vibrations, and were not inner sensations hypnotically produced.

Wonder-workings such as those shown by the Perfume Saint, Yogananda concludes, 'are spectacular but spiritually useless . . . digressions from a serious search for God'. But the true yogi, Yogananda suggests, who has reached his Infinite Goal, exercises his powers as he pleases. 'All his actions, miraculous or otherwise, are then performed without *karmic* involvement. The iron filings of *karma* are attracted only where a magnet of the personal ego still exists.' As an avatar, Sai Baba was said to be beyond the chains of ego, a being unbounded by time, space or the chains of *karma*.

Sai Baba himself has consistently refused to submit to any sort of objective, scientific investigation into his powers, saying they are gifts from God for his followers, not entertainments:

> My miracles are part of the unlimited power of God and are in no sense the product of yogic powers, which are acquired. They are natural, uncontrived. There are no invisible beings helping me. My Divine will brings the object in a moment. I am everywhere.

And this:

> Mine is no mesmerism, miracle or magic. God can do anything. He has all the power in the palm of His hand. My power is eternal, all-pervasive, ever dominant. You call them miracles, but for Me, they are just my way. You cannot solve the mystery; for Me they are no mystery.

Of course, this reluctance to submit to scientific scrutiny has only increased the efforts of the sceptical to prove him a fraud.

Professional magicians have suggested that his materialisation of *vibhuti*, pendants, necklaces and the like are mere tricks. Lawyers have speculated about whether his materialisation of watches of well-known brands, complete with monograms and serial numbers, constitutes infringement of patent rights.

Pondering his claims for omniscient knowledge, sceptics have produced documentation clearly showing discrepancies between Baba's reading of historical events and biblical prophecies and the established accounts. It has been suggested that his ability to 'read the minds' of his devotees is simply achieved through a combination of information being gained by his helpers and the technique of 'cold reading', whereby facts are drawn out of a subject and fed back to them later, without their realising it, questions are disguised as statements, and nods or meaningful silences are used to give the impression that he knew all along what the subject was talking about. In *Miracles Are My Visiting Cards*, an Icelandic researcher, Professor Erlendur Haraldsson, quotes a survey of twenty-nine interviewees on the subject of Baba's mind-reading talents. Of these, nineteen reported that he had done so correctly, and five only partially correctly. Two people considered that the mind-reading was simply clever guesswork. One woman whom Baba advised 'should get married' was married already.

The most indefatigable critic of Sai Baba is the Indian sceptic B. Premenand, the so-called 'anti-guru' and convenor of the Committee for the Investigation of Claims of the Paranormal. In 1995, Premenand produced a video of Sai Baba supposedly materialising a gold chain which seemed to show that the chain had, in fact, been handed to him by an accomplice. Premenand is the publisher of the magazine *Indian Skeptic* which, in 1989, published an investigation into one of Sai Baba's most famous miracles, the supposed resurrection in 1971 of an American devotee, Walter Cowan. The most popular accounts of this, found in sundry literature about Sai Baba, tell of how Walter Cowan fell ill in his Madras hotel with cardiac trouble, and on being taken to a local hospital, the Lady Willingdon Nursing Home, was pronounced dead on arrival. Dr John Hislop, in *My Baba and I*, describes how the body was placed in an empty storage room and covered with a sheet to await daylight and decisions about the funeral.

According to Hislop, Cowan's wife had meanwhile called upon Sai Baba, who was in Madras at the time, and who went to the hospital. Mrs Cowan and a friend came to the hospital the next morning.

To the joy of the ladies, but also to their total amazement, they found Walter alive and being attended to. Nobody saw Baba with Walter, nor has Baba chosen to say how or why Walter was resurrected, but on returning to the devotee family who were his hosts, Baba told the people there that he had brought Walter back to life.

Investigating the case, *Indian Skeptic* reproduced letters from Dr O. Vaz, the physician who attended Cowan in the hotel, and his cardiologist at the Lady Willingdon Nursing Home, Dr R.S. Rajagopalan. According to Dr Vaz, Cowan was 'perfectly conscious' in bed in his hotel, having complained of breathing difficulties and pain in the chest; he was alive when admitted to hospital, and that with treatment 'he showed rapid improvement'.

> That morning [Vaz wrote] Mrs Cowan requested me whether there
> was any objection for Sai Baba ... to pray for him in the room for
> which I said he was most welcome and I was there when Sai Baba
> was offering prayers. Mr Cowan was conscious then and also right
> through.

According to Dr Rajagopalan, Cowan was admitted to the hospital in a state of consciousness with a functioning heart and subsequently suffered a cardiac arrest, but was revived by employing 'standard cardio-respiratory resuscitative procedures'. *Indian Skeptic* also quoted Professor Kasturi's account of the incident in *Sathyam Sivam Sundaram, Vol. 4*, which includes Sai Baba's claim of having saved Cowan.

> Walter had three attacks of heart failure, full and fatal, but I saved
> his life all the three times, for I wished to save Mrs Cowan the
> pain and bother of taking her husband back home dead.

The source of the story about Cowan having died in the first place appears to have been his wife, a devout follower of Baba. It seems unlikely that his two doctors were mistaken in their diagnosis. So did Mrs Cowan simply make it up, or perhaps conclude that her husband's recovery, by whatever means, was due to Sai Baba having answered her prayers? Did Cowan actually die without his doctors being aware of it, only to be revived by Sai Baba? Did Baba himself simply imagine that he had saved Cowan? Or perhaps he was suggesting that it was his intervention that had somehow determined whether the medical processes applied to Cowan succeeded or failed. Or was he simply taking advantage of a story spread by an over-zealous devotee to lead people to believe he had power of life over death? In short, was he lying?

The more spectacular accounts of miracle-working seemed to have declined in recent years. Sai Baba no longer produced *lingams*, for example. The age of miracles, I was told, had passed. Sai Baba had declared 1995 the Year of Service, characterised not by gold watches and trinkets but by gestures of munificence on a grandiose scale. On his seventieth birthday, Baba had made a birthday present of an extensive water project for 700 villages in the state of Andhar Pradesh. (However much this cost, it was surely only a drop in the ocean of donations and offerings that poured in from his millions of followers.)

This theme of service was reiterated constantly in his discourses, the signs and posters on the ashram walls – imprinted on my Hard Rock 'gold card': 'Love All, Serve All'. Some of his aphorisms on the subject were sublime: 'You cannot pronounce a man to be alive judging from the beat of his pulse. He is alive only when he works for himself and others.'

'The rich should sacrifice their wants so that the poor can secure their needs.'

There was something redolent of a muscular, decent, old-fashioned Christianity about his teachings which emphasised the virtues of action over contemplation. 'Two days of social service will do you more good than two months of meditation,' he says; and, 'Liberation lies not in mystic formulas or rosaries, but in stepping out into action.' I could see the attraction of such a direct appeal to love and charity to Westerners, stranded on a plateau of disenchantment with the empty affluence, the greed and the selfishness of Western society. Many of these people were of a generation brought up on the ethic of 'If it feels right, do it' and it had not made them happy. But, 'The secret of happiness,' Sai Baba taught, 'does not lie in doing what one likes, but in learning to like what one has to do.'

'The idea of a high standard of material living has played havoc with society,' he taught. 'The desire can never be satisfied. It leads to a multiplication of wants and consequent troubles and frustrations. We need morality, humility, detachment, compassion, so that the greed for luxury and conspicuous consumption is destroyed.' I thought: This is a hair-shirt for the Western devotees – this emphasis on the duties, rather than the rights, of the individual; the requirement for a moral code and a rejection of the libertarianism of their youth. And, of course, it was an appeal to the idealism which had characterised the Sixties, and which had now been corroded in every sphere of public life. 'All materialistic attempts to equalise society have failed,' said Sai. 'Only spiritual transformation can bring about the revolution in human consciousness, from which alone the desired changes can accrue.'

To have travelled halfway around the world, as these people had done, in order to suffer the austerities of ashram life, sleeping in crowded dormitories, rising at four each morning, sitting in back- and bottom-racking agony on the hard marble floors – all of this, surely, was an act compounded partly of penance, partly of devotion, partly of hope. In a way I admired them; in another I found them irritating, with their white uniforms that made them look less like devout pilgrims on the path than hospital orderlies – or perhaps inmates. I was irritated by their neatly pressed Boy Scout scarves and their silly Sai shoulder-bags-cum-cushions. Irritated by the incessant 'Sai Rams', a smug password among the faithful, and which the pushy guards and the obstructive officials used as an all-purpose verb, meaning, 'Get out of the way,' or, 'Move over there.'

'What is it about this place?' said Erica. 'You're not supposed to have anger, but you have these guards around who just provoke anger.' We had bumped into each other at the café, making the now obligatory joke about the meeting being predestined, and sat sipping our coffee like furtive cynics.

'It's Sai, testing you,' I joked.

But then everything seemed like a test. The pushy guards; the lottery system for *darshan*; the palpable disappointment that registered on people's faces when Sai Baba did not single them out for an interview, a word, a smile, a glance. 'He can see into your hearts,' people said. 'He knows what you need better than you do.'

I was constantly disconcerted by the jarring contrast between the hushed, sanctimonious, almost clinical air of the ashram and the squalid pandemonium of the village beyond its gates. 'The rich man in his castle, the poor man at the gate, God made them, high or lowly, and ordered their estate . . .' The words, I now remembered, came from the hymn, 'All Things Bright and Beautiful', a Victorian apologia for the status quo. This was God's design.

I felt increasingly bothered and uneasy. Those moments that one has cherished of an intense communion with humanity, with something beyond humanity, I did not feel them here. As I walked the streets of Puttaparthi, it struck me that the ashram and the village around it was a catalyst, a pressure-cooker, for almost every human feeling, from the most elevated to the most base. Here came the faithful, the pious, the hopeful, the desperate, the greedy, the healthy and the afflicted – all human life drawn to the promise of deliverance or gain.

Some days I found myself almost fighting for breath. Some days I couldn't wait to get out. Other days I thought: I have never been anywhere more stimulating in all my life. If I had come expecting to find peace of mind, serenity, even revelation, I was mistaken. Everything here seemed designed to irritate, to destabilise, to challenge your preconceptions and make you uneasy with yourself. But perhaps that was the point. Perhaps you weren't meant to like it.

'Have you noticed,' said Erica, 'that during *darshan* only 10 per cent of Sai Baba's time is spent among the women? And fewer women get interviews. And you never see any women up on the platform with the all-important men.' Her tone was cutting. All this was evidently getting to her too. 'I'm leaving tomorrow,' she said.

One of the most frequently told stories of Sai Baba is how, as a young child, he would play with his friends on a hill just outside Puttaparthi, where a tamarind tree grew, materialising on the tree all manner of fruits – apples, mangoes, oranges and figs. The tree still stood on the hill, and had become a shrine for devotees. 'I will tell you a true story about it,' said Mr Dutta. He came from Birmingham. I met him one afternoon, whilst waiting in line for *darshan*, a sprightly elderly man dressed in grey flannels and a brightly patterned shirt. (Indian devotees, I noticed, made fewer concessions to the uniform code that was followed so rigidly, so self-consciously by most of the Westerners; they wore their spiritual aspirations more comfortably, it seemed.)

'Thirteen years ago I knew nothing about Sai Baba,' said Mr Dutta. 'Then a man came and told me everything about Shirdi Baba and Sai Baba. Then I came to India. I was in Bangalore, and my chest was completely choked with asthma, because I was a heavy smoker. So I came here, and on the next day something happened in my mind.

I left my friends here in the *mandir*, and I went to the cliff where the tamarind tree grows. There are many steps, and I couldn't walk, my chest was so bad. Slowly, slowly I went up, and when I reached the top there was nobody there, but on the ground beside the tree was a photograph of Shirdi Sai Baba. When I saw the photo I cried and lay down. I stayed there for a long time, and then came down the hill. And by the time I had reached the bottom my asthma was gone.

'On the second day, Baba gave me an interview. And he said, "Smoking is very bad for you; don't smoke." I hadn't told him anything about my asthma, or going to the tamarind tree, but he knew! I told Baba, I will give up smoking. He gave me a blessing and touched my cheek, and I have not smoked since.'

Mr Dutta beamed with pleasure at the story.

'Is Sai Baba God?' I asked.

'Certainly. With no doubt.'

The next morning, I walked through the village, along a dusty track towards the site of the tamarind tree. A collection of houses stood at the bottom of the hill, with a rough stone pathway between them, marking the ascent to the tamarind tree. In *Sathyam Sivam Sundaram*, Professor Kasturi describes how, as a young boy, Sai Baba would play on the hill with his friends.

> He got up the rocks quick and fast, to the surprise of everyone; indeed, sometimes He did not even climb at all; still, He would be talking to the devotees on the sands one moment and hail them from the tamarind tree the next.

It took me somewhat longer to climb the 500 exhausting steps. Halfway up, I passed a group of young girls, sitting on the steps with baskets of fresh flowers, which they were weaving into garlands. Puttaparthi was spread out below me; a village blossoming into a town, a tangle of rooftops, with the skeletons of new buildings sprouting at its edges – more hotels and apartment blocks, and, beyond, the broad expanse of the Chittrathi riverbed, which had dried to mud, leaving only a small, dirty lake, like an inkstain on sandpaper, in which women could be seen washing their clothes, before laying them out on the sand to dry under the baking sun.

The tamarind tree grew on the very edge of the steepest side of the cliff face. To have reached into its branches to pick fruit would, it seemed, have been a particularly hazardous exercise. People had thrown garlands of flowers, and tied offerings to its lower branches. Two of the girls had followed me up the hill and now held out their garlands. 'Please, sir, if you have worries, give them to the tree.' I paid for a garland and one of the girls stepped across the stones and threw it high into the tree. She pulled some leaves from the lowest branches, and brought them back to me, cupped in the palm of her hand. I sat on a rock, feeling the warmth of the sun on my back, the crumpled leaves clutched in my hand.

What purpose would be served by giving worries to the tree? I thought of a friend in England, who was suffering from a particularly painful illness. I found myself praying for him, without fully knowing to whom or what I was praying. 'Please Baba; if you are who you say you are, make him better, ease his suffering.' The very qualification – 'if you are who you say you are' – was a measure of my lack of faith, my scepticism, my rational self. If he was who he said he was, would he not read the doubt in my prayer, and disregard it? If he was who he said he was would he not take compassion on my friend, despite my doubts? Is there a bargain in prayer? Can one beg to receive without being willing to give?

The girls had been watching me, absorbed in my thoughts. 'Please, sir, another garland?' I reached in my pocket for a handful of coins and made my way back down the hill, the sound of their laughter mingling with the birdsong in the wind.

I sat in my room, reading Yogananda.

> India's unwritten law for the truth-seeker is patience; a master may purposely make a test of one's eagerness to meet him. This psychological ruse is freely employed in the West by doctors and dentists.

The next morning I presented myself at the administration offices of the ashram. They had the somnolent air of some pre-war outpost of colonial bureaucracy. Men in white shirts sat at old-fashioned typewriters, feeding in sheets of paper and carbon, methodically pecking at the keys. A fan gently stirred the air. Forms and orders and numbers; everything in triplicate. The true symbol of India, I thought, is the rubber stamp; its abiding spirit, the requirement for patience.

I took a seat outside the office of the ashram secretary and waited.

Beside me sat a woman, cradling a baby in her arms, which she wished to present to Sai Baba; a yellow-robed *sadhu* clutching a business card, printed with the words 'Eagle Insurance Company'; and a smartly dressed but nervous-looking young woman. At length the door opened, a man poked his head out and waved the young woman and me inside. The ashram secretary sat behind his desk, an elderly man with a thin face, wearied by a lifetime of listening to incessant requests which he could never fulfil. The young woman explained that she was a journalist from Brunei, who wanted to interview Sai Baba.

The secretary gave a practised smile to preface what was clearly a standard reply. 'To request a meeting, this is not possible. If he wishes to meet you then you will meet him. If you write a letter and if you give it to Swami in *darshan*, then perhaps he will choose you.'

'A letter?' The young woman paused. 'Also, I want to ask Baba's help. My mother is going blind.'

The secretary raised an eyebrow. 'Come tomorrow. I will give you a slip to sit in the front row.' He turned to me. 'And you, sir?'

But my question had already been answered, and I had no ailing mother to call upon for favour.

'I'm sorry, no interviews are possible,' he repeated.

Could I then arrange a meeting with the chairman of the trust?

The secretary studied the ceiling carefully. 'I think this is not possible either. This is a very busy time . . .'

Who then would he suggest I should talk to about Sai Baba?

'Mr S—. Yes, go and see Mr S—. He is a most interesting chap . . .'

Mr S— lived in a ground-floor dwelling in one of the ashram's accommodation blocks. I knocked, and a voice from within bade me to enter. The door opened into a small room, little more than a cubby-hole. An old desk was pushed against the wall, with an antique typewriter almost hidden under a confetti of books and papers. Bookshelves lined the walls: the works of Thomas Hardy, G.K. Chesterton, Adam Smith's *The Wealth of Nations*; volumes on politics, economics, philosophy and English literature.

Mr S— was seated at his desk. He rose unsteadily to his feet, a slight, bent figure, dressed in a plain white dhoti, with a shock of white hair. He peered at me myopically through thick spectacles, and reached out his hand. 'Good afternoon, sir. And how can I help you?' The crystalline enunciation seemed to spring from the quads of Oxford sixty years ago.

Mr S— was eighty-two years old, and his life was the history of modern India. A scholar, writer and economist, as a young man he had embraced Marxism, and been imprisoned by the British for sedition. Disenchanted with socialism, he had then become a follower of Gandhi, all the while pursuing his career, in economics, politics and writing. He was a man of substance and good reputation. Sixteen years ago he had become a devotee of Sai Baba, and he and his wife had come to live in the ashram.

'So what is happening in England? It is many years since I was there. Who is the editor of the *Manchester Guardian*? I used to enjoy reading it.'

And so we talked of newspapers and journalism and at length I explained my predicament. Mr S— nodded indulgently. 'Swami has often dismissed journalists because he thinks they are out for sensationalism.' He chuckled. 'Having practised the trade myself I know how difficult things can be.' He waved his hand, as if to suggest there was nothing practical that could be done in this matter. That it was in the hands of providence.

'But tell me,' he asked, 'have you heard in London of a man named Benjamin Creme?'

I had not expected this. You know Mr Creme? I asked.

'Not personally, but I've received *Share International* for many years now. A most interesting journal. I think it is dealing with matters of the highest priority in the world today. But they have these ideas of Maitreya governing the world and all that. If there are Masters as Mr Creme says, then what were they doing when Hitler was massacring six million Jews? That doesn't make sense to me.'

So you do not believe in Maitreya?

Mr S— shrugged. 'I am keeping my judgement suspended, because the world is all a mystery. A long life has taught me this, if nothing else. Some things cannot be explained. For example, I have always been baffled by the phenomenon of Jesus Christ. Are the gospels right in what they say about him? If he did not exist, then it is a miracle that someone could have made up a story like this and that it should have endured so long.' He laughed quietly to himself.

And what did he feel, I asked, about the claims made on behalf of Sai Baba, that he is Christ?

'This is certainly what has been written. Peggy Mason, an Englishwoman – a very *fine* lady – has written that she asked Swami if he was the Father who sent Christ and he replied yes. Well . . . that is an extraordinary thing to say.'

And you do not believe it?

'Believe, believe. Who knows about belief?' He laughed again. 'I came to Swami in 1980, but I am a curious devotee in that I still suspend judgement about many things. Especially about the Creator and the purpose of the Creator in this horrible world. But there is no question in my mind that Swami is a manifestation of the Divine. The powers of divining the minds of others; the materialisations and so forth. These things are very convincing to me. That he has succeeded in creating the impression in so many people's minds is a miracle in itself. Although my feeling is that the Supreme Power is greater than Baba. Or he has not yet revealed all his powers. The question is, how far is he going to change the world, change the minds of those in power? He has firmly declared that there will be no third world war. He has said that.

'I think this consciousness is growing that we are all one family in a global village, as McLuhan said. And by the end of this century I think the human race will come more to a realisation of what it owes to the Divine, to nature and so on. This is building now. And no man is doing more than Sai to make Indians realise their spiritual and cultural heritage. Everyone who comes to him leaves with a greater awareness of this.'

Mr S— had known Gandhi. Did he think Sai Baba was an even more significant figure in Indian national life?

'I have written something on this, some years ago,' he said. He shuffled through a mound of papers, and produced a copy of the magazine *India Today*, which he handed to me. I read the article later in my room:

[Sai Baba's] avowed commitment to the restoration of India's Dharmic ideals in the life of every person in the country will be obvious to anyone who listens to him or watches his students. [Baba provided an answer to] the crisis of character . . . a pernicious disease eating away at the vitals of the nation, offering the prospect of a spiritual reconstruction that surpassed Gandhi's. The attempt to unify a people as diverse as ourselves with a multiplicity of languages, religions, customs and divisions of caste and community which Sri Sathya Sai

Baba is making is something vastly more significant and far-reaching than what Gandhi or others had attempted in the past.

Mr S— folded his hands in front of him and peered at me through his pebble glasses. 'The hospitals and schools and so on which Swami provides – in one sense, these are trivial. Many people have built things like this. They are minor achievements. But he is able to inspire in people a spirit of service, and that is a remarkable achievement. Love and sacrifice are the constant things in his discourses. This is not easy. The entire human civilisation of the last five hundred years has been built on selfishness. I think Baba's concern is to raise the entire level of human consciousness across the world to a sense of God. He says people have forgotten God because of technological progress and materialism. Although the denial of God has an ancient pedigree, of course.' Mr S— leaned back in his chair and chuckled.

'Tell me, have you read the poems of Thomas Hardy? I had not realised until recently what a marvellous poet Hardy was. He seemed to feel that God has written off mankind and is totally indifferent to the fools that we make of ourselves. But I think Baba has relevance from two points of view. One, the arrogance of man that he can solve his problems through science and technology. Swami says the solution is not external, but internal. Turn inwards to solve your problems. He sees the problem in this way. Man is preoccupied with the physical, the sensual, the mental, but behind that is the spirit. That doesn't seem real to people. But he wants to show how the Divine can, in a human form, demonstrate supernatural powers. To my mind, that is the point of the miracles. They are demonstrations of the power of the Divine in action.

'Without the Divine in you, you are merely a lump of clay. So realise that. Then realise the Divine is in everything. Then, the moment you recognise the omnipresence of the Divine, find out how you should behave in such a world.' Mr S— settled back into his chair.

What had most unsettled me in the ashram, I said, was the cult of personality around Sai Baba; the sense that what was being worshipped was not the Divine but the man who was said to be the embodiment of the Divine.

Mr S— nodded understandingly. 'Swami says each man decides the object of his worship. Because the Divine can exist in anything. He says that people are worshipping him, making up songs about him and so forth, without him asking for it.' Mr S— shrugged, as if to say, what can Swami do?

'The exploited creates the exploiter, and the worshippers create the object of worship. Krishnamurti said that. Are you familiar with Krishnamurti?'

'Yes, "Truth is a pathless land . . ."' I said.

Mr S— chuckled to himself. 'He would be outraged by all this. I knew him well. When I told him I was staying with Baba he raised his hands in holy terror. But you have to solve your problems yourself, in your own way.'

But what, I asked Mr S—, had brought him here?

Indian tradition holds that there are four stages in life, he said. First there is *brahmachari*, the life of the young celibate. Then comes marriage and the stage of family man and householder. Thirdly, the stage of renunciation and retirement to a life of spiritual contemplation, leaving behind attachment to worldly things. Fourthly, there is *moksha*, liberation from the endless cycle of life and death.

'As somebody said, an unexamined life is not worth living, and I've been examining my life all the time. I wanted to spend my last days in the third stage of life. And Swami called me, I suppose you could say . . .' He fell silent for a moment. 'But I didn't give up anything. My children were married. I had fulfilled my obligations. Now I live in three rooms. I was living in a house five times this size. But I have my studies, and meeting people who are earnest seekers of God is a wonderful experience. For forty-eight years I was involved with the follies and cruelties of mankind. Now I am spared the cruelties,' he smiled, 'if not the follies.'

We had spoken for almost an hour, and Mr S— was clearly tired. I rose to leave. He shook my hand, and showed me to the door. 'Tell me,' he said. 'Are Shaw and Chesterton still read and respected in England?'

It was another question I could not answer.

One day, a mood of excitement gripped the ashram. It was announced that to mark the Festival of Makara Sankranthi, Swami would be giving the gift of a discourse to his devotees. The *mandir* had been decorated with flowers; music and incense filled the air. The platform was peopled with dignitaries.

A hush fell as Baba walked slowly through the crowd, and settled

himself on his velvet throne. A man came to the microphone –
apparently he had once been a delegate of the Indian government
to the United Nations – and spoke in precise, fluting tones. Baba,
he said, was as 'a great mystery, wrapped inside an enigma and put
into a box ... the visible human manifestation of the power and
mystery and glory of the sun'. It was our 'triple fortune' on this holy
day to be spending it in his presence. In the age of Kali Yuga, the
age of conflict and violence, he said, the remembrance of the Lord
is enough to set you on the road to liberation. 'The most mightily
visible manifestation – natural, divine, splendorous manifestation of
the loving power of the Lord is represented right here.'

As the man spoke, Baba reclined in his chair, apparently
unembarrassed by such superlatives, gently moving his hands in
the air, almost as if orchestrating the speech. The man droned
on, extolling Baba's greatness, his beauty, his grace, his virtue, his
power, in a florid and unrelenting torrent of verbosity. He told a
story, at interminable length, of how Baba had cured his son of illness
– a story laden with addendums and digressions. Baba lolled on his
velvet swivel-chair, lazily swatting the air with his hand, looking for
all the world like a bored potentate. The man told another story of
how Baba had materialised *vibhuti*, and of a private audience where
he had started to write down everything Baba said. 'And Swami
said, why are you doing this? I will give you a guarantee that you
will always remember what I say to you.'

At last, he was finished.

Now Sai Baba rose from his chair and began to chant in Telegu
in a sweet, high, firm voice. An interpreter translated the words
into English. It was a song to the sun. He sang of the harvest
ripening, the flowers blossoming, the houses being full of grain.
Without pause, the song became an oration, the translator rushing
to keep pace. 'We do not need to undertake an exterior journey,'
he said. 'Intellect has to turn to the heart. The internal joy is the
true happiness. That which is external is only temporary. That
which is Atman is eternity. We have to direct our intellect toward
inspiration. This time is highly auspicious.' He spoke rapidly, in a
clipped staccato fashion, not waiting for the translator to complete
his last sentence before he began the next. People craned forward
on their haunches to catch the words.

He talked of Makara Sankranthi as a season of thanksgiving, of
physical and mental rest. 'But man is forgetting the inner meaning

of the festival. Happiness in the physical world will never remain permanent. You can search anywhere and you will realise this. Happiness is within, bliss is within, but we search for it elsewhere. It is not present in a foreign land. It is present within oneself. So long as there is attachment, there will not be liberation. With detachment there will be *moksha*, or liberation.' Spiritual pursuits followed by the mind cannot take you to the heart, he said. No spiritual pursuits can take you fully to happiness without devotion. Now he turned his attention to television. 'Rich people have colour TV. Richer people have Star TV. Since the installation of TV, never was mind so impure, so dirty. And today we find TV in huts.

'As you watch TV, unknowingly you are agitated and disturbed. With the passage of time those seeds will sprout. As we eat we should never discuss hostile things. We should eat observing silence. Bad thoughts affect the heart. We risk ruining man totally. The human mind is completely polluted because of cinema and TV. The radio and television will not teach you to respect your parents. Love your parents. Love others. Respect your elders. Practise good citizenship.'

A man sitting on the ground beside me cradled his son in his arms. The boy was perhaps twelve, listening intently. I wondered what he thought of this tirade against television, and I thought of what Mr S— had written of Baba as a social teacher, a force of moral regeneration in a fragmented and confused India.

He was not a good orator; jumping from point to point, rambling, repetitive, yet for more than an hour his audience sat on the hard marble floor, listening raptly. Now music struck up, and Baba broke into song, while the audience clapped their hands in time to the music. The mood of quiet attentiveness had suddenly turned to jubilation. As the music gathered pace, a bell rang, and Baba began his slow procession out of the *mandir*, people rising as he passed to thrust their gifts and letters towards him. The young students moved among the crowd, distributing cakes, as a chant began, *Govinda, Govinda, Govinda*. Sai Baba paused briefly at the entrance to the temple, lifted his hand in a wave and walked out.

The café at the top of the village had become a place of sanctuary. Nobody talked in the ashram. The code of conduct advised against it. The Western groups, in their uniform whites and scarves, kept largely to themselves. People shuffled around silently, like somnambulists, or buried their heads in books. It was not a place for expressing doubts, but doubt – or at least debate – flourished in the café. The café was full of questioners and back-sliders; people passing through; the sceptical, the disaffected, the not-quite-sure-yet-but-I'm-keeping-an-open-mind-about-it; people who made wisecracks (wisecracks were not encouraged in the ashram) or just needed to talk.

I felt more at home here.

'It's like Groundhog Day,' said Daryl one morning, as we sat drinking coffee. 'Every day you have exactly the same chance. If you can get up, go through the day and keep your centre, keep your God, in this place then you can do it anywhere.' Daryl was Australian; in his early forties, an acupuncturist. He was travelling with his friend Bob, who ran a forest plantation in Western Australia, and Sergio, a small, wiry Italian they had met somewhere on the journey.

Daryl and Bob did not look like typical Sai Baba devotees; they did not look like spiritual seekers at all. They had the brawny, weather-beaten appearance of outdoorsmen, veteran surfies who knew how to look after themselves. If you had not met them in a café at the ashram gates you might have expected to find them in a beach bar, sinking beers and chasing women. They had never heard of Sai Baba before coming to India, but then they had met somebody on a train who had told them about Puttaparthi and . . . it was a familiar story.

Bob was extrovert, laughing and joking, loudly looking forward to the next stop on the tour – 'I'm going to get out on the beach and do Tai Chi, mate.'

Daryl smiled quietly to himself, as all the talk of frustrations and miracles and is Sai Baba God, or isn't he eddied around him. 'The big thing that happens here,' he said, 'is that people look at other people and what they're thinking too much instead of working things out for themselves. The big thing here is people talk too much.' Daryl seemed to be undergoing some form of transformation, and talking about it did not come easily.

Practising acupuncture in Australia, he said, he had noticed that in the last two years more and more people had been coming to him with spiritual problems that he had no idea how to deal with. 'I mean, I'm not a guru, mate. I didn't know what to tell people, but I've been treating fourteen or fifteen people a week and sleeping at the weekends to recover. My chest was constricting, I was feeling really punished. But since I arrived here, Sai's been in my head. He's worked on my psychic space. He's been in my dreams. I've invited him in, and I've been through some real changes. Just in the last week here I've realised that all the people who were coming to see me, what I was doing was taking on their *karmic* sins unconsciously but I wasn't letting them go. Now I realise that I can pass them on to God.' He paused to watch a group of people walk past in their crisp white designer Sai Ram saris and T-shirts. Their neckscarves announced that the group had come from Italy.

So he had found God?

Daryl blinked. 'Well . . . I didn't know I had faith in God, but I do now. This is big stuff . . .'

Once again, I found myself feeling almost envious of somebody else's certainty. 'I feel as if I'm in a washing-machine,' I said. 'Everything just keeps churning round and round and I can't get a focus on any of it.'

'That's what it is, mate, a washing-machine,' said Daryl with a smile. 'It's cleaned me out, that's for sure.'

The beggars were drawn to the café like a magnet. It is one of the great imponderables of India. To give or not to give. But here in Puttaparthi the question took on a particularly vivid hue, the contradiction between the gold-encrusted shrines of the ashram, and the poor outside the gates.

My reading of Yogananda offered sage advice:

> Inner research soon exposes a unity of all human minds – the stalwart kinship of selfish motive. In one sense, at least, the brotherhood of man stands revealed. An aghast humility follows this levelling discovery. It ripens into compassion for one's fellows, blind to the healing potencies of the soul awaiting exploration.
>
> Only the shallow man loses responsiveness to the woes of others' lives, as he sinks into narrow suffering of his own. The one who practises a scalpel of self-dissection will know an extension of universal pity.

Nightly sharpening the scalpel of self-dissection in my room, I fancied that my responsiveness to the woes of others' lives had blossomed like a flower. I would start each day determined to be a saint, eagerly dispensing spare change and soiled rupee notes to almost anyone who strayed across my path. By the end of the day, the scalpel of self-dissection blunted by the incessant demands on my charity, I would be waving the beggars away as if they were flies, snarling at the snotty urchins who tugged relentlessly at my sleeve – 'Get a job.' (Seated in the back of a taxi in a traffic jam in Bombay, a constant procession of the crippled and infirm had knocked on the window, begging for money. Eventually I relented when a man whose arms had been rotted away by leprosy presented himself at the window. I poured some coins in the pocket of his shirt, which he held open with the stub of his elbow. The taxi-driver regarded me sceptically in the rear-view mirror. 'These people don't want to work,' he said. 'But he has no arms,' I said. 'He could use his feet,' said the driver.) On the streets of Puttaparthi, I tried to discriminate: give only to leprous mothers clutching babies in their arms one day, and to those who had actually lost a limb the next.

But even this resolution would crumble in the face of my own uncertainty: handing over money began to seem like an action designed to salve my liberal conscience; but refusing the demands simply made me feel heartless.

'Fuck 'em all,' said Bob, with a cheery laugh. 'Y'know, Baba laid aside a space inside the ashram to feed them, but they stopped going. They can make more on the streets. Some of them have so much money they own shops and rent them out to shopkeepers. You don't believe it?' He laughed. 'It's true, mate.'

I didn't believe it. Nor did I necessarily accept the argument, commonly voiced, that it was simply their own 'bad *karma*' that made them beggars in the first place. Even if that was the case, wasn't it my good *karma* to give them something? But the ethic of self-reliance seemed to hold sway here over the ethic of charity, or perhaps there was something particularly corrosive in the endless demands on one's charity on the streets of Puttaparthi.

'And another thing . . .' Bob was rocking back on his seat, enjoying a cigarette. 'You drinking the milk here? They shoot the cows full of drugs, and they use a crowbar on their uterus to make it flow more freely.' Everybody at the table had put down their coffee cups. Bob was laughing to himself. 'And don't eat the food either. The DDT, it falls like *vibhuti* here, mate.'

Daryl was right. People did talk too much, but it was hard not to. Talking seemed to be a way of keeping things in focus, of stopping everything slipping on to its side. It seemed to be a way of keeping yourself sane, even if sometimes it could drive you mad. Perhaps that was why the ashram guide book counselled you not to converse, and to keep your thoughts to yourself. Other people's experiences might sow the seeds of envy (*Why haven't I been chosen?*); their opinions might sow the seeds of doubt. But wasn't doubt healthy – a prophylactic against the contagion of credulity and superstition?

Everything here contradicted the received ideas about the value of individualism, individual expression. There was something authoritarian about it all. It was the eternal spiritual conundrum: how to surrender the ego, to surrender doubts, without surrendering discrimination.

'He gets in your head, man,' said Sergio, one day as we sat drinking coffee. 'All this Sai Ram, Sai Ram. I tell you, two days ago I thought I was going fucking crazy. They say it's not brainwashing, but everywhere you go you hear his name – Sai Ram, Sai Ram. You say something to someone and they say, "Ah, but Baba says . . ." All these people thinking Sai can read their thoughts: What does Sai want me to do? What does Sai want me to think? They're giving up their freedom. These people have forgotten how to think for themselves. The philosophy is very good, love everybody, be kind, lose your ego, all this. Of course that's good, but the scene is very bad. These people believe these things already, so what's the point of giving the good philosophy to these people? It should go to normal people. These people are like from the army or something.'

Bob chuckled. 'Y'know, Baba planted Sergio in the ashram – the spiritual terrorist – just to keep everybody on their toes.'

'But listen,' said Sergio, 'I try to talk with these people, try to have a dialogue, yes? But all they say is, "Sai says this, Sai says that." They've lost their minds to Sai. They think that Sai is omnipotent, always in their mind, watching them. But they need that. It's a reassuring thing for them. It's like a piece of wood being beaten over their heads. But he's a very clever guy. He understands what they need. It's another form of Nazi spiritualisation. In another couple of years they'll all be fighting for him, you'll see.'

'It might drive you nuts, but there's a lot of good stuff going on here, mate,' said Bob, his face creasing into a grin. 'Keep open to it.'

This was what everybody said. Don't jump to conclusions. Let your intuition be your guide. Keep open. But it was the thing I found hardest to do. 'Just *give* yourself,' said Anneka, as we sat in the café one evening. She offered practical advice. 'In *darshan*, tip your head forward, then you hear. If you lift your head, the mind and body are separated, and the body is where your feelings lie. I find if I lift my head, I don't understand it. If I just drop my head, then I understand.' She laughed lightly. 'I call it my world journey of two millimetres in two seconds.'

We walked back through the village. The shopkeepers were taking in their Sai merchandise and pulling down the shutters; people scurrying back towards the ashram before the gates were locked. We said goodbye at the gate.

'Open your heart tonight,' said Anneka, 'and remember, tomorrow morning tip your head forward, and maybe you feel something.'

If Sai Baba is omniscient, I thought, if he knows everything that is in our minds, all our fears and desires, then surely he will know the contents of the letters before they have been given to him, even as the thoughts are forming, and the pen is moving across the paper. 'But you are not writing it for Sai,' Mr S— told me. 'You are writing it for yourself.'

I sat in my room, trying to compose a letter which I hoped would strike the appropriate note between fawning self-abasement, humble supplication and a brisk and businesslike sense of purpose. Others had told me of their notes – asking for divine intervention in the matter of a friend or relative's illness, for revelation or guidance on some personal trouble. My request for an interview seemed trite and selfish by comparison.

The next morning I awoke with a start, feeling peculiarly exhilarated. I crossed the village, and took my place in line for *darshan*. Coming alive in the softly rising light, the courtyard seemed a particularly beautiful place, touched by an ineffable grace. Next to the courtyard was a gateway, an elaborate tower, sculpted in the marzipan pinks and blues of the ashram; a large monkey lazily climbed its steps and parapets, pausing triumphantly at the summit to look down on the people gathering below, before swinging out of view. I was suddenly overwhelmed by a sense of being in the presence of something far greater than myself; a calm and stillness that seemed to fill the courtyard, spread out beyond the ashram gates and fill the world. I felt strangely purified, strangely whole. The whisper passed back. Three! A place immediately adjacent to the aisle! I had never been so close. Surely this was providence.

With the sound of feet gently scuffling over sand, we filed into the *mandir*, and I took my place on the marble floor, closed my eyes and waited. Was I praying, or simply lost in my thoughts? I hardly knew. I was barely aware of the rustle passing across the hall, signalling Sai Baba's arrival. He came down the aisle, his red robe trailing along the marble, head turning to left and right. Beside me, a man held his note between folded palms, his eyes closed as if in prayer. This is a test, I thought; a test of my faith. Now he was almost upon me. I rose to my feet, the letter clasped between my hands in a gesture of supplication, and reached out to him. His eyes moved past me, settling on the man sitting beside me with a look almost of recognition. He reached for his note, and walked on. I sat down, still clutching my letter in my hands, feeling unaccountably crushed, betrayed, foolish. Whatever belief I had been prepared to put in his divinity had evaporated in the heat of my slighted vanity. I had not been chosen. I could feel a small ball of cynicism suppurating inside me. The atmosphere of reverence in the *mandir* suddenly seemed like the worst kind of sanctimoniousness. Beside me, the man whose letter Baba had taken wore a smile of blissful serenity, and he mouthed a silent prayer of thanks. I hated him.

I walked out of the ashram, feeling rejected and downcast. A young woman with her babe in arms attached herself to me at the gate, and trailed me to the café, her mewling imprecation sounding in my ears, 'Please, sah, babee, babee.'

Sergio was at his usual table, drinking coffee. 'So you write a letter, and he doesn't take it?' He laughed. 'I see a man here, he is dumb and crippled, so I wrote a letter to Sai, to heal him. Not for myself, but for this man. I go to *darshan*, but he didn't take the letter.' Sergio lit a cigarette and exhaled impatiently. 'I tell you, man, I've had enough. I'm not surrendering anything. I'm a free man. An anarchist. I'm not giving my mind to anybody. This is my first time here, and my last. It's all a joke.'

The woman with the baby had stood silently by our table through all this. Now she caught Sergio's eye and her pleading began afresh. 'Please, sah, please, sah, babee . . .'

'So Sai won't help you, eh?' said Sergio. He reached into his pocket and pushed a bundle of notes into her outstretched hand.

The Sai Baba Eternal Heritage museum stood on top of a hill, overlooking the ashram, another place of pilgrimage. It was as berserkly ostentatious as any of the ashram's principal buildings. I joined the long queue to get in, superintended by the customarily pushy attendants, chivvying people into line as we filed at last through the door. A large cardboard cut-out of a smiling Sai Baba greeted me at the entrance.

I found myself in a large, dimly lit hall. A neon Om sign glowed, and the Om chant sounded on a tape-loop. Around the walls were set display cases, and the line shuffled obediently forward, patrolled by attendants hurrying along anyone who stopped too long to inspect what was on view – a clear case, I thought, of efficiency overriding education. We shuffled past a display, spelling out the differing interpretations of creation and the universe, the spiritual and the scientific. I had time only to take in the sub-headings – intuitive consciousness versus scientific reductionism; self-revelation versus logic and deduction; self-experience versus methods and doctrine; permanent versus subject to change and revision – before I was hurried along. The line wound past a series of dioramas of the world's major religions. Buddhism; Islam; Sikhism, Hinduism and Christianity, in which was displayed a drawing of Christ and Sai Baba together, in identical postures of thoughtful repose. 'Baba,' read a caption, 'says that between the ages of twelve and thirty Jesus went to India and learnt meditation.'

A display entitled 'The Ideals of Sri Sathya Sai Baba' showed drawings of young boys studying and praying around a picture of Sai Baba. There were, I noticed, no girls in the drawings. Sai Baba's life unfolded in a further series of dioramas. A sign stated that he had been born with all knowledge of Vedas and religious texts without need to recourse. 'Divinity born, not developed.' There was a frieze of the young Sai on the day of Divine Declaration of Incarnation, 20 October 1940; and a life-sized mechanical model of the young boy contemplating a lotus flower.

I began to feel repelled by the tackiness of the displays; they reminded me of the museums dedicated to Country and Western stars that I had seen in Nashville; there the deification of showbusiness celebrities had seemed merely risible; to see the same gimcrack techniques applied to – whom? A deity? – seemed somehow even more tawdry.

I paused to read the caption under yet another photograph of Baba. 'My power is immeasurable, my truth is inexplicable, unfathomable. I am announcing this about me for the need has arisen.' A group of people clustered around a TV presentation, *Living With Baba*. A solemn voice intoned, 'Baba has incarnated to redeem mankind and release him from the shackles of bondage.'

I quit the line and found my way upstairs to a second range of exhibits. There were fewer people here and I was able to browse at will. In one corner of the room, there was a re-creation of the altar of a Christian church; a cross, surmounted by an image of Christ, and on the walls two paintings of childlike naivety – depicting the Last Supper and Christ on a hill, overlooking Jerusalem. Banal as they were, the images seemed charged with something familiar, reassuring. I stood for a moment lost in thought. A memory came back to me of being six or seven, at primary school, the afternoon of a nativity play – had I played a shepherd? An angel? I could not remember. I could only see myself rushing home from school, the evening darkness illuminated by the sparkle of Christmas decorations in shop windows, a tangible thrill of childish excitement and anticipation of the holiday to come, now rendered as a deep yearning for the simple certainties and unquestioning faith of childhood. Something in the corner of the altar caught my eye. It was a photograph of Sai Baba.

That morning I had read this from one of his discourses:

The human form is one in which every divine entity, every divine principle, that is to say all the forms and names ascribed to God by man, are manifest. Why do you waste time and energy trying to explain Me? Can a fish measure the sky? Do not try to measure Me, you will only fail. Try rather to discover your own measure. Then you will succeed better in discovering My measure. Though I am omnipresent and found everywhere, you can find Me installed, whenever my glory is sung.

The next morning, I left Puttaparthi.

5

THE BOY LAMA

There is a saying in Buddhism: if you wish to know of your past life, look to your present circumstances; if you wish to know of your future life, look to your present actions.

I thought of this as the morning bus from Puttaparthi sped through the dusty countryside, bound for Bangalore. My experience with Sai Baba had left me feeling curiously deflated, disillusioned almost. But then what, after all, had I expected? A personal epiphany? Some experience of transformation? Some proof of his divinity? A trick that would convince me? I could feel none of the certainty that so evidently galvanised his devotees at Puttaparthi. But neither did I feel able to reject him. I wondered, if 2,000 years ago, I had happened to find myself among the congregation for the Sermon on the Mount, would I have recognised Christ? Like Christ, Sai Baba was said to have been born divine, an emanation of God. But I was no clearer in my own mind about the truth of the story of his previous incarnation, Shirdi Sai, and his incarnation to come, Prem Sai. As myth alone, there was something wondrous in this idea of an avatar coming to earth in a series of incarnations in order to continue the work of previous lifetimes. In Tibetan Buddhism the principle of such rebirth as a human, not divine, possibility is taken not simply as an article of faith, but as a living article of practice. Central to all Buddhist teachings is the belief in *karma*, the law of cause and effect, which holds that consciousness begets actions which must be worked out over an endless cycle of lifetimes. Only when all negative *karma* has been eliminated, and with it all the worldly attachments arising from the ego, can the consciousness attain release from *samsara*, the 'wheel of suffering' – and attain enlightenment.

According to Tibetan Buddhist teaching, while reincarnation is inevitable for everyone, there are certain beings who have

so trained their minds through intensive study and meditation
that they can influence the conditions of their next birth. These
tulkus, as they are known, are bound by their vow to return to
lead others to enlightenment. The Dalai Lama, whose lineage can
be traced through fourteen successive rebirths, is the best known.
Historically there were thousands of *tulkus* recognised in Tibet.
Now there are hundreds. Traditionally, such rebirths occurred
within a geographical area where a teacher who was reborn could
be recognised by his former students, in order to carry on his work.
Until 1959, this meant Tibet.

In that year, the Tibetan people staged a popular uprising against
the Chinese who had occupied Tibet illegally since 1950. The uprising
was violently quelled; thousands of Tibetans died, and thousands
more were forced to flee across the border with India into exile with
their spiritual leader, the Dalai Lama. In the Chinese occupation –
or, as the Communists had it, 'liberation' – of Tibet, the secular
land-owning nobility and the religious hierarchy of abbots and *tulkus*
were, naturally, the main target for suppression. And a large number
of lamas and religious figures were among those forced to flee to
India. The diaspora of the Tibetan people, and Tibetan Buddhist
culture, had begun.

For the first time, Tibetan lamas began travelling and teaching in
the West. And now the first Western *tulkus* had begun to appear. In
Sera Je monastery, the largest Tibetan Buddhist monastery in India,
lived one of the first of these Western reincarnates – a Spanish boy
named Osel Hita Torres, who as a young child had been identified
as the reincarnation of a Tibetan lama, Thubten Yeshe.

I had first read about Lama Osel's discovery and his enthronement
at the age of two in a remarkable book, *Reincarnation*, written by a
former Fleet Street journalist, Vicki MacKenzie. But now the boy
was ten, and living in Sera, where he was being tutored simultaneously
in both the centuries-old teachings of Tibetan Buddhism and the
contemporary teachings of the technological West, in what one of
his tutors had described to me as 'potentially the most exciting
experiment in education done anywhere, at any time'.

Throughout my time in India I had been having dreams of
extraordinary vividness, as if the turmoil of my thought processes
was being sifted and filtered. Even by the uncertain standards of
the dream-state, these confounded interpretation: garbled, chaotic
visions of blue-faced gods and phantasmagorical characters, the

panoply of Indian deities depicted in the garish postcards sold
outside temples, commingling with friends from England, work
colleagues; half-familiar places alternating with landscapes of almost
lunar strangeness. I would wake each morning feeling that I had been
catapulted into daylight from a world whose contours and details
had been as real as wakefulness, but which evaporated the moment
I tried to bring them to mind.

In Bangalore I had the most vivid dream of all. I was at home
in London, preparing to go on a journey to some sort of Buddhist
conference or convention. I was in a mood of keen anticipation. Was
I supposed to wear robes? I wasn't sure, but a set had materialised
around my body, and I studied myself in the mirror. I looked
awkward, like an impostor, and the thought occurred that I was
not entitled to wear them. A woman had appeared in the room,
to clean it, or perhaps she had finished cleaning it. I went to the
door to leave and there, sitting in a chair, was my grandmother.
My grandmother died more than twenty years ago. We were not
particularly close, and I now realised, to my shame, that I had hardly
given her a moment's thought since her death. And yet there she
was, exactly as I had last seen her, two days before she died, but
somehow transformed, suffused in a golden glow, and with a look
on her face of such peace, serenity and joy that I felt myself moved
to tears. I said to her, 'Nana, you always come just as I'm about
to go,' although there was no reason for me to say this, for it was
certainly not true. I moved to give her a farewell embrace, and as
I did so I noticed that a small crib stood beside her, with a baby
inside. For some reason, I knew that the woman in the room would
pick up the baby and give it to my grandmother to nurse, and that
this would make my grandmother happy. I awoke in a mood of great
serenity and contentment, feeling that I had somehow been blessed,
and filled with the certainty that everything was for the best.

In Bangalore I had arranged to meet a friend, Peter, a photographer,
who had been travelling through South East Asia, and Peter Kedge,
an Englishman, a former Buddhist monk, one of the trustees of the
Foundation for the Preservation of the Mahayana Tradition, and the
man responsible for the Western aspect of Lama Osel's education.
It was through Peter Kedge that I had arranged a meeting with
the young lama. We hired a car and driver – a stately Ambassador
with wrap-around bumpers and the sort of leather upholstery rarely
found in British cars – and set off for the five-hour drive south,

to Sera monastery. Like most Indian taxi-drivers, it seemed, ours drove incredibly fast, with a reckless disregard for safety, as if his manhood depended on his ability to overtake a bus in the face of an oncoming truck. 'My friends call me Tiger,' he said, smiling around the car. 'Tiger,' said Peter Kedge drily, 'is playing chicken.'

Sera is one of the three great monastic 'universities' of Tibetan Buddhism. It stands near the small town of Bylakuppe, two hours' drive south of the city of Mysore, in an area of land that was given to the Tibetans by the Indian government in the early Sixties, when accommodation was first being made for those fleeing from the Chinese. Writing in his autobiography, *Freedom In Exile*, the Dalai Lama recounts that when they first set eyes on their new home many of the Tibetan settlers broke down and wept, so daunting seemed the task of hewing a livelihood out of the parched Indian earth, and of acclimatising to the baking heat after the cold of Tibet. Thousands died from tropical diseases or illnesses caused by the heat and an unfamiliar diet. When it was suggested that fields should be cleared by burning to plant crops there were objections from many of the settlers: Buddhists hold all life to be sacred, and burning meant the death of insects and small animals.

Sera is less a monastery than a small town, the home to more than 3,000 monks. It was strange to turn off the road, past small Indian villages, and come suddenly upon this collection of temples, surrounded by a tangle of whitewashed houses and barrack-like accommodation blocks, with red-robed Tibetan monks, many of them no more than children, thronging the narrow unpaved streets and pathways.

As a *rinpoche* – an incarnate lama – Lama Osel enjoyed the privilege of his own household. He lived in a bungalow, set in its own grounds, with a carefully tended garden, a blind deer – a pet – grazing contentedly in a fenced paddock. A child's swing stood on the lawn, and mountain bikes rested against the wall. Lama Osel greeted us at the door; a sturdy-looking boy, tall for his age, with a grave, watchful expression illuminated by a shy smile as he reached out to shake hands. That night we sat down to dinner. There was Lama Osel's father, Paco; his brother Kunkyen, who was eight years old, and also dressed in monk's robes; a Tibetan monk, Pemba, who served as the young lama's attendant; and the lama's tutor in Western studies, George Churinoff, a fifty-year-old American Buddhist monk.

The young lama led grace in Tibetan, and there was a moment's pause as everyone, including his father, waited for Osel to begin to eat. The conversation turned to philosophy. George Churinoff began to expound on the nature of reality. What do we mean when we talk of a tree? A table? A body? Do these things have an absolute reality? No, they are merely names for a composite of parts, each of which is a composite of smaller parts, breaking down to a degree where the parts cannot be measured; they are simply energy. The ten-year-old boy toyed with his food, listening intently, then picked up the thread of the argument. 'So a cup is impermanent, the body is impermanent. Only emptiness is permanent . . .' He paused and turned to me. 'You're like me,' he said. 'You eat very slowly,' and laughed.

Lama Yeshe was born in Tibet in 1935 and, at an early age, identified as the reincarnation of an abbess from a convent close to his birthplace. At the age of six he was placed under the care of an uncle in Sera monastery, which then accommodated some 10,000 monks. At the age of twenty-five, following the uprising against the Chinese, he escaped across the Himalayas into India, and spent two years in a monastic settlement called Buxadaur, where he met the man who would become his first disciple, Lama Zopa. Together, the two lamas established a small retreat in Kopan, in Nepal, where their first Western students – mostly travellers on the hippie trail – began to gather around them. As his following grew, he began to travel the world, establishing teaching and meditation centres wherever he went, under the aegis of his organisation, the Foundation for the Preservation of the Mahayana Tradition.

Peter Kedge was one of the first Westerners to arrive at Lama Yeshe's retreat in Kopan. Kedge grew up in a devout Christian family in Birmingham. He studied engineering at university, but in the early Seventies set off with a group of friends in a Land Rover, bound for Asia, imbibing the spiritual handbooks of the day as he travelled. By the time he arrived in Kathmandu he was ready to entertain the prospect of a course in Buddhist meditation taught by Lama Yeshe – if not quite prepared for the change it would wreak in his life. 'Meeting Lama Yeshe was a revelation,' Kedge remembered. 'For the first time in my life I was receiving crisp, clear, scientific answers to all the questions I'd always been asking – why we are born, why we die, why some people have good lives and others bad. And I was struck by the parallel between the Christian path and the graduated path to enlightenment through Buddhism. That was a big relief to me, to see there was some universal validity to religion. But then I found that the lamas were able not only to give clear, logical, crisp answers to all the questions I'd ever wanted to ask, but the origins of the teaching were explained. At the beginning of any teaching its lineage is explained, and this lineage – teacher to disciple – can be traced back to the Buddha. It's a living oral tradition that can be traced back to one man's experience. And that was tremendously reassuring to me.'

Kedge became a Buddhist monk and for four years he was Lama Yeshe's attendant, organising lecture tours and helping to establish the Lama's organisation, the Foundation for the Preservation of the Mahayana Tradition. (Kedge eventually gave up the monkhood, deciding that he could better serve Buddhism as a lay person. He started a material handling business in Hong Kong, donating a large proportion of his income to the FPMT, and to Osel's education.)

It was Lama Yeshe's particular skill, said Kedge, to extract the essence of Buddhist philosophy and psychology – 'what makes you happy or unhappy, the purpose of life and how to solve life's everyday problems' – from its Tibetan packaging and make it lucid and understandable to Western students.

In March 1984, Lama Yeshe died in California of a heart condition. It was assumed that as a great lama he would be reborn in a body recognisable to his students, and the responsibility for finding his reincarnation fell to his student and closest friend, Lama Zopa. In accordance with tradition, Zopa consulted several oracles – mediums who are in touch with the guiding and protecting spirits of Tibetan Buddhism. These indicated that in his next life Lama Yeshe would choose a Western reincarnation, to continue his work of teaching. Zopa studied his dreams. In one, Lama Yeshe appeared, telling his old friend that he was about to take human form. Much later, Zopa dreamed of a Western baby, crawling across the floor towards him. Convinced that Lama Yeshe's reincarnation was now in the world, Zopa began his search in earnest, visiting the centres and monasteries that Lama Yeshe had founded in his lifetime.

At length, he came to the small town of Bubion in Southern Spain, where Paco Hita, a self-employed builder, and his girlfriend Maria Torres, both former students of Lama Yeshe, had helped found a Buddhist retreat. Lama Yeshe had visited the retreat a year before he died and thanked Maria and Paco for their work. 'Even if I die,' he told them, 'I will never forget you. We have much business, much *karma* business between us.'

Six months before Zopa's arrival in the village, Maria had given birth to her and Paco's fifth child, a boy named Osel, after the retreat centre where he was born, Osel Ling, 'Land of Clear Light'. Lama Zopa immediately recognised the child from his dreams. He asked Maria, when exactly was the baby conceived? It was the night of Zopa's first dream. Zopa said nothing then to the parents about reincarnation, only that Osel was a very special child; that he should be kept in an unpolluted atmosphere, and that nobody should be allowed to ruffle his head. In the case of any reincarnate, it is the responsibility of the Dalai Lama to ratify the claim of identification. Zopa informed him of his belief that he had found Lama Yeshe's new incarnation. The Dalai Lama made his own divinations, confirming the recognition. Finally came the public affirmation, when Osel was presented with a selection of handbells and prayer-beads and unerringly selected those that had belonged to his predecessor.

At the age of nineteen months, Osel Hita Torres was proclaimed as 'the absolute and irrefutable' reincarnation of Lama Yeshe. At his enthronement ceremony in Dharamsala, the two-year-old lama, dressed in ceremonial robes and the curved, yellow *pandit* hat, accepted ritual offerings, grinned, yelled, chewed sweets and played with a toy car. At the end of the ceremony, he wriggled off the platform and ran to his father Paco, who carried him out of the temple, his destiny changed for ever. Osel's upbringing, Peter Kedge admitted, had been largely a case of 'trial and error'. Under normal circumstances, a young reincarnate lama would be given up to the monastery at an early age; his parents would welcome it as an honour. But what is appropriate for a Tibetan *tulku* is not necessarily appropriate for a Western child, and trying to strike a balance in Osel's life between the requirements of Tibetan tradition and the expectations of a normal family life had not been easy.

From an early age, Lama Osel led a peripatetic life. In order for students of Lama Yeshe to 'reacquaint' themselves with their reincarnated teacher, Lama Osel travelled to monasteries and centres in Nepal, Australia, America and Europe, usually in the company of one or other of his parents. As Buddhists and students of Lama Yeshe, Paco and Maria had always acknowledged that, at some point, it would be necessary for their son to enter a monastery in order to continue his education. And in 1991, at the age of seven, the young lama left his parents and took up residence in Sera.

At first, a Western monk acted as his attendant. A classics scholar from Yale and her husband answered an advertisement in *The New York Times* and were employed as private tutors. But after less than a year things began to go wrong. The young boy complained of missing his family, and started to kick against the strictures of monastery life. His mother travelled to India and took her son back to Spain. Back in his village, the boy began to eclipse the lama. It was, Paco said, a bad time. 'Lama became an ordinary boy in the village. There was no studying. He speak bad words. He is fighting and playing the pinball machine with the other boys.' Things were complicated still further by the fact that Paco and Maria had now separated. The young boy was sent to London, where his father was working. 'He was a completely changed boy, undisciplined, unbelievable,' said Paco.

A meeting was called between Paco, Maria and the heads of the FPMT in which the young boy decided that he would return to Sera, on condition that Paco and his younger brother Kunkyen joined him. But the family difficulties were not altogether resolved. Barely a year after he had returned to Sera, his mother Maria complained to a newspaper reporter in Spain that her son's monastic education was 'making him a Tibetan', and said that she wanted him to spend more time with her family in Spain. After further negotiations, a timetable was devised allowing for more regular visits home.

It was, by any standards, an unusual household. Responsibility for the young lama's discipline and upbringing was divided between his father, Paco, and a Nepalese monk attendant, Pemba; there was a Tibetan teacher; an American tutor; a male housekeeper and cook. 'It's sort of analogous to someone at boarding school, with a housemaster, tutor, a senior prefect and so on,' said Peter Kedge. The only exposure the young lama had to the opposite sex was when female students came to pay their respects. But then it was assumed by all around him that he would grow up to follow the life of a celibate.

As a Western incarnate, Lama Osel enjoyed considerably more freedom than would have been afforded a Tibetan. He was allowed to ride his bicycle, for example – if only within the walls of his own garden; to play games on his computer. One day, another reincarnate lama – a thirteen-year-old Tibetan boy – came to play football. 'They are old friends,' Peter Kedge explained. He meant, very old friends: in his previous incarnation the Tibetan boy was supposedly Lama Yeshe's teacher. The two young boys clattered noisily up and down a corridor, the ball ricocheting off the walls. Pemba appeared from the kitchen, shook his head in obvious disapproval, but said nothing.

'I think Lama is happy here,' Paco told me one day, as we walked in the garden. 'That is the most important thing, because when he's happy his mind is open and he wants to learn. When he's not happy, learning is so difficult. He has good health, good teachers, a good environment. These are the best conditions for him to become a very good person.'

From the beginning of Maria's pregnancy, Paco said, things had seemed somehow different. His work as a builder had always been irregular and life for the large family was difficult; yet during the pregnancy Maria seemed unusually relaxed, and suddenly there was more work, more money. Paco was able to build extra rooms on his house, with a nursery for the new child. After Osel was born, Paco practised his daily meditation in the baby's room. 'I don't know why,' he said, 'but sometimes I had these incredible feelings. I would open my eyes and many times see Lama Osel looking at me with very wide eyes, and then laughing. When I was first with Lama Yeshe, we didn't speak, but we had incredible communication. And it was the same with this baby.'

When his son was declared as the reincarnation of Lama Yeshe, Paco says he did not know what to think. 'I needed time to meditate, to think about this. I needed to feel it in my heart.'

And now?

'Now I feel it.'

Why, I asked Paco, did he think his family had been chosen?

'Not because I am a good person, no. I think because we are a big family; we have many children and are less attached to them, so for us to give up our son was easier. That way it is easier for Osel to follow the way to help many thousands of sentient beings.'

The last few years had not, I imagined, been easy for Paco. Meeting Lama Yeshe, he told me, had changed his life. It had given it meaning and purpose. Yet he could hardly have anticipated that his devotion to Lama Yeshe would lead to him becoming the father of his reincarnation. Paco seemed to have greeted this with a remarkable equanimity. He was an intensely shy, self-effacing man who went about the household chores of caring for his two sons with a quiet diligence that made him almost invisible; and who gracefully balanced paternal authority with deference to his son's position. He may have addressed his son not as Osel, but as 'Lama', but woe betide Lama if he was late for lessons.

'Lama Yeshe's motivation was always incredible,' Paco told me. 'When I first met him in 1977 I didn't understand Buddhism, nothing – but his compassion, his understanding, reached me. And now we have Lama Osel who speaks English, Spanish, Tibetan, he understands computer. It is as if Lama Yeshe has chosen this incredible body to help the world.'

My room in Sera was in a school administrative building, above the kitchens. It contained only a narrow bed and a table, on which stood a vase of flowers and a single red candle in a holder. On the wall was a glass-fronted cabinet, containing a faded black-and-white photograph of the Dalai Lama, taken, I would guess, some thirty years before. On either side were pictures of two elderly lamas, the Dalai Lama's teachers.

I loved these photographs: the Dalai Lama smiling from behind his wire-rimmed glasses, as if someone had just cracked a very funny joke; his two companions, more serious, almost austere, with a certain quality about their eyes that suggested they were privy to some unfathomable secret. The photographs had a peculiarly contagious serenity about them; faded as they were, they seemed almost alive. It was as if the monks were looking at me, looking at them, and this thought made me smile. It was strangely comforting to fall asleep to them at night, to wake to them each morning.

As a boy I had decorated my bedroom wall with pictures of footballers and soul singers; heroes; people I admired or thought I wanted to become. I did not wish to become these monks, but it occurred to me that I would like to know what they knew. I could watch the faces of the monks in the monastery for hours. Even during the most serious rituals, there seemed to be a glimmer of amusement behind their expressions, as if they were aware of some underlying cosmic absurdity at the heart of everything. They seemed to smile more readily, more openly, than any group of people I had ever encountered anywhere; not smiles that were automatic, or forced, but smiles which seemed to come from the very core of their being. When they smiled at you there was nothing to do but smile back, which caused them to smile back, causing you to smile back, so you were caught in some endless loop of smiling only broken by one of you turning away.

Meeting Lama Osel's teacher Geshe-La, I had been struck by his smile but, more than that, the expression he wore in repose – an expression of something more than serenity, and which somehow implied a depth of what I could only think of as self-knowledge. Watching him, I became aware of the degree to which my own expressions were nothing more than a series of masks – here I am being polite/grumpy/frivolous/serious. Geshe wore no masks. It was as if he knew exactly who he was and, furthermore, knew exactly who I was too. Meeting him, one had the curious sense that here was someone who was not judging, but simply accepting.

I had felt exactly the same sensation on meeting the Dalai Lama two years before. I was in Dharamsala, the town in Northern India, in the foothills of the Himalayas, that had become the centre of the Tibetan community in exile. It was Lhosar, the Tibetan New Year, and the Dalai Lama had been giving a series of teachings in the temple opposite his home, a thirty-two-room bungalow that had once been the home of the British District Commissioner and which had been renamed the Heavenly Abode. A crowd had gathered in the courtyard, to listen to the teachings, broadcast on a public address system, and to pay their respects as he walked back to the house. He came almost at a gallop, a short, squat figure, bobbing along with a train of attendants in his wake, his hands clasped together in a mirror of the gestures around him, laughing and nodding. As low as the people on either side bowed to him, he seemed to be bowing lower in acknowledgement. He seemed a man totally devoid of the slightest hint of grandeur, or, for that matter, of piety; and momentarily – absurdly – I was reminded of Groucho Marx, coat-tails flying.

Since he was awarded the Nobel Peace Prize in 1989, for his commitment to the cause of non-violent resistance against the Chinese occupation of his country, the Dalai Lama had become for many people not only the personification of the cause of Tibetan liberation, but the embodiment of the spiritual possibilities held out by Tibetan Buddhism. These he distilled to the most simple common denominator: the purpose of life, according to the Dalai Lama, is quite simply 'to be happy'. Everyone can understand this: everyone wants to be happy.

In an age of charlatans and despots, he seemed to wear the

demeanour of a saint. As he moved across the temple courtyard
in Dharamsala, many people, I noticed, were in tears. I felt, quite
involuntarily, moved to them myself.

I had travelled to Dharamsala to interview the Dalai Lama for
Esquire magazine, and, at the same time, for a radio programme
for the BBC. A friend and BBC producer, Martin, had flown out
to Dharamsala to record the conversation for radio; an illustrious
Indian photographer had travelled up from Delhi for *Esquire*. The
meeting was conducted in the drawing room of the Dalai Lama's
residence.

Armed soldiers from the Indian army patrolled the gates – a
stipulation not of the Dalai Lama himself, but of the Indian
government. His office was staffed not by monks, but by personable
Tibetans in Western suits. His personal secretary was an urbane
young man, dressed in a navy blazer and club tie, who smoked
Rothman's King Size as we talked. He spoke flawless English. He
explained that he had been brought up and educated in Switzerland.
(Following the Tibetan diaspora in 1959, some two hundred Tibetan
children had been adopted by Swiss families; I assumed he was one
of them.)

The secretary explained the Dalai Lama's daily routine when in
Dharamsala. He rises at 3.30 a.m. He spends an hour meditating
and does prostrations for half an hour. He eats a light breakfast at 5
a.m., then meditates and prays until nine, pausing only to listen to
the six-thirty news bulletin of the BBC World Service. He spends
an hour dealing with state and private papers. His afternoons are
spent on government matters and in meetings. At five he takes
tea, sometimes watching television. His evenings are spent with
scripture and in prayer. He goes to bed at nine. 'His Holiness
always sleeps soundly,' said the urbane young man with a smile,
tapping out another Rothman's. That day's programme included
meetings with a Canadian parliamentarian and representatives of the
Polish government, followed by a public audience for some thousand
people, conducted in the garden of the Heavenly Abode.

For almost two hours the Dalai Lama stood patiently, shielded
from the fierce sun by a multi-coloured umbrella, as the line of people
wound past him. He clasped the hands of each one, exchanged words
with some, nodded sympathetically to particular problems, blessed
children, received notes and letters. One woman, overcome with
emotion, clutched at his hand and was pulled away by attendants,

anxiously glancing at their wrist-watches. The Dalai Lama brushed the attendants aside, called the woman back and spoke soothingly to her for some minutes.

At last, the audience ended. We were shown into a reception room, spacious and airy, comfortably furnished with sofas and armchairs; an enormous golden Buddha stood in an elaborate shrine at one end of the room. He bustled in, for all the world as if he had a bus to catch, bright, curious eyes casting around the room. I had been tutored in the ritual of presenting him with a *kata*, the white ceremonial scarf. He took it with a smile, then thrust out his hand to grasp mine in a vigorous Western handshake. He beckoned me to a chair and sat down beside me, and the interview began. Martin switched on his tape-recorder, monitoring the recording through headphones; the photographer started taking pictures, moving ever closer to the Dalai Lama as he did so. We had been talking for only a couple of minutes when Martin raised his hand. The incessant click-and-whirr of the photographer's motor-drive was impairing the sound-quality of the recording.

Could the photographer perhaps desist until the interview was finished?

The photographer thought not. 'I've come to take photographs. I will take photographs.'

'But perhaps you could be reasonable . . .?'

The photographer obviously had no intention of being reasonable. The discussion continued, growing ever more heated. I had been allocated a little more than an hour, and the precious minutes were ticking away in a fatuous row over a photographer's motor-drive.

I looked at the Dalai Lama. He was wearing a smile of blissful indifference, as if regarding the imbroglio from a vast distance, through the wrong end of a telescope. I realised with a sinking heart that the winner of the Nobel Peace Prize had absolutely no intention of negotiating a truce. For a reason I couldn't quite understand, that responsibility had fallen to me. I could feel my palms sweating. I could hardly believe what was happening. I had travelled 4,000 miles to interview the fourteenth reincarnation of the Buddha of compassion, the wisest man in the world, and the interview was disintegrating in front of my eyes. I pleaded with the photographer, I begged him. Eventually, he agreed to wait, and the interview awkwardly resumed.

What I had not noticed was that at the moment the first voices were raised, the Dalai Lama had placed his hand over Martin's, and let it rest there. Throughout the course of the argument, Martin said, the Dalai Lama's hand remained utterly still, utterly firm, conveying not the slightest flicker of anxiety, irritation or impatience – rather, his resting hand conveyed, as Martin put it, 'an eternity of stillness'.

We talked about the Chinese occupation of Tibet, the Dalai Lama's attempts to introduce democracy into the Tibetan community in exile, and the spread of Tibetan Buddhist teachings to the West. 'West too big a word,' he said, wagging his finger. '*Some* of the West.' He spoke in a guttural English. When the right word failed to come he snapped his fingers and barked at the interpreter, 'English word! English word!' His neck, I noticed, was bullish; his heavy shoulders rolled, and the folds of flesh on his arms shook. There was nothing the least ethereal about him.

The conversation moved to the subject of compassion. All the suffering in the world arises from cherishing oneself, he said, all the happiness in the world arises from cherishing others. Treating other people gently, sincerely, compassionately – this was the source of true personal happiness. 'This should not be considered as a religious matter. It is a basic requirement of human beings. And our very existence, I believe, is based on these human qualities.'

In Buddhism, he said, contentment and peace of mind are the most highly prized things, since these are all that one carries from this life to the next. At the heart of this contentment is motivation: the motivation responsible for unhappiness is selfishness, or 'self-cherishing'. It is this that blinds us to the unity, the inter-dependence, of all things, and the knowledge that our well-being depends on the well-being of others. To hate or hurt others is to hate or hurt ourselves. We should be grateful to our enemies, the Dalai Lama said, for it is they who give us our greatest opportunities to deepen our patience, tolerance and compassion.

He told me a story to illustrate this. In Tibet, he said, he had been friends with a monk a few years older than himself. When the Dalai Lama fled across the border into India in 1959, the monk stayed behind. He was arrested by the Chinese and thrown into prison. Thousands of other monks had suffered the same fate; subject to starvation, beatings and, not uncommonly, a particularly vile form of torture – having electric cattle-prods thrust into the mouth and bodily orifices. Countless Tibetans had died of such atrocities, but this monk survived, and eventually he was released. He walked out of Tibet into Sikkhim, and from there he travelled to Dharamsala, to be reunited with the Dalai Lama and to recount his terrible story.

'And he told me, in all this he occasionally found one danger,' said the Dalai Lama. 'I asked him, what danger? And he said, the danger of him losing his compassion for the Chinese.' The Dalai Lama fell silent for a moment. 'That's wonderful, isn't it? You see, compassion is so important.'

In the Dalai Lama's case, this compassion is not contingent; it is taken to be the fundamental condition of his existence.

According to the Mahayana Buddhist teaching, at the moment of enlightenment the Buddha made the supreme sacrifice by vowing to forgo release into nirvana until all suffering was ended in the world. Thus was established the ideal of the Changchub Sempa, or bodhisattva – the highest goal for which a practitioner can strive – to attain enlightenment and return to the round of rebirth in order to work for the benefit of others. The Dalai Lama, it is believed, represents the highest expression of this ideal – the fourteenth reincarnation of Avalokiteshvara, the Buddha of compassion and a manifestation of the Buddha himself. His very existence is, in itself, testament to an idea of the perfectibility of man.

Buddhism began to infiltrate Tibet from India in the seventh century, but it was not until the eighth century, and the advent of the yogi Padmasambhava, that Tibet began to develop its own particular, esoteric and highly ritualised form of mystical practice, based on the three Buddhist paths, the *Hinayana*, the *Mahayana* and the tantric, or *Vajrayana*.

It was Padmasambhava, or Guru Rimpoche as he became known, who, legend has it, tamed the old animistic deities of the Bon religion and made them subordinate to the Buddha-dharma, and who founded Tibet's first Buddhist monastery, Samye. Padmasambhava became the 'root-guru' of the *Nyingmapa* tradition of teachings – one of the four main schools of Tibetan Buddhism (the others are the *Gelugpa*, the *Kagyupa* and the *Sakyapa*).

While the teaching that all beings are subject to rebirth until they achieve liberation is central to all schools of Buddhism, the theory of identifiable reincarnation is uniquely Tibetan, originating in the twelfth century with the tantric master Dusum Khypena, the founder of the Kagyupa tradition. Kagyu means 'linear oral instruction', and the order prides itself on its teachings having been transmitted in an unbroken line from master to disciple since the eighth century.

The lineage originated with the Indian Tilopa, whose disciple was Naropa. Naropa's teaching was brought to Tibet by Marpa the Translator, who passed it to Milarepa, who passed it, in turn, to Gampopa. Dusum Khypena was Gampopa's disciple. He is said to have attained complete enlightenment in his middle age, after months of solitary meditation and fasting. Recognising his pupil's attainments, Gampopa laid a hand upon his head and told him, 'My son, you have severed your bond with the world of phenomenal existence and henceforth it will be your duty to impart this realisation to others.'

In his early seventies, Dusum Khypena founded Tsurphu monastery, and as head of the Kagyu order took the title of Karmapa. He died at the age of eighty-four, leaving a letter predicting that ten years later he would be reborn as 'Karma Pakshi'. In accordance with this prophecy, Karma Pakshi took birth ten years later, under auspicious circumstances and demonstrating miraculous powers, and was duly recognised as the second Karmapa. The seventeenth Karmapa, who was born in 1985, presently lives at Tsurphu monastery.

In a society where celibacy was fundamental to monastic life, identifiable reincarnation not only affirmed the philosophical ideal of returning to continue work over successive lifetimes; it also ensured the continuity of both a spiritual and a political hierarchy.

Under successive Karmapas, the Kagyupa tradition remained the dominant force in Tibetan spiritual and political life until the fifteenth century, when monastic corruption opened the door to a reforming movement led by a scholar named Je Tsongkhapa, who systematised the Buddhist teachings into one great volume, *The Great Exposition of the Stages of the Path* (the *Lamrim Chempo*). From this grew the Gelugpa order, and the office of the Dalai Lama – a title bestowed by the Mongols on Sonam Gyatso, the abbot of Drepung monastery, at the same time retrospectively bequeathing his two predecessors the same position, making Sonam Gyatso the third Dalai Lama. For the next four hundred years, despite the incursions of the Mongols and the Manchus, and the internecine struggles between the various monastic traditions, Buddhism flourished in Tibet, with the Dalai Lama as its spiritual and political figurehead.

Its remote geographical position – a vast, windswept, mountainous wilderness; two-thirds of the country stands on a plateau at an altitude of 15,000 ft. and Lhasa, standing at 12,000 ft., is the highest capital city in the world – kept Tibet effectively isolated from the world beyond its borders. At the same time, its mythical role as a cradle of esoteric spiritual wisdom made it an object of mystery and fascination to Western explorers. Tibet produced its own fantastic legends of adepts who could fly, or walk through walls and speak in the tongues of birds and animals, of yogis practising *tum mo* meditation, or 'inner heat', able to sit naked in snow, drying off sheets drenched in water with the heat of their bodies, or to travel enormous distances by *gompa* running, using highly developed breathing techniques. Or of 'rainbow body', where, at death, the adept simply 'dematerialises', leaving only a small pile of nails and hair to verify that he was ever there at all. (Attainment of magical powers is known in Tibetan Buddhism as 'the relative achievement'. Attainment of Buddhahood is 'the ultimate achievement'. When, half teasingly, I asked the Dalai Lama whether he would leave the earth in 'rainbow body' he burst into laughter and replied that he didn't think so. 'You need a lot of practice and special training for that. I've not yet reached these things.')

Tibet's place in Western myth as a cradle of spiritual wisdom owes much to the esoteric teachings of the eighteenth and nineteenth century. In Russia, the mythology of 'The Unknown Superiors' – an enlightened hierarchy of beings who were supposed to dwell in Tibet – was an important element in Rosicrucian Masonry, and probably influenced the teachings of Madame Helena Blavatsky. Blavatsky claimed to have spent three years in Tibet, studying with enlightened masters, and her encounter with these *mahatmas*, as they became known, became the foundation stone for the Theosophical Society which was to prove enormously influential in propagating Eastern religious ideas in the West.

In her book *Isis Unveiled* Blavatsky argued that Buddhism was the 'wisdom doctrine' by which science and religion would be united. She described Buddhism, 'even in its dead letter', as 'incomparably higher, more noble, more philosophical and more scientific than the teaching of any other church or religion'. In 1880, Blavatsky and Olcott became the first Europeans to 'take refuge' in Theravada Buddhism, receiving the five Buddhist lay precepts before a *bikkhu* in a temple at Galle in Ceylon.

Blavatsky looked to Buddhism, rather than Christianity, for her belief in the coming of the next great world teacher. Buddhist

legend teaches that while an infinite number of beings may attain
enlightenment and become Buddhas, during this world age, or
kalpa, there will be one thousand fully enlightened Buddhas who
will 'turn the wheel of *dharma*'. Four of these have already come and
gone; Guatama Buddha (or Shakyamuni, as he is known in Tibetan
teaching) was the fourth. The fifth – or Forthcoming Buddha – is the
bodhisattva Jampa, or Maitreya (Jampa means 'loving kindness').

According to legend, until he descends to earth, Maitreya, like
Shakyamuni Buddha, resides in the Ganden paradise, the third
heaven of the senses, where all bodhisattvas await rebirth. The
residents of Ganden are said to be 200 metres in height, and
to live for 4,000 years, each day being the equal of 400 human
years. Maitreya, it is said, will come after the decline of Guatama's
teachings, to lead the world out of the dark age of the *Kali Yuga*. This
prophecy of the Buddha to come became a central preoccupation of
theosophy, eventually leading some years after Blavatsky's death to
the declaration that 'a vehicle' for Maitreya had emerged in the
slight, boyish and diffident frame of an Indian boy named Jiddu
Krishnamurti.

Tibet clung tenaciously to its secrets, but it could not keep the
world at bay, and by the turn of the century the country had become
a strategic pawn in 'the great game' between Britain and Russia. In
1904 a British expedition led by Colonel Francis Younghusband
penetrated as far as the capital Lhasa, looting and robbing from
monasteries as they went. Thigh-bone trumpets, skull caps and
ornate thangkas depicting the most fearsome Buddhist protector
deities were taken as evidence that the Tibetans were godless infidels.
But the British were puzzled at the lack of resistance. Rather than
fighting or negotiating with the conquerors, the thirteenth Dalai
Lama simply left the country, on a missionary journey to Mongolia,
leaving negotiations with the British to his Regent, Lamoshar Lobsang
Gyaltsen, the Abbot of Ganden Monastery (or the Ganden Tripa as
he was known).

Younghusband later wrote to his wife that, when his troops
marched in hollow victory through Lhasa, the people of the city
lined the streets and applauded 'the grand show' of the British
expeditionary force. What Younghusband did not realise was that
the Tibetans were clapping to drive out evil spirits. Younghusband
did not subscribe to the view of his footsoldiers that the Tibetans were
godless savages. 'The Tibetans are excellent people,' he wrote, 'quite

polished and polite and genial and well mannered, but absolutely impossible on business matters.'

On his last day in Lhasa, Younghusband was presented with a small, bronze Buddha by the Ganden Tripa, and the next morning rode out of the city into the surrounding mountains. Seated on a rock, he later wrote, he was suddenly seized by the most intense, untellable joy. 'The whole world was ablaze with the same ineffable bliss that was burning within me . . . I was beside myself with an intensity of joy, such as even the joy of first love can give only a faint foreshadowing of. And with this indescribable joy came a revelation of the essential goodness of the world. I was convinced past all refutation that men were good at heart, that the evil in them was superficial . . . in short, that men at heart are divine.'

Younghusband's expedition was a futile gesture which did little to bring Tibet within the sphere of control or influence of the West. The British withdrew, leaving only a pair of trade agents and a telegraph wire inside Tibet's borders. In 1907, a treaty between Britain and Russia carved up the area of the 'Great Game' between them, with the two great powers agreeing to keep out of Tibet and to conduct any negotiations concerning the country with the Chinese, thus opening the door to China's renewed claims to territorial sovereignty over the country. (Younghusband himself was one of that rare breed of colonial soldiers and administrators who became enamoured of Eastern philosophy; he later sponsored the World Congress of Faiths which brought together a Russian orthodox theologian, Muslim scholars, the Hindu teacher Radhakrishnan and the great Japanese teacher of Zen Buddhism T.D. Suzuki, in London in 1936.

Sir Edwin Arnold was another of the same breed. An educationalist and journalist – he was at one time editor of the *Daily Telegraph* – Arnold was originally sent to India as the principal of a government college in Poona. He became absorbed in Oriental studies and wrote an epic poem on the life of the Buddha, *The Light of Asia*, which was published in sixty editions in England and eighty in America.)

The idea of Tibet as the focal point for a romantic Western yearning for spiritual enlightenment and salvation only increased after the Great War, providing a powerful mythology in the face of the chaos of industrialised Europe. In 1925 the playwright and poet Antonin Artaud published a plea to the thirteenth Dalai Lama in *La Révolution surréaliste*.

We are your most faithful servants. Direct your lights to us in a language that our contaminated European spirits can understand and, if need be, transform our Spirit, make for us a spirit entirely turned towards those perfect summits where the Spirit of Man no longer suffers.

This view of Tibet as a place of spiritual deliverance was compounded in the popular imagination by James Hilton's novel, *The Lost Horizon*, which was published in 1933. Hilton's story told of four Westerners who are flown from India to a Himalayan redoubt – 'Shangri-La' – where the inhabitants devote themselves to lives of art, music and contemplation of the truths of all the great religions. (*La* means 'pass' in Tibetan. Hilton probably took the name from the Changri La, a pass located near the Everest region in Tibet which was frequented by the British climber George Mallory in his attempts to ascend Everest in the early Twenties.) In this peaceful and rarefied paradise, people live for centuries, but anyone who tries to leave grows old immediately. Authority is vested in the High Lama – in Hilton's tale not a Tibetan at all, but a Western capuchin monk, who is more than 300 years old.

Shangri-La has been designed to preserve the world's most ennobling spiritual and cultural values against the impending holocaust which 'will rage till every flower of culture is trampled, and all human beings are levelled in a vast chaos'. The parallels with Madame Blavatsky's teachings about the great brotherhood of Mahatmas, guiding the world's destiny, are inescapable. Hilton's book became an enormous popular success. It was turned into a film and introduced the word 'Shangri-La' into the lexicon as a synonym for a peaceful, idealised Utopia.

Growing up in the Sixties, I can remember being intrigued by the books of one T. Lobsang Rampa. His first book, *The Third Eye*, the autobiography of a Tibetan monk, raised in the Chakpori monastery in Lhasa, was published in 1956. He went on to write a dozen more books, including *The Cave of the Ancient* and *Living with the Lama* (which claimed to be the autobiography of his cat, transmitted telepathically), their enormous popular success apparently unaffected by the subsequent revelation that 'Lobsang Rampa' was not a Tibetan monk at all, but one Cyril Henry Hoskins, the son of a plumber from Plympton in Devon.

Hoskins had based his books on a vivid imagination and the

assiduous study of the writings of Madame Blavatsky and Alexandra David-Neel, who travelled extensively in Tibet and was the first European woman ever to have an audience with a Dalai Lama, the thirteenth, whom she met when he was in temporary exile in Darjeeling in 1912. (Apparently, David-Neel was unimpressed: 'I don't like popes,' she wrote. 'I don't like the kind of Buddhist Catholicism over which he presides. Everything about him is affected, he is neither cordial nor kind.')

But it was neither poetry nor literature that was to bring Tibetan teachings to the West, but the popular uprising against the Chinese, when the Dalai Lama was forced to flee into exile in India, with tens of thousands of his countrymen following behind him. The Tibetan diaspora made possible for the first time on a mass scale a personal encounter between Westerners and Tibetan Buddhist teachings. Buddhism is not an evangelical movement, yet in the last thirty years increasing numbers of Tibetan lamas have travelled in the West, with the result that retreats, centres and monasteries are now to be found in America, Australia and in virtually every country in Western, and increasingly Eastern, Europe. In this, as in all things, I heard it said, could be seen the workings of *karma*. It was the *karma* of the Tibetans to experience the suffering of displacement, and to learn from it; the *karma* of the West to be exposed to the teachings, and to learn from them.

It was a peculiar irony that in the Nineties Tibetan Buddhism had become fashionable. The Dalai Lama had been invited to edit French *Vogue*, and had been the subject of two Hollywood bio-pics. Film stars such as Richard Gere and Harrison Ford sponsored expensive charity dinners for the cause of Tibetan independence. Tibetan restaurants appeared on the streets of New York and London. The attraction of Buddhism to the West can be easily understood: its emphasis on tolerance, compassion and inter-dependence; its combination of intellectual rigour and wholly practical common sense; its advocacy of experience over doctrine – the Buddha himself taught that none of his teachings should be accepted on faith, but only after they had been tested as one would test gold, 'by burning, cutting and rubbing'.

To this Tibetan Buddhism added the particular allure of exoticism and mystery, a centuries-old tradition rich in wondrous tales of spiritually enlightened beings, with the living example of a multitude of lamas and *tulkus* bringing the teachings to the West, with the charismatic and saintly Dalai Lama to the fore. It was as if, having been hidden for centuries, the Tibetan culture had now fluttered into the world like some vividly plumaged bird. It offered something for everyone: spiritual seekers, cultural anthropologists, human rights activists.

Dharamsala had become a mandatory place of pilgrimage on the spiritual tourist trail. Back-packers, tourists and students of Buddhism jostled with maroon-robed monks on its narrow, rutted streets, and joined Tibetans at the small *stupa* in the centre of the village to turn the brightly painted prayer wheels spinning blessings into the sky. A conference of Western Buddhist teachers was being held in the town, to coincide with the Dalai Lama's teachings, and in the evenings the small dining room of my hotel was crowded with Western teachers entertaining visiting lamas to dinner. Some travellers, I noticed, while not monks themselves, seemed to have adopted a sort of monk chic – close-cropped hair and splashes of maroon – in a sort of sartorial solidarity. While the Western visitors discussed Buddhist theology, the younger Tibetan monks toyed with their visitors' Walkmans and Gameboys. The atmosphere crackled with talk of philosophy, politics, the stories of new arrivals from Tibet. People talked of the Dalai Lama with a catch in their breath, as His Holiness, or with a knowing insouciance as simply 'H.H.'.

The Chinese set out systematically to destroy Tibetan culture. In 1950, there were some 2,700 monasteries in central Tibet; there are now fewer than fifty, and religious freedoms are violently suppressed. In the face of this, Dharamsala has become a precious living storehouse of Tibetan culture, as if James Hilton's vision of Shangri-La had been physically uprooted from its Tibetan plateau and transplanted to the foothills on the other side of the Himalayas.

Religious texts and artefacts, smuggled across the border by refugees, are housed in the Tibetan library and museum; schools, monasteries and nunneries have grown up in the hills around; Tibetan shops and restaurants line the streets and prayer flags flutter above the ramshackle wooden buildings, carrying blessings towards the snow-capped Himalayas, and the holy, tragic Tibet beyond.

High lamas, visiting from the monasteries in the south, had requested a consultation with Nechung, the state oracle of Tibet. It was to be held in the temple of the oracle's own monastery, at dawn. I awoke at five and walked for a mile by starlight to the monastery gates.

There were once many hundreds of oracles in Tibet. Few survive, and of these the most important is Nechung, believed to be the voice of Dorje Drakden, one of the 'protector spirits' of the Tibetan nation and the Dalai Lama. Nechung is said to have arrived in Tibet with a descendant of the Indian sage Dharmpala. In the eighth century, it was the protector spirit of the first Buddhist monastery to be built in Tibet, Samye, by the country's supreme spiritual guardian, Padmasambhava. But it was not until 1544 that the spirit first took possession of a human being, Drag Trang-Go-Wa Lobsang Palden, who became the first medium, or *kuten* (literally, 'physical basis'). The present *kuten* is the fourteenth. It is traditional for the Dalai Lama to consult Nechung on affairs of state, and such matters as confirming the claims of rebirth of important *tulkus*. In 1959 Nechung warned of impending danger to the Dalai Lama and told him the route by which he could flee to safety.

The medium of the oracle traditionally holds the position of abbot of the Nechung monastery. The ceremony was to begin at seven in the morning; by six the monastery temple was crowded with monks, sitting cross-legged on the wooden floor, chanting to the accompaniment of trumpets and cymbals. Candles had been lit, and the air was heavy with incense. Flanked by attendants, the *kuten* entered and was guided to his place on a throne on a raised platform in front of a large statue of the Buddha. He appeared to be in a deep trance. A large and elaborately decorated cloak was placed over his shoulders; on his chest he wore a circular steel mirror, surrounded by amethyst and turquoise, and inscribed in sanskrit with the name of Dorje Drakden. Now an enormous helmet was placed on his head, so heavy that it required two attendants to lift it, the *kuten*'s head involuntarily falling back under the weight of it, the helmet resting on the back of a monk, kneeling behind him. As the drumming and chanting increased in intensity, and the possession took hold, the *kuten*'s body began to twitch uncontrollably; his face began to expand visibly and turn purple, and a violent, guttural hissing issued from his mouth.

Now his attendants busied themselves with the helmet, tightening the straps around his throat in a stricture that under normal circumstances would surely have throttled him to death. The air of expectancy in the temple had become unbearable. Suddenly, the *kuten* leapt from his chair with a cry, as if the cloak and helmet were made of nothing more than feathers, and drawing a sword from his cloak began to sketch a graceful and balletic dance around the platform. A gust of some palpable yet indefinable energy seemed to have swept into the temple, agitating the candles and the wall-hangings, pulling the monks to their feet; they were spellbound by the dancing figure, a spirit no longer human. I was suddenly aware that my legs were shaking.

A woman had pushed her way to the lip of the platform, dressed in the robes of a nun, but with a white bandanna around her head. She too appeared to be in the grip of some violent possession, taunting the spirit in front of her. He raised his sword as if to smite her down. She was pulled, writhing and screaming, back into the crowd. His dance completed, the *kuten* fell back on to the chair. A high, urgent voice filled the air; the voice of Dorje Drakden, delivering his message. The lamas gathered round the *kuten*, temporarily obscuring him from view, while a scribe hurriedly wrote down his message.

Now the monks pushed forward to receive the oracle's blessing. I found myself being jostled up the steps of the platform and standing in front of him, a deranged, purple-faced figure, his head lolling violently from side to side under the weight of his enormous helmet. An attendant had materialised beside him, holding a large bowl filled with seeds. The *kuten* scooped up a handful and threw them into my outstretched palm. The urgent weight of the crowd behind me pushed me on. At the door of the temple a monk tied a scrap of red silk around my neck. 'The blessing of the oracle,' he said. 'You must wear for three days.'

The flash of silk chafing at my throat, I visited the *kuten* the following afternoon. His name was the Venerable Thupten Ngodub. He greeted me in a drawing room, a fresh-faced monk in his late thirties with an air of implacable calmness; he was barely recognisable as the possessed figure of the previous day. I asked how he had come to be chosen as the *kuten*.

Nechung had chosen him, he replied. When the previous *kuten* died, he was a mere attendant to His Holiness. Then one day, during *puja*, he had felt something strange, 'Like an electric shock. For five minutes I could remember nothing. Everybody said this was very strange, but they couldn't be sure 100 per cent it was the oracle. So then His Holiness called to me and asked me about this feeling. I told him everything. He asked me if I'd had a special dream, and I had.' The young man smiled. 'But this is a secret which I don't tell to anybody, I'm sorry. So then I was sent on a retreat, to say 400,000 mantras; they gave me a series of tests, His Holiness and the high lamas. And after this they announced that I was the medium . . .' He smiled. 'I think it is some *karma* . . .'

Dorje Drakden, he said in faltering English, was, 'Like the wind. He is all around us, at all times. You can't see him. When he comes in the medium body, then you can see him. He uses my body. It is a higher awareness that speaks through me. As it comes it is like an electric current, and after that I feel nothing.' He laughed. 'I am no more there.'

Had I felt anything in the room when he was in the trance, he asked.

I replied that I had.

He laughed. 'That is Dorje Drakden.'

The oracle, he said, spoke in an ancient Tibetan tongue, and the *kuten* had no memory of what was said through him. He knew only what he was told, and sometimes he was told nothing. But this much he knew of yesterday's message. The oracle had predicted beneficial changes in the situation with China. 'He said that His Holiness has given good advice to the people, and the Tibetan people must maintain non-violence, without losing heart. He says the oracle and the protectors do not have form, but they will do their duty by changing the heart and minds of the Chinese. The freedom of Tibet is the responsibility of both the people and the deities.'

Personally, he said, he could remember nothing of being in the trance. After Dorje Drakden leaves his body, he falls into a faint. When he comes to, he feels ill for hours afterwards, tired and vomiting, 'And great pain here . . .' He rubbed the veins of his arms. 'Where spirit comes.'

I had been told, I said, that the exertions of being a *kuten* exact a terrible physical toll, and that mediums usually die young.

Yes, the *kuten* said. This is true. He smiled. 'This too is *karma*.'

In Sera, I woke each morning in darkness, to the sound of pots and pans clattering in the kitchen below, a cock crowing, the murmur of voices, and the hacking and clearing of throats on the path outside my window. The monks gathered each morning in the main temple for prayers, and to break bread together. Most of the monks in the monastery sat cross-legged on the floor, in long lines, facing each other. Each monk was given a large piece of unleavened bread and sweet Tibetan tea was poured into their metal mugs. They sat chomping and slurping, the crumbs falling to the floor. After the meal, a young monk distributed brushes, and the monks swept the crumbs in front of them into a pile, pushed it along, skidded the brush further down the line, and in this way all the crumbs were gathered into large piles, which the young monks then swept into pans and carried away. This domestic ritual occurred, as everything occurred, in silence, save for the coughing and clearing of throats, and the click of the brushes, working their way across the temple floor. It seemed to me that this ritual must have been taking place for hundreds of years.

Now the monks fell to chanting, while two officer monks walked along the lines, keeping a beady eye open for anyone slacking in their duties or falling asleep. One young monk, caught with his eyes closed, was thrashed soundly about the head with the officer's mala. The violence of the beating was shocking, a sudden jolt to the idealised view I was forming of monastery life. But later that day, as I stood on the roof of my building, overlooking the school yard, I saw an elderly monk pummelling a young boy about the head and body with all his might, the boy struggling to get away, but raising not so much as a whimper in protest. I would arrive each morning at Lama Osel's for breakfast, to the sound of the young lama chanting prayers in his room, and leave after supper to the same sound, like a thread that ran through each day, connecting it to the next. 'In a world filled with suffering, please grant me the blessings to help all sentient beings. In a world filled with suffering, please grant me the blessings to help all sentient beings. In a world filled with suffering . . .'

A timetable taped to the door of the study described Lama Osel's regime: a fifteen-hour working day six days a week. English, science, history, Spanish, mathematics; Tibetan script, memorisations, philosophy, debate. Sometimes I would sit in on his lessons, watching as he and George pored over books on history and grammar, or concocted schoolboy experiments with the chemistry paraphernalia stored on the shelf in his study. On his desk was the latest Apple powerbook, hooked up to the Internet. Most people have screen-savers of stellar constellations, shifting abstracts or shoals of electronic fish. Lama Osel's screen-saver, I noticed, was a picture of the Dalai Lama.

During his break-times, Osel would bolt for the computer and load a game. One day he suggested that he, Peter and I should play Sim-City – a game that involves planning and building a city from the power-supply up. 'But before we build anything,' he said, 'we all have to agree. If two say yes and one say no, we do it. If two say no, we don't.' Such diplomacy, it seemed to me, was unusual in a ten year old. He allocated an area of forestland – 'For the animals to live in – do you agree?' He installed schools, hospitals, a police station.

'Perhaps we should raise taxes to pay for all this,' I said.

'The people don't like it,' he said. 'We must keep the people happy.'

From the moment I arrived at Sera, I had found myself looking for signs that would indicate that this young Spanish boy was, indeed, what he was claimed to be: a reincarnation of a Tibetan lama.

According to Tibetan teaching, after death the subtle consciousness – which exists in all of us but is generally dormant – remains, carrying traces, or imprints, shaped by the thoughts and actions of the life just ended, into the next one. This could be one explanation, Peter Kedge believed, for child prodigies who demonstrate an unusual facility for, say, mathematics or playing the piano. 'The more habitual the activity, the stronger the imprint. This is why religious practice has to be followed; what one is doing is strengthening a certain kind of imprint, and avoiding strengthening another kind of imprint.'

Our culture does not accommodate the idea that such talents are imprints from a previous life. But in the case of a *tulku* who has 'chosen' his reincarnation, these imprints are thought to be unusually developed, and are carefully looked for. These imprints are said to be more recognisable in the early years; there are countless stories in Tibetan Buddhist lore of young reincarnates crawling from their houses towards the monastery where they lived in their 'previous life', or commanding their playmates to make prostrations in front of them.

Shortly after the Dalai Lama's identification at the age of two he was brought from his birthplace in Eastern Tibet to the Potala Palace in Lhasa. It is said that in the state bedroom, he noticed a box and exclaimed, 'My teeth are in there.' They were – the false ones of his predecessor.

'Very complicated . . .' said the Dalai Lama with a gust of laughter, when I raised the question of reincarnation. Whether he is the reincarnation of previous Dalai Lamas, or the living embodiment of the Buddha of Compassion, he said, 'is not for me to say. Some reincarnations can be the same person or same being; some reincarnations can be as a representative of that being. In some cases, the previous being asks one of his or her close friends and says go there instead of himself or herself; that's also possible.

'This much I can say. Through previous lives I do believe there is some special connection between my being and the Tibetan nation. My spiritual work and the freedom of Tibet are inextricably linked. And I feel, with some confidence, some connection with previous Dalai Lamas, particularly the fifth and thirteenth Dalai Lamas.'

It was the 'Great Fifth' who first consolidated the unification of Tibet under Buddhist rule in the seventeenth century, securing its independence in the face of manoeuvres by both the Mongols and the Chinese. It was the thirteenth who, in 1912, declared Tibet independent, and made the first cautious steps towards internal reform, and too the first tentative contacts with the outside world, sending Tibetans abroad to study.

'The purpose of reincarnation is to continue the work of the previous life which is not yet accomplished,' the Dalai Lama said. 'The thirteenth Dalai Lama at an early age fought with the Chinese.' He chuckled. 'And the British also . . . So I believe I came to continue the accomplishment of his plan. Firstly, to continue the reforms of Tibet; and secondly the cause of Tibetan freedom.

'I think there is some special connection there, through my dreams and feelings. On a few occasions I have dreamt of the thirteenth, and the fifth also, and discussed something; and sometimes some vague instructions, not very clear.' He burst into laughter. 'I always wish it could be clearer.'

Certainly, identifying reincarnates seemed an inexact science. In Dharamsala I took tea with the Dalai Lama's youngest brother, Tenzin Choegyal – or Geyri Rinpoche, to give him his reincarnate title – in his cottage in the grounds of the Heavenly Abode. I expected a robed monk. Instead, I was greeted by an affable man in sweater and slacks, smoking Benson and Hedges (lit by a cigarette lighter stamped with a dollar-bill motif), who spoke in a fluent English, peppered with Americanisms acquired from his years studying in America. 'I was a college drop-out!' he said with a laugh. His older brother had already been identified as the Dalai Lama before he was born, he told me. His own birth followed shortly after the death from illness of another brother. Immediately before his death, the brother's body was marked with yak's butter. When Tenzin Choegyal was born, he bore the same marks, in the same place – 'On my butt, actually,' he said with a laugh. 'Very inconvenient.'

He was taken to be a direct reincarnation of his dead brother, and, simultaneously, of a previous Rinpoche. 'That's what they tell me, anyway.' He sounded sceptical. He had entered a monastery at the age of seven – 'I was taken hostage!' he laughed – and remained a monk until the age of twenty-five, when he renounced his vows of celibacy. 'To be a monk is a vocation rather than an occupation, and I just felt I didn't have the stuff to be a celibate. To be celibate without being in the spirit of it . . .' He smiled. 'It creates inner conflict.

'As a Buddhist, I believe that reincarnation of consciousness is totally possible. But as to the question of identification, I'm not so sure. I can't rule out the possibility, and in the Dalai Lama's case the signs are very clear, but in my case, there's a mistake for sure. I don't feel any different, and I don't remember anything of a previous life.' He paused to light a cigarette. 'This question of reincarnation is very complicated, and I think there's a danger now that it's being degraded. There are reincarnations being declared all over the place; it's become almost a fashion. A teacher dies and the pupils decide they have a reincarnation among them.

'My brother, His Holiness, has spoken about this; he's said that *tulkus* are growing like mushrooms. You have all these lamas in the West now, forming their own little fiefdoms. It's like a cult. I'm totally against these. Some of these people are degrading the teachings. There's a lot of money involved, a lot of ego. To be a teacher, there's a lot of power. Particularly if your pupils are blind-faithers – people who just follow the words of the teacher without using their own common sense. You find that in Buddhism too.'

He regarded me with an amused expression. 'I can tell I've disappointed you. But you should beware of Shangri-La syndrome.'

Shangri-La syndrome?

'Yes,' he chuckled, 'thinking everything about Tibet is magical and romantic. You people in the West, you like the mystery of it all, the magic, the talk of reincarnations, all the costumes and the rituals. It's very exotic, yes? But these things aren't important. The real miracle of Buddhism is how a person can change, from a very empty person to a person who's full of compassion.'

In the days I spent with Lama Osel I became aware that he was watching me watching him, and it struck me that he was someone who had grown up under perpetual scrutiny. From the moment of his recognition by Lama Zopa, people had been looking for signs, correspondences – imprints. At an early age, Lama Osel was said to have behaved unusually, enacting ritualistic gestures quite spontaneously, 'recognising' old friends. Unusually for a Spanish child, he had demonstrated a liking for Tibetan food, and Tibetan tea (definitely an acquired taste). Like Lama Yeshe, when eating fruit he would suck out the pulp and throw the rest away. Lama Yeshe loved gardening; Lama Osel had enjoyed playing with gardening tools, and shown an interest in flowers. Lama Yeshe was often to be found in the kitchen, lifting the lids on pots and pans, tasting food; Lama Osel showed the same traits.

I had read that Lama Yeshe had a habit of rubbing his head for no apparent reason. At the dinner table one night I noticed with a start that Lama Osel was doing exactly the same thing. We were discussing the lama's studies; he had been reading about the Aztecs. 'It's so interesting,' he said. 'I read it and immediately go right into it.'

'Why do you like it so much?' I asked.

'It reminds me of Tibet,' said Lama.

He had never been to Tibet, although Lama Yeshe, of course, was born there.

'Lama Osel is not Lama Yeshe, he is himself,' said Paco one day as we walked in the garden. 'In some ways there is no similarity. But I do feel there is incredible compassion and love there, and a very clear, lucid mind. I am surprised sometimes. He'll ask me a question and then challenge my answer; he has an incredible ability to show me aspects of myself. And his relationships with others are interesting. I've noticed that when people around him are proud, his attitude to them is very hard. But when people are humble, he responds with great sympathy.'

I had noticed this. The young lama had an uncommon awareness of others' moods and a mindfulness of their well-being. 'Are you OK?' he would ask at odd moments – which would be unusual in an adult, let alone a ten year old. Watching him at his studies, conversing at the dinner table and playing with his Lego set, I found myself torn between wondering if he was a child pretending to be a grown-up, or a grown-up pretending to be a child.

The theory of reincarnation, it seemed, added a further imponderable to the timeless question of nature versus nurture. To the outsider, it was impossible to tell how much Lama Osel's obvious intelligence and composure, his readiness to volunteer opinions, was 'karmic imprint', and how much the consequence of being brought up in an environment which was, by any standards, unusually scholastic and serious-minded. There was no television in the household; no pop music. One sensed that everything that was said to the young lama – everything he was exposed to – was carefully weighed and considered.

As his student and attendant, Peter Kedge had known Lama Yeshe as well as anyone. Their relationship, he said, was essentially a practical one, revolving around the development of the FPMT, the building of a new monastery in Kopan, a retreat in Dharamsala. 'We'd walk around together, and Lama Yeshe would point to things and we'd discuss them.'

Here in Sera, a new temple was under construction. 'Yesterday,' said Kedge, 'Lama Osel took me there. And we walked around and he pointed out all the features and he was discussing what had been done well, what was a mistake and so forth. And it was just like walking round with Lama Yeshe; exactly the same dialogue, exactly the same format . . .'

George Churinoff, Lama Osel's American tutor, who had also been a student of Lama Yeshe, told me another story.

'Shortly before Lama Yeshe's death,' George said, 'one of the last things he said to me was intellectual verbiage doesn't mean kaka – doesn't mean shit; in other words, being a scholar for its own sake is not spiritual progress.

'The first time I met Lama Osel, he was about three and he was cycling around on his tricycle; I bent down and asked if he had anything to say to me, and he whispered, "I don't know anything about kaka." Now, if you take that out of context, it doesn't mean anything. But to me it suggested that Lama was on the same line – not caring whether people thought he was a high scholar or whatever.'

I didn't know what to make of such stories. Were the people around Lama Osel deluding themselves, seeing what they wanted to see? I wanted proof, but what proof could there possibly be? I was adrift in a sea of divinations, intuitions, signs and wonders where the compass of rationalism was useless.

I talked with Geshe-la. A venerable teacher, he was responsible for the education of a college of 1,000 monks in the monastery. Lama Zopa, I was told, had conducted many divinations to establish that Geshe-la was the best teacher for the young lama.

'At first, I asked not to,' he told me. 'Because he is a Western child, I had some fear and doubt that I might not be able to fulfil what was wanted. But Lama Zopa said that his divinations had come out well, that there would be a good result in the future. So I believed that, and promised to carry on.'

But was he convinced that Lama Osel was indeed a reincarnation of Lama Yeshe?

He considered the question carefully. 'From my own side I don't have any personal experience or divination that he is a reincarnation, but because it has been validated by the Dalai Lama, and because from my own side I can see imprints of the *dharma* there, then yes, I believe it. When I try to explain the teachings he sometimes grasps them very quickly and actually elaborates from his own side. For me, that shows there is some imprint.'

Geshe-la arrived each afternoon to take the young lama's class in Tibetan language and dialectics. The little Spanish boy and the elderly Tibetan faced each other, cross-legged, on the floor of the lama's room, overlooked by a portrait of the Dalai Lama and a mask of the cartoon character Captain Haddock. They enacted a ritual with dorge and bell, made offerings to the Buddha and the deities, and the lesson began.

Today's lesson, in Tibetan, was on the law of *karma*. Plant the seed and the wheat grows, said Geshe-la. From a good seed, good wheat grows. Merit arises from good actions; negative *karma* from bad ones. The young boy debated vigorously, following the ritual of slapping his palms each time a point was made, chastising himself with a slap on the head when he faltered, collapsing into laughter. The chirrup of a Mickey Mouse alarm clock marked the end of the lesson.

When he is older the young lama will go to the debating courtyard, where as many as 500 monks at a time gather to debate the most abstruse points of Buddhist philosophy. Osel must be ready for this, said Geshe-la. 'He must be good.' My room in the school building

was close to the debating courtyard. At five-thirty in the evening, as
the sun dipped behind the roof of the main temple, turning the huge
relief of the Wheel of Life on its roof to gold, the monks would file
in to begin their debate. At midnight they would still be there. I lay
in the darkness, listening to the voices raised in raucous argument
and laughter, the sound of hands hitting palms, like waves slapping
against rocks, rising from below.

I liked George Churinoff from the moment I met him. He was a
brawny, heavy-jowled man with the build of a wrestler, yet the
gentleness of a child. He lived in a small bungalow, set on a hill
overlooking the monastery. The path to his house led past villas,
with gardens, new houses in development – the homes of senior
lamas, *rinpoches*, monastery dignitaries. 'It's Sera's equivalent of the
upscale neighbourhood,' George joked.

His bungalow was filled with stacks of *Newsweek* and *Scientific
American* magazines; a computer, and volumes of Tibetan texts, the
shape of elongated house-bricks, bound in gold cloth. In his spare time
George was translating texts from Tibetan into English. George came
from Chicago. His father, he said, was 'a philosopher truck-driver', a
self-educated man, who taught George that the most important thing
in life was to think. George attended MIT, then studied physics at
graduate school, with a view to becoming a research scientist.

'I always thought when I was a kid that by understanding the laws of nature you could find happiness and control
your destiny. Then I found so many people who were in that
profession that were unhappy. I realised they didn't have the
answers at all.' He smiled. 'Now I think, maybe I was a monk
in previous lives, and it was just a question of finding that
out.'

He discovered Sufi-ism and the works of the Russian mystic
Gurdjieff, and dropped out of graduate school to pursue his
interest in philosophy, at the same time heeding Gurdjieff's
imprecation to 'do something with the left foot' whilst pursuing
your spiritual practice, by teaching physics at Choate, a Wasp
preparatory school in Connecticut, where John F. Kennedy had
been a pupil. But after two years he became restless. He took
a job in Beirut, teaching in an American community school,
then travelled through the Middle East, studying Sufi philosophy.

In 1974, he found himself in India. 'Somebody told me about Lama Yeshe's meditation course in Kopan. I didn't know anything about Tibetan lamas, but I was told they were authentic; that they weren't interested in collecting Rolls-Royces like the Maharishi.' He made his way to Kopan. 'At the end of the course I wrote in my notebook: "Now I'm ready to get off the race-track of Samsara."' The following year he made the decision to become a monk, and in 1976 took ordination as a novice.

'People in the West have reached the end of the line,' said George. 'We've seen that all of this wealth, this technological knowledge, doesn't bring happiness. If wealth, status or the pleasure of the senses were the source of happiness we should be the happiest people since the birth of civilisation. But you have a very strong feeling as you look at the world that many people in those positions aren't happy at all. The Buddhist path doesn't say you should disdain material development, but the main cause of happiness is interior, the development of the mind. That's what we should be pursuing.'

George had the most humble heart, the most noble aspirations of anyone I had ever met. He wore his innocence like a child, and yet he was a born teacher. As we talked I found myself falling easily into the role of student. Sometimes, in the break periods between his lessons with Lama Osel, I would make the short walk to George's bungalow, or we would sit on the veranda in the sunshine at Lama's house, talking of Buddhist philosophy.

'*Karma* is not something we can see with our own eyes,' George told me one day. 'OK, we can see it on a superficial level: you punch someone in the mouth, they get mad and punch you back. But the actual *karmic* results of punching someone in the jaw will come sometime in the future. What you cause now with negative actions, negative thoughts, is just a condition for other negative *karma* to ripen. Think about anger. In our society we see two kinds of responses to anger; you repress it, or you express it, you act it out. We oscillate between those two responses, depending on what's in vogue. But Buddhism talks about the middle way.

'When we repress something our lives don't seem authentic. A lot of psychologists note this; when people repress things it might come out in psychosomatic illness or anger directed at someone else. But when Buddhism talks about the middle way, it's not like letting out the anger halfway. It's a completely different paradigm.

The middle way talks about developing through wisdom a state of mind that analyses those situations.

'See the anger-provoking situation as the result of past *karma*; so it's not only the other person who is making you angry – it is your past actions that have brought you to this situation. Recognise that the person who is making you angry wants to be happy *just like you*. Treat this situation as a lesson; not that this is something I can do without, but that this is something I *need*. When you start to have this frame of mind, the anger begins to disappear.'

When bad things happen to you, said George, welcome them as the ripening and exhaustion of the bad *karma* you have accumulated in the past. The joy you feel will sow the seeds of good *karma* to come. 'Rather than the negative mind thinking how much I'm suffering, think: My store of negative *karma* has actually gone down! If I can experience this suffering with equanimity, with a positive attitude, with enthusiasm, I can actually create virtuous *karma*, rather than create negative *karma* by complaining and blaming others. Look at the Dalai Lama and the Tibetan people, who have experienced tremendous loss, but even in this lifetime, with that attitude, they have flowered. Rather than the response of the people in 1929 who lost their money in the Stock Market crash and jumped out of the window.'

George was a fund of such imprecations. One day, we hired a motor-rickshaw and made an expedition from the monastery to a nearby lake, where the carp were enormous, and came to the very water's edge to snatch the food from your hand. 'Here's a little devotion you can do,' said George, as he crumbled biscuits in his palm and threw them into the water. 'Just pretend that as you're feeding the fish, you're feeding the world.'

We crumbled biscuits and threw them into the water, watching the giant fish thrashing below us, and, heeding George's words, I tried to imagine that I was feeding the world. On the way back to the monastery, Lama Osel rode shotgun, next to the driver, waving and shouting. A short distance from the monastery, he stopped the rickshaw and clambered into the back. It would not be appropriate for a lama to be seen by other monks riding shotgun in a rickshaw.

There were moments in Sera when I thought I was as happy as I had ever felt in my life, lulled by the peace and serenity of the surroundings, the smiling faces, the bracing conversations about the meaning of things. One evening, I came across a ceremony in a courtyard outside one of the smaller temples. It was an initiation ceremony for a geshe. Perhaps two hundred monks sat cross-legged on the stone, under a canopy of trees, threaded with light bulbs. They chanted for what seemed like hours, while I sat to one side, my thoughts drifting away on the undulating waves of sound. I was enjoying being a tourist. I returned to my room, with its simple bed, its flowers, its picture of the Dalai Lama. I began to feel austere; purified.

One day, I struck up conversation with a young Westerner. His head was shaved, like a monk's, but he wore jeans and a T-shirt. Chris was from Australia. He was twenty-one. He had become a monk two years ago in Australia and taken the name Jampa Chodrag. Then he came to Sera. He had been here for six months, living in a small cell in a dormitory block, and it had driven him to the brink of madness. He had given back his robe and was making the transition from being Jampa Chodrag back to plain old Chris. 'I think,' he said with a note of weariness, 'I threw myself in the deep end.' He complained of the loneliness, the isolation, the struggle to learn Tibetan, the omnipresent feelings of sexual desire, the endless conflicts with himself. 'I think the important thing is to be happy while you practise; you can't practise when you're angry and distracted. I realise now I was thinking idealistically; that because I needed to change all my habits I would automatically be able to and it would be easy. But it's not easy.'

He laughed. 'You know what I'm looking forward to doing now? Sitting on the beach with a few beers watching the girls go by.'

I asked Paco if I could have a private conversation with Lama Osel. 'You must ask Lama,' he said. 'It's up to him.'

Lama said, 'Four-thirty tomorrow.'

It was his break period; he was playing Sim-City on his computer and dragged himself away with palpable reluctance when I reminded him of our appointment. We sat on a sofa in his room and talked about his studies – what he enjoyed (English, science, history) and what he didn't (Tibetan grammar). Did he understand, I finally asked, what people said about him being the reincarnation of Lama Yeshe?

He nodded gravely. 'Yes, I understand.'

And were they right?

He laughed. 'I don't know.'

Did he feel any particular connection?

He gave the question some thought. 'I think when I was younger, perhaps, but now I've forgotten.'

Did his dreams give any clues?

'You know, I never remember my dreams.'

Did he enjoy living in the monastery, I asked.

'I remember the first time I came here. I was seven. And when they talked to me about coming here I said, "Bah, India." But then I came and I realised it was a very nice place. Now I think this is the best place for me. It's a very good place to study.'

And that was what he wanted to do, to study?

His answer was immediate and emphatic. 'Yes, that's what I want to do. So that in the future I can teach other people. That's what I want to do.'

'What do you want to teach?' I asked.

'Buddhism,' he said. 'It's a good thing to teach, because I think it would help to make people happier, and I believe that's my job, to help people.'

'And how do you feel about that?' I asked.

'I like it.' He paused, and then smiled. 'Well, actually, I've still not tried it yet, but I think I'll like it.'

Peter Kedge had a clear vision for the young lama's future. He would be educated to university level, going on to take a degree, possibly at MIT, Oxford or Harvard – or more likely through an Open University course; by the time he was twenty he would already be 'out on the road', supervising the FPMT activities.

This, I said, seemed a daunting prospect for the young boy to consider.

'Yes, Lama is aware that he has a big load to carry. But I've never heard him express any hesitation. It was Lama Yeshe's work, and Lama Osel has always been quite clear that his role is to carry on.

'We've done the material thing in the West; we're so materially sophisticated, yet despite all that we have increasing social problems, as a result of people not understanding what makes the mind happy, what makes the mind miserable – that basic. Mind as a topic is not something that ordinary people are brought up to know anything about. Nowhere in my fifteen years of the best education in England did anyone ever mention mind, once. I was fitted for doing a job, but as far as helping myself through life my formal education did nothing at all. So I think there is tremendous scope within our education system to introduce into the curriculum something about mind, how it works, what it is, and even practical meditation – how to help yourself in life, and that all exists in the Tibetan Buddhist tradition.'

This, said Kedge, was the process Lama Yeshe was engaged in before his death, to take the essence of Tibetan Buddhism, 'its universal psychology', and make it accessible to the West. 'Lama Yeshe conceived of what he called "universal education", which means developing activities in which the essence of the Buddha's experience is fundamental – in hospitals, teaching, education. He foresaw a curriculum for kids which included, within every subject, the implications of mind – of *karma*.

'In history, for example. History with an understanding of *karma* is different from history as fact; but let's study history from the point of view of facts and *karma*. What happened to these people; why as a group did these things happen to them? Why is it when a building falls down or an aeroplane crashes, two people come out unscathed and one hundred don't? These are very profound questions, but Buddhism provides an answer. Healing with an understanding of *karma* is different from just giving medicines to arrest the symptoms; you look for the cause. In this sense, an understanding of the mechanics of mind can change every aspect of life. This is the work that Lama Yeshe started in his lifetime, and that Lama Osel will continue in his, as an innovator of projects, and a person who understands both cultures.'

But, I wondered, did the young lama have a choice?

In a sense, said Kedge, the choice had already been made. 'Any *tulku*, in previous lives, has already vowed to dedicate their existence to the benefit of others. So choice is limited. And it's conditioned by that wish, that aspiration, that vow to make one's existence, even beyond one's life, beneficial.'

But suppose, I said, that he expressed a desire to be something other than a universal teacher; suppose he expressed a desire more in keeping with the usual adolescent ambitions, to be, say, a professional footballer?

'I don't know,' Peter Kedge replied. 'We are pioneering something that clearly you can only pioneer if you have some vision of the future. We would have to be flexible to accommodate something that didn't necessarily fit into that. But a professional footballer? I just don't know . . .'

When I asked Paco the same question he considered it carefully.

'I think it is not possible for him to go the wrong way,' he said at last. 'Whatever he chooses, even if we don't understand it immediately, he will have chosen it because it is the best way to help people. This is what Lama wants.'

Sitting in his bungalow, talking of *karma*, the obligations of the bodhisattva, our destiny over many lifetimes, George Churinoff gave life the epic quality of an adventure story.

There is a common misconception that *karma* means surrendering to fate, the acquiescent acceptance of your lot. But, as George talked, it struck me that it actually means accepting responsibility. You carry the responsibility for your past actions in your present circumstances; you sow the seeds of future circumstances – in this life and lives to come – in your present actions. It is a belief that eradicates blame; a valuable corrective, it seemed to me, in a time in which people increasingly held others – parents, school, government, the great amorphous mass of society – responsible for their misfortunes.

'Everything is bound for dispersal,' said George. 'All birth results in death. This is what the Buddha was saying. Clinging, attachment, is futile. It's inevitable from the moment that we meet a loved one that we will be separated, if not sooner then later. It's inevitable from the moment we are born that we will die.'

Life is a preparation for death.

This is not a comforting thought. Leading our lives as if they will go on for ever, forgetting that we could die tomorrow, is the most common human vanity. I had always done my best to avoid thinking about death. It frightened me. The thought of dying itself; the thought of what lay beyond death. But lately I had found myself becoming more preoccupied with the fact of death, not as something abstract, but as tangible and real. My father had died many years ago; as had my grandparents. Now I was at an age where friends and contemporaries were dying: cancer; alcoholism; suicide.

The certainty that I too would die began to prey on my mind, almost to a point of morbidity. I would sometimes lie in bed measuring the rhythm of my own breath, the methodical rise and fall of my chest. I could feel my heartbeat, sending the blood surging through arteries and veins, and the sensation made me terrified at the fragility of my own body, and how easily it might be destroyed or lost. I would try to push the thoughts away, terrified afresh that the fear of death was in itself some warning of its imminence, as if simply to think of death was enough to make it happen.

'That's good,' said George.

Good that I try to push the thoughts away?

'No,' he chuckled, 'good that you fear death.'

Buddhism teaches that we must cultivate a constant mindfulness of death, said George; that we should live in the fear not of losing our loved ones or our possessions, but the fear that at the time of death we have not sown the seeds for a favourable rebirth. To die consumed by regret, remorse, hatred, is to ensure our next rebirth will be an uncomfortable one.

The Tibetan Buddhist teaching on death and rebirth is very precise. In a normal death, the senses lose their power in a particular sequence. Gross mind – the day-to-day mind – ceases. The subtle mind – the dream-state mind – begins to lose its abilities. Clinical death comes at a certain point when the gross mind ceases; when the breath stops. Vision, touch, recollection, discrimination, all cease. The mind is still in the body; it has withdrawn from the senses, but still there are coloured visions to the subtle mind. These occur in a specific order, white, copper-red and pitch-black. Then comes a state of swoon before the final clear light of death, which is mind being aware of its own nature without any projections or delusions. For an ordinary person these stages are passed through almost without being noticed. For a yogi, who has rehearsed the techniques of dying sufficiently, these stages are recognisable; he will know that the clear light is a state in which he can rest in meditation, and even attain release from *samsara*, the endless cycle of death and rebirth. It is at this point that the subtle mind leaves the body, through one or other bodily orifice. For an ordinary person, this may be after a couple of hours. In the case of a practised meditator it may be weeks.

After death, the being enters into the intermediate state, or *bardo*. In this state the being is formless but has clairvoyance and can travel unobstructed through matter. It exists in this state for up to seven days, its condition and its eventual destiny shaped by the forces of *karma* from its previous existence. During the first seven days, if it meets with the circumstances appropriate for rebirth, the being will take that birth. If not, it will 'die' and arise again as an intermediate being. This can happen up to seven times, but after forty-nine days it can no longer remain as an intermediate being and must take rebirth.

Among the most powerful *karmic* forces is sex, and it is the habituated attraction to the act of sex which draws the intermediate being back to life, through the medium of a couple engaged in an act of procreation, the mixture of semen and ovum. Buddhism teaches that there are six realms into which a being may be born: human; animal; hungry ghost; the hell realms, and one of two forms of 'celestial beings', the lower and the higher. The lower celestial beings experience great pleasure, but are characterised by envy and jealousy; the higher experience immeasurable bliss which so blinds them to their condition that they 'burn up' their accumulated *karmic* merit. Shades of all six realms can be seen in human experience – the bestiality of the executioner and the tyrant; the purgatory existence of the 'hungry ghosts' enslaved by drugs and alcohol; the hell of those who are victims of war or famine; the apparently 'celestial' existence of the rich, the beautiful and the gifted, squandering their talents or their good fortune.

Imagine a wide ocean with a golden yoke adrift upon it. In the depths of the ocean swims a blind turtle who surfaces for air once every hundred years. How rare would it be for the turtle to surface with its head through the hole in the yoke? The Buddha said that attaining a human rebirth is even rarer than that. In short, it is an opportunity not to be squandered, for only in the human realm can one work towards enlightenment and liberation from *samsara*.

The traditional Buddhist depiction of the hell realms as places of extreme heat or extreme cold is as terrifying in its own way as anything that medieval Christianity has to offer. According to ancient Tibetan scriptures, the hell realms are located at a great distance directly below Bodh Gaya, the place in India where the Buddha attained enlightenment. Commenting on these scriptures, the Dalai Lama has pointed out that this would theoretically place hell in the middle of America – a fact that anybody who has been stranded in Des Moines, Iowa on a wet Sunday night would immediately recognise. But the physical location of hell is, of course, intended as metaphor, not fact. 'The purpose of the Buddha coming to this world was not to measure the circumference of the world and the distance between the earth and the moon,' says the Dalai Lama, 'but rather to teach the Dharma, to liberate sentient beings, to relieve sentient beings of their suffering.'

'Fear can be both paralysing and instructive,' said George. 'But *wisdom* fear is good, because it discourages you from creating negative *karma*. It's said that the way to understand *karma* is by observing morality; if you wish to be reborn as a human you must determine to lead a moral life. Let's say, I know that going to the disco is not real happiness; it's only temporary medicine. Spend your life in a disco and you'd get bored after a week. So Lama Yeshe would say, within that context, when you feel you need relief, you say Buddha I'm not yet able to overcome this thirst, this attachment, just through meditation-wisdom, I'm going to take a little bit of the medicine, but keeping mindfulness of is this *real* happiness? So that you don't overdo it, get drunk, thrown out and so on. And that's a very good first step; and when you realise that it didn't really satisfy you, you get more and more strength and resource to build on that.'

George, I noticed, seemed particularly to relish the hell and damnation aspect of Buddhism. If his idea of serious moral slippage was going to a disco and having one too many beers, where did this leave me?

'I remember when Lama Yeshe was alive, he and Lama Zopa were very much like a good cop/bad cop combination,' said George. 'Lama Zopa was the tough cop. Heavy *karma*; hell realms; suffering; you'd better get your act together; future lives are so much more important than this one, and so on. Then Lama Yeshe would look on the bright side; what is the result of good practice? A happy, contented mind.'

I lay awake in my room, watching the shadows from the candle-light playing on the ceiling, my mind turning restlessly, envisioning myself hurtling through timeless space, like a computer smart-card, encrypted with all my failings (too numerous to mention) and merits (none that I could immediately call to mind), struggling through the universal stew of lost and seeking souls, in search of rebirth. All of my habitual anxieties – about work, career, family, relationships – had receded, or rather coalesced into one abiding concern: my *karma*. Every unkind word, every wrongdoing, every blemish and sin, every act of selfishness and indifference became vivid in my mind. The vigilance required for goodness seemed terrifyingly pressing. Every avenue of thought seemed to lead to the same conclusion; that I was in terrible shape.

Lama Zopa, George told me, used to say that if you knew about your next rebirth you wouldn't sleep at night. I had no idea what my next rebirth held, but I was already having trouble sleeping. I lay in my bed, vowing to be good.

I thought back to what George had said, that when bad things happen to you you should regard them joyfully. I thought: It's easy to think that here, where everything is serene and wonderful. It was a beautiful theory when things were going right, because when things are going right the fact of things going wrong seems almost unthinkable. How rapidly our feelings fluctuate and change, lending us the illusion at any time that they are permanent. When you are happy it is impossible to remember and imagine sadness; when trapped in the depths of sadness and depression, it is hard to imagine what it means to be happy.

I knew only too well the seductions of self-pity and the culs-de-sac of despair, those moments when whichever way your mind turns it seems there is nothing but frustration and anger and boredom; when everything seems as sour or as pointless as everything else; when your mind seems like a prison and every thought a small instrument of torture. Perhaps, I thought, it is this sadness that leads people to the spiritual path. Not a desire for transcendence, or enlightenment, but simply a weariness with all the tricks and frustrations of the self, what George called 'a revulsion for *samsara*' – the wheel of suffering created by the illusions of the ego; the belief that we have a 'self' that is anything more than a series of illusions, bound together by the fragile thread of our thoughts, which are illusions in themselves. Buddhism teaches that beyond the self, beyond the ego, there is only emptiness, *sunyata*, and that recognising this – or rather experiencing it moment by moment, for recognition presumes a 'self' to do the recognising, and there is no 'self' – is enlightenment.

> The truth of emptiness is the understanding that everything – the body, the consciousness, the world, the self – is like a flame [the American Buddhist scholar Stephen Butterfield writes in *The Double Mirror*]. There is no entity of a 'flame' apart from the constantly dissipating light, heat, and gas, which arise each second from the changing conditions of temperature, fuel, oxygen, and wind. It is no more possible to maintain a self in this conflagration than it is to preserve a log which fire is converting into embers and smoke.

But how could one glimpse the possibility of enlightenment if one was not enlightened oneself? How could one taste it? Smell it? Experience it if it was a condition beyond appraisal by the 'self'? What did enlightenment *feel* like? Chogyam Trungpa had described it as 'much, much better than Disneyland', and cautioned devotees against what he called 'spiritual materialism', desiring 'enlightenment' as if it were a new car, a bigger television set or a more prestigious and powerful job – as something that fortified the ego.

But was Trungpa enlightened? How could one tell?

I had asked the Dalai Lama the same question when I met him in Dharamsala: what is enlightenment? He roared with laughter – a laugh that suggested *that* in itself was enlightenment – and replied, 'I am just a simple monk . . .' He *always* says this, a reply that is both the literal truth and yet as far from the truth as could be imagined.

'There are many various levels of enlightenment,' he said. 'Buddha stage is the highest. But at the first stage, or foundation of enlightenment, according to my own little experience, usually much of the time our mind goes outside, it is distracted by things. But through deeper meditation the grosser levels of mind eventually dissolve, and at a certain stage you reach some peace or calm, and also some kind of deep self-confidence, deep satisfaction – and energy, also; sometimes I call it inner-strength. So that experience is very useful in our daily work. So, pure and open-minded and compassionate nature – that I can call the first sight of enlightenment.'

One evening in Sera I sat with Geshe-la on the veranda of Lama Osel's house. His lessons in Tibetan with the young lama had finished for the night. Osel was playing with his computer, and the clatter of dishes from the kitchen announced that supper would soon be served. The sound of a Tibetan long-horn echoed mournfully through the fading light. (This horn was blown at the same time each evening. Intrigued, I had once followed the sound to a site on the furthest perimeter of the monastery, beyond the monks' living quarters. The horn was a huge instrument, some six feet in length, propped on a stand. Three monks were gathered around it, taking turns puffing up their chests and blowing into the mouthpiece, then falling away in laughter, like children. I could not tell whether they were blowing it for any specific reason, or simply because it was there and they liked the sound.)

It was a cool night, and Geshe-la gathered the folds of his robe around his shoulders. He spoke no English; Pemba, Lama Osel's attendant, had agreed to translate. Geshe-la told me that he had been a monk since he was eight years old. He was now fifty-five.

'All my life has been spent in the monastery. I've never lived with a family.' He tilted his shoulders and laughed, apparently satisfied with this state of affairs.

And in that time, I wondered, did he feel he had made any progress along the spiritual path?

He chuckled good-naturedly at the naivety of the question. 'Perhaps I've developed some understanding. Buddhism is very profound and deep, so my understanding has increased. But so far I've never gained any realisations.'

And was that disappointing?

He smiled. 'No, I'm not disappointed. I feel very fortunate. Through these vast, deep studies I've come to the knowledge that realisations can't be achieved in a short time.'

His answer reminded me of a passage from *Autobiography of a Yogi*, in which Yogananda asks a venerable *rishi* whether he has seen God. 'God is eternity,' the *rishi* replies. 'It would be foolish to think you could see him in forty-five years.'

Geshe-la nodded when I told him this story. 'The Buddhist goal is that oneself becomes the Buddha, so in that case to achieve that goal is not simple; it takes infinite aeons to achieve that.'

It was hard to have these conversations with Tibetans. I always felt as if I had been thrown overboard without a lifebelt. Whatever one asked seemed stupid and naive. I wanted simple answers to complicated questions.

I turned again to George.

'One of the four root vows of being a monk is never to tell the Great Lie: to say you have realisations when you don't.' He paused. 'And a subsidiary of that is not to say you have realisations even when you do.'

So what, I asked, did George think he had achieved in twenty years of practice? Was he less susceptible to desires, to lust, to anger?

'Anger has been in our minds from beginningless time. It's not something that goes easily. But if one recognises through the teachings that one is less *prone* to anger ... One doesn't break one's vows by feeling those things, but one becomes less prone to them, one understands them with more equanimity.' He paused.

That was it? After twenty years all that had been achieved was to recognise that one was prone to anger? I felt deflated. And then I thought how quickly I was roused to anger myself.

'Changes come slowly,' said George. 'We in the West always want everything to happen yesterday. But in Buddhism you've got until infinity.'

The days in the monastery passed like weeks. I sat in on lessons with Lama Osel, or I walked to George's house and we talked. One day I walked out of the monastery into the forest. A group of boy monks stalked through the woods in their maroon robes, halloo-ing and kicking a football.

I had gradually become aware over the days that Sera had become a stop on the spiritual tourist trail. The rooms next to mine, above the school, were now occupied by three chic-looking Swiss guests. The monastery guest-house was full. In the evenings its small restaurant, where, on the hour, a clock played the chorus of 'Santa Claus is Coming to Town', and which was usually frequented by monks and the odd Westerner, was now filled with back-packers, clutching maps and books of Buddhist philosophy.

On our last night at the monastery, Peter and I arranged to meet George at the café for dinner. We arrived early. There were few enough tables that one invariably had to share, and tonight the café was even more crowded than usual. Some new visitors had arrived, and were chattering loudly among themselves. One man was dressed in a garish T-shirt and Bermuda shorts, as if he had set off for the beach and strayed into the monastery by mistake. He looked incongruous, idiotic. An Australian woman named Diane sat at our table, and we exchanged small talk. She gabbled excitedly, making me realise how my short time in the monastery had slowed my own metabolism and conversation to something like snail's pace.

'Yeah, I mean I've done India before as a tourist, y'know,' she said. 'But this time it's different. This time I've come to find out about myself.'

I nodded.

'I mean, I didn't even know what this place was; I thought it was a Vipassana meditation centre, because I've been doing Vipassana in Melbourne, but this is, like, Tibetan, right?'

As we were talking, George arrived at the table; he looked disconcerted and anxious. 'I'm sorry. I didn't realise, you're with someone. I'll go.'

Before I had a chance to say anything he had turned and walked out of the door. I caught Diane's eye. 'I think it's me,' she said, looking crestfallen.

I ran out of the café and caught up with George, walking alone in the darkness. 'I'm sorry, it's nothing personal, but I don't feel comfortable sitting in there.' He sighed. 'It's not right; the atmosphere in there. The people coming to this place now, like hippies or something, as if it was on the tourist trail. Who are these people?' There was an awkward silence.

I didn't know what to say. But I was suddenly aware of the stillness of the night, and the clamour of the outside world, rushing in to fracture the silence. George, I felt, had his own, private reasons to do with his religious practice for not wishing to mix too closely with the outside world. I simply resented the presence of the newcomers in the café, with their loud voices and garish clothes. I had been in the monastery only a few days, but I was already possessive of its serene magic, already holier-than-thou.

'I'm sure we can find another table,' I said.

We walked back to the café. Diane had gone; the café was almost empty now and George seemed happier. As we ate, he held forth on the subject of bodhisattvas, *karma*, rebirth, Buddha nature. There were Buddhas among us now, he said, bodhisattvas who had deliberately chosen rebirth in order to help mankind. What greater act of selflessness could there be than to forgo one's immersion in Nirvana in order to lead others on the path to enlightenment? What better choice could a man make than to follow that path himself?

'This is wonderful,' I said, 'but what if none of it is true?'

George took the question in good spirit. 'If it's not true, I still can't think of a better way to lead your life. The Buddha said that without good practice the life of a monk is a prison. But with good practice, the life of a monk is bliss.'

There had been a power-cut. We left the café and walked back by torchlight. Where our paths divided, we bade each other good-night, and George vanished into the darkness. In my room, I lit a candle and lay on my bed, watching the shadows flickering on the ceiling. There was shouting, wailing and the sound of laughter from outside. The monks were playing games, scaring each other in the darkness. Drawn by the light, a moth skittered about the candle, then flew too close, and immolated itself upon the flame. It struggled briefly, then surrendered, blackening in the heat until it was no longer a moth at all, but a part of the candle, and the candle became the flame, and the flame became nothingness, while the yelps of laughter quietened, and the night closed in.

6

MOTHER, MOTHER

The bus to Bangalore was crowded beyond capacity. A young woman squatted beside my rucksack on the dirty floor of the bus. Her husband had taken the seat beside her. Throughout the journey she rested her hand gently in his, staring ahead with a look of phlegmatic resignation on her face. The stoicism of Indian women on these journeys never failed to move me: they would silently stand for hours, or squat on hard metal floors, children clutched in their arms, quickly averting their eyes whenever your glance happened to meet theirs. They never talked, they never read, they seemed hardly even to look out of the windows. It was as if they were enclosed in their own secret world, drawing their children in with them. It occurred to me that I had never heard a child cry on a bus, or display the slightest sign of fractiousness or ill-temper. Patience seemed to be learned at the mother's breast. But then India is an endless round of waiting.

At Bangalore I queued for an application form to buy a ticket to Pondicherry, then queued again for the ticket. These were always undignified scrums, people pushing at the window, a test of patience and endurance. When a young man tried to push in front of me my temper finally snapped. 'Can't you see there's a queue?' I shouted. He melted away.

A familiar figure tapped me on the shoulder. 'Hey!' It was Diane. 'Is this *karma*, or what?' I hadn't seen her since leaving the restaurant in Sera on the unfortunate evening with George. 'It was me that drove him away, right?' she said. 'No, not really . . .' I replied.

'Well, I guess it was meant to happen.' She shrugged. 'But it's strange us meeting up again like this, isn't it? Do you think it means we have something to say to each other?'

But if it did mean that, evidently we could neither of us think what it could possibly be.

'Well, maybe we'll see each other further down the line,' said Diane.

'Maybe,' I said.

The privately run 'luxury' air-conditioned bus that would run to Pondicherry was fully booked. All that was available was the state-run bus, considerably less comfortable, and necessitating a change halfway, at a town I could not even find on the map. It was a journey of some 350 kilometres. The ticket cost little more than £1. The bus left at nightfall. No sooner had I sat down than a man seated behind me engaged my attention. He was in a state of high excitement, prodding and chattering, reaching out his greasy hand for me to shake, showing his cracked brown teeth in a lop-sided grin. Perspiration streamed down his face. He pressed peanuts and a fragment of cake into my hand, which I chewed politely, pantomiming gratitude, while silently fearing the consequences. What was my name? Where was I going? Where had I come from? I mentioned the name Sai Baba. His eyes rolled upwards, he touched his forehead with his hand, grabbed my hand and kissed it fervently, as if, through having been in Sai Baba's presence, I was somehow a repository of his grace. I realised that he was either drunk or mad, and I did my best to ignore him.

The bus bumped and lurched through the darkness. The lunatic had turned his attention elsewhere and was now engaged in a heated argument with the passengers around him. Soon the excitement got the better of him, and he began to cough violently, a heaving, wheezing, hawking sound, the phlegm rattling in his chest and spraying out of his open mouth. I could feel it on the back of my neck. I leaned forward in my seat, burying my head inside my shirt, trying to sleep. I came awake as the bus lurched to a halt. A sliver of moon barely illuminated the fields on either side of the bus, but there was no sign of habitation. We had stopped at a level-crossing. I stepped out and breathed in the cool night air.

After a few minutes, the light of a train appeared in the distance, and the tracks began to sing. Its bell chiming mournfully, the train rolled slowly past, passengers silhouetted in the small squares of light, dozing, or gazing blearily into the darkness. A shiver ran through me; that curious thrill of displacement – I had no idea where we were, what time it was – mixed with a feeling of exquisite melancholia at the sight of the passing train, its chiming bell transforming the enveloping darkness into a vast and impenetrable ocean. I watched for what seemed like an age as the train went by, its tail-light rocking slightly, then finally blinking once and fading into the night.

I climbed back on to the bus, and hunched down in my seat in front of the madman. The bus bumped slowly through the night, as if down a long, dark tunnel, illuminated by splashes of sudden and confusing light – roadside halts, lit by a string of bare light bulbs or tungsten lamps, figures huddled over fires, their shadows dancing against the walls of low, mud buildings – tableaux of medieval squalor. In one village a ramshackle stage had been thrown up beside the road; beneath a gaudy canopy, players in fancy-dress were acting out some sort of pantomime to a crowd of appreciative onlookers – a wedding party perhaps.

We shuddered to a halt in a bus station. I had no idea where we were. It was 2 a.m., but India never sleeps. The bus station was as crowded as if it were midday; hawkers sold fruit and drinks, and bent over small kerosene stoves; the air was filled with the squawk of transistor radios and the blare of bus-horns, and pungent with the aroma of food, garbage and fetid humanity. People slept on platforms and against walls, their sacks and parcels beside them; children ran to and fro. It was a scene from every bus terminus and railway station I had passed through. I could never decide if these huge swathes of India's population were in a state of permanent transience – forever waiting for buses and trains to arrive and depart – or whether these were more permanent encampments, the homeless and the dispossessed huddling together for comfort in public space.

Despite his threats that he would see me safely to Pondicherry, the lunatic had vanished. But you are never alone in India. A well-dressed man carrying a small suitcase now appeared at my shoulder. Politely enquiring if I needed assistance, he steered me through the crowds and on to a bus and waved goodbye. Even by the erratic standards of Indian transport, the bus was the most uncomfortable I have ever travelled on. The seats were of a scarred and lumpen metal, the bars at the window put one in mind of a prison vehicle and a smell of sweat and urine hung heavily in the air. People filled every available inch, clutching at poles and seat-backs to steady themselves as we bucked and skewed over the pot-holed road. And yet I felt filled with a mood of unaccountable joy and happiness – a palpable sense of purpose, although to what end and for what reason I could not say – as if there was no better experience in all the world than being jolted through the Indian night in a ramshackle tin-can, the head of a total stranger slumped on my shoulder as he snored peacefully. I fell into a fitful sleep, the sound of Hindi pop from the driver's radio weaving in and out of my dreams, and came awake to a helium voice singing what sounded like 'bouncy, bouncy', over and over again. Dawn was breaking through the barred windows, a thin mist veiling buildings, a filling station and a broad, deserted street. Twelve hours after leaving Bangalore, we had arrived in Pondicherry.

A motor-rickshaw took me through the streets of Pondicherry, stirring in the smoky half-light of dawn, to the sea-front. I found a hotel on the promenade, and fell into a deep sleep.

I awoke, still feeling physically exhausted. My stomach ached and my spirits felt at a low ebb, as if the feeling of exhilaration that had carried me halfway across India had mysteriously drained away. I was becoming accustomed to this. A peculiar effect of India was the almost violent mood-swings, between frustration and exhilaration, sudden bursts of energy and an equally sudden and inexplicable torpor. I roused myself and went for a walk by the sea. Pondicherry is a former French colony, and there is a long, sweeping promenade, designed, it seems, to stir memories of Deauville or Biarritz. It was mid-morning, not yet so hot as to drive people in search of shade. A handful of Westerners, and track-suited Indians jogged slowly past. Nowhere else in India would I see people pursuing this peculiarly Western, early morning ritual.

I sat in a café on the promenade, drinking coffee and eating dried toast, watching the bathers in the sea; the boys and men stripped down to their shorts, energetically splashing each other and striking out into the depths, the women tentatively immersing themselves in the water, their saris spreading out around them like vividly patterned water-lilies.

In Bangalore I had met two girls, one Dutch, one Australian, on the cosmic shopping trip. 'Have you been to the "hugging ashram"?' the Dutch girl asked. We were sitting in a café, eating honeyed pancakes and drinking orange juice.

The 'hugging ashram'?

'Yeah, Guru Ma something. She gives *darshan* by hugging . . .'

I had heard of Mata Amritanadamji – or Ammachi, as she was known. She was forty-two years old and lived in Kerala, in the south.

She was born, it is said, with an unusual dark-blue complexion, reminiscent of images of Krishna and Kali, and at the age of seven she had been gifted with an apparition of the Divine Mother as 'a mass of effulgence' merging into her. From this day on, Ammachi declared, 'Nothing could be seen as different from my own formless Self, wherein the entire universe exists as a tiny bubble.'

'There were all these people standing in a line waiting to be hugged,' said the Dutch girl. 'It's mostly women – Western women, all in their thirties and forties, y'know. And some of them carry round these little dolls that look like Ma, hugging them as if they were babies.' She pulled a face. 'They're obviously feeling the absence of their mothers. But what I found really disconcerting was that there seemed to be a lot of . . .' She paused, looking for the right word, '*Cattiness* there. People were vying against each other to be Ma's favourite, or to curry favour with her. At Christmas they put on a play about Francis of Assisi. It was a really nice play, but I noticed that nobody was watching the play at all; they were all just watching Ma to see what she thought of it.'

And did you get hugged, I asked.

'No. I get hugged enough already.' She paused. 'People go there and they think they feel better.'

Isn't that better than nothing, I wondered – to think you feel better?

'No,' she said, 'you must *be* better.'

The musician Sting had also been to see the Hugging Mother, not in Kerala, but in Sydney, Australia. He had told me about it.

'She came into the room, this lovely little lady, and she smiled and she gave me a hug and rubbed my back, and then smelled my hand and my cheek. I sat down in the lotus position, and just entered this state of real . . .' He smiled and made a buzzing sound between his teeth. '*Consciousness*. And she was giving this *stuff* off . . . I was with my manager, who is not sophisticated in any sense of the word; he's never had an experience like that. And he was saying, "What's happening to me?" He was feeling it as well.

'This feeling of *presence* lasted for about five minutes, and then we talked for about another thirty minutes. I asked her, was she optimistic, about the world in general. And she said, the future is pretty gloomy, but there is reason to be optimistic. Then we talked about grace and how human intent is only part of the solution to any problem; and how grace from somewhere else is really the major part of any action, and how you get grace. And she said, you have to create grace with good work. That made a lot of sense to me.'

And did he think she was Divine?

Sting shrugged. 'Who knows? But I do know that what I felt was very real, and that she's very powerful. I'm not looking for a guru, but at the same time this woman was an extraordinary person.'

People said this was the time for Holy Mothers. It was the time of the Divine Feminine; of manifestations of female divinity. The time of the Mother. The emerging feminine principle. If the Sixties and Seventies had been marked by the coming of male Indian gurus and teachers to the West – the Maharishi Mahesh, the Guru Maharj Ji, Rajneesh, Sri Chinmoy and many more; then the Eighties and Nineties were the age of women saints.

There were Holy Mothers everywhere.

There was Sri Ma of Kamakhya, who arrived in the United States at the request of her guru Ramakrishna Paramahansa, and established her own temple, Devi Mandir, in California. Anandi Ma, who arrived in America in 1976 with her guru Dhyanyogi Madhusudandas and stayed on to establish teaching centres in Maine, Connecticut and California. And Bhagavati Sri Vijayeswari Devi – or Karanumayi, 'the compassionate one' – revered as an incarnation of Saraswati, the Goddess of Knowledge, Creativity and Eloquence.

Then there was Gurumayi, who had come to America as a disciple of Swami Muktananda, and found her own following. Her principal ashram in Fallsburg, New York includes an auditorium with chandeliers and plush velvet seats but she travels the world on a schedule that would exhaust the most seasoned rock band. I had missed an appearance in London, a two-day initiation in Siddha Yoga at the Wembley conference centre, in which Gurumayi promised to bestow '*shaktipat*, the spiritual awakening that enables us to begin the great journey of inner realisation'. The cost was £250 (Master and Visa cards accepted) – 'Cheaper than Deepak Chopra,' as a friend pointed out, but expensive nonetheless, although I suppose plush velvet and chandeliers do not come cheap.

Foremost among these was Mother Meera, who had become one of the best known of the new generation of spiritual figures. (Sufficiently notable to have been listed in a nonsensical English newspaper article about 'celebrity gurus', between the Dalai Lama, and a psychic and 'faith-healer' who had entranced the Duchess of York.) Meera, who was born in India but now lives in Germany, is said to be an avatar, an embodiment of the Divine Feminine, the creative, sustaining force of the universe. It was an interest in Meera that had brought me to Pondicherry, for it was here that she had first emerged in the late Seventies, drawing a small group of Western devotees around her.

But to understand Mother Meera it was necessary to learn something of yet another Mother – an enigmatic French woman named Mirra Alfassa, who was born at the end of the last century, and lived in Pondicherry for some fifty years until her death in 1973, but whose presence dominates the town still.

Mirra Alfassa, or 'Sweet Mother' as she is known, was the companion of Sri Aurobindo, one of the most remarkable figures that modern India has ever produced: a political revolutionary, a poet, an educator, and spiritual teacher, the founder of 'integral yoga' – a system which, he believed, would raise a ladder to the divine, and thereby carry mankind to a higher stage of evolution.

The Sri Aurobindo ashram dominates the old French quarter of Pondicherry. Some 2,000 people live in the ashram permanently. It owns some 400 buildings, and runs its own post office, bank, various shops, a travel agency, and many of the guest-houses. It is a major employer, with its own farms, construction companies, electrical repair shops, and sheet-metal works. But while the ashram which draws thousands of pilgrims each year to Pondicherry bears Aurobindo's name, it is his companion of almost fifty years, Sweet Mother, who seems to have laid the greater claim to posterity.

Her portrait hung above the reception desk in my hotel. (Not one, as it happened, that was owned by the ashram: perhaps the proprietor felt it prudent, or commercially expedient, to display a photograph nonetheless.) It showed the Mother in late middle age. A striking face rather than a beautiful one. A long, aquiline nose; a wide mouth with protruding teeth; dark, bulging, almond-shaped eyes. Beneath the benign expression, I thought, lurked the face of a woman used to commanding attention, and getting her own way.

I had tried three guest-houses, all owned by the ashram; all were full, and the welcome in each was less than friendly. The statutory noticeboard of rules and regulations in each of them – about visitors, closing time, drinking and smoking – made me grateful for my own small, scruffy hotel on the promenade, where the manager and his friends sat all day in the reception area smoking and talking and watching game-shows on a tiny, migrainous television set, and where a houseboy snatched away my dirty clothes and returned them two hours later, washed and neatly pressed.

I hired a bicycle, evidently the preferred mode of transport in the town, and set off to explore. Pondicherry is divided into two distinct sections, bearing the legacy of colonialism in their unpleasant nomenclature: the old French – or 'white' – quarter, around Government Square, and closest to the sea; and the more traditional Indian 'black' town. The two districts are separated by a fetid, litter-strewn canal, only a few metres wide; yet the contrast between them is so striking as to be almost comical. On the 'black' side of the canal is to be found the characteristically noisy, chaotic, haphazard press of Indian life, riotously colourful markets, the streets congested with cars, buses and squawking mopeds. On the 'white' side, the colonial buildings are fading like a distant echo from the past, and the streets seem almost deserted, save for earnest-looking Westerners on bicycles, commuting between the various ashram classes, workshops and businesses, lending the area the air of some half-forgotten European university town.

The house where Sri Aurobindo and the Mother lived for thirty years is a handsome, whitewashed villa in the French colonial style, set behind a high brick wall, on a side-street close to the promenade. A crowd of schoolchildren milled around outside, clutching clipboards and notepads, evidently on an outing. I slipped off my shoes and stepped through the gate.

Although born in Calcutta, in 1872, Aurobindo Ghose spent his formative years in Britain. His father, a senior civil servant, was a great anglophile, and at the age of seven Aurobindo was sent with two brothers to be educated in England, where he was to spend the next fourteen years. He was educated at St Paul's public school in London, and at King's College, Cambridge. He had ambitions to join the Indian Civil Service, but was denied a place because he was a poor horseman. In 1893 he returned to India, where he worked for thirteen years in Baroda, in the Revenue Department and Secretariat, then as a professor at Baroda College, where he developed two interests: Indian nationalism and yoga. For Aurobindo the politics of nationalism were inseparable from a renaissance of the spiritual message of Hinduism, embodied in the lives and teachings of the great saints Ramakrishna and Vivekananda.

India [he wrote] cannot perish, our race cannot become extinct, because among all the divisions of mankind it is to India that is reserved the highest and most splendid destiny, the most essential to the future of the human race. It is she who must send forth from herself the future religion of the entire world, the Eternal Religion which is to harmonise all religion, science and philosophies and make mankind one soul.

For Aurobindo this 'eternal religion' was based on a recognition and worship of 'the Mother' – the divine, animating force of all creation. The Mother, he believed, was the spiritual force that would regenerate mankind; and 'Mother India' would be its engine.

India [he wrote] has always existed for humanity and not for herself and it is for humanity and not for herself that she must be great. I look upon my country as the Mother. I adore Her, I worship Her as the Mother. What would a son do if a demon sat on his mother's breast and started sucking her blood? Would he quietly sit down to his dinner, amuse himself with his wife and children, or would he rush out to deliver his mother? I know I have the strength to deliver this fallen race. It is not physical strength . . . but the strength of power.

In 1906, Aurobindo left Baroda for Calcutta, where he threw himself into campaigning for total independence from British rule, editing a Nationalist newspaper, *Bande Mataram*, while continuing with his yogic studies. In 1908 he was arrested, and remanded in custody, following an explosion in which two British women were killed. He spent a year in Alipur jail, awaiting trial.

A year before his imprisonment, Aurobindo had his first experience of Nirvana, or 'silent Brahman'. He described it thus:

An absolute stillness and blotting out, as it were, of all mental, emotional and other inner activities – the body continued indeed to see, walk, speak and do its other business, but as an empty automatic machine and nothing more. I did not become aware of any pure 'I' nor even of any self, impersonal or other – there was only an awareness of That as the sole Reality, all else being quite insubstantial, void, non-real. As to what realised that Reality, it was a nameless consciousness which was other than That . . . Neither was I aware of any lower soul or outer self called by such and such a personal name that was performing this feat of arriving at the consciousness of Nirvana . . .

In Alipur jail he had his second decisive spiritual experience, seeing 'God present in all things', and was able to understand, he would later write, 'what Sri Krishna demanded of Arjuna . . . to be free from repulsion and desire'.

Acquitted of all charges laid against him, Aurobindo was released from jail. He withdrew from politics, and in 1910 moved to Pondicherry, then still under the control of the French, sent, he would claim, by 'higher command' to follow the life of a yogi. It was there that Aurobindo began to formulate his theories of 'Integral Yoga' – a yoga concerned not only with inner change but with the transformation of the outer man. This was based on Aurobindo's ideas of 'the five levels of the spirit' – manifest in the physical body: the life; the mind and understanding; what Aurobindo called 'the Supermind' and the Ananda, or Godhead.

> Man grows by gradual growth in nature and each has to realise his own Divine person which is in the Supermind. Each is one with the Divine in essence, but in nature each is a partial manifestation of the Supreme Being. By the Supermind is meant the full Truth-Consciousness of the Divine Nature in which there can be no place for the principle of division and ignorance, the truth of that which we call God.

The objective of Integral Yoga was to bring about the descent of this 'Truth-Consciousness' into one individual – namely himself – to prepare for its general manifestation on earth. The ultimate result, he wrote, would be the transformation and divination of mind, life and matter. 'It would mean for man his transfiguration into Superman.'

Aurobindo was aware of the writings of Frederick Nietzsche, but his idea of 'Superman' was somewhat different from the German philosopher's. Nietzsche was right, he said, in his belief that a new kind of man would evolve, as different from man as man is from ape. But Nietzsche's belief that the strong deserved to flourish at the expense of the weak was essentially anti-Divine. Aurobindo's 'Superman' is a cosmic being, conscious of the unity of all existence, acting free from the ego in harmony with universal laws.

*   *   *

It is not for personal greatness that I am seeking to bring down
the Supermind [he wrote]. I care nothing for greatness or littleness
in the human sense. I am seeking to bring some principle of inner
Truth, Light, Harmony, Peace into the earth consciousness . . . I
believe the descent of this Truth opening the way to a development
of divine consciousness here to be the final sense of the earth
evolution.

In Pondicherry he began to gather around him a small group of
disciples – a *sangha*, to put his philosophies into practice.

Politics, industry, science, poetry, literature, art . . . we must give
them a new soul, a new form. I do not want hundreds of thousands
of disciples. It will be enough if I can get a hundred complete men,
purified of petty egoism, who will be the instruments of God.

His dream was of nothing less than 'a divine paradise on earth'.

In 1914, he met the willing accomplice for his dream when Mirra
Alfassa came to call. Born in Paris in 1878, of an Egyptian mother
and a Turkish banker father, Mirra had been, from an early age, an
unusual and precocious child. She claimed to have embarked on a
life of yogic contemplation at the age of four.

There was a small chair for me on which I used to sit still, engrossed
in my meditation. A very brilliant light would then descend over
my head and produce some turmoil inside my brain. Of course
I understood nothing, it was not the age for understanding. But
gradually I began to feel: I shall have to do some tremendously
great work that nobody yet knows . . .

By the age of eleven, she would later claim, she was in the grip of a
series of psychic and spiritual experiences that 'revealed to me not
only the existence of God, but man's possibility of uniting with Him,
or realising Him integrally in consciousness and action, of manifesting
Him upon earth in a life divine'. She claimed to have been visited in
her sleep by several teachers, or 'Beings' as she called them, one of
whom she called Krishna; and of taking rhapsodic journeys out of her
own body, 'clad in a magnificent golden robe', which would stretch
to form 'a kind of immense roof over the city, under which the old
and the sick would shelter for comfort'. It is not recorded if she

ever shared these visions with her parents, or what their response was if she did.

Pursuing the life of an educated and affluent member of the Parisian haute-bourgeois, she studied painting at the École des Beaux Arts, and was exhibited several times at the Paris Salon. At the age of nineteen, she married Henri Morriset, a disciple of the painter Gustave Moreau. But it was clear that mysticism had her in its grip. Between the ages of eighteen and twenty, she would later claim, she had attained 'a conscious and constant union with the Divine Presence and . . . I had done it *all alone*, with *absolutely nobody* to help me, not even books'. Not until she was twenty-one did an Indian acquaintance give her a copy of the *Bhagavadgita*, and encourage her to envisage Krishna as the immanent Godhead, the Divine within ourselves. She followed this advice and, apparently, 'in one month the whole work was done'.

Mirra's interest in Vedic mysticism soon led her to the occult. In 1905 she left Paris for Algeria, to join an occultist named Max Theon, and his Scottish wife Alma. Theon's real name was Louis-Maximilien Bimstein; he was a Polish Jew who had been Grand Master of an occultist group in Cairo known as the Hermetic Brotherhood of Luxor, with which Helena Blavatsky and Colonel Henry Olcott are believed to have been associated before they founded the Theosophical Society. When that group disintegrated, Bimstein and Alma moved to France, and thence to Tlecmen, Algeria, where they published a periodical, *The Cosmic Review*, espousing the 'Cosmic Philosophy', which Mirra would later remember was based partly on the Kabbala.

Mirra spent three years in Tlecmen, apparently cultivating, among other things, such useful skills as communing with spirits and quietening tempests. She would later recount how she was given the opportunity to put her new skills to some practical use on the boat journey back to France. Halfway across the Mediterranean a storm blew up which threatened to sink the ship. Mirra retired to her cabin and, in a meditative trance, left her body. On the open sea she discovered the mischievous vital entities that had caused the storm. After a stern talking to from Mirra, the 'entities' left the scene, and the storm abated.

Her marriage with Henri Morriset had, by now, come to an end, and back in Paris, she took a new husband, Paul Richard, a philosopher with a particular interest in Vedantic Yoga. In 1910

Richard journeyed to Pondicherry. He had political ambitions which he thought could be furthered in the French colony, and a wish to consult an advanced yogi. He was introduced to Sri Aurobindo. Mirra, meanwhile, kept herself busy conducting another study group called Cosmique, studying Indian scriptures, the Upanishads and the Yoga-Sutras. (One of its members was the Tibetologist Alexandra David-Neel, who in 1924 became the first European woman ever to set foot in Lhasa.)

Mirra's address at Cosmique's first meeting struck a messianic tone, stating, 'The general aim to be achieved is the advent of progressive universal harmony.' She referred to 'states of being which have so far never been conscious in man', and, in connection with the earth, to 'several sources of universal force which are yet sealed to it'. The objective was to found an ideal society in a place suited to the flowering of the new race, 'The Sons of God'. She and Aurobindo had yet to meet, but it was already clear they were made for each other.

When Paul Richard returned to France, Mirra struck up a correspondence with Aurobindo, and in 1914 she set sail to India with Richard to meet him. *En route* she berated a priest who was on his way to China to be a missionary. 'What are you going to teach them?' she demanded. 'To be insincere, to perform hollow ceremonies instead of following a profound philosophy and a detachment from life which will lead them to a more spiritual consciousness?'

In Pondicherry, as she came face-to-face with Aurobindo for the first time, she apparently experienced a profound pang of recognition. 'I recognised in him the well-known being whom I used to call Krishna,' she would later write. 'And this is enough to explain why I am fully convinced that my place and my work are near him, in India.'

> It matters little that there are thousands of beings plunged in the densest ignorance [she recorded in her diary]. He whom we saw yesterday is on earth; his presence is enough to prove that a day will come when darkness shall be transformed into light, and Thy reign shall actually be established upon earth.

Mirra was in Pondicherry for less than a year before her spiritual idyll was interrupted by the inconvenience of war. Paul Richard was called into the Army reserve, and the couple returned to Paris. Mirra was apparently undeterred. At the height of the hostilities, she was to be found sitting in her deckchair in Paris, convalescing from an illness, yet recording in her diary how by her occult facility she was still able to do her 'work' in 'France, America and other places. I could see that nothing could stop the work: even without my body the work could go on. Wherever the call was, I could attend.'

In 1917 the Richards again set sail for the East. They spent time in Japan, and in 1920 returned to Pondicherry. Mirra now declared her intention to stay. Unable to withstand the strain of her devotion to Aurobindo, the marriage to Richard dissolved. For the first six years of her time in Pondicherry, Mirra was an unobtrusive presence, merely a disciple among disciples, as Aurobindo bent to his work of connecting with the Supermind. Then, on 24 November 1926, Aurobindo made a historic declaration. Krishna, he said, had descended during a group meditation. 'Krishna is not the supramental Light,' he explained. 'The descent of Krishna would mean the descent of the Overmind Godhead preparing, though not itself actually, the descent of Supermind and Ananda. Krishna is the Ananda-Maya; he supports the evolution through the Overmind leading it towards his Ananda.'

In other words, the Supermind was on its way. It was shortly after this momentous occasion, which was thereafter known as the 'Day of Siddhi', that the ashram moved to its present site on the Rue François Martin, where Aurobindo was to spend the rest of his days. He would never set foot outside the ashram again.

Aurobindo had, by now, stopped referring to Mirra by her given name: she had become Sweet Mother. For the next twenty-four years, until his death in 1950, he lived in almost complete seclusion, seeing only her, leaving the material and spiritual charge of the ashram completely in her hands. All approaches to Aurobindo, all communication from him, would go through her. He would allow himself to be seen by disciples only on certain days: his birthday, the Mother's birthday and the 'Day of Siddhi', when he and the Mother would sit in a small *darshan* room, while devotees approached, offering flowers and prostrating themselves at their feet. She became, in effect, his only contact with the outside world, his agent, his emissary, the point of transmission of all his ideas.

For Aurobindo, the Divine Mother, the animating force of the universe which he had acknowledged and praised from his earliest years as a yogi, and which had once been embodied in the cause of

Indian self-determination as 'Mother India', now began to take on an increasingly corporeal form. In 1928 he published his masterpiece, *The Mother*, in which he extolled this divine force in rhapsodic language:

> Four great Aspects of the Mother, four of her leading Powers and Personalities, have stood in front of her guidance of this Universe and in her dealings with the terrestrial play. One is her personality of calm wideness and comprehending wisdom and tranquil benignity and inexhaustible compassion and sovereign and surpassing majesty and all-ruling greatness.
>
> Another embodies her power of splendid strength and irresistible passion, her warrior mood, her overwhelming will, her impetuous swiftness and world-shaking force. A third is vivid and sweet and wonderful with her deep secret of beauty and harmony and fine rhythm, her intricate and subtle opulence, her compelling attraction and captivating grace. The fourth is equipped with her close and profound capacity of intimate knowledge and careful flawless work and quiet and exact perfection in all things. Wisdom, Strength, Harmony, Perfection are their several attributes and it is these powers that they bring with them into the world . . . To the four we give the four great names, Maheshwari, Mahalaki, Mahalakshmi, Mahasaraswati . . .

Aurobindo let it be known that in writing the book he was referring not only to the 'cosmic' entity of the Divine Mother, but to Mirra. The metaphysical idea of the Divine Mother, and the person of the small, wiry and purposeful French woman had somehow become one. Although there is no suggestion that there were ever intimate relations between them, read in that light *The Mother* emerges as a love letter of transcendent grace and rapture.

Aurobindo's usual method of answering questions from devotees was to scribble his replies in the margins of their letters to him. In 1938, the following exchange took place:

> Do you not refer to the Mother, our Mother (i.e. Mirra), in your book *The Mother*? *Yes*.
>
> Is she not the individual Divine Mother who has embodied 'the power of these two vaster ways of her existence' [a quotation from part one of *The Mother*] – transcendent and universal? *Yes*.

Has she not descended here amongst us into the darkness and falsehood and error and death in her deep and great love for us? *Yes.*

There are many who hold the view that she was human but now embodies the Divine Mother, and her prayers, they say, explain this view but, to my mental conception, to my psychic feeling, she is the Divine Mother who has consented to put on her the cloak of obscurity and suffering and ignorance so that she can effectively lead us, human beings, to knowledge and bliss and *ananda* and to the Supreme Lord. *The Divine puts on an appearance of humanity, assumes the outward human nature in order to tread the path and show it to human beings, but does not cease to be the Divine. It is a manifestation that takes place; a manifestation of a growing Divine consciousness, not human turning into Divine. The Mother was inwardly above the human even in childhood, so the view held by 'many' is erroneous.*

Aurobindo was declaring that the Mother was an avatar – that is to say, not a human who has *become* Divine through spiritual development, but the Divine coming down into humanity in a living incarnation. The Mother made the same claim for Aurobindo, although neither made such claims for themselves.

Under the Mother's control, the ashram took on an unusually Western aspect. There were no *sadhus*, no ascetics, no deities or statues. Meals were eaten with a knife and fork. There were improving talks on such subjects as yoga and morality, Gandhi-ism and Indian politics, Ouspensky and Shaw's St Joan. All of this conformed less to the traditional Indian idea of the ashram as spiritual sanctuary than to the Western idea of community, emphasising Aurobindo's belief not in retreat from life, but in transformation, and divine fulfilment on earth. Mirra wrote to her son André in 1933:

The life we lead here is as far from ascetic abstinence as from enervating comfort; simplicity is the rule here, but a simplicity full of variety, a variety of occupations, of activities, tastes, tendencies, natures.

Tennis, a game of which Mirra was inordinately fond, was introduced as part of the ashram curriculum, along with callisthenics and a sort of spiritual flower-arranging, in which flowers served as metaphors for the human qualities – Purity, Faith, Surrender. The Mother, it was said, could divine the essence of flowers by holding them in the palm of her hand.

In the absence of Aurobindo, secluded in his chambers, grappling with the Supermind, the Mother inaugurated the practice of appearing each day on the balcony for *darshan* – a tradition that was to last for thirty years. She explained:

> Every morning at the balcony, after establishing a conscious contact with each of those who are present, I identify myself with the Supreme Lord and merge myself completely in Him. Then my body, completely passive, is nothing but a channel through which the Lord passes freely His forces and pours on all His Light, His Consciousness and His Joy, according to each one's receptivity.

It was said that even her appearance altered from day to day. Aurobindo wrote: 'She has many personalities and the body is plastic enough to express something of each when it comes forward.'

The ashram became a point of pilgrimage for both Indian and Western seekers. Among its students was Sri Chinmoy, who lived in the ashram from the age of twelve until the early Sixties, when he moved to New York, establishing his own teaching centres, and attracting such followers as the rock musicians John McLaughlin and Carlos Santana.

The distinguished French photographer, Henri Cartier-Bresson, the founder of the world-famous Magnum agency, visited in 1950, shortly before Aurobindo's death. He had come from the ashram of the great saint Sri Ramana Maharshi. He had been there the day Sri Ramana Maharshi died. At nine-thirteen, Cartier-Bresson would later recall, he had looked at his watch, then looked up to see a huge fireball crossing the sky. A few minutes later an emissary from the ashram arrived on a bicycle to say the Bhagwan had died.

Compared to the ashram of Ramana Maharshi, Pondicherry, Cartier-Bresson remembers, was 'a completely different world'. He photographed the Mother playing tennis and in repose, and then asked if he might also photograph Aurobindo. Aurobindo had not been photographed for thirty years. Cartier-Bresson was taken upstairs where the sage greeted him in almost total darkness. Cartier-Bresson fired off a handful of exposures in the gloom, then later photographed Aurobindo at *darshan*. The photographs were subsequently published with an article in *Illustrated* magazine, to which the Mother apparently took great exception. To placate her, Cartier-Bresson agreed to sell the negatives to the ashram. It was the only time in his career that he had ever surrendered the copyright on his photographs. The fee, he would later recall, had saved Magnum at a time of crippling financial difficulty.

Aurobindo died on 5 December 1950, at the age of seventy-eight. Three years before his death he had seen the fulfilment of his dream of 'Mother India' winning her independence from the British. 'Another dream, the spiritual gift of India to the world, has already begun,' he wrote. 'India's spirituality is entering Europe and America in an ever increasing measure. That movement will grow; amid the disasters of the time, more and more eyes are turning towards her with hope.'

Claiming to be in continuing contact with him from the other side, the Mother continued his work. She inaugurated a school in his honour, the Sri Aurobindo International Centre of Education, and set to the task of calling down the Supermind. On 29 February 1956, during a group meditation in the school playground, she made the momentous announcement that the Supermind had finally descended. 'I had a form of living gold, bigger than the universe, and I was facing a huge and massive golden door which separated the world from the Divine. As I looked at the door, I knew and willed, in a single movement of consciousness, that "the time has come", and lifting with both hands a mighty golden hammer I struck one blow, one single blow, on the door and the door was shattered to pieces. Then the Supramental Light and Force and Consciousness rushed down upon earth in an uninterrupted flow.'

The sensation was so profound that the Mother believed all the students around her would be felled to the ground by the sheer force of it. But, rather anti-climactically, nobody else felt anything.

The Mother was undeterred. Nothing revolutionary could be expected immediately, she announced, but the process towards a new super-race had begun. She now set to work on a yoga to transform her own body cells, through 'cellular consciousness', striving to realise the age-old dream of immortality. Before his death, Sri Aurobindo had prophesied that 'the supramental consciousness will enter into a phase of realising power in 1967'. In that same year, the Mother announced, 'Since a few months ago the children born, among our people, are of a special kind.' Taking note of the burgeoning hippie movement – a fulfilment in part, perhaps, of Aurobindo's prophecy of the spread of Indian spirituality to the West – she observed that, 'In America . . . the entire youth seems to have been taken up with a sort of curious brainwave which would be disquieting for reasonable people, but which is certainly an indication that an unusual force is at work. It is the breaking up of all habits and rules – it is good. For the moment, it is rather strange, but it is necessary.' She could hardly have failed to be aware of the hippies, for Pondicherry had by now become an obligatory stop on the pilgrim trail, and the guest-houses were full to overflowing with long-haired, tie-dyed back-packers.

As her health deteriorated, the Mother gradually withdrew from ashram life, but she continued to talk of her work of the transformation of consciousness. In January 1969 she announced that there had been a descent of the 'Superman-consciousness', an intermediary between man and the supramental being. The special characteristic of this force, she noted, was its material character and impact on the body. 'During these few hours I understood absolutely what it was to have the divine consciousness in the body . . . But that state, which lasted for several hours, nothing similar to that happiness has this body ever felt during the ninety-one years it has been here upon earth: freedom, absolute power and no limits.'

Three years later she claimed to have had direct experience of her 'supramental body'. It was sexless, she reported, slim, but with broad shoulders. 'The two things very, very different; first, procreation, of which there is no possibility there; secondly, the food . . . And now the question is to find a food which needs no complicated digestion . . . Evidently, what will change very much, which had become very important, was breathing. It is upon this that this being greatly depended.'

Presumably still striving to answer the questions raised by this visitation, she died on 17 November 1973, at the age of ninety-five. Her body was laid in state in the meditation room, and over the next three days, thousands of devotees processed past it. Reflecting on the Mother's life, one could only admire her enormous industry. She was a prolific author, a skilful painter, an indefatigable administrator (not to mention, a useful tennis-player). Her vision and determination had fostered the growth not only of the Sri Aurobindo Ashram, but also – and this was perhaps her most remarkable achievement – the founding of Auroville, the Utopian community that had been carved out of a tract of tangled, arid and inhospitable forestland some eight miles from Pondicherry, and where 900 people from twenty-seven nations now lived.

But alongside her idealism, her unquenchable faith in the innate divinity of man, lay a clear streak of Messianism, and an unnerving tendency to place herself in the forefront of history – if only after the event. Her occult powers, she suggested, were not simply confined to the everyday business of taming malevolent spirits at sea; they had also come in useful in changing the course of the Second World War. At the outbreak of war, many in India took a pro-German, or at best neutral stance, reflecting the bitterness of a country still under colonial rule. But both Aurobindo and the Mother declared their support for the allies, seeing the Axis powers as a force that was actively opposed to the progress of divine evolution.

Hitler, the Mother claimed, was in contact with a being that he considered the Supreme, but who was actually an *asura* – a force of evil – called 'the Lord of Falsehood', who appeared to the Führer 'wearing a silver cuirass and helmet; a kind of flame came out of his head, and there was an atmosphere of dazzling light around him', and who played with Hitler 'as with a monkey or a mouse'. When Hitler was going from success to success in Europe, the Mother claimed, she had used her occult power to check the Lord of Falsehood, leading to Hitler opening the second front against Stalin in the East – a decision which had resulted in his eventual defeat. Curiously, this contribution to the allied victory has been overlooked in most conventional histories of the Second World War.

At the house where the Mother and Aurobindo had shared their lives, I joined a line of people, processing up the stairs to the first-floor rooms which had been the Mother's private quarters. We filed through a sitting room and into the holy bedroom. People knelt in momentary reverence beside her bed, heads inclined towards the turquoise bedspread; beside the bed stood two china bowls, one containing blossoms, the other a collection of small envelopes, each containing a portrait of Aurobindo and the Mother. Keepsakes. We filed back into the sitting room, crowded with furniture, a carved sideboard, a display case crammed with knick-knacks and *objets d'art*, and the divan, covered with a tiger skin, on which Aurobindo and the Mother had once been photographed sitting together. There was nothing the least bit ascetic about it. Whatever her spiritual qualities, it was clear the Mother also had a good eye for furniture and antiques.

Downstairs, a bookshop sold volumes of teachings and biographies and an assortment of photographs. Like the house and the furnishings these seemed to be informed by a particularly European sense of good taste. The books, produced by the ashram, were models of classically simple and effective design; the postcards and photographs, including those taken by Cartier-Bresson, were of the quality one might expect to find in galleries in New York or Milan rather than an ashram in India. Studying the photographs of Sweet Mother, the idea that the Divine Feminine principle, embodied in Isis, the Earth Goddess, the Virgin Mary and Shakti, should have manifested in the form of a lugubrious-looking French woman, living in faded, post-colonial gentility beside the lapping waves of the Bay of Bengal, struck me as a peculiarly pleasing felicity.

At the back of the house was a paved courtyard, edged with flowerbeds. In its centre, under the shade of a large, spreading tree, stood the *Samadhi*, the marble plinth under which Sri Aurobindo and the Mother are buried. A simple cotton canopy shielded it from the sun. The *Samadhi* itself was exquisitely decorated with flowers, arranged in a circular symbol of eternity. It was the most dazzling floral arrangement I had ever seen – a riot of blues, purples, reds and yellows. The smell of burning incense, mingling with the perfume of the flowers, was overpoweringly heady. People wandered into the courtyard, knelt in front of the *Samadhi*, touching their heads to the marble and murmuring prayers. Stone benches lined the courtyard walls, and I sat in the shade, lost in thought. The simplicity and beauty of the *Samadhi*, the palpable mood of serenity and reverence, were profoundly touching, and I felt moved in a way that I had not felt in the *mandir* at Puttaparthi, as if the absence of the subjects of this veneration were a more palpable force than the presence of Sai Baba had been. The thought occurred to me that it was somehow easier, more satisfactory, to revere a teacher who was dead than one who was alive. Death sanctified them, blurred their fallibility and weakness. They were enlarged, made more holy, by memory. The problem with the living was they could always let you down.

Kamala Reddy, a young Indian girl who would later become known to the world as Mother Meera, arrived in Pondicherry for the first time shortly after the death of the Mother. Like 'Sweet Mother' herself, Kamala was evidently a highly unusual child. The daughter of a farmer, she was born in the village of Chandepalle, Andhra

Pradesh on 26 December 1960 – thirteen years before the death
of Sweet Mother in her room at the Sri Aurobindo ashram in
Pondicherry.

From an early age Kamala was said to have demonstrated signs
of divine communication: at the age of two or three she would talk
of going to 'different lights' when in need of comfort; at six she is
said to have had her first experience of *samadhi*, or meditative bliss,
falling senseless for a whole day. 'From then on,' she would later
say, 'I knew myself to live only in the Divine and by the Divine's
will and help.' At the age of thirteen, she came under the guidance
of her uncle, Balgur Reddy. At the time Mr Reddy was living in
the Sri Aurobindo ashram. Mr Reddy was immediately struck by
the young Kamala's presence and aura. In 1974, he took Kamala
to Pondicherry for the first time, to pay homage at the *Samadhi* of
Aurobindo and the Mother. Here, Kamala had a vision of Aurobindo
and the Mother, later described in her biography, written by her
secretary and constant companion, Adilakshmi.

> I saw Sri Aurobindo as a young boy surrounded by members of his
> family [Kamala recounts]. And then I saw Sweet Mother and Sri
> Aurobindo waking up, as if from a trance. Sweet Mother walked
> to a chair under a tree in the ashram and sat down. I ran to Her.
> Sweet Mother caressed me, took me into Her Lap, and blessed me.
> She handed me the flower 'Prosperity' . . .

So begins an extraordinary (and extraordinarily protracted) description of her communion with the two dead saints, in which she travels
with them, in visionary form, through the highest and lowest spiritual
realms, in preparation for her life's work:

> Once, Sweet Mother gave me a rose. I took the flower to Sri
> Aurobindo's *Samadhi*. I knew it was not an ordinary flower. It
> was my soul. I held on to it fiercely. But as I was walking, Sri
> Aurobindo snatched it from me without my knowing.
> I was very sad because I had lost my soul. Then Sri Aurobindo
> called me and asked me why I was so sad. I told him that I had
> lost my soul. He said, 'Your soul is not lost and could never be,'
> and then he showed me the flower he had stolen. Then he replaced
> Sweet Mother's rose with a golden rose and told me that this golden
> rose was his soul and that it would stay with me always. And then he

blessed me. I merged in Sweet Mother and Sweet Mother merged in me. I was told by Sweet Mother that I must look after the affairs of the world, and that I must bear very heavy responsibilities and work unceasingly for the Divine.

After some months in Pondicherry, Mr Reddy took his niece to Hyderabad, entrusting her to a girls' hostel to be educated. It was here, it is said, that she had her first experience of the *Paramatman* Light, the Light of the Supreme Lord. There followed a series of encounters with deities, in which, it is said, Mahakali, Mahasarastai and Mahalakshmi merged into her, and she was blessed by Krishna, Brahma, Vishnu and other gods, Vivekananda and Ramakrishna and other saints, ascetics and *rishis*.

She travelled, she would later say, to 'the Supramental Regions, the Kingdom of the Supermind', and encountered 'Supramental Beings . . . different from God and from men. They were very tall, and they had a white and rose-tinged complexion. Their bodies were soft, slender, delicate, shining like mirrors and transparent, without bones or nerves. There was no way of telling male from female.'

By the age of sixteen, we learn, she had merged with 'several Divine powers'; she had experienced *Nirguna, Parabrahman* and *Paramatman*; she had received gifts from gods and *rishis* of all kinds, and she had visited the world of Supramental Beings and learnt their language.

One time [she writes] I saw that Sweet Mother was working in a vast field of earth consciousness and was cleaning it. Sweet Mother had cleansed one fourth of the field, but three-fourths remained. Sweet Mother gave me this work, asked me to finish it. That is what I am doing. Into this unfinished part the light must be mixed. By this light the whole earth will be transformed into something as soft as butter. When that is accomplished the Supramental Beings will descend and a new creation will begin.

Reading these accounts, one is immediately struck by the naivety of their tone. They are a child's version of visionary experience, a fairy-tale: one is unsure whether she is describing genuine mystical revelations or flights of the most vivid adolescent imagination.

In 1977, Kamala and Mr Reddy returned to Pondicherry. They took a small house in the Indian quarter, across the canal from the Sri

Aurobindo ashram, where Kamala began to gather a small group of followers around her, predominantly Europeans. She was no longer known as Kamala, but as Mother Meera. In Hindi, *meera* means 'miracle'. The similarity to Sweet Mother's given name, Mirra, is, perhaps, coincidental. It was here that Meera began explicitly to define her mission as a continuation of the work of Aurobindo and Sweet Mother, to call the Supramental Light down to earth. According to Meera, on 21 November 1978, the Supramental Light descended to earth, infusing the atmosphere with an immense force for one minute. Two months later, in January 1979, inspired by Aurobindo and Sweet Mother, it is said that she 'called down' the *Paramatman* Light, to make the transformation of the world 'go much faster'. By the end of that year, we read, Meera's

> ... identification with the Supreme Mother was complete. She had succeeded in bringing down to earth the light of the Supreme Lord that makes transformation certain; she had been assured of the Paramatman's help and protection and power in everything she undertook.

Her mission was established.

It was in her small, bare room in Pondicherry, among a gathering of devotees, that a young English academic named Andrew Harvey first took *darshan* with Mother Meera:

> I had never knelt to anyone else [he would later write in his book about Meera, *Hidden Journey*] yet nothing in the worship that I saw before me struck me as blasphemous. Meera seemed to know intimately each head she took into her hands; and her eyes changed for each person who approached her. She did not take the worship offered for herself. There was no self in her; only a Presence like the red-gold sunlight and warm wind that filled the room. To kneel to this girl in this room seemed even familiar. It was like kneeling to the sea wind, or to a sudden vision of snow in the mountains, or to a moment of supreme eloquence in music.

Hidden Journey is one of the most remarkable spiritual testaments of modern times. (And, deservedly, one of the most widely read: I have seen it in bookshops in San Francisco, Bombay, Dharamsala and Paris.)

Harvey begins by describing his idyllic upbringing in India as the son of English colonial parents; the trauma he experienced at the age of eight, when he was sent away by his mother to England to be educated at boarding school; his brilliant academic career, which had seen him become, at twenty-five, one of the youngest ever Fellows of All Souls, Oxford, but which left him feeling hollow and dissatisfied; his feelings of sexual confusion and suicidal depression; and his meeting with Meera, and his transformation over the next ten years under her guidance, firstly in India, and then in the small German village of Thalheim, where Mother Meera now lived. Meera, Harvey concludes emphatically, is the living embodiment of the Divine Feminine, the human mask of the universal creative force – 'in her case, a very beautiful tender mask'.

Hidden Journey is an extraordinary book for two reasons. First there is the magnitude of its assertions and the experiences recorded – a sort of metaphysical roller-coaster ride. Second, Harvey brings intellectual rigour and a refined literary sensibility to a subject more usually marked by uncritical, credulous awe.

A friend in publishing gave me page-proofs of the book before it was published. As soon as I read it I knew that I wanted to meet Andrew Harvey. He was no longer living with Mother Meera at Thalheim. He kept a flat in Paris, but earned his living teaching English literature in America, at the university in the small town of Geneva in upstate New York. I travelled to see him. Geneva was a one-horse college town of clapboard buildings and filling stations. I made my way to Harvey's lodgings. He greeted me at the door; I saw an unruly mane of black hair, a velvet jacket and jeans. He was garrulous, charming and funny, a man of almost operatic enthusiasm; I liked him immediately. Within an hour of my arrival, Harvey was whisking me off to the only French restaurant for miles around. A friend who had studied with him at Oxford had warned me that Harvey was 'effortlessly clever; more clever than you or I will ever be'; and I could see immediately what he meant. Over dinner, he held forth on Shakespeare, Buddhism, the Sufi poet Rumi. All seemed to be his *Mastermind* subjects. He ordered another bottle of wine and cadged cigarettes. The fact that his spiritual transformation had apparently not made him altogether immune to petty vices made me warm to him even more.

A friend of Harvey's had joined us for dinner, a French woman who also taught at the university. She told me that, infected by Harvey's enthusiasm, she too had visited Mother Meera in Germany, and the effect had been palpable. In Meera's presence she experienced immediate feelings of uplift and serenity, but the long-term consequences were more remarkable still. She was not by nature, she said, a gregarious person, and certainly not someone whom others sought out for advice or comfort. 'But when I came back from Germany, for some reason, I felt more confident in myself, I could cope with my own life more, and gradually I noticed that people were coming to me and asking my advice on things. It was as if I had found the strength to give people something and they sensed that without needing to be told.' She paused. 'Does this sound crazy? But I think there's some universal law operating there which says if you have the strength to help people then it will be asked of you.'

The next day, I sat with Harvey in his small study, overlooking a rambling garden, blossoming in the spring afternoon, while he recounted his story. Books on Hindu and Buddhist philosophy lined the walls, and on his desk stood a framed photograph of Mother Meera. As a child growing up in India, he said, the stories of Hindu saints and gods were his fairy-tales. To be transplanted to England at the age of eight had been a miserable, isolating experience. Clever and quick at school, he had glided effortlessly into Oxford. A glittering academic career had been followed by a professorship at Cornell. He had published poetry, novels, given every appearance of being a blithe success. But it was all, he said, a total sham. 'I was a brittle, vain, very difficult young man who had found nothing worth serving in the culture around him, and I was very frightened by that. I was intellectually ambitious. I wished very much to be a great artist. I didn't want fame so much as I wanted respect.' He laughed quietly to himself. 'I was still naive enough to believe that those things mattered.'

In a state of emotional and spiritual crisis he had returned to India. He was twenty-six when he was taken by a friend to meet Mother Meera, on Christmas Day 1978. The effect on his life had been profound. Returning to Cornell he had tried to explain to colleagues that he had found his guru in a seventeen-year-old Indian girl. 'Many of them,' he notes in the book, 'thought I was on the verge of a nervous breakdown.' Over the next ten years he had engaged in an epic, often fraught, but eventually revelatory relationship with Meera, sometimes denying, eventually succumbing to the fact of her divinity, and his own role as her disciple.

This transformation is vividly described in *Hidden Journey*. During *darshan*, he hears 'a great vibrant humming curtain of burning silence'; before his eyes the Mother's body seems to glow 'red, fiery, a burning gold'. Alone in his room light streams from her photograph in 'a diamond white torrent'. Days pass as though in a dream, punctuated by moments of profound self-revelation.

Her teachings are seldom verbal. The Mother, or 'Ma', as he calls her, hardly speaks, and then only to interpret his thoughts and experiences, seldom to direct or instruct. The impression Harvey gives is of awakening to some deeper voice within himself.

> My room downstairs, when I returned to it, was full of Mother's gold light [he writes]. As soon as I walked in I heard Ma's voice: *Look at the dot between my eyes.* Turning to the photograph of Ma on the wall, I gazed at the large red dot on her forehead . . . Ma's eyes became two whirlpools of fire, and the large red circle started to vibrate and hum. Her Force seized me and began to pour itself into me. I felt as if the lid of my head and my entire face had been peeled off and molten radiance was being poured directly into my mind and body . . .

What Harvey describes is a sort of spiritual surgery, a laceration of the ego, forcing him to discard the intellect and consider a deeper sense of self. Readers of a sceptical persuasion, I suggested, might wonder if he wasn't confessing to taking leave of his senses.

Harvey rocked back in his chair with laughter. 'If you were reading Eastern literature, created out of a religious civilisation, the experiences I describe, while I hope they would be moving, would not be extreme; many, many people have experienced such things. What seems improbable to the rational mind is actually natural in that dimension of mystical knowledge.

'It was very startling at first, because these experiences came so very fast. I think she was extremely merciful to me – she realised that my intellectual resistance was great. I was given experience after experience, vision after vision, that I could not refute or deny. There is no way irony or mockery can survive that.'

Reading the book, I said, anyone with a little knowledge of Freud might see in it a case of the sensitive child, sent away by his mother at an early age, brooding on his loss and finding the ultimate symbol of replacement.

'It's the obvious construction,' said Harvey. 'But it's just not true. What is true is that I think whatever pain my mother's abandonment caused became the psychic wound that made my search essential.

'Where Freud is very helpful is in analysing how the ego takes an original trauma and then repeats it. So I always chose in my emotional life people – lovers – who would repeat that abandonment. But what happens is you repeat and repeat until you realise you are trapped. That, possibly, is the beginning of many people's spiritual search – when they realise they are repeating an old record, and that repeating it will be fatal to their lives.'

We talked about gurus, good and bad. The West, said Harvey, had been hideously misled by some dangerous and self-absorbed people setting themselves up as spiritual teachers. 'But the advantage of this is that it's shown us what false gurus are like. Mother has never forced me, never demanded anything, never asked for anything, never imposed any kind of relationship on me that wasn't chosen by me; she has always been all-loving, all-patient, all gentle.'

At her home in Thalheim she lived in virtual silence. She cooked; she tended the vegetable garden; she had even climbed on to the roof to lay slates, much to the consternation of local villagers. 'There is no cult of adoration around her, no special clothes, no medallions . . .' Harvey paused. 'She is interested only in bringing the world to its senses. She is the only normal being I've ever met. Totally normal. Totally sane. And her message is very simple. We must live in harmony with the environment and with each other. No hierarchy. No dogma. Love alone. Fraternity alone. One large family. It's so simple it makes one want to roll on the floor. But that's it. That's the entire teaching.'

Thinking of Harvey's academic and literary career, I said that I admired his decision to publish the book. I suggested jokingly that it was tantamount to a suicide note to him ever again being embraced by the sceptical, chattering classes of London's literary establishment.

'Good!' He laughed. He had turned his back on what he called 'the concentration camp of reason'. The 'old biography' of Andrew Harvey, suffering poet and author, was gone. 'I've come home.'

I found Harvey's testimony, as I had found his book, deeply moving. A week after meeting him, I flew to Germany to see Mother Meera for myself. Mother Meera first came to Germany in 1980, at the invitation of a group of devotees. When her uncle and guardian Mr Reddy fell ill, requiring constant hospital treatment, Meera took a house in the small village of Thalheim, an hour's drive north of Frankfurt. When Mr Reddy died, she married a German devotee (presumably for purposes of citizenship) and remained in the country.

I rented a car in Frankfurt, and drove north on the autobahn, through the flat north-German countryside. I booked into a guest-house in a neighbouring village (there were none in Thalheim itself) and made my way to Mother Meera's house for evening *darshan*. Thalheim was a small, anonymous place under a dreary grey sky; stolid houses, fenced in behind tidy gardens; a gloomy-looking Gothic church; a Spar grocery, a knot of bored-looking teenagers loitering outside a café. The idea that an incarnation of the divine should have marooned herself in such an unprepossessing place seemed slightly surreal.

The Mother lived on a quiet residential street in a former farmhouse, set at the end of a long gravel drive and backing on to fields. An outbuilding had been converted into the *darshan* room. It was decorated with creamy flock wallpaper, and set with plastic seats, of the kind found in institutional canteens, arranged around a white armchair, set in the centre. I took a seat and waited as the room began to fill, some people sitting on chairs, others cross-legged on cushions on the floor, perhaps sixty in all. At seven, the door opened and Mother Meera entered. A slight figure, dressed in a red silk sari, she walked serenely to the white armchair, eyes cast down – a gesture, it seemed, of the utmost humility. She looked far younger than her thirty years – almost a child. It was as if a breath of wind had passed across the room, enveloping it in a still, pristine silence.

One by one people came forward to kneel in front of her. Beside the Mother was an empty chair. As one person knelt before her, another would occupy the empty chair, awaiting their turn. There was no signal, no order, to come forward and await your turn, yet neither was there ever a time when the chair was empty, nor when two people were heading for it at the same time. I found this ritual – like silent clockwork – curiously absorbing, while the familiar doubts and questions circled in the back of my mind. Could the Divine manifest in human form? Was Mother Meera genuine? A fraud? What did any of this have to do with my life?

But of course! I was a journalist. I did not have to believe anything. My role was objective and dispassionate observer. But wasn't this simply a posture? Self-defence? A barrier that would effectively neutralise whatever effect her powers, if powers she had, would have on me?

I took my place in front of her. She held my face in her hands, cradling it there for perhaps a minute, then tilted it upwards to meet her gaze. I could sense my thoughts flapping behind the wall of my eyes like flags. Are you a fraud? Well, are you? She read my doubts without blinking, and continued to stare fixedly into me; as if she was cancelling them out with her gaze, discarding them as too trivial to bother with. I had the curious sense that she was forgiving me.

I seemed to have been staring at her for hours. But I knew that it could have been no more than a minute. I could feel my heart galloping. She lowered her gaze, released her hold on my head; I rose and made my way back to my seat.

It took another hour for everybody in the room to take their turn in front of her, then she rose silently from her chair and left, glancing neither to the left or right. There was a moment's pause – an unwinding, almost – and then people began to file out. Across the corridor was a room where you could buy books, posters and photographs of Meera and postcards of her paintings. These were swirling abstracts in blues, purples and pinks, cosmic symbolism that bore a curious resemblance to Benjamin Creme's paintings which I had seen hanging in his home. Apart from the charge for these items, no one asked for money, and as far as I could see there was not so much as a plate for those inclined to make donations.

I bought a copy of a slim volume of quotations by Meera, *Answers*, and stepped out into the cool German night. I could feel the warmth where she had touched my face, as if I was running a temperature. I felt a curious mixture of light-headedness and exhaustion; as if I had just sat a particularly arduous examination. I drove back to the guest-house and ordered a coffee in the lounge. It was full of people who had taken *darshan*, talking among themselves, or simply sitting, lost in thought.

A man caught my eye and brought his drink to my table. 'Do you mind?' He was German, in his fifties, a florid, well-shaven face, casually, but expensively dressed. If I had met him anywhere else I would have taken him to be a dealer in paintings or antiques. Perhaps

he was. I did not catch his name. He too had been in *darshan*, he said
– although I had not noticed him there. He was a student of yoga, he
said, a seeker of sorts. He waved an expansive hand, as if this took
in all manner of possibilities. He had been coming to take *darshan*
with Mother Meera for more than a year, he said. 'Of course, she
is an avatar, yes. I believe this. I have seen the changes in myself.
There is a lot of power there, a lot of power.' He smiled. 'I think
you have felt it, yes?'

Was the dazed look on my face that obvious? I could still feel it
burning from where Mother Meera had held it. But that had been
more than two hours ago.

'She has cut you open now, opened you up. If you are receptive
then she will pour all her love into you.'

So, he asked me, I was a seeker too, yes?

I shrugged and said I was a journalist. Seeker is not a word I
am happy with.

'One has to beware of seeking,' he said. 'All the great teachers say
that searching is an obstacle to finding. It's the paradox. The ego
drives you to search in order to satisfy itself. But the true meaning
of spirituality is to transcend the ego, and transcend the quest.'

He laughed. 'Don't expect searching to make you happy.'

I excused myself and stepped outside to get some fresh air. The sky
was as black as pitch. I could see the lights from some neighbouring
houses through the trees. A phrase came into my mind. Starless
and Bible black. Dylan Thomas. A gale of laughter rose up from
inside the guest-house and I turned back to go inside. My eye fell
on a small hand-printed sticker which someone had attached to the
door. It read: 'Maitreya is here.'

The German was sitting where I had left him in the lounge,
drinking an orange juice. Had he heard of Maitreya? I asked.

'Ah yes, you know about Maitreya?' He sat back in his chair,
warming to the theme. 'These are very special times. There are
many avatars now in the world, because the world needs them.
Soon, all this will be revealed.'

You think that soon Maitreya will be revealed?

He nodded. 'Undoubtedly. And you, my friend, as a journalist,
you have some part to play in this. Why do you think you have
come here? To satisfy your curiosity, to find something out for
yourself? Maybe. But it's your job to tell people about this. All
your accomplishments, what you've done in your job and your life,

has brought you to this, and you can't turn back. You would make yourself very unhappy if you did.'

The conversation made me uneasy. The German had made what I was doing seem somehow important, and I always shied away from the belief that anything I did was important. I didn't want the responsibility. Nor did I believe Maitreya was here, waiting in the wings to reveal himself to an incredulous world. I thought it was a myth, a folk-tale. Perhaps everything here was a myth. I no longer knew what to believe.

In my bedroom I thumbed through the book I had bought at Meera's home. It was in question-and-answer form, and I was struck by the simplicity of her answers, and the enormous complexity of what they implied:

Q: Did you incarnate knowing that you were divine?

MM: Before coming here I knew who I was, knew that I would incarnate and what my work would be. The Mother is beyond time.

Q: Have you ever been a human being?

MM: No.

Q: Did you know who you were, even as a baby?

MM: Yes, I always knew.

Q: Why do you live so normal and simple a life in a quiet German village?

MM: To show the world that the transformation is normal, can be done anywhere and in daily life.

. . .

Q: How can I realise 'Who am I?'?

MM: Give up that 'I' and you will know.

Q: What is love?

MM: To go on doing for people what they need, without expecting anything in return, that is love.

Q: What is sin?

MM: There is only one sin and that is not to love enough.

I went to sleep, my mind buzzing. I awoke with the feeling that sunlight was streaming in through the window. Something curious had happened. I felt serene, light-headed – more light-headed than I had ever felt in my life. I drove back to Frankfurt. I flew to London. I negotiated the rush-hour crowds going home. It was all completely

effortless. Unnaturally so. The next morning I took the underground
to the offices of the *Daily Telegraph*. I was aware that I was smiling
absurdly, aware that people on the tube were giving me strange
looks, as if I was on drugs. The truth was that I felt happier, far
happier, than I had ever felt on drugs, as if some vast reservoir of
well-being and beneficence had been tapped inside myself. I could
barely constrain myself from leaning across to the complete stranger
sitting opposite me, clasping him on the shoulder and telling him
that life was undoubtedly, indescribably, wonderful. People in the
office kept asking me, 'What are you on?' 'Well, there's this woman
in Germany . . .' Try again. 'What are your feelings about gurus?'
No, that was no good either.

   This feeling stayed with me. I felt suffused with love for my
fellow man; tolerant; benevolent. I felt that everything was in its
place. Something had happened, but I knew not what. I wasn't
used to feeling this good, and it made me uneasy. I telephoned
Andrew Harvey to tell him about it, and could hear him laughing
indulgently down the line. He was much too polite to say, 'I told
you so . . .'

   Looking back, I should have used this experience; done something
with it. Gradually, over a period of days, the feeling of exhilaration
subsided. I did not place a photograph of Mother Meera by my
bedside; I did not meditate on the memory of her image. Her voice
did not speak to me. The sky did not open. Life went on, much
as before. But I knew what I had felt; I knew that the feeling was
genuine, and in some curious way I felt heartened by that knowledge.
The world cannot be altogether explained. There is something more.
It was enough.

'What,' I asked the trustee of the Sri Aurobindo ashram, 'are your
feelings about Mother Meera?'

   He was a slender, austere-looking man in his early sixties, with
sleek white hair, dressed in perfectly creased khaki trousers and an
immaculate linen shirt. He received me in his office, wood-panelled,
and lined with books. He sat behind a desk which was completely
empty; I imagined him sitting in the same position before I arrived,
and long after I had gone, as static as an exhibit in a museum. He
had the sanguine, imperious and opaque manner of a civil servant,
a government bureaucrat. I found this disquieting. Simplistically,
I had always believed that the best measure of the efficacy of any

faith was the temperament and behaviour of its practitioners. If someone believes in harmony, this should somehow reflect in their behaviour. But India produced its own particular breed of religious officialdom. At the Sai Baba ashram in Puttaparthi, the uniformed guards had been no different from people in uniforms anywhere; bossy, impatient, quick to throw their weight around. This man was a bureaucrat of an altogether more subtle, but no less obstructive order. I struggled to formulate the question more pointedly. 'Does the Sri Aurobindo ashram *endorse* Mother Meera?'

The lids came down over his eyes like blinds. 'It is true that she was here at the ashram, and it is said that she too is an emanation of the Divine Mother. But we do not endorse the claims she makes.'

'So you do not believe that she is an avatar?'

'That is what she says; we do not say this . . .' He waved his hand lazily in the air, as if shrouding the claim in a veil of scepticism.

Meera's biography, *The Mother*, is explicit in cementing a connection between Meera and the Aurobindo ashram. While living in Pondicherry, it says, she had received 'two visits from leading Ashramites. Each time Mother was asked certain very searching questions. All of those who came were convinced by her'. But the trustee had evidently not been one of them – or if he was, he wasn't going to tell me. There was something distinctly proprietorial in his manner. He was a guardian of Sweet Mother's tradition; I sensed that he felt Meera was a usurper.

What, then, of Sweet Mother, I asked. Had he known her personally?

His face clouded, as if my mention of her name had caused him pain. 'I knew her, yes.'

'And what were your feelings about her?'

He stiffened slightly. 'It's difficult . . . I have my own feelings about her, as all those who knew her had. But I think in these matters it is better to go to the source.' He waved towards his bookshelves. 'The ashram library is most helpful.'

But was she an avatar?

'This is what Sri Aurobindo said, and I believe it.' He sighed. 'But you should really read the books.'

I walked out into the somnolent midday sunshine. The pavements outside the ashram were deserted. I crossed the road, past the ashram post office, and turned into a narrow side-street. A crowd of people were milling outside the door of a Hindu temple, more like a cavern, lit by candles, the smell of incense and the clamorous chanting of prayers and devotions billowing into the street. The contrast with the studied formality of the ashram that I had just left could hardly have been greater. A souvenir stall stood outside, laden down with statuettes, posters and postcards of deities, among them a handful of pictures of Aurobindo and the Mother, evidently pirated, and tricked out with tinsel borders and the garish colours more attuned to local tastes. The inevitable beggars slumped in the shade along the temple wall, leprous hands clutching metal tins, silent babies crawling in the dust. The gate to the Aurobindo ashram, arguably a more profitable pitch, was less than fifty yards away, and it suddenly dawned on me that the pavements there had been deliberately swept clean of such discomforting and unsightly human wreckage.

I threaded my way through the streets and found the building housing the Sri Aurobindo Archives and Research Department. A sign on the wooden gate read: 'Please close the door to keep the goats out.' The chief archivist was an American named Peter Heehs, a dark, wiry and intense-looking man in his late forties. He led the way through the library and on to the roof and fetched two chairs. An Indian woman brought tea.

Heehs first discovered the teachings of Sri Aurobindo in New York when he was a student. He had come to India in 1971 to visit the ashram, and stayed. 'I was a kind of hippie, I guess,' he said. 'But reading the books, they clicked with me. They're satisfying intellectually as well as going deep into the spirituality.'

Did he believe that Sri Aurobindo was an avatar, I asked.

He shrugged. 'These things aren't clear-cut. There's a tendency to describe any realised being as an avatar. It's one of those words that gets bandied around rather too casually. I mean, who's to say who's an avatar and who isn't? The concept is a paradox: that the whole Divine is incarnating in a single human being – that this being would simultaneously have what makes us human and what is divine. That's a difficult thing to get hold of . . .'

So what of Sweet Mother?

'Well, Sri Aurobindo said she was an avatar.'

And Mother Meera? Did Heehs believe she was an avatar too?

He laughed. 'Why not? The field is kind of open. She says she's connected to Sweet Mother but whatever connection she feels herself and may have spoken of can be given whatever value you're inclined to give it. But there's nothing from the side of Sri Aurobindo and the

Mother that would corroborate that. The majority of the people living in the ashram had never heard of her when she was in Pondicherry. But there's no belief in the ashram that in order to continue the work it was necessary for the Mother to be reincarnated. There's no waiting around here for a Messiah or something like that. People here see the thing going forward with the power of Aurobindo and the Mother still being here directing things in a disembodied way, and that there is no need for anything further.'

What Aurobindo was trying to do, he said, was 'climb the ladder' between lower nature and the Divine. After his death in 1950, the Mother had continued that work. Her declaration in 1956 that the 'Supermind' had finally descended was not the end of the work; it should be taken as just the first step in an evolutionary purpose.

'At one stage the tendency in the ashram was somewhat millennial. People living here in the Thirties really thought they weren't going to die. They believed this change would happen through Aurobindo and they would be the first to feel it. But it didn't turn out the way people expected. And after Sri Aurobindo and the Mother passed away people began phasing back their expectations. So I don't think anyone expects that everyone is going to wake up golden the next day. Being an evolutionary process it might very well be quite gradual.'

So the death of the guru necessarily modifies expectations?

Heehs sipped at his tea. 'Well, it depends what you had in mind in the beginning. A lot of people, myself included, think of the whole process in more personal terms; that everybody's got lots of work to do on himself, whatever might be happening in the cosmos. And so this is a better place than most to be doing that work. On a day-to-day basis people in the ashram are just concerned with going to work, meditating on a daily basis, that sort of thing. People have plenty to do without worrying about cosmic processes. Nobody expects to wake up tomorrow morning suddenly transformed.'

We were joined by his colleague, Bob Zwicker, a tall, angular man with a bony face and dreamy eyes. Bob was forty-nine, another Sixties searcher. Dissatisfied with life in America, he said, he had travelled to Europe. In France he was introduced to Sri Aurobindo's theories of 'integral yoga'. He filed it away in the back of his mind, and moved on to Rishikesh, where he had studied *raja* yoga. 'Then I read about Sweet Mother. I thought it wasn't for me. Too many sweet words, and too much nomenclature – overmind, supermind. I didn't get it. But I came here anyway.' After three weeks in Pondicherry, he caught his first glimpse of the Mother, giving *darshan* on the balcony of the ashram.

'When she came out I felt a burst of awe, of religious reverence, going towards her from everybody there. But the truth was I wasn't changed, and that put some doubt in my mind. Then three weeks later I had an interview. Before going in, I was composed. I'd decided it didn't matter, because I was a good person. If it was for me, fine. But if it wasn't, she was still a good lady who could run a good show. For me, I didn't want a queen, somebody with a calculating mind.

'And then I saw her. The first thing, she was very small. And she was completely white, stooped over, with her mouth open. She was ninety-three years old, and instead of being a queen she was like a baby, so vulnerable. But she was looking at each person so attentively. She was *all there*. The room itself was like a force-field, dense with peace and sweetness. All my mind and senses seemed to slow down. I got to her, and her attendant gave me a beautiful smile of recognition. Then I knelt before her and looked into her eyes, and it was like looking into a clear blue sky. And I could feel that all of my questions, all of my worries and doubts were just melting. My mind was full of gladness and wonder. And my mind was moving into this blue sky, like a kite.

'After about fifteen seconds, the thought came to me: there are no walls here. It was like looking into infinity. I just kept looking for twenty to twenty-five seconds, and then I became aware that she was looking at me. And what I felt was, she knew everything; she knew me entirely; she knew me better than I knew myself, and she could see my goodness. I had gone in there fearing that she would somehow try to take me and put me in her little world, but instead she was saying wordlessly if there's anything I have that you want, take it; anything I can do, tell me.

'I felt a pure unconditional love streaming into me. I felt she really cared for me. I was like a cup that had been enlarged and was being filled up with the nectar of her love. My eyes started to glaze over, and I closed them and tilted my head down. Then she put her hand on my head for about fifteen seconds. It was firm and soft. The perfect hand. And I looked up and she was just pouring herself into me. And after about fifteen seconds, I suddenly thought: She's doing it all – she was there for me. My cup filled up and I just broke down and started crying. She gave me a sweet smile, and a bouquet of flowers. I walked out of there, and my feet weren't touching the carpet. I was just in a mood of sublime gratitude. And it lasted for three days. I would listen to someone who was boring, and I didn't care. I was listening intently, and finding contact with that person. For about three days I was living in a world where whatever was happening to me was filled with some meaning that the world just doesn't have in an ordinary state.

'It showed me what a human being could become. I think she was living in a state like that all the time, which is pretty amazing. I mean, I'm just a *sadhak*, a disciple. But when you have a spiritual experience like that it's a glimpse of a higher truth. A clarity. A sense of connection.'

As Bob talked my mind went back to Thalheim, kneeling before Mother Meera. I could recognise something of what he described in my encounter with Meera, although his experience had evidently been infinitely more transformative, and more enduring. The memory of it had nourished him for some twenty years. It had changed the entire course of his life. Bob had spoken without pause or interruption for more than twenty minutes, and by the time he had finished there were tears coursing down his cheeks. I got the sense that it was a scene he had replayed many times in his own mind, cherishing each detail. I was unsure what to say. Peter was staring into the middle-distance, looking slightly embarrassed.

Had he too met the Mother? I asked.

'Yeah, I had an interview. And I felt some sort of link, but the opening wasn't anything like Bob had. My attraction was always towards Sri Aurobindo. I never doubted that. I got connected with the work.' He smiled. 'I'm a head guy. Bob is a heart guy . . .'

I asked Bob, had his experience returned at all in the years since the Mother's death?

'Yes, when I talk about it, and sometimes . . .' He fell silent.

The Mother had written, I said, that after her death she would continue to project her love and protection.

'Yes, she said that. For those in the ashram, you follow the work and sometimes, just sometimes, connections are made. You have to be open. "Being open" is a phrase you hear spoken a lot around here. You have to be in a condition to receive it.'

But were these experiences of connection qualitatively any

different from the experiences that everybody occasionally has, of feeling completely at one with oneself and the world?

'Qualitatively, no,' said Peter. 'But when you get those feelings . . . Sometimes your intellect gets in the way. You're thinking about the experience as you have it. And there is a difference between thinking about it and simply having it.'

Bob was listening intently. 'I've seen the Mother,' he said, 'and whatever she says I believe.'

After my meeting with Andrew Harvey, and my visit to Mother Meera, I wrote a piece for the *Telegraph* magazine. It prompted an enormous mailbag, and I dutifully supplied her address to anyone who requested it. Subsequently, a number of these people wrote to me, saying that they too had experienced some effect at *darshan*; others wrote that they had experienced nothing. There seemed to be no rules here. Andrew Harvey, meanwhile, became something of a spiritual celebrity. He collaborated with the Tibetan Lama Sogyal Rinpoche, helping to ghost-write *The Tibetan Book of Living and Dying*; he published a book about the Sufi poet, Rumi; he gave lectures, and featured on television programmes.

Then came the news that he had renounced Mother Meera. Harvey spelt out his reasons in an interview with the American magazine *Common Boundary* in October 1994, which was later included in his book *The Return of the Mother*. He had broken with Meera, he explained, because she wished him to sever his relationship with his lover, Eryk. Meera, Harvey alleged, told him that he had the choice either of remaining celibate or of marrying a woman, and 'writing a book about how the force of the Divine Mother transformed [him] into a heterosexual'. After a period of 'tremendous suffering and confusion, thinking that all this might be a divine teaching of some kind', Harvey had finally severed all connections with her.

Reflecting on his period of devotion to Meera, Harvey writes, 'I'd been so battered as a child and so disappointed in love in my twenties and thirties that I thought the only relationship with any hope was the kind of exotic, intense, subtly sadomasochistic relationship I had with Meera.' Meera, he said, fulfilled his desire for the perfect parental relationship which his own mother could not provide; she represented India in 'its essence . . . its sweetness'; and too his fascination with 'powerful female stars'. In a sense, he wrote, 'Meera is the Garbo of the spiritual Hollywood.' In short, Harvey had been star-struck.

> I no longer believe at all in Meera. I believe in the experiences I had *with* her, but I no longer believe they came *from* her. The Divine Mother gave me them *through* Meera and when it was becoming dangerous to go on following Meera and being her spokesperson, the Divine Mother smashed my relationship with the false 'Mother' to reveal the real one, beyond names and forms . . . It is extremely important to understand exactly what the Sacred Feminine is not. It is not power or achievement, it has nothing to do with dominating others, it has nothing to do with having millions of disciples.

The Return of the Mother is an anthology of writings on the Sacred Feminine in Hinduism, Islam, Buddhism, Taoism and Christianity; a plea to dismantle 'all the old habits of dependence, hierarchy and authority'. If there is to be a future, Harvey writes, 'it will wear the crown of feminine design'.

At every turn, while affirming the principle of the Divine Feminine, and the necessity to acknowledge it if the world is to be saved, it is a personal refutation of his own experiences with Mother Meera, thoroughly saturated with his disenchantment with the whole notion of guruhood. It is a demolition job, written with all the persuasive eloquence and force which he used to praise her in *Hidden Journey*. Ashrams, he writes, are 'lunatic asylums, filled with jealous and needy people'. The guru system is merely a perpetuation of the patriarchy – even in the female form of so-called 'Divine Mothers' – or 'Jehovahs in drag'. Gurus 'divide and rule. They are the magical "other" – everybody's in love with them, everybody's focused on them, and everybody hates whatever position the others have with them'.

He talked of Western seekers who had bought 'a cheap Hollywood version of the Indian trip'.

> A lot, perhaps most, of those we now call 'enlightened gurus' are nothing of the sort. They are not divine or divinised beings at all, but extremely powerful occult manipulators, who through certain kinds of spiritual exercises have attained certain *siddhis*, or powers, which enable them to dominate the minds and actions of others. They masquerade as 'gods' giving 'experiences' and doing 'miracles' . . . Mother Meera simply wanted me to remain her devotee and to

go on 'using' me, and her lies prove she is not enlightened (to say the least).

It was as if Paul, having undergone his Damascene conversion, had turned round and denounced Christ.

Harvey's denial of Meera made me wonder how much one could trust other people's testimony in these matters. Obviously, not at all. Had his enthusiasm put me in a receptive frame of mind to feel what I did when I visited Mother Meera? Were the experiences I had the result of 'occult power'? Something more? Or perhaps, something less – figments of my imagination, my yearning?

I made plans to return to Thalheim. It was almost three years since I had last visited. Andrew Harvey's denunciations, if they were widely known, seemed to have done nothing to diminish Meera's following. Such were the numbers of people now wishing to see her that it was no longer possible simply to arrive at her home for *darshan*. It was now necessary to book some weeks in advance.

I spent the night in Frankfurt, in a hotel near the railway station. I had brought *Hidden Journey* with me and sat in my room reading it afresh, in the light of all that had happened. Harvey's view of Meera as all-knowing, all-encompassing, all-seeing took on a sudden poignancy. 'I will always be here in the garden of your soul,' Meera says to him at one point. 'No force in heaven can shake that now.' But some force obviously had. I remembered how moved, and how convinced, I had been by Harvey's account on first reading it, and thought how bewildering his change of heart had been.

I wandered the streets around the station, looking for somewhere to eat, and realised that I was in the middle of Frankfurt's red-light district. It struck me that where once I might have found something intriguing, even exhilarating, in its seedy, picaresque garishness, now it only heightened my mood of depression. The cold-eyed, predatory hustlers outside the peep-shows and porno-cinemas; the drunks capsised on the pavement or huddling in small groups, passing bottles around – all seemed to be living symptoms of some appalling sickness afflicting humanity.

I sat in a bar drinking coffee – I did not feel like beer – the walls decorated with posters of James Dean, Marilyn Monroe and Elvis; the dead, but ubiquitous icons of popular culture. Only two weeks earlier I had been writing about Dean for a magazine – a previously unpublished set of photographs had appeared. Now I felt faintly disgusted by the posters around me, symbols of an adulation steeped in necrophilia, a veneration of the secular saints of tragedy and self-indulgence, and faintly disgusted with myself for being part of the industry that perpetuated it. What compelled us to seek solace in the doomed, the tragic, the dead?

The next day I took the train north to Limburg. I had booked into a guest-house near Thalheim, and the proprietress was waiting at the station to meet me. Ursula was a cheerful woman in her early fifties, with blonde hair, a musical laugh and an idiosyncratic grasp of driving skills: we sped down the autobahn at 70 m.p.h. without leaving third gear, the engine howling in protest.

She was a divorcee, she explained, who had run her guest-house for tourists until a friend had told her about the growing numbers of pilgrims making their way to see Mother Meera. 'For a long time I did nothing about it, then I tell the Mother Meera home to put me on their list. Huh! I should have done it sooner! Now they are coming from America, Italy, South Africa, all over.' She steered the car on to the raised cats-eyes running along the edge of the road – just for the fun of it – whooping joyfully like a child.

Had she been to see Mother Meera herself?

'Ya, ya. Three times. Very good woman. She is very open, yah? No make the organisation, but she is for everybody. Christian, Jewish, Hindu. This very good. Super.'

That evening Ursula drove me to Thalheim and waved goodbye. The arrangements for *darshan* had changed. Instead of simply turning up at the house, as had previously been the case, people now had to gather in the car-park of the village, to be led to the house in groups of twenty by aides. A German man stood at the door with a clipboard, ticking off names. People who had lost members of their party since booking in were reprimanded fiercely. 'Places are limited,' he said. 'You are denying others.'

The *darshan* room had been extended since my last visit. There were perhaps 120 people there – twice the number of my previous visit: predominantly middle-aged and middle-class, clutching handbags and bandaged in brightly coloured cardigans and anoraks. But for the handful of people sporting Mother Meera badges, it could have been a meeting of the National Trust.

At seven precisely, she entered the room, looking straight ahead. She looked older than I remembered, her features slightly drawn.

She took her seat, under a portrait of her guardian, Mr Reddy. One by one, people began to come forward, kneeling in front of her for a few moments, then turning away. Some had tears in their eyes. I thought about Andrew Harvey's denunciations, then put them out of my mind. His attachment to her, and his subsequent rejection, was to do with his own life; nothing to do with mine. I must decide for myself about this. The familiar doubts and questions began crowding in. Could the Divine manifest in human form? Was she it? I reflected on my family, my job, the constituents of my life, and for a moment it seemed sufficient unto itself. What exactly was I doing here anyway? Every spiritual text I had ever read had talked of the necessity of shedding one's skin, casting aside one's old biography. And the more I thought about this, the more uneasy I felt. I was aware of the fact that much of what I wrote as a journalist seemed artificial, a constructed vision of what the world was about. Journalism often bred those feelings, I found. Now the intensity of the realisation seemed unignorable. But it was the rhythm of my work, the boundaries it drew, which had given my life bearings. The thought that I would find my life pointless, meaningless, without them was a terrifying one.

I sat in my chair and tried to still my mind, but to no avail. My thoughts churned madly. I formulated a question for myself. How should I approach her? And a voice in my head said: Go to her as if she were your own mother. At the thought of my mother, I could feel a wave of sentiment, of love, pass over me. Meera is your mother, the voice said.

I took my place in front of her, rested my head in her hands, then turned my gaze upwards to meet her eyes. I found myself asking her with my eyes: Pour your grace into me, although I have no idea where the thought came from. I returned to my seat and closed my eyes. I could feel the pressure on the sides of my head from where her hands had held me. I was suddenly aware of my own heartbeat, and my eyelids were fluttering uncontrollably. I tried to track the thoughts passing through my mind. I thought of my family and friends, and felt a great love welling up inside me. I thought: My mind is never still, and at that moment I saw an image of a lake, and I held it there. The lake became a mirror, reflecting my thoughts on its surface. It occurred to me: I have spent my life as the watcher of my thoughts, the watcher of my actions; my career as a journalist had given me an excuse to stand on the sidelines of experience, to avoid commitment to anything. I looked in the mirror, and thought of my duplicity and pride, the pride in writing about this, in writing anything. The realisation that as much as I wanted to tell the truth, so I was also weighing the praise, or hostility, with which it would be received made me feel faintly depressed.

Then banality took over. A woman seated in front of me fumbled in her bag and produced a boiled sweet, which she unwrapped and began to suck on noisily. I felt unaccountably angry with her, then suddenly aware of feeling acutely uncomfortable in my seat. I glanced at my watch and was surprised to see that I had been sitting in the room for more than two hours. I had completely lost track of time. Irritably, I wondered how many more people were waiting to come forward. I glanced at the portrait of Mr Reddy on the wall behind Meera and he said: The Divine is always patient. I sat for another hour, lost in thought.

Afterwards, people milled around in the corridor outside, collecting coats and bags. In the adjacent room where you could buy souvenirs of Meera, the German who had stood on the door counting people in now stood behind the counter, collecting money. I asked if I could talk to Mother Meera or her secretary.

The German shrugged. 'You can write a letter, and maybe an appointment will be made.'

Ursula was waiting outside to give me a lift back to her guest-house. It was part of the service. Another of Ursula's guests had come to see Meera, an Indian woman named Krishna. We set off into the darkness. A heavy mist had descended, totally obscuring the passing scenery. The *darshan* with Mother Meera had left me with a feeling of dislocation and weightlessness, as if I had been smoking a particularly potent strain of grass. Ursula seemed to be driving with her foot flat down on the accelerator; it was as if we were travelling through time. I asked Krishna, had she felt anything taking *darshan* with Mother Meera?

'I'm thinking about it,' she said, and fell into silence. Then she began to talk of Sai Baba. 'The first time I went to see him, I can't tell you how disappointed I was, because I'd been asking for this, that and the other thing – give me an interview, give me a sign and so on – and, of course, I got nothing.' She laughed. 'I was like a child, you know; not getting the toys she wanted for Christmas. But now I'm convinced.'

And what had changed her mind?

'Faith, belief, certainty . . .' She paused. The car headlights
reflected back in a solid wall of mist, but Ursula sped on, brow
furrowed against the onrushing darkness. 'You know, Sai Baba
helped me to give up smoking,' said Krishna. 'I used to smoke
forty or fifty a day, a real puffer, always coughing and bronchial
and asthma trouble the whole time. Then one night I dreamed
of him. You know that Sai says nobody ever dreams of him by
accident; that if you dream of him it is because he has come to you
for a reason. Well, in this dream he told me to stop smoking, that I
was killing myself. So I said to him, well, it's an addiction, a habit,
hoping that I could be forgiven for that, you see – let off the hook.
But he made it clear that it was suicide for me. And we Hindus, we
believe that suicide is very bad for your *karma*. It throws you back.
And I wanted a cigarette very badly afterwards, but I thought why
should I wipe out fifty-five years of work on myself with cigarettes,
and I haven't smoked since.'

Back at the house Ursula made coffee and tea.

I asked Krishna again: had she experienced anything during
darshan with Mother Meera?

She gave the question some thought. She said at last, 'To me,
she feels authentic.' She produced some *vibhuti* from her bag, 'from
Sai Baba's ashram', and encouraged us to taste a little. She turned
to Ursula. 'I think you have some pretty strange people here, yes,
with all this talk of God and dreams and miracles.'

'Very *nice* people,' said Ursula with a laugh. 'Everybody who
comes, there is so much gentleness, so much love. I feel I am
wrapped in love.' Tomorrow morning, Ursula said, she would take
me to the station. It was all part of the service.

'Yesterday, I try to call you from the telephone at the station and
I lost seven marks,' said Krishna. 'There was no refund.' We fell
silent considering this, the small dances of *karma*.

'Tomorrow morning,' said Ursula, 'we go there and smash it.'

I returned to London. Shortly afterwards, I received a letter from
Andrew Harvey. It was cordial, but noncommittal. Since turning his
back on Meera, he wrote, he had received letters of vilification, and
even death threats. He had taken the precaution of placing affidavits.
Everything he had to say about Meera, he wrote, had been said in
detail in *Return of the Mother*. I was free to quote liberally from
the book. 'I have nothing at the moment to add, and am fed up
with the horror and violence and lies and would prefer to get on

with my life.' He added a postscript. 'My advice to you is not to believe one word (or syllable of a word) coming out of Thalheim! But you do as you want.'

There was not one word, or one syllable of a word, to believe or disbelieve. I wrote to Mother Meera, requesting some response to Harvey's denunciations, but received no reply. Eventually I spoke to Meera's secretary, Adalakshmi, on the telephone. Mother, she said, was not against any religion, any relationship. 'She says that whatever your inner voice says you must follow it.'

But on this matter, would it be possible, I asked, to speak to Mother herself?

'In this case,' said Adalakshmi, 'Mother wants to be silent.'

One morning in Pondicherry, I decided to cycle to Auroville. At the end of the promenade, the road curved inwards to meet the main road heading north. I turned off and followed a rough, unmade track, which ran a few hundred yards from the beach. The sturdy brick buildings of the town quickly gave way to more rudimentary dwellings, improvised from clay and corrugated iron. Children ran beside me, screaming delightedly and trying to keep pace with me. Three women sat in a circle outside their homes brushing and picking nits out of each other's hair.

At a crossroads, I came upon a large group of people, gathered around an open-sided shelter, fashioned from wood and palm leaves. As I drew closer, I suddenly realised that a body was laid out on an elevated platform under the shelter. It was a middle-aged man, wrapped in a white shroud, heaped with garlands of flowers, surrounded by mourners. Nobody seemed to care that a stranger had happened upon their grief. Here, death, like life, was out in the open for all to see.

I found my way back to the main road, and cycled on towards Auroville. Fields and palm groves stretched out on either side, the occasional small hamlet. A stream of heavy-goods lorries thundered along the road in both directions, furiously sounding their horns at every opportunity, throwing clouds of dust into the faces of small children playing at the roadside. I shuddered to think of the statistics for traffic fatalities.

The dream of Auroville was launched in 1964 during the World Conference of the Sri Aurobindo Society. It was to be the summation of the Mother's ideals of a Utopian community, a place where seekers from all over the world could live a life in the service of Truth. 'The purpose of Auroville,' the Mother announced, 'is to realise human unity.' An area of land of fifteen square-miles was purchased a few miles outside Pondicherry. A French architect, Robert Anger, began drawing up blueprints for the new city, dividing it into four zones – residential, industrial, cultural and international, arranged around the centrepiece of the community, the Matrimandir, or 'Temple of the Mother'. The site was particularly inhospitable; a thick tangle of jungle and uncultivated land; hot and arid; no water supply, no electricity. For the first settlers it must have been rather like building a new world.

By mid–1967, the first colony, Promesse, had already been established on the margins of the site, and in February 1968, the Mother made an inaugural declaration from her room in the Aurobindo ashram. 'Greetings from Auroville to all men of goodwill. Are invited to Auroville all those who thirst for progress and aspire to a higher and truer life.' The first article of the Auroville charter was read out in sixteen languages. 'Auroville belongs to nobody in particular. Auroville belongs to humanity as a whole. But to live in Auroville one must be the willing servitor of the divine Consciousness.'

Construction of the Matrimandir started in 1970. 'The Matrimandir will be the soul of Auroville,' the Mother announced. 'The sooner the soul is there, the better it will be for everybody, and especially for Aurovillians.'

But the first, faltering steps towards Utopianism immediately sank into the disputive quagmire of human nature. Shortly after the death of the Mother a dispute broke out between the Sri Aurobindo Society, who owned the land on which Auroville was being built, and the new colonists over who was in charge. The power struggle was to continue over the next fifteen years, amidst claims and counter–claims of corruption, sexual shenanigans and drug-taking, and periodic bouts of fisticuffs. In 1976, the Society tried to starve out the Aurovillians by withholding funds, and the governments of France, Germany and the United States were obliged to send food-parcels. In 1980, in an attempt to solve the dispute, the Central Government took charge and nationalised Auroville. In 1988, a panel of nine people was set up to administer the project.

The population now numbered some 900 people, drawn from some twenty-seven countries. French, Germans and Indians pre-dominated. To describe Auroville as a 'city' is misleading, for there is no urbanised conurbation, merely a nexus of small sites and communities set amongst fields and forestland. The Auroville directory listed them: Acceptance (residential); Aspiration (education); Auro-Orchard (farming); Felicity; Fertile; Gaia; Grace; Revelation; Sincerity, down to Verité and Vikas – eighty-four in all. There was a choir, dolphin-watching, sundry environmental groups. There were health centres, schools, the manufacture of clothing and furniture. Much emphasis was placed on the principles of renewable energy (solar, biomass and biogas); appropriate technology, eco-friendly methods of agriculture.

Under the Auroville contract, incomers must have enough money to support themselves for a year; to build their own house, and to provide transport. In other words, they were, in the main, professionals with a reasonable income. And for the majority of people, it seemed life in Auroville was a short-term proposition, a temporary Utopian respite from the compromises of bourgeois life.

I cycled along its roads, past well-tended fields, every now and again a residence or centre visible through the trees. Clearly, something remarkable had been achieved, the carving of a community out of such a forbidding wilderness, and yet I could feel myself growing increasingly antagonistic. While I could see Indian people working in the fields, the majority of Europeans seemed to be roaring around ostentatiously on motor cycles. There seemed to be something rather precious about it all; it smacked of the idealistic indulgence of a middle-class, educated elite. I was not surprised to be told that there had been tension between the Westerners and the Indians – a problem someone attributed to 'too much separation'.

There was a visitors' centre with a museum, displaying the various developments and objectives of the community; a gift shop, selling handicrafts and community produce – T-shirts, sandals, and a small selection of books by Sri Aurobindo and the Mother – and a distinctly Westernised cafeteria, such as you might find in a museum or art gallery in Seattle or Amsterdam.

The Matrimandir was set in the middle of a botanical garden, which had been carved out of the forest. The building itself was a huge concrete globe, studded with what looked like portholes, and a cluster of large, golden metallic circles, like satellite dishes. Construction materials were littered around the building. Twenty-six years after construction began, it was still unfinished. It struck me as ugly and preposterous, less like a spiritual shrine than the sort of exercise in triumphalist vanity – a 'cultural' or sports centre, dedicated to some Marxist-Leninist despot – that you might have found in Eastern Europe before the fall of the Wall. A single tree, I thought, would have been more appropriate. 'But just wait till you get inside,' somebody had told me. 'Wait until you see the crystal.' The crystal was the centrepiece of the Matrimandir, which was the centrepiece of Auroville. It was said to be huge; reflecting the light in a certain way, suffusing the interior of the Matrimandir in a glow that was both holy and beautiful. I wanted to savour it for myself. It was only four in the afternoon but a uniformed guard told me the Matrimandir was closed, and would not open again until tomorrow morning. Tomorrow morning I would be gone. The bureaucracy was maddening, impossible.

I cycled down to the beach, thinking a swim would calm my mood. There was a small guest-house at the water's edge, run by the community: a handful of thatched cottages among the palms, a beach bar serving food and fruit juices. Sunburned Westerners, naked children, women with blossoms in their hair. It seemed like a cliché of paradise.

'This,' I said to the woman serving drinks behind the bar, 'is a wonderful place.'

'It is,' she said. She had lived in the community for twenty-three years. 'But you must work; you must contribute something to the community. You must be adaptable. Some people, they are nurse in the morning, teacher in the afternoon; painter in the morning, farmer in the afternoon. There are no rules, no laws. Guidelines, yes. But it depends on everyone having the same vision.' She paused. 'In the Sixties a lot of Americans were coming here for the peace and love trip, and the first years were very hard, a lot of difficulties, and hard work. They left.'

A wicker fence separated the compound from the beach. I walked through the gate on to the sand, submerged myself in the crashing surf, then fell on the beach to dry. A small boy, wearing only a raggedy pair of shorts, appeared beside me, making awkward, pidgin conversation about my country, his country.

'You give me pen,' he said at last.

A pen?

Yes, a pen.

I had left my bag beside the beach bar. 'I don't have one,' I said.

He stood silently, watching me as I made my way back. An Italian woman and her American companion sat at the bar, and we fell into conversation. All of this, the woman said, reminded her of Findhorn, the alternative community in Scotland. 'Have you been there?'

I hadn't.

'I didn't like it so much,' she said. 'And I think they're having problems. They were growing cabbages, which was fine; now they're growing human beings, and that's more difficult. And they're living in caravans; it's like living on a caravan site.'

We shook our heads at the very idea of trying to carve out Utopia on a caravan site in a windswept corner of Scotland. We were sitting under palm trees, with the sand under our feet, drinking hibiscus syrup – 'power juice' – the roar of the ocean less than fifty yards away beyond the wicker fence.

I asked the woman, what brought you here?

She laughed. 'I am looking for happiness.'

And have you found it? I asked.

She looked at me evenly. 'No. Have you?'

There was a shout. It was the small boy from the beach, standing at the gate. Evidently he was not allowed on this side of the fence. I had forgotten about him, but he had not forgotten. He waved at me. 'A pen! A pen.'

I scrabbled in my bag for a biro, trudged across the sand and handed it to him. His face broke into a broad grin and he walked away, waving his thanks, easily pleased.

7

HER MASTER'S VOICE

Dawn rose in a viscous, milky haze as I waited at the bus station at Pondicherry for the bus to take me to Madras. At a ramshackle stand, a man served tea in rough clay cups, and an old woman meticulously swept around my feet with a broom made of twigs. The clouds of mosquitoes, enjoying the last moments of the receding night, were so thick that I bought a packet of sweetly scented *biddhis* and chain-smoked them in the futile hope that the smoke would keep the insects at bay. The 'luxury' bus to Madras took the same road that I had cycled along the day before to Auroville. I watched India stream past the window, and thought of gurus.

In the late Sixties, the failure of political idealism and the burn-out of drugs saw a generation turning inwards in search of deeper, more enduring satisfactions. The embrace of Buddhism – particularly Zen Buddhism – in the Fifties by such Beat writers as Jack Kerouac and Gary Snyder had been crucial in introducing Eastern philosophical teachings to a young Western audience. But the psychedelic revolution opened the door to a mish-mash of occult teachings, Eastern wisdom and esoteric literature: the i ching, *The Tibetan Book of The Dead*, The Way of the Tao, the novels of Hermann Hesse, native American Shamanism.

Lysergic acid – LSD-25 – had been developed in 1943 by a Swiss chemist named Albert Hoffman, and by the mid–Fifties it was being regularly used in California among a small community of psychologists, intellectuals and inner travellers, who christened the mind-altering chemicals 'psychedelics'. Foremost among them was Aldous Huxley, who had first taken mescaline in 1953, famously observing in his account of the experience, *The Doors of Perception*, that he had seen 'eternity in a flower, infinity in four chair-legs and the Absolute in the folds of a pair of flannel trousers'.

The Doors of Perception became one of the primary handbooks of the psychedelic movement, but Huxley took a mandarin view of the experience. Mescaline and LSD were tools for self-transcendence which could bring the user to the realisations of inner bliss, of unity with the Cosmos, known by religious mystics. But this experience, he believed, should be treated with caution, and restricted to the small coterie able to cope with it.

This put him at odds with the great evangelists of psychedelics, Timothy Leary and Ken Kesey. Leary too saw psychedelics as tools of applied mysticism, arguing that 'pursuing the religious life today without using psychedelic drugs is like studying astronomy with the naked eye'. But where Huxley advocated caution, Leary championed what he called 'the American open-to-the-public approach'. While acid proved to offer only a short-term trip to heaven (or hell, depending on your state of mind), for many it opened a window to the East. The jazz musician Maynard Ferguson, who was a regular visitor to Leary's psychedelic commune at Millbrook in upstate New York, went on to become a devotee of Sai Baba.

Richard Alpert, a professor of psychology, the head of Harvard's Centre for Research in Personality, and Leary's closest colleague, was an ardent proselytiser on behalf of LSD until he made a trip to India. There he was taken in hand by a twenty-three-year-old former surfer from Laguna Beach, who introduced Alpert to his own guru. Alpert was confronted by a small, wizened man seated on a blanket, whose opening gambit was to enquire whether Alpert was a rich American. When Alpert replied that he 'did OK', the man immediately asked for a car. 'I had come from a family of fundraisers for the United Jewish Appeal, Brandeis and the Einstein Medical School and I had never seen hustling like this,' Alpert later wrote. Alpert offered him 900 micrograms of Oswald Owsley's best LSD. The guru took it without blinking. Alpert returned to America as Ram Dass, and a new vocation as a spiritual teacher.

Michael Murphy, who started the Esalen Institute in California, a foundation-stone of the 'human potential' movement which would grow through the Seventies, characterised the times thus: 'I've always thought of the Beats as the first wave on the beach. The hippies were the second and now maybe we're getting the third, the *sadhaks*, who will become more experienced meditators. A lot of people have been done in by drugs, I think. Now that has passed its peak. The interest is here to stay but wisdom is coming in.'

By then, a wave of Eastern gurus had already begun to arrive in the

West, their teachings seized on almost as a kind of 'morning-after' cure for a hangover. Foremost among them was the Maharishi Mahesh, who had appeared at the side of the Beatles, draped in white, garlanded in flowers, smiling beatifically, and promising that it was not necessary to pursue a life of renunciation in order to attain enlightenment; through 'transcendental meditation' practitioners could enjoy 'the positive experience of Heavenly Bliss' in their lifetime. The news that you could have your cake and eat it proved immediately attractive. Notwithstanding the fall-out with John Lennon over charges of sexual impropriety (never proved) and the disillusionment of Paul McCartney – 'We thought there was more to him than there was,' McCartney said. 'He's human, we thought at first he wasn't' – the Maharishi went on to build a world-wide organisation, shrewdly dispensing with the Eastern trappings and the references to 'Heavenly Bliss' in favour of flow-charts and statistics demonstrating TM's benefits to health and business efficiency.

In his wake came the Guru Maharaj Ji, the chubby-faced teenaged 'boy god', who made a spectacular public debut in Britain in 1971, when he arrived at the Glastonbury Festival in a white Rolls-Royce (hired for the day by his first English devotees).

'It was very odd,' remembers Michael Eavis, the dairy farmer who runs the Glastonbury Festival. 'Somebody said God had arrived and could we put him on stage, and my thought was: Well, the festival's for everybody really, so why not? By the time he went on stage everybody in the audience was completely stoned out of their minds, and you could hear this ripple going around, "Wow! That's God!" Then he started preaching against drugs, which I think everybody there found a bit disconcerting.'

Maharaj Ji was the youngest son and heir of Param Hans Yogiraj Shri, a spiritual teacher who had built a large following in India, establishing several ashrams, the largest at Hardwar, named Premnagar, 'the city of love'. Maharaj Ji promised instant bliss through a process that he called 'the knowledge', which involved simple meditation and yogic techniques. His Divine Light Mission Organisation quickly flourished in Britain. The former Odeon, East Dulwich, became 'The Palace of Peace', the headquarters for a range of 'divine' businesses, including a haulage business, punningly called GM Motors. Maharaj Ji moved on to America, on a ticket paid for by the writer Alan Watts, establishing residences in Denver and Los Angeles. In 1973 he rented the Houston Astrodome, for

'Millennium '73', describing it as 'the most significant and holy event in the history of mankind'. While a rock band played on stage, the electronic scoreboard flashed 'G-O-D', 'Enjoy! Enjoy!' and 'Sugar Is Sweet, So Are You, Guru Maharaj Ji'.

His most celebrated devotee was Rennie Davis, the former leader of the radical Students for a Democratic Society (SDS). Davis had been a leading campaigner against the war in Vietnam, and one of the 'Chicago 7', along with Abbie Hoffman, Huey Newton and Bobby Seale, who stood trial in 1969, on charges arising out of disturbances at the Democratic Convention. But he had grown disenchanted with radical politics. Davis described the arrival of Guru Maharaj Ji as, 'The greatest event in history . . . If we knew who he was we would crawl across America on our hands and knees to rest our heads at his feet.' The San Francisco *Sunday Examiner* publicly wondered whether Davis had undergone a lobotomy: 'If not,' an article on the op-ed page declared, 'maybe he should try one.'

In 1974, Guru Maharaj Ji married his American secretary. The Divine Light Mission began a steady decline, and the Denver headquarters closed in 1979. In 1992, in a deliberate attempt to distance itself from its Indian origins, and its own history, the name of the organisation was changed to Elan Vitale. Maharaj Ji continues to travel the world, lecturing to private audiences, distributing his teachings on video and tape and politely declining to talk to the media. Even the word 'meditation' is discouraged.

While Westernisation had overtaken both the Maharishi Mahesh and Guru Maharaj Ji they at least avoided the worst taint of scandal. The Indian guru who most inspired ridicule and opprobrium, and tainted the whole idea of Eastern teachers with disrepute, was the man popularly known as 'Bhagwan'. Rajneesh Chandra Mohan came from no particular religious tradition, declaring instead, 'I am the beginning of a totally new religious consciousness.' His teachings bore the traces of an eclectic reading list: Lao Tzu, the Bible, Buddhism, Plato, Freud and, not least, Gurdjieff.

He claimed to have attained enlightenment, spontaneously, at the age of twenty-one, following a prolonged bout of mental illness, and, after working as a teacher of philosophy at the University of Jabalpur, travelled throughout India, lecturing and gathering a small group of followers around him. From 1971 he styled himself as 'Bhagwan', the incarnate God. He established an ashram at Poona, where he taught the techniques of 'dynamic meditation', and by the mid-Seventies the ashram was accommodating up to 6,000 visitors at any one time, the majority of them Westerners, and generating an income from books, fees and donations of up to $200,000 a month.

His following bore all the trappings of a cult. Devotees were encouraged to dress uniformly in orange or red, to wear a *mala* bearing Rajneesh's image, and to accept his authority unconditionally. Central to Rajneesh's appeal was the licence he granted to sexual activity. Rajneesh drew on tantric doctrines to argue that sex was a way to enlightenment, and devotees were encouraged to swap partners and participate in sexual orgies, with predictably deleterious consequencies. The tantric path presupposes a detachment from the snares of *Angst* and possessiveness which bedevil inter-personal relations. Many devotees simply felt abused and unhappy, and sexually transmitted diseases proliferated. (Eventually, the use of condoms and rubber gloves became compulsory.) Rajneesh himself claimed to have made love to more women than any other man on earth, but the accounts of disenchanted disciples suggest that his principal sexual activity was voyeurism.

The antics at Rajneesh's ashram eventually brought him into conflict with the local authorities. When the Indian government revoked the tax-exempt status of the Rajneesh Foundation and attempted to collect $4m in back-taxes, he flitted to America. Declaring, 'I am the Messiah America has been waiting for,' he established a new base on a 64,000-acre farm in Oregon, married a Greek millionaire's daughter to secure American residency and announced his intention to build a holy city, 'Rajneeshpuram', housing up to 50,000 *san–yasins*. Rajneesh quickly began to vanish in clouds of hubris. From 1981 he ceased speaking in public altogether, apparently concentrating instead on amassing personal wealth, and adding to his collection of Rolls-Royces (which eventually numbered ninety-three). Rajneesh made no secret of his enthusiasm for capitalism: 'The materially poor can never be spiritual. Capitalism is not an ideology, it is not imposed on society, it is natural growth. Capitalism simply gives you the freedom to be yourself, that's why I support it.'

As in Poona, the activities at the ashram quickly aroused the hostility of its neighbours. Paranoia began to infect his inner circle, some of whom armed themselves with assault rifles and semi-automatic carbines. Devotees were subject to an increasingly authoritarian regime of personality worship and hard labour, which left many sick and exhausted.

Eventually, Rajneesh brought himself into direct conflict with the local authorities when he tried to rig local elections to increase the political power of the ashram. Under investigation by the police, the FBI and immigration officials, Rajneesh fled Oregon in 1984, *en route* to Bermuda, but was arrested in Charlotte, North Carolina. Among his possessions were thirty-five platinum-and-gold watches and some $58,000 in cash. He was deported to India, where he died in 1990, having announced that he no longer wished to be known as either Rajneesh or Bhagwan.

His ashram at Poona still entertains hordes of Western visitors, and his teachings continue to be published under the name of Osho. In my bag I had a copy of a volume entitled *My Way: The Way of the Clouds*. The author's note makes mention of 'Osho's' birth, the founding of the Poona ashram, the development of his philosophy, and his death. But curiously, it makes no mention at all of his experiences in America, the armed guards, the platinum watches and the pursuit by the forces of law and order – even of the fact that he was once known as Rajneesh. The bad old Bhagwan has simply ceased to exist.

Tibetan Buddhism, too, had seen its share of scandals. The first teacher to establish Tibetan Buddhist centres in Britain and America was Chogyam Trungpa, known as 'the roaring tiger of crazy wisdom'. Trungpa taught in the tantric, Vajrayana, or 'diamond vehicle' tradition of Buddhism – sometimes characterised as 'the expressway to enlightenment', because it is believed that by following the teachings a student may attain enlightenment within a single lifetime. The eleventh Trungpa Tulku, and head of the Surmang monasteries in Eastern Tibet, Chogyam Trungpa followed the Dalai Lama into exile in 1959, when he was just twenty. A brilliant scholar, he was awarded a scholarship to Oxford, where he studied comparative religion and philosophy. He became the first Tibetan to receive British citizenship, and in 1968 he founded the Samye-Ling Tibetan centre in Scotland – the first Tibetan-Buddhist centre in the West. Trungpa quickly acclimatised himself to the more liberal mores of his new home. He returned his monastic vows, and married an eighteen-year-old English girl, then moved to America where he founded that country's first Tibetan meditation centre, in Colorado, and, later, the Naropa teaching institute.

Trungpa was nobody's idea of the ascetic and saintly holy man.

He walked with a pronounced limp, the result of a car accident when he drove into the window of a joke-and-novelty shop in Newcastle. Explaining to his pupil, the poet Allen Ginsberg, that 'I come from a long line of eccentric Buddhists,' he ran his organisation like a medieval court, surrounding himself with an elite bodyguard and sometimes amusing himself and his followers by dressing in a pseudo-military uniform of his own design. Hierarchy is important, he once explained, because it creates a setting for the development of compassion and devotion. In a good society, the upper class displays compassion to its inferiors; the lower class maintains devotion to its superiors. Hierarchy, Trungpa argued, was necessary to cultivate these virtues.

'The real function of the guru,' he once said, 'is to insult you.' In Trungpa's case, this often meant turning up late for teachings, or sometimes not bothering to turn up at all; giving teachings reeking of alcohol and exercising virtual *droit de seigneur* over female students – one of whom would later describe him as 'a spiritual stud'. But passion, Trungpa argued, was a legitimate expression of basic goodness and of experiencing enlightenment; he was fond of referring to arousing *bodhicitta* – the seed of enlightenment in us all – as 'tickling the clitoris of the heart'.

His teachings demonstrated an astute understanding of the culture that had shaped his students. His most famous book, *Cutting Through Spiritual Materialism*, expounded on the danger of regarding the goal of 'enlightenment' as just another consumer commodity, and how the spiritual search can itself become ensnared in illusory ideas of status and self-esteem – a way of reinforcing the ego even as one attempts to understand and train it.

Trungpa died in 1987, from complications arising from alcoholism. Before his death he appointed his favourite disciple Thomas Rich, an American who had taken the name Osel Tendzin, as his successor. Osel later died of Aids, having allegedly passed the virus on to several of his students.

Among many Buddhists, Chogyam Trungpa was regarded as a wayward embarrassment – a symbol of the dangers that can arise when Eastern teachers are exposed to the glamour of Western personality worship. To his students, however, he remains an exemplar of the tradition of 'crazy wisdom', where a teacher frequently acts with an apparently cavalier disregard for any moral, ethical or social propriety – 'completely shaking your programme', as one former

pupil of Trungpa puts it – in order to force the pupil to realise
the true nature of self. Not all of Trungpa's students followed his
bidding with an easy conscience. 'A lot of people at Naropa would
do anything that Trungpa told them to do without question,' one
former student remembers, 'but they didn't always like it.' But if
some women felt coerced into sexual relations for fear of incurring
his disapproval, their disgruntlement was never expressed in the law
courts; in the Seventies, the legal concept of sexual harassment was
yet to come.

The dubious honour of being the first Tibetan lama to face a
Western court action was to fall instead to Sogyal Rinpoche. Widely
regarded as one of the most gifted and enlightened teachers of Tibetan
Buddhism in the West, Sogyal left Tibet in 1958, a year before the
Dalai Lama. He was educated at university in Delhi, and at Trinity
College, Cambridge, arriving in London in the late Seventies, where
he began to gather a small group of students around him. In 1981
the Rigpa Fellowship (Rigpa means 'innermost nature of mind') was
founded to propagate his teachings.

In 1992 Sogyal achieved worldwide fame with the publication of *The
Tibetan Book of Living and Dying*, his interpretation of the traditional
Tibetan Buddhist ideas on death. Rightly praised as a masterpiece, it
has since been widely adopted by hospice organisations and doctors
working with the dying. Psychologists and philosophers have queued
to commend it not simply for its insights into death, but as a complete
blueprint for an ethical and compassionate life.

Three years after the publication of the book, Sogyal was served
with a law suit in California, alleging that, using the justification
of his spiritual status, the lama had sexually and physically abused a
female student, turning her against her husband and her family, and
seeking $10m in damages. The case was subsequently settled out of
court, but not before other female students of Sogyal came forward
to say that they too had felt obliged to sleep with him in the belief that,
because he was their teacher, he had their best interests at heart.

The case galvanised a wider debate within the Western Buddhist
community about the role of Tibetan teachers in the West, and the
conflicts that may arise between an ancient spiritual tradition and
contemporary standards of secular behaviour. How does a religion
dating back hundreds of years, and coming from a country rooted in
feudalism, adapt itself to modern society where political correctness
is high on the agenda? More than anything, the law suit crystallised

the often confusing conflict between ideas of 'devotion' without limits in the Eastern tradition and our ideas of 'individual rights' in the West.

Like Chogyam Trungpa, Sogyal Rinpoche is a lama, but not a celibate monk. He is unmarried, and there are, theoretically, no constraints on his private behaviour other than the third Buddhist precept not to engage in 'sexual misconduct'. Also like Trungpa, Sogyal claims to teach in the Vajrayana tradition. This teaching is founded on a relationship which demands the total trust of the pupil in the teacher's selfless motives – and total integrity on the part of the teacher. The relationship between teacher and pupil can often be one of extreme emotional and, in some cases, even physical intimacy – a relationship of 'no boundaries', in which sex may sometimes, but by no means necessarily, play a part. In short, it demands a surrender of self which can seem anathema to Western ideas of individuality, equality and free will.

In his book on Vajrayana, *The Double Mirror*, Stephen Butterfield, a former student of Chogyam Trungpa, writes:

> Without the guru, enlightenment is impossible. The guru is the Buddha. Anything that happens to you, whether good or bad, is the guru's blessing and compassion. If it is good, be grateful to the guru; if it is bad, then it helps to wake you up and so you should also be grateful to the guru.

In this context, scepticism is defined as neurosis; and actually to sever oneself from the teacher is to risk entering '*vajra* hell' – a state of subtle, continuous emotional pain much worse than divorce. Insanity, Butterfield writes, is one of the risks that comes from Vajrayana.

Even before the law suit against Sogyal Rinpoche there had been concerns about the conduct of Buddhist teachers, both Western and Asian, in the West. In 1993, when an organisation called The Network for Western Buddhist Teachers met the Dalai Lama in Dharamsala, the matter of sexual ethics among teachers was high on the agenda. In the course of that meeting the Dalai Lama agreed that miscreant teachers threatened to bring the whole teaching of Buddhism into disrepute. Misbehaviour should be publicised, he said, and errant teachers made 'regretful and embarrassed' about their conduct. 'As the expression goes,' he added, 'someone who has already fallen down cannot help someone else stand up.'

According to Tibetan teachings, students should not enter lightly into a relationship with a teacher. The Dalai Lama has suggested it can take as long as fifteen years for a student to determine which teacher is right for them. And he has been quite specific on the subject of tantric teachings. Historically, he says, there have been teachers who may have engaged in conduct 'which appears disgraceful, but which may have had some kind of deep realisation or knowledge of the long-term benefit to the person involved'. He has suggested that a good test of the qualifications of a tantric master who is beyond attachment and the temptations of self-gratification is whether the master can drink alcohol and urine with equal indifference. Asked which Tibetan teachers were of a sufficiently high level to do this, the Dalai Lama replied, 'As far as I know – zero.' In *The Return of the Mother* Andrew Harvey writes:

> I believe that we are at the end of the guru system and that its current abuses disqualify it from the business of serious spiritual transformation. The next five years will see a blizzard of financial and sexual scandals which I am certain will make this point painfully clear even to those who now believe implicitly in the guru system and are prepared to fight dirty to preserve it.

Indeed, it was depressing to reflect on these stories of vaunted promise and deep disappointment. Clearly, the longing for some panacea for the pain and confusion of modern life had been the Trojan horse that countless charlatans had used to ride into the West, to dupe and swindle countless credulous devotees.

Rajneesh, it seems, was a wise man, whose judgements and talents were corrupted by power and the adulation of his followers. Unthinking devotion seemed as dangerous to the guru as it was to the follower. In pursuing a romantic idea of the 'spiritual perfection' of the teacher, devotees seemed all too often prepared to leave their powers of discrimination, even basic common sense, at the ashram door. The moral, surely, was that a teacher is only as enlightened as his acts. There will always be charlatans ready to exploit the gullible, just as there will always be the gullible whose insecurities or genuine hunger for knowledge will make them ripe for exploitation. But the fact that some gurus are charlatans does not mean that *all* gurus are charlatans. And to dismiss all Eastern teachers as deluded fantasists or rank opportunists is the height of folly.

In his illuminating book *Feet of Clay*, the psychologist Anthony Storr speculates on whether the extraordinary views that some gurus have of themselves may be the consequence of schizophrenia, or manic-depression. In clinical terms, Storr writes, the voices, messages, the messianic beliefs of the mystic, the sense that they are somehow special or chosen, the propounding of theories about the universe that have no basis in scientific fact, are all classic symptoms of delusional behaviour. Yet such characteristics, of course, are also the foundation stones for most of the world's great belief systems.

Storr makes the point that idiosyncratic belief systems that are shared by only a few adherents are likely to be regarded as delusional. Belief systems that may be just as irrational but which are shared by millions are called world religions. If there were only a hundred believing Christians in the world, he writes – wedded to doctrines of the Virgin Birth, the Resurrection and the immortality of the soul – we would think of them as eccentric.

Tradition and belief concretise the scientifically implausible. It is an oft-repeated saw that if Jesus Christ wasn't the son of God then he was almost certainly mad for claiming he was. If Sai Baba is not an avatar, then he too is either mad, or a charlatan. Mystical experience, like faith itself, is not amenable to reason. But then nor are most of the defining experiences of being a human being: love, loyalty, self-sacrifice, the feeling of being inexpressibly moved by a piece of music, a painting, a smile. Everyone is familiar with the sense, however fleeting, of some inexplicable yet tangible unity with the world, a momentary sense of being in a state of grace, as if every atom in your body was smiling – 'intimations of immortality', as Wordsworth put it.

Charles Kingsley wrote:

When I walk the fields, I am oppressed now and then with an innate feeling that everything I see has a meaning, if I could but understand it. And this feeling of being surrounded with truths which I cannot grasp amounts to indescribable awe sometimes . . . Have you not felt that your real soul was imperceptible to your mental vision, except in a few hallowed moments?

Aldous Huxley touched on this conundrum in *The Perennial Philosophy*. The nature of the 'ultimate reality' – described and acknowledged by mystics in all the great religions – is such that it cannot be immediately apprehended except by those who have chosen to fulfil certain conditions, making themselves 'loving, pure in heart and poor in spirit'. Only by making physical experiments, Huxley wrote, can we discover the intimate nature of matter and its potentialities. So only by making psychological and moral experiments can we discover the intimate nature of the mind and its potentialities. To realise them we must fulfil certain conditions and obey certain rules that experience has shown empirically to be valid.

The most important of these is the experience of 'ego-lessness', for central to every mystical tradition is the belief that it is the ego that obstructs our vision of the truth – which separates 'thou' from 'that'. To know God, Huxley wrote, it is necessary for the self to die, and with it the separative life of craving and self-interest, of egocentric thinking, feeling, wishing and acting. (Huxley, of course, was ridiculed for his interest in mysticism, scorned by the literary intelligentsia as soft-headed, a squandered talent; Christopher Isherwood suffered the same fate for his espousal of Ramakrishna. Their indifference to the criticism made me admire them more.)

Anthony Storr advances the theory that the illumination of the guru often follows a period of acute psychic distress; that new ideas spring from the chaos of the mind, as an answer to the problems of the mind. But you do not need to be a mystic, or a psychologist, to see this. Sometimes it takes a crisis to make us realise the truth about our lives, ourselves. A heart attack may tell us that the life we are leading is too stressful; the discovery of betrayal in a relationship may bring to a head long-running and suppressed grievances or misunderstandings.

Crisis can be catharsis, a prelude to a necessary change. I thought back to my conversations with George in Sera monastery, about 'revulsion for *samsara*', and how a weariness and frustration with the world is often the first step on the path to change. When the Buddha gathered his first disciples around him in Deer Park, he did not start by teaching about the beauty of enlightenment or liberation, but with the First Noble Truth – the Truth of Suffering; that discontentment, unhappiness and disappointment are universal, that all the things we desire and cherish, not least our own lives, must eventually come to an end, and that attachment is therefore futile. The essence of Buddhist teaching is to reflect on the nature of this suffering, and through this reflection to come to terms with the transience of all things. To surrender the illusion, the pretence, of permanence –

the clinging of the ego – is painful, but ultimately less painful than the illusion itself.

To change the self it is necessary to confront the truth about oneself. This too is painful, but from that purging comes realisation. It occurred to me that this small but universal truth was a paradigm for the great religious myths of destruction and regeneration: the Vedic Kali Yuga, and the Christian Apocalypse, in which turmoil, destruction and suffering are seen as the necessary prelude to a new order of peace and harmony. Death, and rebirth. Out of darkness will come light.

In *Cosmos, Chaos and the World to Come*, the historian Norman Cohn suggests that the belief that the order of the cosmos will triumph over the disorder of chaos is one of the fundamental convictions of mankind. It is, perhaps, a necessary conviction, for without hope we would not go on. The Christian revivals sweeping America and the Far East, the faddism of the 'New Age', the rising interest in Eastern spirituality as we approach the millennium could all be seen as symptoms of the increasing uncertainty of the modern world, and the search for some confirmation that the order of the cosmos will triumph over the disorder of chaos: a collective nervous breakdown of the old systems, giving birth to a renewed search for consolation, meaning and deliverance.

I had never seen a city as dirty as Madras. I found a hotel on a small side-turning off Triplicane High Road, a busy commercial thoroughfare lined with wedding shops and haberdashers, which, after nightfall, took on the appearance of an enormous squatters' camp. Outside the shops selling textiles, fancy goods and religious tracts, whole families squatted on blankets thrown on the pavements, their laundry draped over walls, cooking utensils scattered around them. Men pissed on street corners and lifted their dhotis to crap against walls. People with dismembered bodies and vacant eyes stared as I threaded past. I felt oppressed by the squalor, exhausted by India's intractability, its hopelessness, its endless demands on one's patience and charity.

My hotel was in the Muslim quarter. There were political meetings on the street, police brandishing truncheons on the corners, excited shouting, the constant blare and jangle of music and the sound of firecrackers exploding. Out walking one evening, I was kicked hard on the legs by a man, who melted into the crowd as I turned. It was the first time I had experienced any hostility directed against me in India. In my hotel, young men loitered on the landing, watching silently as I padlocked my door each morning. I could never decide whether they worked in the hotel, or were there for some more nefarious purpose. They looked disconcerted when I smiled. I returned each evening half expecting to find that my hotel room had been looted, but it never was.

It was a Sunday. I walked to the beach, across a river – a slick brown mess, with a stench so overpowering that I could feel the nausea tugging at the bottom of my throat. At the promenade police were holding people back to let a procession pass. It was two or three hundred strong, mostly youths and schoolchildren, the boys in uniform blue shirts, the girls in blue saris, superintended by bossy adults. They were chanting and handing out leaflets, calling for moral rearmament, a return to family values and faith in God. A rearguard action, I thought, in the face of encroaching Western materialism.

It was a familiar paradox, but one that constantly intrigued me. Everywhere I had gone in India I had met Westerners, not unlike myself, in search of some antidote to the materialism and despair of their own culture – in search of some corroboration of Aurobindo's vision of India as the spiritual engine-room of the world. And everywhere too there was evidence of India's eagerness to embrace the values of Western consumerism. Since 1991, when the government of P.V. Narasimha Rao liberalised economic controls, Western goods, and investment, had been flooding into India. It was a curious transaction. India had given the world its ancient truths. The West was offering motor cycles, cosmetics, computers, the glitter and jangle of the commercial market-place in return.

In bars and hotel rooms across India you could see the Western ideal being transmitted on Star television, with its shoddy American and Australian soap-operas and glib Hollywood fantasies, its endless cycle of commercials for the products of the global supermarket which few in India could afford, but more and more now dreamed of. Among these commercials was one prepared by an organisation called the International Advertising Association, with a strident message: 'Your Right to Choose', educating this new, entranced audience in the role of advertising as the lubricant of a consumer society. To the sophisticated eye it had all the crudeness of propaganda. In a Madras newspaper I read an evaluation by a government psychiatrist predicting that India would soon be suffering the same incidence of mental illness as the West. The shelves of American self-help books in Madras's largest bookshop, offering advice on maximising the power of positive thinking and contacting your inner-child, suggested that the problem was bringing its own 'cure'.

The beach was a heaving carnival of humanity, bleeding into the green ocean. A line of cargo ships queued on the distant horizon. Pedlars moved among the crowds selling food and plastic toys, including an ingenious catapulted boomerang. I bought one, found a space on the sand and sent the boomerang soaring into the sky and circling over the crowd, until a group of small boys confiscated it for their own pleasure.

The procession had evidently come to an end. Freed from their duties as the praetorian guard of moral rearmament, a flock of schoolgirls in blue saris floated across the beach like gorgeous butterflies, their laughter like music, and dipped themselves tentatively in the sea.

I had come to Madras to explore one of the most intriguing stories about this transaction between East and West – the story of the philosopher and teacher Krishnamurti, who, at the beginning of the century, was hailed as 'the vehicle' for the great world teacher, Maitreya, and who subsequently turned his back on his anointed role, in the process denouncing the very idea of guru-dom.

It is a story that begins with Madame Helena Blavatsky, the co-founder and presiding spirit of the Theosophical Society. Brash, mercurial, a vivid and fascinating mixture of genius, huckster and fabulist, Blavatsky ranks among the most extraordinary figures of the nineteenth century. Perhaps more than any other single individual, she was responsible for introducing the spiritual teachings of the East to the West by promoting theosophy as a syncretism of the world's great religions into one unified philosophy. Her ideas of a 'Hidden Brotherhood', or Hierarchy of Spiritual Masters, watching over man's evolutionary progress, have been echoed in many of the beliefs of what we now call the New Age Movement. Echoed too in the teachings and prophecies of the congenial Mr Creme.

A life-size marble statue of Helena Blavatsky stands in the great hall at the headquarters of the Theosophical Society at Adyar, two miles south along the coast from Madras. The statue is of a stolid, rotund woman, primly buttoned in Victorian dress; she has a currant-bun face, eyes staring impassively into the middle-distance. She is seated. Beside her stands Colonel Henry S. Olcott, the erstwhile civil-war soldier and journalist and Blavatsky's co-conspirator in the spread of theosophy, a portly, bearded gentleman in a frock coat, his hand resting in a fraternal fashion on Blavatsky's shoulder. A motorised rickshaw had carried me from the clamour of Madras to the Theosophical Society estate. At the gate, the inevitable guard in a khaki uniform scrutinised my letter of introduction and nodded me past. A long, winding avenue of palm and tamarind trees led to a large handsome whitewashed building in the colonial style. The atmosphere was somnolent and still. I had made an appointment with the secretary of the TS, but I was early. A factotum in a white dhoti gestured me into the cool surroundings of the great hall and pointed to a wicker plantation chair, set under a gently turning fan.

Plaques set in the wall commemorated the strands of esoteric teaching from which theosophy had been woven: Quetzalcoatl; Ashtaroth; Asshur; Freemasonry; Moses; Guatama Buddha; Christ; Sri Krishna; Shinto; Islam. And the legends: There Is No Religion Higher Than Truth, and Universal Brotherhood. As I waited, two women arrived and, bossily supervised by a man in a crisp white shirt, began to arrange chairs around a large circular cloth on the floor, decorated with the theosophical symbol of the six-pointed star, evidently in preparation for some form of ceremony. 'That side,' said the man, 'straighter, straighter,' as the women carefully smoothed the cloth, under the beady gaze of Blavatsky.

She was born Helena Petrovna von Hahn, in Ekaterinoslav, Ukraine on 12 August 1831. Her father Peter Alexeyevitch was an army colonel, descended from minor German nobility; her mother, Helena Andreyevna de Fadeev, was a romantic novelist, who died when Helena was nine. She was raised by her maternal grandparents. The young Helena, it seems, was a headstrong and highly imaginative child, a keen reader and an accomplished pianist.

According to her sister, Vera, even as a child Helena was subject to clairvoyant powers.

For Helena, all nature seemed animated with a mysterious life of her own. She heard the voice of every object and form, whether organic or inorganic, and claimed awareness and being, not only for some mysterious powers visible and audible to herself alone in what was to everyone else empty space, but even for visible but inanimate things, such as pebbles, moulds and pieces of decaying phosphorescent timber.

In 1848, at the age of sixteen, Helena married Nikifor Blavatsky, the vice-governor of Yerevan province in Armenia. Her husband was thirty-nine. It was evidently not a happy marriage, for within a matter of weeks, having refused her husband conjugal rights, Helena had fled the marital home, and was *en route* to Constantinople on a cargo ship. It was the beginning of an extraordinarily peripatetic life that over the next twenty years would take her through Europe, Asia and America.

Like her contemporary Gurdjieff – another self-styled spiritual teacher about whom argument still rages as to whether he was a genius or a charlatan (the likely answer is probably something of both) – the fine details of Blavatsky's travels are shrouded in mystery and often fanciful speculation. It is said that she toured as a concert pianist; worked as a decorator to the Empress Eugenie, managed an ink factory and even rode bareback in a circus. She is said to have consorted with bandits in Mexico and Red Indians in Canada, and there is some evidence that she fought with Garibaldi against the papal army in the Battle of Mentana in 1867, in the course of which she sustained a serious injury to her arm. She had a taste for foul-smelling cheroots and a volatile temper – believed to have been at least partly attributable to the cystitis that plagued her throughout her life. But she was also given of an extraordinary personal magnetism, with a particular gift for story-telling and self-publicity.

More pertinent to her life as a theosophist was a compendious knowledge of occultism and mysticism, the seeds of which had been implanted early in her life. Her great-grandfather, Prince Pavel Dolgorukii, was a Rosicrucian Mason, and as an adolescent the young Helena would spend many hours in his library. After leaving her husband, she travelled extensively in the company of an American artist and orientalist named Albert Rawson, who had some association with Egyptian Masonry and Rosicrucianism. In Cairo she was associated with the occultist 'Max Theon' (Mirra Alfassa's early associate). In later years she would tell a friend, Charles Johnston, that she had known 'adepts of many races, from Northern and Southern India, Tibet, Persia, China, Egypt; of various European nations, Greek, Hungarian, Italian, English; of certain races of South America . . .' She was familiar with Sufism, the Kabbala, necromancy, astrology, voodoo, crystal-gazing and spiritualism, as well as Buddhism and the Vedas – an eclectic range of enthusiasms which suggests that Madame Blavatsky has some entitlement to the claim of being the world's first spiritual tourist.

Out of this esoteric brew Blavatsky distilled her revelation of what she described as the Hierarchy of *mahatmas*, or spiritual 'Masters', that was to become the foundation stone of her philosophy and ultimately lead to the forming of the Theosophical Society. These 'Masters', Blavatsky claimed, were not spirits, but 'living men', beyond the laws of physics, for whom 'the highest interest of humanity, as a whole, is their special concern', and who had guided the course of man's evolution over millennia. Foremost among the 'Masters' were two men whom Blavatsky called Morya and Koot Hoomi. The names, she said, were pseudonyms, designed to protect the Masters' privacy from the inquisitive or the sceptical. They were Indians, but lived, Blavatsky claimed, in a remote valley in Tibet. Etchings of the time, drawn from her descriptions, and those of other theosophists who claimed to be in contact with them, suggest that both men were fine-featured, bearded fellows with suitably saintly expressions.

There is some doubt as to exactly where Blavatsky first encountered the Masters in person. According to Blavatsky herself, the Master Morya had long been a frequent visitor in her dreams, but her first physical encounter with him took place in 1851. Constance Wachtmeister, the widow of a Swedish diplomat, and a close friend of Blavatsky, described this encounter as taking place in the month of July, during London's Great Exhibition. Blavatsky, it seems, was travelling as the companion to a Russian countess. Walking along the street one day Blavatsky supposedly saw a tall 'Hindu' in the company of an Indian prince. She immediately recognised him as the figure from her dreams. The next day, strolling in Hyde Park, the Hindu, whom Blavatsky called Morya, approached her, explained that he had come to London on a mission with the prince and that he required Blavatsky's co-operation in an important work which he was about to undertake. To prepare for the task, he said, she must journey to Tibet.

(Mysteriously, Blavatsky would later claim in her diaries that this encounter had actually taken place a month later in the improbable location of Ramsgate. Constance Wachtmeister would attempt, somewhat implausibly, to explain away the discrepancy by saying that the story of the London encounter was a blind 'so that anyone casually taking up her book would not know where she had met her master'.)

Most people, perhaps, would think twice about making an expedition to the other side of the world on such a flimsy premise, but Blavatsky was evidently made of stronger stuff. Following the Master's instructions, she made her way east once more, where, she would later claim, she resided in the vicinity of Shigatse, and was initiated into the esoteric mysteries of Tibetan Buddhism. Blavatsky's fascination with Tibetan Buddhism had possibly been aroused as a young girl by her exposure to the Kalmuck tribe, which practised Tibetan Buddhism in a region near Astrakhan. Her maternal grandfather was the government-appointed administrator for the Kalmuck settlers in the area. The Mahayana Buddhist teachings of Tibet became a central plank in Blavatsky's ideas. In later life, it is known that Blavatsky visited the Himalayan principality of Ladakh – known as 'Little Tibet' – and also Sikkim, where she would also have been exposed to Tibetan Buddhism teachings. But whether she actually penetrated Tibet itself is, like so many of the details of her life, open to question.

Not only was the terrain notoriously inhospitable, but foreigners were not welcomed by the Tibetans, who were intensely protective of their culture and suspicious of outsiders. Following Blavatsky's death, a British soldier, a Major-General Murray, testified in writing that he had encountered Blavatsky near the Tibet-India border in the mid-1850s, but Murray's account has never been independently corroborated.

What is known is that by 1871 Blavatsky was to be found in Cairo, studying snake-charming, founding a short-lived 'Society of Spiritists' and smoking hashish in the company of the American Albert Rawson. In a memoir published in Frank Leslie's *Popular Monthly*, in February 1892, Rawson recalled Blavatsky remarking, 'Hasheesh multiplies one's life a thousandfold. My experiences are as real as if they were ordinary events of actual life. Ah! I have the explanation. It is a recollection of my former existences, my previous incarnations. It is a wonderful drug, and it clears up a profound mystery.'

In 1873 she arrived in New York, where she supported herself working as a seamstress. Blavatsky's arrival in New York was timely.

Like Britain, America had been convulsed with a fad for spiritualism and table-rapping, and it was through spiritualism that she was to meet the man who was to become her partner, confidant – and sponsor – in the next, and most important, phase of her life. Colonel Henry Steel Olcott had developed an interest in spiritualism by way of consolation for an unhappy divorce and the uncertainties of advancing middle age.

In 1874, Olcott wrote a series of articles for a New York newspaper about strange goings-on at a farmhouse in Vermont belonging to the Eddy family, where, it seemed, a variety of spirits were being 'conjured' by the three Eddy children. It was at the Vermont farmhouse that Olcott met Blavatsky, apparently drawn there by reading Olcott's newspaper reports.

Blavatsky immediately impressed Olcott by introducing into the seances the materialised spirits of her uncle, a Kurdish warrior and a Persian merchant. Olcott quickly fell under Blavatsky's formidable spell; she, after all, did not deal in mere disembodied voices from 'the other side' as most spiritualists did; she had the voices of her own living 'Masters' to draw on, and a deeper knowledge of the occult – the esoteric science concerned with 'the hidden laws of the universe'. In 1875 she and Olcott founded the Theosophical Society – with Olcott as president and Blavatsky as 'Corresponding Secretary' – as a forum for disseminating 'knowledge of laws which govern the universe', and promoting the teaching of Eastern religions in the West.

The Concise Oxford Dictionary defines theosophy as 'Any of various philosophies professing to achieve a knowledge of God by spiritual ecstasy, direct intuition or special relationships'. The word originated among the third-century philosophers of Alexandria, descended from Pythagoras, Plato and the Neo-Platonists. Blavatsky, more fancifully, described it as ancient teachings communicated by 'the angels' – meaning not angels in the Christian sense, but living men in higher states of consciousness.

The objectives of the Society were set out as follows:

1. To form a nucleus of the Universal Brotherhood of Humanity without distinction of race, creed, sex, caste or colour.

2. To encourage the study of Comparative Religion, Philosophy and Science.

3. To investigate unexplained laws of Nature and the powers latent in man.

The essence of Blavatsky's conception of theosophy was contained in her first book, *Isis Unveiled*, published in 1877. According to Blavatsky, this was partly her own work, and partly written under the psychic influence of the 'Masters'; some sections of the book, she claimed, simply 'appeared' on her desk, handily materialised by the Masters overnight while she slept. (In her subsequent work, *The Secret Doctrine* (1888), she would invoke the words of Montaigne to describe the influence of the Masters: 'I have here made only a nosegay of culled flowers, and have brought nothing of my own but the string that ties them.')

Isis Unveiled is divided into two sections, 'Science' and 'Theology'. In the first section, Blavatsky challenges Darwin, Hume and Huxley, by arguing that there are laws of nature, accessible to occult wisdom, which exist beyond the proof of scientific materialism. The second section is an essay in comparative religion, in which Blavatsky argues that Buddhism is the wisdom doctrine by which science and religion can be united.

Blavatsky had emerged at a critical juncture, a time not so unlike our own, when traditional certainties were subject to question. The rise of scientific rationalism, and Darwin's theory of evolution, appeared fatally to undermine the authority of Christian teachings founded on faith. It was no longer possible to believe the world had been created in six days. But while science appeared to have answered the fundamental questions of creation and evolution, it could, as yet, provide no answers to the timeless and worrying questions about creation, life's purpose, the meaning of death and the possibility of an after-life. Blavatsky's quasi-scientific theories of the origins of man, her teachings of a hidden Brotherhood, which has existed throughout history to oversee the spiritual development and evolution of the planet, and theosophy's emphasis on universal brotherhood – its idea of 'the One Life' – not a sectarian God, struck a nerve.

> A religion in the true and only correct sense [Blavatsky wrote] is a bond uniting men together – not a particular set of dogmas and beliefs. Now religion *per se* in its widest meaning is that which binds not only *all* men, but also *all* beings and *all* things in the entire universe into one grand whole.

She also refuted the theories of 'social Darwinism' which had grown from Darwin's teachings on evolution:

> The pseudo-law of the survival of the fittest is a 'pretended' law indeed, as far as the human family is concerned, and a fiction of the most dangerous kind. 'Self-preservation', on these lines, is indeed and in truth a sure, if slow suicide, for it is a policy of mutual homicide, because men by descending to its practical application among themselves merge more and more by a retrograde reinvolution into the animal kingdom . . . Once this axiomatic truth is proved to all men, the same instinct of self-preservation only directed into its true channel will make them turn to altruism – as their surest policy of survival.

Rather than flatly contradicting Darwin, Blavatsky argued that he had not gone far enough, and that in formulating a theory of biological evolution he had neglected to consider the mental, creative and visionary aspect of the human race – consciousness. In her *magnum opus*, *The Secret Doctrine*, Blavatsky trumped Darwin's ideas of evolution through natural selection by introducing her own phantasmagorical theories about mankind's origins in spiritual form on the moon, and his evolution on earth through a series of 'root races'. The first of these root races, she claimed, had been little more than multiplying cells, which had gradually evolved into physical forms, helped to a higher stage of development by the benign intervention of a group called the Lords of the Flame, who had descended from Venus nineteen million years ago. Then came the age of Lemuria which had given way to the age of Atlantis, each destroyed by man's own stupidity or by natural disasters.

According to Blavatsky, each age experienced a cycle of darkness and light, modelled on the alternation of day and night. Borrowing from the Vedas, she placed modern man in the Kali Yuga (the dark age). This, said Blavatsky, was the age of the Fifth Root Race, which had started in 3102 BC, with the death of Krishna; it would be followed by man's evolution through the Sixth Root Race, and culminate in the Seventh, when mankind would finally realise its innate divinity and become a race of God-men. Borrowing from Buddhist legend, she saw this golden age coinciding with the emergence of a great teacher, Lord Maitreya. Maitreya, she wrote in *The Secret Doctrine*, was the secret name of the Fifth Buddha, and the Kalki avatar of the Brahmins – 'the last messiah, who will come at the culmination of the Great Cycle'. Blavatsky was always very careful not to specify exactly when this would be – although those who came after her would not be quite so cautious, as we shall see.

The colourful implausibility of Blavatsky's ideas about Moon-beings and Venusians, Atlantis and Lemuria, was no impediment to her theories about man's evolution towards spiritual perfection receiving a respectful hearing, at least among some. The Theosophical Society would eventually embrace such disparate sympathisers as Darwin's collaborator, Alfred Russel Wallace, the inventor Thomas Edison, and W.B. Yeats, as well as the modernist painters Kandinsky and Mondrian, heeding Blavatsky's prophecy that in the twenty-first century, 'This earth will seem a paradise compared to what it is now,' and that, 'Literature, music and art are the first and most sensitive spheres in which the spiritual revelation will be felt.'

Both Kandinsky and Mondrian were inspired by the idea of exploring what Kandinsky called 'the spiritual possibilities of art', employing abstract designs as symbols to express the higher levels of reality. 'Through theosophy,' Mondrian wrote, 'I became aware that art could provide a transition to the finer regions which I will call the spiritual realm.'

The Theosophical Society was to become a seed-bed for the growing enthusiasm for Eastern teaching in the West. The Buddhist Lodge of the TS, for example, was later to become the British Buddhist Society, under the presidency of Christmas Humphries, author and High Court judge. Humphries was an early mentor of the young Alan Watts, who in turn was to be enormously influential in popularising Zen Buddhist teachings in America in the Sixties. (Humphries also makes an unexpected appearance in one of Van's songs, his memoir of his Belfast childhood, 'Cleaning Windows' – 'I went home and read my Christmas Humphries book on Zen/Curiosity killed the cat/Kerouac's *Dharma Bums* and *On the Road* . . .' Alan Watts is similarly memorialised in the song 'Alan Watts Blues'.)

But it was in India that the main stem of the Theosophical Society found its home, and ultimately, its greatest following.

Blavatsky and Olcott arrived in India in 1879, allegedly under the instructions of one of her Masters (at the same time escaping the satirical attentions of the American press, who had made considerable sport lampooning Blavatsky's claims of communion with Masters and spirits). Blavatsky initially set up home in Bombay, where she founded a magazine, *The Theosophist*, but by 1882 the TS was sufficiently prosperous to acquire a new headquarters in a colonial manse, Huddlestone's Gardens, set in 27 acres of land, at Adyar, a few miles south of Madras. (Over the years the estate has grown to its present 200 acres.)

Blavtasky's amalgam of occultism and Eastern philosophy not only began to find an audience among those retired colonels, colonials and European expatriates sympathetic to the religious philosophies of their new home; its political message of pacifism and universal brotherhood and its embrace of Hindu and Buddhist philosophy also attracted many members in India and Ceylon, chafing under the yoke of colonialism. The support of Annie Besant – who succeeded Henry Olcott as president of the TS in 1907 – for the cause of Indian nationalism would ensure that the Society's ideas would continue to hold sway in that country long after theosophy had gone into decline in Europe.

Installed at Adyar, Blavatsky continued communing with the Masters. They wrote her letters, which were sometimes received in a cabinet called The Shrine, located in 'the Occult Room', next to Blavatsky's bedroom, or appeared in 'precipitated' form in the margins of sealed correspondence and, on occasions, even dropped from the ceiling. And all the time the questions as to whether or not the Masters actually existed, or were simply the fruits of Blavatsky's fertile imagination, continued to grow. Only Blavatsky, Olcott and a few close associates had ever seen these 'Masters'. If they were in the world, bent on improving man's spiritual lot, why didn't they make themselves more widely known?

Writing in *The Theosophist* in 1884, Blavatsky ventured the explanation that while the Masters were indeed physical beings, their special qualities may not always be apparent to the sceptical lay-man. A *Mahatma*, she wrote, was:

> . . . a personage who, by special training and education, has evolved those higher faculties and has attained that spiritual knowledge, which ordinary humanity will acquire after passing through numberless series of reincarnations during the course of cosmic evolution . . . The real *Mahatma* is not his physical body but that higher *Manas* which is inseparably linked to the *Atma* and its vehicle . . . a union effected

by him in a comparatively very short period by passing through the
process of self-evolution laid down by the Occult Philosophy.

When, therefore, people express a desire to 'see a *Mahatma*', they
really do not seem to understand what it is they ask for. How can
they, by their physical eyes, hope to see that which *transcends* that
sight? Is it the body – a mere shell or mask – they crave or hunt
after? And supposing they see the body of a *Mahatma*, how can
they know that behind that mask is concealed an exalted entity? . . .
Higher things can be perceived only by a sense pertaining to those
higher things . . . Whoever wants to see the real *Mahatma* must use
his *intellectual* sight. He must so elevate his *Manas* that its perception
will be clear and all mists created by *Maya* must be dispelled. His
vision will then be bright, and he will see the *Mahatmas* wherever
he may be . . . for the *Mahatmas* may be said to be everywhere.

But the storm clouds were already gathering. Not only had the
suspicions that had surrounded Blavatsky in America followed her
to India. She made new enemies among missionary societies in
Ceylon and Madras, resentful of Blavatsky's apparent contempt for
Christianity and her embrace of Buddhism and Hinduism. Before
arriving in India, Blavatsky had become enamoured of the teachings
of Swami Dayanada Sarasvati, the founder of the reform group the
Arya Samraj, which promoted a return to the pure teachings of the
Vedas. There was even talk of a merger between the TS and Arya
Samraj, but it came to nothing when Blavatsky discovered that any
contacts with Parsis or Sinhalese Buddhists – or, indeed, anyone
who was not Hindu – would not be tolerated. However, the TS
was affiliated with a Sikh reform organisation, the Sing Sabha, and
a coalition of Sikh and Hindu maharajas opposed to the work of
Christian missionaries. In Madras, the Society even began to attract
students from the Madras Christian College. Blavatsky, in a phrase,
was bad for business.

But a more dangerous enemy still was Blavatsky's own housekeeper,
Emma Coulomb. It seems that Blavatsky and Coulomb first met in
Cairo about 1871 and became friends. Nine years later Coulomb
and her husband turned up in Bombay, penniless and homeless and
beseeching Blavatsky's help. Blavatsky appointed Coulomb as her
housekeeper and her husband as general factotum, but the friendship
evidently began to deteriorate. While Blavatsky and Olcott were
abroad in Europe, Coulomb and her husband were arraigned

by the TS board of control and dismissed for misappropriating housekeeping expenses. Without money or references, Coulomb approached Blavatsky's enemies, the Madras Christian College, offering evidence that Blavatsky's clairvoyant feats and her contact with 'the Masters' were a fraud. A number of letters, purportedly written by the Masters, but allegedly written by Blavatsky herself, were published by the Madras *Christian College Magazine*. Coulomb further let it be known that she had acted as Blavatsky's accomplice in a series of psychic stunts involving 'precipitated' letters and materialised saucers. Letters received in The Shrine, Coulomb alleged, had actually been inserted through a sliding panel in the back. Blavatsky, in turn, alleged that the letters produced by Coulomb were, at least in part, forgeries.

Coulomb's broadside could not have come at a worse time for Blavatsky. In 1884, the Society for Psychical Research in London dispatched a researcher, Richard Hodgson, to India to investigate Blavatsky. Hodgson was not initially hostile to Blavatsky, but relying largely on the personal testimony of Madame Coulomb, he produced a report damning Blavatsky's phenomena as forgeries, deceptions, hallucinations or misunderstandings. Blavatsky, Hodgson's report concluded, should be regarded as 'neither the mouthpiece of hidden seers, nor as a mere vulgar adventuress: we think that she has achieved a title to permanent remembrance as one of the most accomplished, ingenious and interesting impostors in history'.

The argument did not finish there. For the next 100 years theosophists continued to argue that Hodgson's report had been inaccurate and inconclusive.

In 1986, the Society for Psychical Research opened the case again, publishing the results of an investigation by Dr Vernon Harrison, a former president of the Royal Photographic Society, and, for ten years, Research Manager to Thomas De la Rue, printers of banknotes, passports and stamps. Harrison's verdict was published in the SPR Journal in April 1986. After studying handwriting samples used as evidence in the Hodgson report, Harrison had concluded that Hodgson was '. . . prepared to use any evidence, however trivial or questionable, to implicate HPB; he ignored all evidence that could be used in her favour. His report is riddled with slanted statements, conjecture advanced as fact or probable fact, uncorroborated testimony of unnamed witnesses, selection of evidence and downright falsity.

'His case against Madame H.P. Blavatsky,' Harrison concluded, 'is not proven.' Of course, it came too late to save Blavatsky. Her reputation dented, she resigned from her post as Corresponding Secretary for the TS and, in 1885, she left India for Europe.

Blavatsky settled in London, initially living in the suburb of Norwood, and then in her own house at No. 17 Lansdowne Road, Holland Park. She founded her own Blavatsky Lodge, started a journal, *Lucifer*, and published *The Secret Doctrine*. The book was widely derided by critics, but there was one particularly favourable notice, in the *Pall Mall Gazette*, by a young woman named Annie Besant. By the time she encountered Blavatsky, Besant was already famous in Britain as an orator and social campaigner. She was a leading light in the Fabian movement; an intimate of George Bernard Shaw (he actually proposed marriage, but she refused). She was also something of a lost soul.

Besant was three-quarters Irish, strong-willed, idealistic. Her businessman father had died when she was just five. She was deeply religious as a child, but her marriage, to an Anglican clergyman, Frank Besant, was loveless and oppressive. The birth of their first child, Arthur Digby, followed a difficult pregnancy, and a second child, Mabel, nearly died from whooping cough. This catalogue of misfortune was sufficient to raise doubts in Besant's mind about both the existence of God, and the wisdom of her marriage. She left her husband, in the process losing her two children to his custody. She channelled her unhappiness into the cause of social reform, speaking out on such issues as women's rights in divorce, birth control and trade union organisation. Encountering theosophy for the first time, with its emphasis on the Brotherhood of Man and its idealistic visions of human redemption, reawakened Besant's spiritual yearnings.

Besant became a regular visitor to Blavatsky's West London home. In a letter to the American theosophist, W.Q. Judge, Blavatsky described her new protégée as 'the soul of honour and uncompromisingly truthful'. Besant's heart, Blavatsky wrote, is 'one single unbroken diamond . . . transparent so that anyone can see how filled to the brim it is with pure, unadulterated theosophy and enthusiasm'.

Besant was soon made co-editor of *Lucifer*, and President of the Blavatsky Lodge; and before long she was having her own visions

of the Masters. It was at this point that Besant encountered a
man who would play a crucial role in shaping the theosophical
movement for years to come. The official version of the life
of Charles Webster Leadbeater, as told by Leadbeater himself,
promulgated by his admirers, and for many years the established
text within the TS, had it that Leadbeater could trace his family
line back to Old Norman stock, who had arrived in Britain at the
time of William the Conqueror. According to Leadbeater, he was
born in 1847, the son of the director of a railway company. At the
age of twelve, he travelled with his parents and younger brother
Gerald to Brazil. Here, in the course of travels into the interior,
Leadbeater survived attacks by Indians and was forced to watch his
brother die by the sword at the hands of the leader of a rebel army.
Leadbeater avenged his brother by bettering the rebel in a sword
fight, and then saw the man shot dead in front of him. Returning
to England, Leadbeater entered Queen's College, Oxford, but his
studies were terminated by the tragic loss of his family fortune. He
then worked as a ship-broker and in a bank, until being ordained
into the Church of England.

Save for the facts that his father worked for a railway company
and that Leadbeater was ordained, the remainder of this account is
complete fantasy – bearing the hallmarks of the vivid imagination
and the talent for spinning yarns that would characterise Charles
Leadbeater all his life. Leadbeater's father was not a director of
a railway company. He was a humble book-keeper. There is no
evidence of the family ever having visited South America, far less
of Leadbeater duelling with rebel soldiers or being forced to watch
his brother die. He did not have a brother. Nor is there any record
of him having ever attended Oxford, and the 'family fortune' seems
equally fictitious. Even his alleged birth date – 1847 – appears to
have been a fabrication. Leadbeater was actually born in 1854, in
Stockport. An undistinguished child, he seems to have occupied a
number of lowly clerical jobs before entering the church, through
family connections, and taking up the position of curate in the village
of Bramshott in Hampshire.

Leadbeater was evidently an energetic curate. He took a particular
interest in the moral improvement, and physical fitness, of young
boys – an enthusiasm which would rebound on him with unfortunate circumstances later on in his life – taking responsibility for
church-affiliated groups like the 'Union Jack Field Club' and the

Church Society, in which members had to promise not to lie and to be 'pure and good'.

But his vivid imagination made him ill-suited to the dull rounds of country parish life. Before long he was dabbling in spiritualism and the occult, keenly trying to make contacts with the spirits of the departed. This enthusiasm soon led him to the Theosophical Society, and eventually to a meeting with Madame Blavatsky, who was then visiting London. Soon, Leadbeater too was claiming to be in communion with the Masters. Blavatsky, who took a hostile view of orthodox Christianity, was quick to recognise the 'propaganda' value of having an Anglican clergyman come over to theosophy, and invited him to travel with her to Adyar. There, Leadbeater claimed, the Master Koot Hoomi began teaching him the techniques of Kundalini meditation, with some assistance from the Master Djwal Kul. This, Leadbeater suggested, was simply renewing an old acquaintance: apparently, in an earlier life, the Master D.K. had been Kleineas, the chief pupil of and successor to Pythagoras, and Leadbeater had studied under him in his school in Athens. Blavatsky, it seemed, took a somewhat equivocal view of her sensitive and excitable young protégé; presenting a copy of one of her books to him she signed it to 'W.C.' Leadbeater, although this was possibly accidental.

Following Blavatsky's hasty departure for Europe in 1885, Leadbeater decamped to Ceylon, where he edited a theosophical journal called *The Buddhist* and continued his war of attrition against his former Anglican beliefs by theatrically burning the Catechism of the Church of England at a TS meeting.

In 1889, he returned to England, bringing with him a young Ceylonese boy, Jinarajadasa, whom Leadbeater claimed was the reincarnation of his 'dead brother', Gerald. He worked as a private tutor to the sons of two fellow theosophists, and then met Annie Besant. The two immediately struck up a close friendship. Galvanised by their mutual enthusiasm for the possibilities of occult exploration, they began to make regular visits to the Masters on the astral plane. Leadbeater became particularly interested in the exploration of past lives and, claiming the help of the Masters, was able to furnish members of the TS with their spiritual histories, gleaned, it was said, by psychically leafing through the Akashic Record, a sort of astral library which is said to contain all the history of mankind.

On the basis of these psychic excursions, Leadbeater's star rose rapidly in the TS following the death of Blavatsky in 1891. He toured America, lecturing to theosophists, and maintained a steady stream of books and pamphlets drawn from his astral explorations, including such works as *Man Visible and Invisible*; *The Other Side of Death Scientifically Examined and Carefully Described*; *The Life After Death – Purgatory*; and *The Life After Death – Heaven World*.

But Leadbeater's clairvoyant endeavours did not altogether eclipse his other, abiding enthusiasm, for the education and spiritual uplift of young boys. In 1906, he became embroiled in scandal when a Society member alleged that Leadbeater had been using the cover of esoteric teachings to teach her son to masturbate. Leadbeater replied to the charges in a letter to the General Section of the American TS. It was true, he said, that he had taught masturbation to two boys in his care, but this was strictly in the interests of their moral improvement. For some boys, he suggested, 'huge masses of undesirable thought forms' could torment the youthful imagination, allowing 'disembodied entities' to act upon the child. 'Experience has shown,' Leadbeater wrote, 'that if the boy masturbates at stated intervals he can comparatively easily rid his mind of such thoughts.' He went on to quote St Paul's maxim that while it is best to remain celibate, 'it is better to marry than burn' (apparently not an option that much appealed to Leadbeater himself – he professed to find women physically repulsive).

Leadbeater's explanation temporarily defused the scandal. His final undoing was the discovery of a letter written to one of the boys, containing a coded reference to his preferred form of combating 'disembodied entities' and concluding, 'Glad sensation is so pleasant. Thousand kisses, darling.' A TS committee was convened to investigate the matter, and Leadbeater was obliged to tender his resignation. Even Annie Besant, who had described him as 'a man on the threshold of divinity', temporarily turned against him. But his exile would not last for long.

In 1907, Colonel Henry Olcott died. Annie Besant succeeded him as President, and in 1909 Leadbeater was officially reinstated in the TS. While Madame Blavatsky had always emphasised that her Masters were 'living men', under Besant and Leadbeater's influence, the Masters began to take on a more fantastic, supernatural hue. Leadbeater, in particular, was keen to place them in the context of a galaxy of realised beings stretching back into millennia, whom he had encountered in his journeys on the astral plane, or leafing through the Akashic Record. As his biographer Gregory Tillett puts it, Leadbeater's Masters resemble nothing so much as 'supernatural upper-classes who pontificated with the air of Victorian Anglican bishops addressing candidates for confirmation'. Bishops, it might be added, who showed an agreeable tendency to approve or corroborate anything that the erstwhile curate thought or said.

Out of this cosmic stew, the expectation of the coming of Maitreya, the new Messiah, or World Teacher, began to grow with renewed vigour. Buddhist legend conspicuously fails to put a date on the arrival of Maitreya. And Blavatsky was no more specific. But she did write in a sonorously prophetic tone about the shifting moods of spiritual expectation, and the role which 'the Masters', and the Theosophical Society, had to play.

Writing in *The Key to Theosophy* in 1889 she noted:

> I must tell you that during the last quarter of every hundred years an attempt is made by those 'Masters' of whom I have spoken to help on the spiritual progress of humanity in a marked and definite way. Towards the end of each century you will invariably find that an outpouring or upheaval of spirituality – or call it mysticism if you prefer – has taken place. Some one or more persons have appeared in the world as their agents, and a greater or lesser amount of occult knowledge and teaching has been given out. [The next century, the twentieth, would see the coming of a] torch bearer of truth . . . He will find the minds of men prepared for his message, a language made ready for him in which to clothe the new truths he brings, an organisation awaiting his arrival, which will remove the merely mechanical, material obstacles and difficulties from his path.

Blavatsky was quite specific that no such 'torch-bearer' would arrive in the immediate future, stating, 'No master of Wisdom from the East will himself appear or send anyone to Europe or America . . . until the year 1975.'

What exactly did Blavatsky mean by the words 'torch-bearer'? Was she referring simply to a messenger who would come in the last quarter of the twentieth century, to further spread the teachings of theosophy? Or would this 'torch-bearer' actually be the World Teacher to come, the Buddha Maitreya himself? Besant and Leadbeater, at least, were in no doubt that it was the latter. Under their influence, Blavatsky's vague and unspecific prophecies were inflated into a more or less immediate expectation of Maitreya's arrival.

Leadbeater's astral excursions had furnished him with a picture of the Occult Hierarchy more elaborate and specific than even Blavatsky had advanced. According to Leadbeater, there are ten distinct grades, or Great Initiations, between ordinary, mortal man and what in occult terms is known as the Logos, or God.

Even the most diligent occult pupil, in coming under the apprenticeship of a Master, might expect to reach only as far as the fifth initiation, Asekha, where he would attain the status of Superman, or Adept.

Beyond this level lies the Occult Hierarchy. The Seven Masters responsible for the government of the world – Koot Hoomi and Morya among them – exist on the Sixth Initiation. On the Seventh exist the three principal Officers responsible for the Occult administration of the world – the Mahochohan, the Bodhisattva and the Manu. On the eighth is the Buddha, above whom comes the Lord of the World, and at the very top stands the Trinity of the Logos.

According to Leadbeater, the Bodhisattva is the World Teacher, responsible for the spiritual development of mankind. This position was once held by Guatama Buddha, but was now held by Lord Maitreya. In his role as the Bodhisattva, Maitreya had visited earth twice before – manifesting first in Sri Krishna, and then in the body of Jesus, who became Christ. Thus did Leadbeater unify the occult expectation of the coming of Maitreya, and the Christian expectation of the Second Coming of Christ. If Maitreya was to return to earth a suitable vehicle would have to be found in whom the World Teacher might manifest himself.

The first candidate to present himself was a young American boy, Hubert Van Hook, the son of a theosophist doctor from Chicago, whom Annie Besant decided had the requisite qualities of spiritual purity. But even before Hubert arrived at Adyar in 1909, his place had been usurped by another, altogether more surprising, candidate.

The story of Charles Leadbeater's discovery of Krishnamurti on the beach at Adyar, Krishnamurti's subsequent elevation to the role of vehicle for the World Teacher – and his eventual disavowal of it – might stand as a parable for the romantic Western notion that spiritual deliverance is to be found in the East.

One day in 1909, Leadbeater and some friends decided on a swim at the beach adjacent to the TS estate. There, they were joined by a group of Indian boys, among them thirteen-year-old Jiddu Krishnamurti and his brother Nitya. Krishnamurti in particular caught Leadbeater's eye; he patted the boy's head and told one of his companions that he felt a particular sense of well-being when he was with the boy. Suspicious minds might attribute Leadbeater's interest to his sexual enthusiasms, but Jiddu Krishnamurti was a pathetic, unkempt, emaciated slip of a boy, infested with lice even in his eyebrows. What impressed Leadbeater was the fact that Krishnamurti was a being 'devoid', as the dreamy Englishman would put it, 'of any particle of selfishness'.

Krishnamurti, as he would become universally known, was born in 1895 into a Brahmin family in the small town of Madanapalle, Andhra Pradesh in Southern India, the son of a revenue collector, one of eleven children, only four of whom survived to adolescence. Krishnamurti's mother died when he was ten, and his father, who was a theosophist, moved the family to Madras. He took a minor secretarial post in the TS, living in a state of semi-impoverishment in a hut close to the Society compound.

Outwardly, there was nothing about Krishnamurti to suggest a divine calling. Slack-jawed and vacant-eyed, he evinced a vagueness which, by his own later admission, bordered on the moronic. Yet Leadbeater was adamant that here was the vehicle for the eagerly anticipated Universal Teacher, and before long he was claiming that the Master Koot Hoomi had instructed him to train the boy. With Jiddu and his brother Nitya installed at Adyar, Leadbeater set to the task of investigating his young protégé's past lives in the Akarshic records, publishing his findings in the book *Lives of Alcyone*. This revealed that, in 40,000 BC, Leadbeater and Annie Besant had been man and wife, and Krishnamurti and Nitya were among their numerous children. Some ten thousand years later, Leadbeater, apparently, had been married to Nitya (presumably in female form), and given birth to a daughter who subsequently married Mrs Besant (presumably in male form). Most importantly, it seemed that Krishnamurti had once been a close associate of Guatama Buddha – surely a propitious omen for his role as the vehicle for the coming Lord Maitreya.

Before long, Krishnamurti himself was said to be making nightly excursions to the astral plane, communing with the Master Koot Hoomi, and returning to jot down his findings in what would become his first published work, *At the Feet of the Master* – a book which some theosophists thought bore an uncomfortable resemblance to Leadbeater's own writings.

Under Besant and Leadbeater, the TS began to take on an increasingly messianic, and hierarchical, bent. Proximity to the Masters – and no one was closer than Besant and Leadbeater – was taken to confer a sort of spiritual authority on 'the Path' of spiritual development. The Masters gave their messages to the TS hierarchy; the hierarchy passed them on to the rest. Ideas of world brotherhood began to give way to a frenetic spiritual one-upmanship.

Showing a hitherto dormant enthusiasm for titles, sashes and badges, Annie Besant set about inaugurating a number of orders within the orbit of the TS – the Theosophical Order of Service, the Temple of the Rosy Cross, the Order of Theosophical *Sannyasins*, the Order of World Peace, and most importantly, the Order of the Star in the East, established to promote the claim of Krishnamurti as the new World Teacher.

Krishnamurti and his brother were sent to Europe, dressed like young lords in stiff collars and suits from Savile Row (instilling a sartorial exactitude that would stay with Krishnamurti for the rest of his life), and paraded before the TS membership. Krishnamurti's slender, elegant figure and liquid eyes, his air of dreamy vulnerability, proved particularly compelling to female members of the Society, not least Lady Emily Lutyens, the wife of the architect Edwin Lutyens, and a recent convert to theosophy. She and Krishnamurti struck up a friendship which would last until her death, with Krishnamurti addressing her as 'Mum'.

Under the tutelage of Leadbeater and Besant, Krishnamurti became a kind of religious superstar. The membership of the Theosophical Society began to mushroom – by 1928 it numbered 45,000. Thousands attended Krishnamurti's lectures in India and Europe, eager for evidence that he was indeed the 'vehicle' for the coming Maitreya. Excitement became pandemic when in 1925, addressing a meeting under the giant banyan tree in the grounds of the Society's headquarters in Adyar on the subject of the World Teacher, Krishnamurti slipped from saying 'he', to 'I'. 'He [the World Teacher] comes only to those who want, who desire, who long . . . and I come for those who want sympathy, who want happiness, who are longing to be released, who are longing to find happiness in all things. I come to reform and not to tear down, I come not to destroy but to build.'

But at the same time it was becoming worryingly obvious to some theosophists that Krishnamurti's talks were beginning to deviate from the party line espoused by Leadbeater and Besant. His lectures, delivered without notes in a calm, unwavering voice, increasingly emphasised self-knowledge and the requirement for each individual to find their own way to the truth – a teaching directly at odds with Leadbeater and Besant's ideas of there being just one 'path of discipleship', regulated by a self-styled elite of initiates. Leadbeater quietly began to express the view that, 'The Coming has gone wrong.' Krishnamurti, it seemed, was beginning to find the burden of expectation placed upon him increasingly intolerable, wearying of the internecine battles within the Society, with members jockeying for favour with the Masters, and the way it had degenerated into a quasi-military movement, with its spurious offices, orders and costumes which could make Adyar seem like a particularly esoteric outpost of Ruritania. He was being hailed as the World Teacher by an organisation that he was finding increasingly ridiculous and reprehensible; but at the same time he was also imbued with a belief in his own specialness – the sense that he had somehow been chosen – and that some higher power was, indeed, speaking through him.

In 1927, addressing a gathering of theosophists in Ommen, Holland, Krishnamurti returned to his argument that people should seek the truth within themselves, rather than relying upon any external authority – namely Besant and Leadbeater. 'Until now,' he said, 'you have been depending on the two Protectors of the Order for authority, for someone else to tell you the Truth, whereas the Truth lies within you.' In what amounted to a fundamental heresy against theosophical thought, he declared that the descriptions of the Masters proposed by the theosophical hierarchy were delusional mental images conjured by the imagination, and largely irrelevant. Krishnamurti talked instead of the ultimate reality, which he called 'The Beloved'. 'To me it is all – it is Sri Krishna, it is the Master K.H., it is Lord Maitreya, it is the Buddha, and yet it is beyond all these forms. What does it matter what names you give?'

Claiming that he was now in union with the Beloved, Krishnamurti strived to put yet more distance between himself and the theosophists' insistence that he was the Messiah. 'What you are troubling about is whether there is such a person as the World Teacher who has manifested Himself in the body of a certain person, Krishnamurti; but in the world nobody will trouble about this question.'

In 1929, at another gathering in Ommen, in front of Annie Besant and 3,000 members of the Order of the Star, Krishnamurti made the final break with his past, dissolving the Order and making his famous proclamation: 'Truth is a pathless land . . . You cannot approach it by any path whatsoever, by any religion, by any sect . . . That is my point of view and I adhere to that absolutely and unconditionally. Truth being limitless, unconditioned, unapproachable by any path whatsoever, cannot be organised; nor should any organisation be formed to lead or coerce people along any particular path.

'I do not care if you believe I am the World Teacher or not. That is of very little importance . . . I do not want you to follow me . . . You have been accustomed to being told . . . what your spiritual status is. How childish! Who but yourself can tell if you are beautiful or ugly inside.'

It was the end of Krishnamurti's association with the Theosophical Society. From that point on, he would constantly reiterate that any belief system, 'the circus' of organised religion, was a trap to ensnare us, and that henceforth his only concern was 'to set men absolutely, unconditionally free'. Krishnamurti left India, to start a new life in America. He would not set foot in the TS compound in Adyar for the next thirty years.

The secretary of the international section of the Theosophical Society in Adyar was Pedro Oliveira, a slim, studious-looking Brazilian in his late thirties. He told me that his particular path to theosophy had begun when he was seventeen. 'My philosophy teacher led a class discussion on the book *Jonathan Livingstone Seagull*. It opened my eyes.'

He offered to show me the rooms where Krishnamurti had lived in the TS headquarters. We climbed two sets of stairs to the top of the building, and he unlocked a door. Stripped of his personal belongings, the quarters had otherwise been preserved exactly as Krishnamurti had left them. There was a large, airy sitting room, with a tiled floor, inlaid with the mystic star; in an adjacent room stood a simple four-poster bed; a mahogany sideboard and a wicker-backed rocking-chair. Like Krishnamurti himself, the impression was of asceticism and elegance. From one side of the veranda, one could look down on to the roof of the octagonal bungalow, where Charles Leadbeater had lived, and where he had undertaken his clairvoyant investigations into Krishnamurti's previous lives. The other side offered a view over the broad, muddy expanse of the Adyar river, at its estuary with the sea. 'Krishnaji used to swim in the river,' said Pedro with a wry smile. 'Nobody would swim in it now. It's far too polluted.'

What, I asked, did Oliveira make of the claims made by Leadbeater and Besant that Krishnamurti was the World Teacher?

'Madame Blavatsky talked of the coming of "the new torch-bearer of truth", who would expound some essential teaching in tune with the ancient wisdom. Personally, I have no doubt that Krishnamurti, in his role as the chosen vehicle, was the instrument for this new revelation. Both Leadbeater and Mrs Besant were very sure about it. After Krishnaji started speaking on his own behalf, then Leadbeater had his doubts. But Mrs Besant's faith never wavered; she always believed that the tremendous intelligence that was functioning through Krishnaji's body was Lord Maitreya.'

And did he believe that himself?

Oliveira smiled. 'Mrs Besant was a very intelligent woman, and a woman of great faith.'

He led me back down the stairs and through the great hall, into the Society's museum. Portraits of theosophist alumni gazed down from the walls, and Society ephemera crowded the display cases: Krishnamurti's gold watch; Annie Besant's fly-whisk. Sundry badges, orders and stars. Exquisite statues of the Buddha from Sri Lanka, Thailand and Sikkim. The urn in which the ashes of Helena Blavatsky were carried from London to Adyar: the ashes themselves are placed under the statue of her and Olcott in the main hall.

One case contained the china cup supposedly 'precipitated' by Blavatsky at a tea-party in Simla in 1880. (Olcott told the story in his book *Old Diary Leaves*: staying with a fellow theosophist, A.P. Sinnett, Blavatsky organised a tea-party. The table had been laid for six guests, but then a seventh arrived unexpectedly. What to do? Blavatsky instructed the visitors to dig near a shrub, where, lo and behold, they found a cup and saucer.)

Oliveira led me back through the corridors of the old house. In one spacious room, three elderly European women sat at evenly spaced desks, poring over paperwork; in another Indian clerks pecked methodically at antiquated typewriters, while fans circled lazily above them. It was a scene which, I fancied, could hardly have changed since Krishnamurti left Adyar more than sixty years before.

The TS boasted an extensive library, a stone's throw from the giant banyan tree under which Krishnamurti had sat and delivered his discourses. Computerisation and microfiche had not yet arrived in Adyar. I ploughed my way through the card-indexes, submitted a list of the books I wanted on a piece of paper, and had ample time to stroll through the grounds and take lunch in a small, darkened restaurant beyond the gates, before returning to find the books waiting for me. There was something particularly evocative in reading about Blavatsky and Krishnamurti, knowing that the principal dramas of their lives had unfolded in the very place where I was now sitting.

I wanted to put flesh on the ghosts of the Masters who lay at the very core of Blavatsky's teachings. The debate about whether the Masters actually existed, and if so in what form, or whether they were simply figments of Blavatsky's, and others', imaginations, has continued to rage in theosophical and esoteric circles ever since Blavatsky's death.

In 1994, an American scholar K. Paul Johnson published a book, *The Masters Revealed*, which suggested that 'the Masters' were, in fact, a combination of the numerous adepts and teachers whom Blavatsky had met in her travels in Asia and the Levant, and fictionalised personae based on living people whom Blavatsky was known to have associated with in India. The Master Morya, Johnson suggests, was possibly inspired by Ranbir Singh, a Maharajah of Kashmir, whose rule was characterised by scholarship, public works and social reform. While Koot Hoomi may have been Thakar Singh, a Sikh aristocrat who devoted his life to restoring and purifying the Sikh faith, and fortifying it against the influence of Christian missionaries.

According to another scholar of theosophy, Daniel Caldwell, at least twenty-five people testified to having met the Masters during Blavatsky's lifetime. In his diaries, Colonel Olcott describes meeting Morya at the theosophical headquarters in Bombay in 1879. Five years later, Olcott testified to members of the Society for Psychical Research that Morya was flesh and blood: 'He put his hand upon my head, and his hand was perfectly substantial; and he had altogether the appearance of an ordinary person. When he walked about the floor there was the noise of footsteps . . .' Olcott went on to testify that he had seen Morya 'at least fifteen or twenty times'.

In *Old Diary Leaves*, Olcott also refers to meeting Koot Hoomi, at Lahore:

He took my left hand in his, gathered his fingers of his right into the palm, and stood quiet beside my cot, from which I could see his divinely benignant face by the light of the lamp that burned on a packing-case at his back . . .

In 1883, an Indian *chela*, Damodar K. Mavlankar, testified that he too had met Koot Hoomi in Lahore, whilst travelling with Olcott.

Him whom I saw in person at Lahore was the same I had seen in astral form at the headquarters of the Theosophical Society, and the same again whom I, in my visions and trances, had seen at His house, thousands of miles off, to reach which in my astral Ego I was permitted, owing, of course, to His direct help and protection. In those instances with my psychic powers hardly developed yet, I had always seen Him as a rather hazy form, although his features were perfectly distinct and their remembrance was profoundly graven on my soul's eye and memory; while now at Lahore, Jummu and elsewhere, the impression was utterly different. In the former cases, when making *Pranam* (salutation) my hand passed through his form, while on the latter occasions they met solid garments and flesh. Here I saw *a living man* before me . . .

R. Casava Pillai, the Inspector of Police in Nellore, joined the TS in May 1882, and three years later offered his account of encountering the Masters while travelling:

In the course of these travels, just about Pari or Parchong on the northern frontier of Sikkim, I had the good fortune and happiness to see the blessed feet of the *most venerated Master Koot Humi and M.* in their physical bodies. The very identical personage whose astral bodies I had seen in my dreams, etc, since 1869, and in 1876 in Madras and on the 14th September 1882 in the headquarters at Bombay. Besides, I have also seen a few advanced *chelas*, among them, the blessed Jwalkul also, who is *now* a Mahatma.

Madame Blavatsky herself was always clear that the names she attributed to the Masters were pseudonyms, designed to protect them against unwanted intrusions. Writing to a friend in 1884 – at the time the Society for Psychical Research were researching her claims – she elaborated on the Masters' existence and whereabouts. The letter was subsequently published in the magazine *Thesophia* in 1947:

All depends, you see, on what each of us means by *Mahatmas* or *Masters*. To a Hindu, no doubt . . . a 'Mahatma', Guru or Master, is a naked *Yogi* with a *chignon* of entangled and unkempt hair on the top of the head . . . For me and those who *know* the Masters *personally* our 'Mahatmas', so-called, are *nothing of the kind*. Olcott is home, and you may ask him what our *Masters* are like, whether from the description he had from me in New York and which has never altered to this day, or from the two Masters he met personally – one in Bombay and the other in Cashmere. My Masters and *the* Masters are Yogis and Munis *de facto*, not *de jure*; in their life not in appearance.

They *are* members of an *occult* Brotherhood, not of any particular School in India. One of their highest Mahachohans lived in Egypt and went to Tibet only a year before we did (in 1878) and he is neither a Tibetan nor a Hindu; this 'Occult Brotherhood' has not originated in Tibet, nor is it *only* in Tibet; but what I always said and maintain to this day is *that most of its members and some of the highest are*, and live constantly, in Tibet, because of its isolation and freedom from Christians; that its origin is of untold antiquity, and is as much Masonic as present Masonry is *little* Masonic . . . I said and repeat, that they are *living men* not 'spirits' or even *Nirmanakayas*, that their knowledge and learning are immense, and their personal holiness of life is still greater – still they are mortal men and none of them 1,000 years old as imagined by some. What I said and say, was and is, the truth; those who will have it, all right; those who see in what I say a cleverly concocted romance by me, are also welcome.

The person who perhaps claimed to have the most dealings with the Masters was Charles Leadbeater. Leadbeater died in 1934 (five months after Annie Besant) with opinion heatedly divided within the TS on whether he was genuinely clairvoyant, or simply an astounding fabulist and liar, with sufficient force of will to draw his students and followers into a hall of mirrors of his own creation.

In 1966, the Theosophical Publishing House in London published an examination of Leadbeater's psychic powers by a distinguished theosophical historian, E.L. Gardner, which has some bearing not only on Leadbeater, but on those who followed him claiming clair-voyant contact with Masters. Gardner wrote of the phenomenom of *kryashakti*, the power of the mind to create thought forms and then to perceive them as if they were real. Gardner – who seems to have believed both in the Masters and, to a limited degree, in Leadbeater's clairvoyant powers – theorised that in the case of the Masters, such thought forms were created as images and communicated to the minds of their pupils. However, he cautioned, this visualising power of *kryashakti* may be unconsciously distorted by the clairvoyant who creates a seemingly real world in his own mind which obstructs the true objects of his perception; what he then 'sees' clairvoyantly becomes merely a reflection of his own unconscious creation. In other words, Gardner theorised, Leadbeater unconsciously created an alternative world, based on his strongly held beliefs and wishes, and, again unconsciously, viewed this clairvoyantly believing it was real.

Towards the end of her life, Blavatsky regretted the way in which the cult of the Masters had grown to epidemic proportions, and that her description of them as normal human beings, albeit with highly developed faculties, had somehow been overlooked in the rush to see them as some kind of all-powerful supernatural brotherhood. 'One may be a perfect Theosophist,' she wrote in a letter to a TS member in 1889, two years before her death, 'without giving one's allegiance to our Master, but simply to one's Higher Self, in essence above the Masters.'

Writing in one of her later books, *The Key to Theosophy*, she lamented:

> Every bogus swindling society, for commercial purposes, now claims to be guided and directed by 'Masters', often supposed to be far higher than ours . . . had we acted on the wise principle of silence, instead of rushing into notoriety and publishing all we knew and heard, such desecration would never have occurred . . . But it is useless to grieve over what is done, and we can only suffer in the hope that our indiscretions may have made it a little easier for others to find the way to these Masters.

In this at least she was prophetic. Some thirty years after her death, a book would appear claiming to be the next chapter in the Hierarchy of Masters' great design. Its title was *Initiation, Human and Solar*; its author an Englishwoman named Alice Bailey.

If Blavatsky was the most influential figure in esoteric history in the nineteenth century, it might be claimed of Bailey that she was among the most influential of the twentieth century. Under the guidance of a Master whom she referred to as 'the Tibetan', Bailey produced twenty-two books in thirty years, expounding an esoteric cosmology even more dense, complex and rambling than Blavatsky's.

The essence of Bailey's teaching was this: the world teacher, whom Bailey referred to as 'the Cosmic Christ' rather than Maitreya, was nigh. The teaching planned by the Hierarchy to precede and condition the coming 'Aquarian age' fell into three categories: the Preparatory, given between 1875 and 1890, and written by Blavatsky; the Intermediate, given between 1919 and 1949, and written down by Bailey herself; and the Revelatory, which would emerge after 1975, Bailey said, to be given on a worldwide scale, 'via the radio' (television not being the ubiquitous medium when she made the prediction that it is now).

Bailey was born in 1880, in Manchester. Her father was an engineer, who died when Bailey was eight, and she was brought up under the care of a governess at her grandparents' country house, Moor Park in Surrey – a comfortable, but, one imagines, claustrophobically stifling background. By her own admission she was a morbid, unhappy and highly-strung young woman, who found some comfort in a fervent religiosity in the orthodox Christian sense.

She claims to have had her first contact with the Masters at the age of fifteen, in the improbable setting of her aunt's house in Kirkcudbrightshire, Scotland. The story is recounted in her book *The Unfinished Autobiography* (Bailey died in 1949 before completing it). It was a Sunday morning, she wrote, and she was alone in the house. 'The door opened and in walked a tall man dressed in European clothes (very well cut, I remember) but with a turban on his head.' The visitor told her that there was work that she must do in the world, spoke of her 'future usefulness to Him and the world', and told her she would travel the world 'doing your Master's work all the time'. He then left. As she recounts, Bailey was, at the time, much enamoured of the legend of Joan of Arc, and took the visitation as a sign of being 'chosen', although she seems soon to have put this conceit aside.

At the age of eighteen she was sent to finishing school in London, where she spent the next four years, taking part in the endless round of garden parties and dances which comprised the London 'season', none of which, it seemed, made her particularly happy. She became enamoured of good works, and imbued with Christian zeal made her way to India where she engaged in evangelical work with British soldiers. Here too she met the man who would subsequently become her husband. They married, and settled in America, where he became an Episcopalian minister. But it was an unhappy marriage – her husband, it seemed, frequently beat her – and they separated. Bailey was obliged to support herself and her three daughters by working in a sardine cannery.

Living in Los Angeles, she was introduced to theosophy. At the TS headquarters in Hollywood she recognised a picture of the man who had appeared in the living room at Kirkcudbrightshire when she was fifteen. It was Madame Blavatsky's old friend, the Master Koot Hoomi. Bailey's fellow theosophists were not, it seems, overly impressed when she let this be known, accusing her of 'glamour' and delusions. Notwithstanding this hiccup, Bailey took to theosophy like a duck to water, energetically immersing herself in the endless wrangles between the 'old' Blavatsky and the 'new' Leadbeater-Besant factions which were then tearing the TS apart. She married Foster Bailey, who became National Secretary of the American TS, and Bailey herself became editor of the American theosophical magazine. Then, in November 1919, she made her first contact with 'the Tibetan' whom Bailey would later reveal to be Djwhal Khul, a disciple of Koot Hoomi. (Presumably the same 'Jwalkul' encountered by R. Casava Pillai, the former Inspector of Police in Nellore.)

> I had sent the children off to school and thought I would snatch a few minutes to myself and went out on to the hill close to the house [Bailey wrote in *The Unfinished Autobiography*]. I sat down and began thinking and then suddenly I sat startled and attentive. I heard what I thought was a clear note of music which sounded from the sky, through the hill and in me. Then I heard a voice which said, 'There are some books which it is desired should be written for the public. You can write them. Will you do so?'

Bailey apparently refused the offer, wanting no truck with psychic voices. However, three weeks later the voice came again. This time she agreed to write, 'for a couple of weeks or a month and then decide what I felt about it'.

It was to become her work for the next thirty years.

Under the Tibetan's direction, Bailey would produce books on such matters as 'personality rays', spiritual healing and the Hierarchy's 'Plan', culminating in the coming of 'the Christ' to usher in the age of a new world order. Bailey described this process not as automatic writing, but as a mixture of clairaudience and telepathy:

> I am only a pen or pencil, a stenographer and a transmitter of teaching from one whom I revere and honour and have been happy to serve . . . I simply listen and take down the words that I hear and register the thoughts which are dropped one by one into my brain . . . I do not always understand what is given.

Bailey's claim of a privileged communion with a member of the Hierarchy almost immediately put her at odds with the TS. A few chapters of *Initiation, Human and Solar*, were published in *The Theosophist* in Adyar. But then, according to Bailey, 'the usual theosophical jealousy and reactionary attitude appeared', and no more was printed.

She drifted away from the TS, and in 1923 founded her own Arcane School – the name, she claimed, that Madame Blavatsky had always wanted to call the esoteric section of the TS. The Arcane School was an esoteric group that taught 'prompt obedience to the dictates of the soul'. According to Bailey, initiates would find that 'as the voice of that soul gets increasingly familiar it will eventually make them members of the Kingdom of God and bring them face to face with Christ'.

Central to Bailey's teachings was a Utopian vision of the future.

> The future [she wrote in *The Destiny of Nations*] will see right relationships, true communion, a sharing of all things . . . and goodwill; we have also a picture of the future of humanity when all nations are united in complete understanding and the diversity of languages – symbolic of differing traditions, cultures, civilisations and points of view – will provide no barrier to right human relations.

The ending of the Second World War, she believed, cleared the stage for the dawning of this 'New Age' when a 'new world religion' would emerge, which would fuse the ideas of the teachings of Buddha and the Christ. Her work – the work of the Masters with whom she was in communication, 'the Tibetan' and Koot Hoomi – was 'to prepare the world on a large scale for the coming of the World Teacher': 'the Cosmic Christ'. Bailey's works are littered with references to 'the coming of Him for whom all nations wait'.

Christ and his disciples, the Masters, would be seen again on earth when man had developed enough free will to accept them. In *The Unfinished Autobiography* she wrote, 'This has taken place on such a large scale that it now appears possible that within the coming century the Masters may emerge from Their silence and again be known among men.'

Bailey divided opinion within the theosophists: some saw her as the heir of Blavatsky's teachings, others as a rank imposter. (Carl Jung opined that 'the Tibetan' was the voice of Bailey's 'personified higher self'.) She was accused of distorting the teachings of Blavatsky by perpetuating the 'World Teacher propaganda' developed by Leadbeater and Besant, and further distorting that by putting a new and distinctly Christian twist on it. Authorities on Buddhism within the Society came forward to say that 'the Tibetan' didn't sound like a Buddhist at all, even that he was a mask for a group of Christian theologians.

In *A Treatise on Cosmic Fire* Bailey (or perhaps one should say 'the Tibetan') attempted to clarify matters. Within the Occult Hierarchy, she wrote, 'The Buddha held office prior to the present World Teacher and upon his Illumination His place was taken by Lord Maitreya whom the Occidentals call Christ.' By 'Christ' Bailey did not mean the actual figure of Jesus who had walked on earth some 1,900 years before, but the principle of 'the Cosmic Christ'. In *Initiation, Human and Solar*, Bailey explained that, 'The Master Jesus', who had been the vehicle for 'the Cosmic Christ' in Palestine, had already returned to earth in 'a Syrian body. [He] is rather a martial figure, a disciplinarian, and a man of iron rule and will. He is tall and spare with rather a long thin face, black hair, pale complexion and piercing blue eyes.'

'The Tibetan' himself entered the fray, justifying Bailey's work in a pamphlet entitled *My Work*. This suggested that under Madame Blavatsky, the TS had taught the existence of the Masters, but that teaching was misinterpreted by later theosophists, and had fallen into the hands of 'entirely mediocre people with no influence outside the

Theosophical Society itself' (an opinion which chimed conveniently with Bailey's own views).

According to 'the Tibetan', 'The Masters, as portrayed in the Theosophical Society, faintly resemble the reality and much good has been done by this testimony to Their existence, and much harm by the foolish detail at times imparted.' 'The Tibetan' offered further illumination. The Hierarchy, he emphasised, were concerned with 'humanity and world service', not spiritual one-upmanship:

> The name given to us by some disciples in Tibet gives the clue to our point of attainment. They call the Hierarchy 'the society of organised and illumined minds' – illumined by love and understanding, by deep passion and inclusiveness, illumined by a knowledge of the plan and aiming to comprehend the purpose, sacrificing their own immediate purpose in order to help humanity. This is a Master.

In his office at the Theosophical Society headquarters at Adyar, Pedro Oliveira arched a sceptical eyebrow when I raised the matter of Bailey and her teachings.

'Personally, I find it difficult to believe that a Master dictated all that. Annie Besant was once asked whether a Master had really given all that to Alice Bailey, and she replied that, if they did, the Masters have become very wordy.' Oliveira chuckled quietly to himself.

Bailey's ideas had never quite had the universal purchase that she expected. An organisation, the Lucis Trust, continues to propagate her teachings, through newsletters and pamphlets, incorporating such topics as spiritual healing, ecology and animal rights, and an almost evangelical enthusiasm for the United Nations. Along with the works of Christmas Humphries and Jack Kerouac, some echo of her teachings could also be found in Van's songs: the lyrics of 'Dweller on the Threshold', and 'Aryan Mist,' on his album *Beautiful Vision* were inspired by Bailey's *Glamour – A World Problem*. And 'Ancient of Days' and 'A New Kind of Man' both suggest her influence – although one doubts that the hundreds of thousands who have played and enjoyed the songs would have any idea who Alice Bailey was.

Reading Bailey's *The Unfinished Autobiography*, it is hard to see why she should have been singled out by a Hierarchy of Masters to spread the word of their existence. The book suggests that she had a purse-lipped, prissy, somewhat *haut en bas* quality about her.

For all her talk about world brotherhood she seems never to have escaped the prejudices of her caste, making lofty and patronising pronouncements on the 'Negro problem', the 'Jewish problem', and the 'sex problem' – on which she believed that the best teaching was, 'The wages of sin is death.'

Yet, at the same time, there was something curiously cheering in her view of humanity, painstakingly climbing up the evolutionary ladder towards enlightenment, guided and watched over by a fraternity of *mahatmas*, indulgently smiling at our foibles and weaknesses, offering encouragement at our every faltering step; something reassuring in her unquenchable optimism about man's destiny. Writing of W.B. Yeats' interest in theosophy, the American critic Frederick Crews has pointed out that Yeats felt that gnostic beliefs and rituals were less a rearguard protest against the iron rule of science and materialism than the advancing edge of an emergent consciousness. In this, at least, he was prophetic.

In a sense, the Masters have never gone away, their disembodied presence hovering over what we have come to call the New Age Movement. They are to be found in the teachings of the Summit Lighthouse organisation, founded by the Americans Mark and Elizabeth Clare Prophet. As a child, Mark Prophet claimed to be visited by angels and spirits; as a young man he studied Rosicrucianism and theosophy, eventually setting himself up as a teacher, publishing letters to his students under the title *Askram Notes*, which he claimed were dictated by the Master El Morya – presumably Madame Blavatsky's Morya.

He founded the Summit Lighthouse in 1957, and was joined in his work by Elizabeth Wulf, a former Christian Scientist, who claimed to have enjoyed a similar encounter with another Master, Saint Germain, whilst studying political science at Boston University. The Prophets married in 1963, and under the instruction of Saint Germain their organisation began to grow, claiming to propagate the teachings of what Prophet called 'the Great White Brotherhood', as dictated to them by the Masters. As well as El Morya and Saint Germain the 'Brotherhood' is said also to include Christ, Buddha, St Michael the Archangel, Maitreya, 'the Mother Mary', and Madame Blavatsky's and Alice Bailey's old friend the Master Koot Hoomi.

Following Mark Prophet's death in 1973, the organisation was renamed as the Church Universal and Triumphant, establishing itself on a 33,000-acre ranch in Montana, where followers were encouraged to participate in a regime of prayer and hard physical labour, and address Elizabeth Clare Prophet as 'Guru Ma'.

A more genial heir to the tradition of Blavatsky and Bailey was Mr Creme, whose prophecies of the coming of Maitreya were in the direct tradition of the teachings about the Masters; indeed, could even be interpreted, by those so inclined, as the 'Revelatory Phase' of the Hierarchy's teachings prophesied by Bailey herself. (Mr Creme reserved a jovial contempt for Elizabeth Clare Prophet – 'Elizabeth Clear Profit, we call her,' he said with a laugh – and for the New Age movement at large, with its paraphernalia of crystals, rune stones and aromatic oils. 'And New Age music, which is supposed to put you into a quiet, tranquil, meditative state makes me climb walls! It's just terrible. I don't know anything less *real* than New Age music . . .')

Within the Theosophical Society itself, there is little talk nowadays of Masters, other than in the domain of recondite academic study. In the Fifties, under its international president, N. Sri Ram (the father of the present incumbent, Mrs Radha Burnier), the Society had entered a new phase in which all talk of Masters and communications had come to an end. This was not, Pedro Oliveira said, because the communications had necessarily ceased, '. . . but because these are things people don't talk about; otherwise they just become a sort of sideshow, a circus.

'One of Krishnamurti's criticisms of the TS was that sacred things had been made public. People were talking too freely of initiations and Masters and so on. These things are not to be taken lightly, because they are sacred. Krishnamurti always said it was important how you lived, not whether you talked about Masters or not.' He paused. 'The real work of the Masters is to change humanity from within, to revitalise the human consciousness – through love, selflessness, compassion. I have absolutely no doubt the Masters are with us still.

'Radha Burnier says it is for each individual to find out. Obviously the Masters would be interested only to maintain a connection to an individual that embodies this spirit of compassion and selflessness.' He fell silent for a moment. 'My stay here has reinforced my conviction that they are with us, and that they can be felt by anyone who is sensitive in their heart.'

Sitting in the library at Adyar, reading these antique accounts of precipitated letters, materialising tea-cups, disembodied voices with garrulous literary ambitions, I experienced the same feelings of vertigo I had experienced in Mr Creme's front room, and in the café at Puttaparthi, hearing accounts of Sai Baba's miracles. The same feeling of navigating a darkened room, bumping into tables, chairs and unidentified obstacles, while engaged in a futile search for the light-switch.

And yet, reflecting on Blavatsky's teachings on the Masters, root races, Lemurians and Atlanteans, the embellishments added by Leadbeater and Besant, and the body of Alice Bailey teachings that had followed them, I could recognise their seductive appeal. They posited a cosmic order, a structure, a whole mythology with infinite possibilities of exploration. They concretised the ineffable, and in the process offered a spiritual equivalent to the obsessive behaviour that characterises collecting railway numbers – or matrix numbers on rare blues recordings – the magnetic drift into a vortex of arcane information with no limit. You could get lost in the talk of Masters and root races, stumble happily through the occult and cosmological labyrinth, without ever once having to stop and address the basic question of what spiritual growth meant and entailed, and the requirement to look to oneself and one's own actions.

Which, of course, was one of Krishnamurti's objections. Certainly his experience with the Theosophical Society had disabused him of a belief in any rigid spiritual dogma, system, discipline, or hierarchy. But he had never fully disavowed a belief in the Masters, and continued to allude to his personal experience of a higher power over and above himself.

Throughout his life, Krishnamurti was afflicted with a peculiar sensation, part physical and part mystical, which his brother Nitya called 'the Process'. This would take the form of acute feelings of pain and weakness which would begin in the neck and spread down his spine, and which sometimes resulted in a total loss of consciousness. Along with this would come alternate sensations of leaving his body, of being profoundly at one with everything around him (not unlike the mystical experience of *samadhi*) but also of mental distress, and of a disgust with his physical surroundings. In later life, he would talk of waking to feelings of rhapsodic joy, and the sense that the room was filled with 'eminent holy beings'.

His biographer, Mary Lutyens (the daughter of Lady Emily Lutyens, 'Mum' to Krishnamurti), recalled being with him on one occasion when he drew her attention to a 'sudden extraordinary throbbing' which filled the room, and which she was able to recognise, even though quite devoid of any psychic gift. 'What *is* this thing?' she asked. 'This power? What *is* behind you? I know you have always felt protected, but what or who is it that protects you?'

'It's there, as if it were behind a curtain,' Krishnamurti replied. 'I *could* lift it, but I don't feel it is my business to.'

In later life, conveniently perhaps, Krishnamurti professed to have no memory of his discovery on the beach at Adyar, his early tuition by Leadbeater; no recollection of his visits to the astral plane, or his authorship of *At the Feet of the Master*. Indeed, the idea that memory is a trap became a central tenet of his philosophy, allied with the desirability of emptying the mind of everything but facts. 'A mind that is not empty, can never find truth.'

'Thought is the response of memory, the past,' he wrote in *The Urgency of Change*:

> When thought acts it is this past which is acting as memory, as experience, as knowledge, as opportunity. All will is desire based on this past and directed towards pleasure or the avoidance of pain. When thought is functioning it is the past, therefore there is no new living at all; it is the past living in the present, modifying itself and the present. So there is nothing new in life that way, and when something new is to be found there must be the absence of the past, the mind must not be cluttered up with thought, fear, pleasure and everything else.

This is an exacting description of how we act on conditioned impulses, but for most of us such freedom from memory seems a remote, unattainable goal, even if it is a desirable one. However illusory they may be, memories are the components of who we believe ourselves to be; they give us a sense of our own biography, our own history. But it is easy to acknowledge that they may equally be a prison, for as much as we draw solace and consolation from our memories, so they also remind us of what we have lost; friends whom we shall never see again, moments of innocence or happiness that can never be retrieved. There are few words in the English language more poignant than *longing*.

But Krishnamurti was talking of something more subtle than our tendency to dwell nostalgically in the past. What Krishnamurti was advocating was a stilling of the mind, living completely in the moment, in a condition – 'a sacredness' as he put it – 'which is not of thought, nor of a feeling resuscitated by thought . . . It is not communicable.'

He was vehemently opposed to any systemised form of study or meditation designed to realise this state. He would not read any religious, psychological or philosophical books. 'One can go into oneself at tremendous depths and find out everything,' he said. And he scorned 'conscious' meditation techniques:

> Sitting cross-legged or lying down or repeating certain phrases, which is a deliberate, conscious effort to meditate . . . such meditation is nonsense. It is part of desire. Desiring to have a peaceful mind is the same as desiring a good house or a good dress. Conscious meditation destroys, prevents the other forms of meditation.

He was equally contemptuous of the whole idea of 'gurudom':

> When a guru says he knows, he does not. Enlightenment is not to be attained. It is not something you can reach step by step as if you were climbing a ladder . . . One does not like to use the word 'enlightenment'; it is so loaded with the meaning given by all these gurus . . . Whether they are Eastern or Western gurus, doubt what they are saying, doubt also what the speaker is saying – much more so, because although he is very clear about these matters it does not mean he is the only person who knows, which is absurd.
>
> The mind must be free from all authority – no followers, disciples and patterns . . . nobody can give guidance, give light to another. Only yourself can do that; but you have to stand completely alone.

It was a message he repeated tirelessly. In the last years of his life, Krishnamurti was insistent that after his death there should be no interpreters of his teachings; that no one should speak in his name; that no church or dogma should arise from his teaching. 'Truth is not yours or mine. It has no country, no race, no people, it has no belief, no dogma. I have repeated this *ad nauseam*.'

From the Thirties onwards, Krishnamurti made his home in Ojai, California, where his affairs were looked after by his childhood friend Rajagopal, and Raja's wife Rosalind. He continued to travel the world, lecturing and writing, unable to reconcile the paradox of arguing against the idea of gurus while having a large and devoted following hanging on his every word – 'the licensed guru of the wealthy classes', as the writer Peter Washington put it, whose engagements looked 'more like *Jennifer's Diary* than a guru's'. Certainly, whether by chance or design, he was drawn into the orbit of the wealthy and the famous, and enjoyed a distinctly comfortable life, while all the time insisting that it meant nothing to him. He drove expensive cars provided by devoted friends. He never lost his taste for Savile Row suits and hogskin gloves. When in London he would lunch at Fortnum and Mason.

The actor Terence Stamp told me of meeting Krishnamurti in Italy in the Sixties, when Stamp was a rising young film star. 'We went for a walk. I remember I was gabbling away, asking him all sorts of questions, and he would just touch me on the shoulder and say, "Look at the clouds; look at the trees." Just getting me to stop my mind, y'know.' Stamp became a student of Krishnamurti's teachings.

'Whenever I met him, he'd never talk about spiritual progress or anything like that. We'd talk about clothes. "Lovely shirt, Terence; where'd you get that?" "Lovely suit, Krishnaji." We were,' Stamp remembered fondly, 'like a couple of birds . . .' One may charitably assume that Krishnamurti had discovered the secret of enjoying beautiful things without being ensnared by them.

Among the wisest and most beautiful things that Krishnamurti had to say was this, on the subject of love:

> Fear is not love, dependence is not love, jealousy is not love, possessiveness and domination are not love, responsibility and duty are not love, self-pity is not love, love is not the opposite of hate any more than humility is the opposite of vanity. So if you can eliminate all these, not by forcing them but by washing them away as the rain washes the dust of many days from a leaf, then perhaps you will come upon this strange flower which man always hungers after.

These words take on a particular poignancy in the light of the revelation, some years after his death, in the book *Lives in the Shadow with J. Krishnamurti* by Radha Rajagopal Sloss – the daughter of Raja and Rosalind, and effectively Krishnamurti's 'god-daughter' – that Krishnamurti had actually enjoyed a long and clandestine affair with Rosalind.

The affair should not, perhaps, be judged too harshly. After the birth of Radha, Raja and Rosalind had apparently ceased sexual relations altogether; Krishnamurti, it seems, brought her a comfort and love that she was unable to find in her marriage. And she brought him an intimacy that he was unable to find among his respectful and adoring followers. The revelation of the affair seems only further to humanise a man who had spent much of his life shrugging off the burden of divinity.

But while his insistence that he was not 'the World Teacher' remained throughout his life, so too did his belief in his own spiritual singularity. Shortly before his death, in 1986, in his last tape-recorded conversation, he said, 'For seventy years that super energy – no – that immense energy, immense intelligence has been using this body . . . You won't find another body like this, or that supreme intelligence operating in a body for many hundreds of years. You won't see it again. When he goes, it goes . . .'

I returned to my hotel, under the watchful gaze of the young men on the landing. An urgent request for toilet paper was met with blank, uncomprehending stares. I pantomimed my mounting desperation. Thirty minutes later a boy arrived at my door, and ceremoniously presented me with three sheets.

The Maharaja Hotel, where I ate breakfast and dinner, was crowded with Westerners – a curious whiff of the Glastonbury Festival on the streets of Madras. Bearded hippies in matted Afghan sweaters; New Age punks with shaved heads; travellers in shorts, brandishing maps and guide books, bum-bags bulging at their waists. I fell into conversation with a man sharing my table – the conversation you always had with Westerners.

'The first time I came to India,' he said, 'I thought: The poor, poor people. I felt bad for them. The second time I came, I just thought: Poor people, and felt less bad. Now I think: It's just the way it is. You can't feed India; India must feed India.' He shrugged his shoulders. 'If you don't give you feel guilty. If you give you feel guilty, because what are you doing? You are throwing two rupees to get them out of your life, to give yourself some peace for a moment. My friend, charity is hypocrisy.'

His name was Maurice; he was a French-Canadian from Montreal. He was fifty, short and stocky with a face like a wrinkled apple. In Montreal he worked as a taxi-driver, but mostly he travelled. 'Once

I had a regular job. I was married . . .' He shrugged. 'Now I drive a taxi, because that way I'm independent. I got to forty-five and thought: Who am I? I wanted to know. A lot of people go through life without ever knowing who they are. This is a terrible thing.'

So, you have come to India to find yourself, I said teasingly.

He grinned. 'Maybe. I sometimes think I've come to be as lost as I ever was – but in more interesting surroundings.' He had come from Calcutta, he said, where he had been working in the hospital of Mother Teresa. 'I was washing people, washing the floor. In the West we don't like to touch each other, we are all in our little prisons – we move away on the subway or the bus. But in India nobody cares. There's no private space. So I am washing old men, their bodies, their privates, the shit, washing with the bare hands. You learn a lot about yourself doing that, because I believe if you are doing things for other people, really you are doing it for yourself. To really love other people, it's hard.' He paused. 'There was an Australian boy there, and people loved him very much. He would hold them and wash them and they would smile because they knew he loved them.' Maurice rapped the table for emphasis. '*He loved them*. With me, it wasn't so easy.'

And what, he asked, was I doing in Madras?

I talked about the Theosophical Society, Blavatsky, Krishnamurti, the Masters.

'And they're supposed to be looking after us, yes?' he said with a smile. 'They're not doing such a good job of it, I think.'

He was on his way to the south, he said, to do a course in Vipassana meditation. 'I'm not so interested in God, this and that. But to know myself, you know – get a perspective on myself. Like, my feelings. I'm trying to watch myself have my feelings now. It's possible, yes, to stand back. There are two yous; the way you see yourself and the way you really are. So with your feelings, watch them come and go, and realise those feelings are not really you; they will pass. Don't become attached to your feelings. Like, I used to be very aggressive when I was younger. I get angry, I could kill someone. But now, not. If I have a feeling I don't fight it, but I don't give in to it. I just watch myself having it. The middle way, you know?

'Seriously, this is happening for me. Last week I was sick, and for days I was able to do that – just remove myself from it. Now, twenty minutes, half an hour a day I achieve it.'

And what, I asked, do you want from this?

'What does anyone want? No pain, my friend.' He smiled and scooped up some vegetables. 'No pain.'

I spent my last day in Madras at the Theosophical Society. It was a glorious afternoon, the sky cloudless and bird's-egg blue; a light breeze tempering the heat of the day. I walked through the grounds, curious to see the beach where Leadbeater had discovered Krishnamurti. The path led through some woods, ending at a high brick wall, with a stout wooden door, which was bolted and padlocked. A uniformed guard lounged nearby. The door was opened at five o'clock, he said, so that members of the Society could walk on the beach. He looked at his watch. It was three-forty-five. Could he unlock it for me now? He gave the question some thought. Yes, he said at last, but the door would be locked behind me.

The guard's prevarication had invested my walk to the beach with an improbable sense of adventure. I stepped through the gate, feeling absurdly as if I was stepping into the wardrobe that would lead to Narnia. An expanse of pure white sand ran down to a turquoise sea. I walked along the beach, and settled myself on a rise in the sand. I was quite alone. To my left, where the broad inlet of the Adyar River met the sea, the beach was utterly deserted; to my right, squinting, I could make out the dark shadows of some fishermen's huts several hundred yards away; some figures at the water's edge, shimmering in the heat haze.

The warmth of the late-afternoon sun on my face, the water lapping creamily against the beach, I tried to picture Leadbeater, the eccentric, dreamy Englishman, discovering his messiah. I reached for my notebook intending to scribble notes about Mahatmas and avatars and Krishnamurti, then put it to one side. I stared out to sea, losing my thoughts in the gentle undulation of the water and the shards of sunlight playing on its surface, dissolving the separation between the sea, the sky, the light, the sand into an indistinct mass of dancing particles, of which I myself was a part. For a moment I was suffused with a feeling of calm and perfect contentment, of being submerged in some eternal present. It was as if I had forgotten myself. But no sooner was I aware of it than the feeling began to dissolve as more mundane thoughts began to crowd in. I should be making my way back to Madras soon. Rickshaw or taxi? Would my belongings still be in my hotel room? I was flying to Bombay tomorrow, to catch my flight to England. I don't like flying . . . I was aware of the

familiar sensation of hearing my own thoughts, skittering around
in my mind like rats trapped in a cage.

The blissful isolation, which moments before had put me at my
ease, now seemed to be having the opposite effect. All I could feel
was a growing sense of dissatisfaction with my own company, the
degree to which I was anchored by the contingencies of my own
life. Absurdly, inexplicably, a sudden feeling of vulnerability began
to come over me. The beach was utterly deserted, the gate behind
me locked; if I was set upon here, what would I do? But the thought
was absurd. Nothing bad had happened to me in India. Nothing bad
would happen to me. There was no one else here but me and my
groundless, ridiculous fears.

No sooner had I thought this than I heard voices. Where seconds
before, it seemed, there had been no one on the beach, now there
was a group of young men, seven or eight in all, in their late-teens
by the look of it, pushing and jostling one another as they tracked
across the sand. Catching sight of me, they changed direction. It was
almost as if my fears had brought them here. I froze momentarily,
and then they were upon me, falling on the sand beside me, reaching
out their hands to shake mine. 'Good sir, good sir . . .' They were
as playful as puppies. Who was I? What was I doing here? I came
from England? Ah, England very good, very bad at cricket. They
laughed delightedly among themselves. And on we talked for what
seemed like ages; about their studies, their families, about Michael
Jackson, about English girls (in which they were greatly interested);
about their dreams. One wished to repair televisions, another to be
an engineer, to leave India, to travel. They wanted motor bikes,
and sound-systems and to marry the girl of their own, not their
family's, choosing. All of the things I would have wanted if I had
been them.

At one stage, I motioned towards the gate in the wall; the
Theosophical Society. Had they ever heard of Krishnamurti, I
asked. They had not. It was too complicated a story, too remote,
to tell them. And anyway, it occurred to me that they would have
found the story absurd; they were not interested in the abstractions
of philosophy – why should they be? They were interested in making
lives for themselves.

One of the boys spoke better English than the rest. He was not
the eldest, nor the noisiest, but it quickly became obvious that he
was the one to whom the others deferred. 'And please tell me, sir.'

He regarded me gravely. 'You come from England, you are a writer. Tell us, what advice would you give us for our lives?'

They had fallen silent and were seated around me, looking at me expectantly. What could I tell them? Work hard at your studies. Life is yours to do as you choose. It was all platitudes, but they listened intently – much more intently than the advice was worth.

I returned to my hotel room. Of course, it was exactly as I had left it. I lay on the bed, thinking of the meeting on the beach, and reading Krishnamurti. I came upon an address he had given in 1927.

What are you seeking . . . you who strive and struggle and ache eternally with unsatisfied longings? Is it money? Is it possessions? Is it fame? Is it physical comfort? Is it love? Is it spiritual safety? . . . Yes indeed, you *think* it is one of these things. But I tell you it is not. What you are seeking for ceaselessly, day and night, is Happiness . . . *The thing you seek is ever at your hand.* Be Happy, and then whatever you do will be worthwhile . . . Do that which makes you happy to do, and you will do right.

Do that which makes you happy to do, and you will do right.

That is what I should have told them.

And, always trust to goodness. I should have told them that too.

8

A TALL MAN IN THE MOSQUE

England seemed pallid and monochromatic on my return, the morning joust on the London underground a particularly Kafkaesque form of torture. I found myself yearning for India. My thoughts turned to Mr Creme. Little it seemed had changed in the saga of Maitreya. Mr Creme was still giving lectures, and his 'transmission group' was still meeting in the shed at the bottom of his garden on a regular basis, transmitting cosmic energy.

The pronouncements of Mr Creme's Master in the pages of *Share International* maintained their customary air of sonorous prophecy and impenetrable ambiguity:

> Trust then the skill in action of the Lord of Love. Chafe not at the seeming delay of His appearance – in the all-embracing Now no such delay exists. Ere long, the Son of Man will assume His rightful place as the teacher of mankind . . .

There were bulletins of further appearances by Maitreya in Morocco, Volgograd, Equador and Flagstaff, Arizona. The letters pages were full of tales of mysterious strangers and miraculous deeds. A correspondent from Ljubljana, Slovenia told of encountering a man 'near a goldsmith's shop', holding a placard bearing the legend 'Happiness is free', and offering 'loud and heartfelt' greetings to passers-by. The italicised footnote had Mr Creme's Master explaining that the man was 'the Master Jesus'. In short, nothing had changed.

I sat in Mr Creme's living room, among the paintings, books and classical records, drinking tea. I was eager to tell him news of my travels, particularly to hear his views on the subject of avatars.

'There are always avatars in the world,' said Mr Creme. 'Krishna

was an avatar, Ramakrishna, the Babaji who was written about by
Yogananda . . .'

Did he think Sai Baba was an avatar?

'Sai Baba is a Spiritual Regent,' said Mr Creme.

And Maitreya?

Mr Creme reached to his bookshelf, pulled down one of his own
volumes and began to scrutinise the index. The Cosmic Hierarchy,
he explained, was based on degrees of initiation, a scheme of gradation
which had been revealed by Madame Blavatsky, elaborated on by
Alice Bailey, and further illuminated by his own Master. The highest
degree of initiation was 9. The Buddha is an 8th-degree initiate;
Maitreya is a 7th-degree initiate. The average point of evolution of
the educated, but not spiritually orientated, human being, he said,
could be 'anything from 0.2 or 3, to 0.5 or 6'.

'As soon as you've taken the 1st initiation you're a member of
the Hierarchy even at a very low level. You are then a 1-degree
initiate. In the various groups around the world I'm dealing with
they'd be 0.8 to 2. There are not many who are 2.'

I found myself silently wondering where I stood in this cosmic
pecking order. Not very high, I suspected. The potential for elitism
was depressingly apparent.

But not everybody who claimed to be an avatar, cautioned
Mr Creme, could be taken as such.

I asked, what about Mother Meera?

'She's seen as an avatar, and she allows people to see her as an
avatar, but she's not at all. She's a disciple of one of the Masters.
She does good work, but the glamour of the illusion is that she's an
avatar. If she believes it herself, it's illusion. She doesn't contradict
people when they say she's an avatar. But neither did Rajneesh. He
let it be believed that he was Maitreya Buddha, but he was only 2.3.'
Mr Creme flicked through his book. 'Look at this. Picasso was 2.4
. . . Rajneesh was misled by glamours. He did a lot of good work.
But what happened around him, and in terms of what he allowed
others to believe about him, has to be corrected.'

He ran his finger down the list. 'Here we are. Meher Baba. 2.4.
The same as Picasso.'

But Meher Baba claimed he was an avatar, I said.

'Yes, well, at his level it's somewhere between glamour and illusion.
Glamour is illusion on the astral plane; and illusion is illusion on
the mental plane. You would assume that anybody who's 2.5 would

probably no longer have the glamour of anybody up to that point. But they could from then on suffer from mental illusion, rather than astral glamour. It's all the same form but on different planes. Anyway, I think Meher Baba was completely deluded. A religious genius – but mad.'

Many followers of Sai Baba, I said, had told me that *he* was the awaited Christ. Was this Maitreya?

'No, Maitreya is Maitreya.' Mr Creme gave a small sigh – the schoolteacher diligently struggling with a particularly dull pupil – and settled back into his chair. 'Sai Baba is not a Master of our Hierarchy. He does not come from our earth at all. Maitreya is a Master who comes out of our earth Hierarchy, and all the Masters at the present time, except for a few high *kamaras*, they're called, come out of our earth Hierarchy.

'Sai Baba is one of the greatest, highest avatars who have come to this earth. He is the embodiment of cosmic love. Maitreya is the embodiment of that same energy of love but at the *planetary* level. Maitreya could be anywhere in the solar system he chooses to be, but he chooses to stay on earth to do his work. He is the embodied soul of humanity – the Christ principle is the consciousness principle, which is the nature of the soul.

'Now, Sai Baba does the same thing at the cosmic level. So they're both the Christ. And they're both in the world at this extraordinary time together. And they work together all the time. Sai Baba is like a benevolent uncle to the Hierarchy.'

As so often when I listened to Mr Creme, I was confused. I wanted to ask him what I always wanted to ask him – how did he *know* all this? I told Mr Creme my reservations about the ashram at Puttaparthi – the pushy guards, the commercial circus at its gates, the hunger of devotees to be close to Sai Baba, and the air of almost hysterical adulation around him. And I told him of my disappointment that Sai Baba had not taken my letter.

'Well, he probably did that deliberately,' said Mr Creme matter-of-factly. 'Of course, he knows what's in the letter anyway.'

That, I said, is what everybody had told me.

'Well, he is omniscient, of course. He's a Master. A Master *plus*!' Mr Creme beamed. 'It's a terrible thing, but the glamour surrounding a being like Sai Baba is just colossal. He is seen as the creator of the universe. If you were to ask him, are you the creator of the universe, as many people have asked him, he'd say yes – but so are you. But people forget this *so are you.* They get carried away with this idea that "I am a devotee of the creator of the universe; this man is ruling everything." I know people who can't cross the road or have spaghetti for lunch without thinking they've got the OK from Sai Baba.' Mr Creme's face was crinkling up in laughter. 'They think he's directing their every thought and action! As if he hasn't got more important things to do! It's a travesty of truth! It's not like that at all.'

He paused. 'But that sort of thinking is inevitable among devotees. You see, I'm not a devotee. I'm deeply respectful, of course. Some people are devotees, but I'm not. I don't much *like* devotees, I must say. I'd rather talk to sceptics than to devotees. I'm more interested in the world. And I've devoted twenty-one years to making the story of Maitreya known, but to the world. And in a way it's for Maitreya, but I don't think of it in those terms. I was just asked to do it. I do it for the Plan. I associate myself with the Plan, rather than with individuals. Maitreya's energy can bring tears instantaneously to my eyes; he can move one in the deepest sense, but it doesn't inspire devotion. It inspires love, but to me that's a different thing.'

I wondered, had Mr Creme ever been tempted to go and meet Sai Baba for himself?

'I have, yes, but I'm asked by my Master not to go for the time being. When Maitreya's out in the world and so on, maybe I'll slip off when nobody's looking. But I have no need to go – and I hate the conditions, the crowds, the mosquitoes . . . I'm seventy-three and shudder at the very idea. But he comes to me.'

He comes to you?

'Oh yes, he overshadows me at my lectures, if anybody asks me a question about him, which often happens. Let me tell you a story . . .' Mr Creme settled back into his chair and I felt a familiar tingle of anticipation. I enjoyed Mr Creme's stories.

'There was a woman in Paris, in the French group, one of the number-one workers, all her rays blazing with aspiration. Then she went to her doctor, who happened to be a fundamentalist Christian, and he talked her out of it. She withdrew from the group, and ran it down, ran me down. It was terrible.' Mr Creme shook his head. 'Totally emotional, of course, both ways.

'And then she got hold of Sai Baba, and went off to India. And she came back and told a colleague of mine who was running the French group that she had been to see Sai Baba, and he had told her that Benjamin Creme had tried to get to Puttaparthi and Sai Baba wouldn't even let him in the ashram. I was sitting with a group of people in Switzerland when I heard this, and it absolutely rocked me with laughter. Because it was totally untrue, of course. And at that moment Sai Baba suddenly overshadowed me, and he said, "When you treat me with respect I will treat you with respect." And I knew exactly what he meant. Because when I'm talking about Sai Baba I make jokes about him. I once called him the stunt-man of the Logos – the Lord of the World – because he stands in for Him, and he does stunts, you see, producing the *vibhuti* and the miracles and so on. But for me this is a way to make Sai Baba human, to take away this . . . adulation. I make jokes about Maitreya and the Masters, to demystify the whole thing. So he said, "When you treat me with respect I will treat you with respect, and if you come to India, and if you come to Puttaparthi, and if you can get your decrepit old body through the gate, then I will let you in."'

Mr Creme was roaring with laughter, wiping the tears from his eyes with the back of his hand.

And then? I prompted him.

He grew more serious. 'And then he overshadowed me with this tremendous power for all the people there. This is humour, you see? This is what the great ones are like. They have this extraordinary sense of humour.'

Mr Creme's story reminded me of one of my own: the story of the Christmas card that I had received from my friend Stephen in Australia, and the mysterious disappearance of the portrait of Sai Baba that was inside the envelope.

'I know this sounds crazy,' I said (hardly a necessary *caveat*, as it happens, in any conversation with Mr Creme), 'but for a moment I actually found myself believing that Sai Baba had made the card disappear himself.'

I expected Mr Creme to chuckle at this, but he regarded me indulgently. 'I'll ask him,' he said. He closed his eyes and sat silently on the sofa, hands folded peacefully in his lap. Outside the window, a car changed gear as it made its way up the hill. Mr Creme was nodding his head, as if engaged in some private and silent conversation. 'Oh yes,' he said at last. 'Sai Baba says he made the picture vanish. It was an encouragement.' He smiled. 'They have a wonderful sense of humour, these people.'

*   *   *

There had, in fact, been a development in the ongoing saga of Maitreya: a development as nebulous, and as unbelievable, as anything I had yet encountered. It was Patricia Pitchon – the journalist who claimed to have seen Maitreya all those years ago in Brick Lane, and who had introduced me to the prophetic Mr Patel – who told me the story.

Henri was a Frenchman with a small import/export business in fruit and vegetables, in Perpignan. Some years ago he had come into contact with Benjamin Creme, started his own meditation group and become involved with various schemes to help the homeless and unemployed. Then he came to London on 'a pilgrimage' to find Maitreya, walking up and down Brick Lane with the photograph taken in Nairobi and published in the *Kenya Times* in 1988, showing it to shopkeepers and passers-by. In a tea-shop in Brick Lane, an 'unusual-looking' man claimed to have recognised the figure in the picture, and told Henri that the man could be found at Friday evening prayers in a nearby mosque, where he was recognised as a great teacher.

That Friday, Patricia and her husband accompanied Henri to the mosque. Glancing through the window in a downstairs office, Patricia told me, she had seen a man, wearing a turban and dressed in white, so tall that he seemed 'like a giant'. This, said Patricia, was a distortion, 'which I realised was happening because of the power emanating from this man'. Before she had a chance to approach him, she said, a mosque official had noticed her staring, and hurried her away. Later, inside the prayer hall, Henri had seen the same man, but he had vanished into the crowd, leaving the mosque before they had a chance to talk to him. Mr Creme, said Patricia, had consulted his Master, and confirmed that the tall man dressed in white was indeed Maitreya.

Like everything to do with the legend of Maitreya, the story was absurd, implausible, completely without proof or verification. I telephoned Mr Creme. 'My Master says the man will be at the mosque this Friday,' he said.

The mosque was situated on a dreary arterial road in East London, lined with clothing wholesalers and sweatshops. Litter gusted along the pavement; heavy-goods lorries and commuter traffic thundered past. I arrived too early, and sat in a pub opposite the mosque, drinking orange juice, a game show jangling on the television in the corner.

There were curious looks when, at last, I entered the mosque, slipped off my shoes and stepped into the prayer hall. Unsure what to do, I stood to one side as the faithful arranged themselves in lines, knelt and chanted their prayers. As always, I felt myself moved by the solemnity and power of ritual, and aware of the absence in my life of what it symbolised – faith. I scanned the congregation, unsure exactly what I was looking for. It was uniformly Asian. A number of the men were turbaned; a number wore white; a number were also tall.

My presence in the prayer hall had not gone unnoticed. At the conclusion of prayers, a man approached and asked what was I doing there. I asked if I might speak to the secretary of the mosque. I was shown to an office. The secretary was a young man, no more than thirty-five, who listened impassively as I struggled to formulate my questions. Best, I thought, not to mention Maitreya, Mr Creme or telepathic messages from a Hierarchy of Himalayan Masters. I was looking for a man, I said, a special teacher. The secretary looked at me blankly. A tall man, I said, especially wise. He shrugged his shoulders. I had a sudden realisation that he thought he might be dealing with a madman.

I tried a different tack. Islam, I said, believed in the coming of a redeemer, the Mahdi. He nodded. Was there a particular time when this was expected?

'Not immediately . . .' He shuffled in his seat, obviously anxious to bring this strange interlude to a close. Perhaps, he said, I wished to learn more of Islam? Instruction could be arranged, but in the meantime . . . He reached behind him to a bookshelf and pulled out an introduction to the Koran which he passed to me. 'Please, take it.'

The conversation was over.

I telephoned Patricia to tell her of my visit. She was resiliently upbeat about my lack of success. 'You have to realise that it's very difficult for them. The Muslim community. They feel under siege already. If they had people saying they claimed Christ was living in a mosque in East London who knows what would happen.'

I spoke to Mr Creme.

'My Master says you saw Maitreya there,' he said with a laugh. 'He says you were looking right at him.'

I was getting used to this.

*   *   *

Whenever I spoke to Mr Creme, sooner or later the subject would turn to miracles. The pages of *Share International* were littered with the latest accounts of this extraordinary occurrence, that amazing apparition. Not least among them was the phenomenon of 'healing waters'.

The first healing waters appeared on a ranch in the small town of Tlacote, two hours' drive north of Mexico City, in 1991. The healing properties of the water were first discovered by the ranch owner when his injured dog drank the water and quickly recovered. Since then some three million people have made the pilgrimage to Tlacote, and twice that number are estimated to have drunk the water. It is claimed that it has healed a variety of ailments including diabetes, epilepsy, arthritis, cancer and even Aids. The ranch at Tlacote had been turned into a vast well for hopeful pilgrims. The Mexican government provided a pumping station; the water was stored in huge stainless-steel tanks, volunteers packaging it for distribution around the world and giving medical advice.

The fame of the Tlacote water has spread throughout the world. In London it is available in a homeopathic potency. Tony Pinkus, who manages Ainsworth's Homeopathic Pharmacy, told me the water had no discernible material or chemical peculiarities; it simply seemed, he said, to be 'blessed'. It was used as a general panacea, a 'cleansing or healing device', and seemed particularly effective for restoring energy after illness. 'It works consistently with the homeopathic principle of catharsis, reversing the passage of an illness along the lines it developed, but unlike conventional homeopathic remedies, which have a discrete application – something works for the eye, something else for the stomach – the water's effects seem to be completely open-ended.'

There was no ready explanation for this, said Pinkus. 'The explanation is that it seems to work.'

Mr Creme had no doubt about its explanation. Wherever he appeared around the world, said Mr Creme, Maitreya would 'charge' water in the area. Similar sources of 'healing water' had been found at Nordenau in Germany, at Nadana in India and elsewhere. These 'healing waters' were among a whole panoply of phenomena, said Mr Creme, which are signs given by Maitreya to create a climate of hope and expectancy for his arrival. They included the increasing Marian apparitions throughout the world, the miraculous disappearance of milk offered to statues of Ganesh in New Delhi and elsewhere. They were, said Mr Creme, part of 'the Plan'.

Among the most intriguing of these phenomena were the so-called 'Crosses of Light' – quite literally, crosses of light, looking rather like holographic images, which appear apparently suspended in mid-air between frosted glass and a light-source. The first Crosses of Light appeared in 1988 in the bathroom window of a house in the predominantly Hispanic suburb of El Monte, Los Angeles. The householder had taken it as a blessing. Before long, healings were being reported in the immediate vicinity. The house had become something of a shrine. Crime in the area began to drop. The window had been removed to the sanctuary of a local church. The Crosses of Light had vanished, only to reappear when the window was reinstalled in the bathroom where it had originally been. If it was a sign it seemed to be one directed at pious individuals rather than the institution of the Church.

Since their first appearance in El Monte, similar crosses had been reported elsewhere in America, Canada, New Zealand and the Philippines, always in people's homes. Now the crosses had appeared for the first time in a church, the Copper Ridge Baptist Church, in the town of Knoxville, Tennessee. These were said to be the most vivid and spectacular crosses of all.

'I'm told that Maitreya has appeared there too,' said Mr Creme. 'And the Master Jesus.'

I had read an account of the crosses in a copy of *Share International*, and I telephoned its author Buddy Piper at his home in California.

Buddy came straight to the point. 'When I was six years old,' he said, 'I knew that before I died I would see something major for Planet Earth.'

He was now in his seventies, and believed that something major had arrived. Buddy had an eclectic curriculum vitae. He had been a scriptwriter and a comedian. He had been a regular on the Red Skelton show on American television. He was the co-creator of what he claimed was the longest-running game show on American television, *Classic Concentration*; the co-host of *Winky Dink*, a network children's show, and the creator/writer/host of a television programme called *The Bible Story Game*. He had organised public information programmes on drink-driving, and 'The Art of Creating Self-Esteem'. At some stage in his eventful progress through life,

Buddy had come across the books of Benjamin Creme. Mr Creme's teachings on Maitreya as the teacher who would unify the world under a creed of love and sharing had struck a chord.

'I knew that religion wasn't going to solve the world's problems, because they're all exclusive – y'know, we're the only ones that know the way.' I could hear Buddy's sigh of exasperation down the telephone line. 'What the world needs is something *inclusive*. When Ben said, we are not bodies with souls, we are souls with bodies – we are all sparks of God – that spoke to me.'

Then he heard of the crosses in El Monte. He visited them himself, and was convinced they were a sign. When he heard news of the crosses in the Copper Ridge Baptist Church in Knoxville, he knew that too was a miracle. He had travelled to Tennessee, witnessed for himself the crosses flaring in the windows, met the pastor of the church, Joe Bullard, and been convinced of his sincerity. The pursuit of the miraculous had given Buddy a new career in the autumn of his life. Styling himself as 'the Cross Chaser', he energetically promoted news of the crosses, and the coming of Maitreya, to whomever would listen. He had appeared on 100 radio and TV shows in the last eight months alone.

Buddy faxed me his literature. Its somewhat excitable tone seemed perfectly attuned to the jaded attention-spans of radio and TV programmers: 'The X-Files? UFOs, Angels, Healing Crosses, the Alien Autopsy . . . **Startling Supernatural Messages We Can't Ignore**.' There was no mention that I could see of Maitreya. That was deliberate, Buddy explained. Get on the programme with the kind of headline-making material that people could understand, and *then* you could start talking about the world teacher to come. The literature was illustrated with a photograph of Buddy, a puck-faced man with a crinkly, beaming smile and a head of silver hair. He looked uncannily like Benjamin Creme's younger brother.

Another leaflet dealt explicitly with the Crosses of Light. It read: 'Gifts of Love they will cherish for ever . . .! Take your family to see the **Amazing Flaming Miracles** in Knoxville, Tennessee – before they disappear.' (The addendum struck an uncharacteristic note of pessimism, I thought.) 'Locals believe no one sees these without experiencing physical, emotional or spiritual healings immediately or in the near future.' A footnote added:

More Miracles
* Where to get drinking water that heals
* Weeping Madonnas, Crop Circles, UFOs and Angels
* How to get on a free mailing list for new miracles

Need a last-minute guest? Piper is available on a moment's notice 24-hours-a-day!

I added my name to Buddy's mailing list, and set off for America.

9

THE CROSSES OF LIGHT

I arrived in Knoxville, rented a car at the airport and drove north, following the freeway signs to Lexington. I found a Christian station on the radio, a speaker urging moral uplift and a return to family values, interleaved with the customarily saccharine, atrocious devotional music. The freeway skirted the town, a handful of obelisks etched against the darkening sky.

I had passed through this part of East Tennessee once before, many years ago. It was a place that I associated, perhaps improbably, with charity. Stranded in California without the price of an airfare, my wife and I had offered to drive someone's VW Beetle across America to New York. It was a hair-raising experience; it was late November, and from the moment we crossed the state-line into New Mexico I was driving in blinding snow, the car buffeted like a leaf on the freeways by an endless caravan of heavy-duty trucks. East of Knoxville, near a small town called Bristol, the car finally expired under the exertions of the journey. It was a Sunday night and we were stranded on a roadside, seemingly miles from anywhere. I trekked through the snow to a road-house, looking for help. Of course, no garages were open, but there was a local man, I was told, Jesse, a mechanic, who knew about VWs. Jesse was called on the telephone. He arrived an hour later, fixed a rope to our car and towed it back to his house through the snow. We pushed it into his garage. While Jesse worked on the car, his wife cooked supper. Food had never tasted so good. They would not hear of us setting off into the darkness in search of a motel room, but put us up for the night, under a quilt hand-stitched by Jesse's wife. Nor would they take any money. It was enough to make you believe in angels – or at least in the fundamental generosity of one's fellow man.

That was more than twenty years ago. We had exchanged letters and Christmas cards, and then Jesse and his wife had divorced and we'd lost touch. I thought of them now as I followed the road, beyond the city limits, and into the outer suburbs. A forest of signs at the roadside signalled a colony of travellers' motels, restaurants and service stations. I turned off, and found a room in a Howard Johnson's. Strolling across the parking-lot, I noticed a huge golden cross, suspended in the sky above signs for an Outback Steak House and the sulphurous arch of McDonald's. But this was a cross not of light, but of gold neon. Tennessee, after all, is Bible-belt country. I telephoned Joe Bullard, the pastor of the Copper Ridge Baptist Church, and arranged to meet him at the church the next day. It was raining as I drove north, along a road lined with car dealerships, exhaust centres and strip-mall plazas, decorated with plastic flags flapping in the stiff autumnal breeze. The suburban detritus gave way to woods. In summertime it might have looked pretty, but under the scudding clouds, the cloak of drizzle, the spray from cars and pick-up trucks, it looked louring and oppressive. A sign on the roadside, beside a dirt track, said: 'Party here this Friday.'

A few miles further on, I turned on to a side road, which dipped up and around into the hills. Single-storey ranch houses and trailer-homes dotted the hillside, some neatly tended, others littered with ramshackle collections of old automobiles and domestic junk.

The Copper Ridge Baptist Church was set in a shallow fold in the hills; a simple, but handsome, white clapboard building. I turned into the parking-lot, climbed out of the car, and tried the door of the church. It was locked. I walked around the church. There were three windows on the left-hand side, two on the right. They were sash windows, made of a rippled, opaque glass, set in aluminium frames. The bottom half of each window was covered with a fine metal-mesh screen. On either side of the church were tall street-lamps, to illuminate the parking-lot. I sat in my car waiting for Joe Bullard, watching the rain fall on the church and thinking this looked nothing like the setting for a miracle – but, then again, what did? A blue Cadillac turned into the parking-lot, and the Reverend Bullard got out. He was a tall, rangily-built man in his seventies, blinking behind spectacles. He was wearing a blue windcheater jacket and trainers. A bumper sticker on his car read: 'My boss is a Jewish carpenter.' (Later, I would notice his licence plate bore another legend: 'The church with the unexplained crosses.')

Joe let me into the church, flicked on the lights and the heating, and said, 'This is it,' like a curator showing me a museum exhibit. It

was a neat little church, freshly painted and carpeted, with a dozen or
so scrubbed-wood pews on either side of a central aisle. At one end
was a raised stage, with a simple wooden lectern, flanked by the stars
and stripes and the state flag of Tennessee. On the wall, facing the
congregation, was a picture of Christ, kitschy, sentimental, adorned
with a flounced curtain, like an opera set. I could see no crosses in
the windows. 'Well, there's no light to fire 'em up yet, y'see,' said
Joe. 'When it's dark, you'll see them. And when the sun's out too.
But now it's raining.'

We sat in one of the pews, and Joe told me his story, speaking
in a thick, strangulated Southern accent. He was born in Knoxville,
and had been a Baptist minister (*Bab-dist*) for fifty-two years, in
which time he had founded rescue missions and started and built
six churches. He was all set to retire (*re-tah*) when, thirteen years
ago, he was asked to take over as pastor of Copper Ridge.

'This here is a Methodist community, and when I came in this
church was dying. We had a tin roof (*ruff*). There was maybe twelve
other people in the congregation besides my wife and myself.' The last
thirteen years had been hard, he said. 'I had prayed and prayed that
God's wisdom and knowledge would help us to do something.'

Then came the crosses.

'It was 8 November 1995, at approximately three minutes after
six. I was fixing to preach. Now this blind was down . . .' He
gestured to the window closest to the lectern. 'And all at once
I see a light come shining through the blind. I went over and
pulled the blind up – and that blind's never been touched since
– and I looked out and saw a small cross, no bigger than 12 inches
tall. And all at once the cross started growing, and well, now some
people say they look like they're 40 feet tall. Now the winders has
been in the church for twenty-seven years. So I asked the people
in the church, what do you want to do? You want to show this to
people, or forget it? We studied about it, and some of them said,
let's open the doors.

'I said, before we do we gonna talk to the man who put the
winders in. Horace Gray is his name. He was the contractor. I
had Mr Gray to meet me here at the church and identify that
these were the winders he put in the church, and he said definitely
they were. Now, thirteen years we been looking out the winders
and there's been nothing out there. Now you can look out and see
those beautiful crosses in every winder in the church.'

I asked Joe, what about the street-lights outside the church? Didn't he think they had something to do with it?

'Now the street-lights was put in in September, two months before the crosses came. But between September and November you still didn't see anything in the winders.'

But the crosses are made by the street-lights?

'Any light will make those crosses,' Joe said. 'You gotta cigarette lighter?' He took my lighter and stepped out of the door. I could see his body as a vague shape on the other side of the glass, then a spark of light flaring into a perfect crusader cross, about twelve inches high.

I couldn't understand this. To me it proved that the cross was simply a refraction of the light in the glass, and I said as much to Joe.

'But see, it wasn't happening before November,' he said.

Well, maybe you weren't looking for it, I said.

'I'd be looking through the winders all the time. And my wife, Mildred, she was *always* looking through them. She's crazy about keeping those winders clean. She'd have seen if it was there.'

But a sceptic, I said, would say that this is just a simple refraction of light.

Joe looked at me evenly. 'Waahl . . . I tell everybody, believe what you want to. I'm not going to argue with it. I've never claimed this is a miracle. But God put breath in our bodies, that's a miracle. Man made the aeroplane, that's a miracle.' He shook his head and chuckled. 'But you wouldn't catch me in one of those things . . .'

I wasn't quite sure what to say, I wasn't sure whether Joe was being simple or disingenuous, or whether I was missing something.

After the crosses appeared, Joe said, word started to spread. More people started coming to the church. 'We've had 45,000 people through here. We get them to write their name in a book. Some do, and some don't.' He paused. 'I can't think of any other way to do it, so that's what we do.'

A TV crew came, he said, and that report was shown on stations all over America. That's how Buddy Piper had heard about this. Buddy came to the church and met Joe and they got on just fine, Joe said. They had appeared on radio shows together, talking about the crosses. It had become quite an industry. I remembered the cheery voice I had heard on the telephone from California and thought what an unlikely couple they made, the self-styled 'cross-chaser', looking for signs of the coming of the world teacher, and the dry, canny Baptist minister. I found it hard to believe that Joe Bullard would have embraced the idea of the coming of Maitreya.

'Well, Buddy talks about this fella, but I don't know anything about him really.' Joe rubbed his chin thoughtfully. 'I've been looking up books trying to find out something about him. But as far as him having something to do with this, I don't think so. But Mr Piper and me, we may not agree on doctrine, but we do agree on the main point which is that these crosses are here for a reason. And the reason first of all is that people changes their lifestyle, and the other reason is that people are healed. And we've got a lot of that. Yessir, we've had a lot of miracles here; a whole bunch of them. We had two deaf boys, and one of them seen Jesus on the cross, and they were healed. We've had people whose marriages were failing who've patched up their differences after seeing these crosses. Then there was Mrs Anderson, from Kokomo, Indiana. She had a brain tumour; she knelt down outside the church and prayed. And things begin to change. She actually came down here last week, thinking you'd be here then, because she wanted to tell you about it.

'But the strangest one was we had a lady drove up in a Cadillac. I'd never seen her before, but she said she'd come to meet her husband here, and he was dead. Now he died before the crosses came here, apparently; and on his deathbed he'd told her to come up here on this date and look through the window for him. So I told her to go ahead. She looked through the window and she talked and talked. Then she called me over to talk to him, but I couldn't see anyone. She just talked to him until it overcome her emotions and she just fell on the floor, right there by the window. We picked her up, and she got back in her Cadillac and just drove away, and I never did see her since.'

Joe told me this story as if he was talking about the weather, or describing having his front door painted, with no hint in his voice of embroidery or exaggeration. I looked for some glimmer in his eye that would tell me he was pulling my leg, but he simply blinked back at me through his spectacles. I couldn't make up my mind whether he was a straight-shooting, good old boy, or a masterful con-man.

I asked Joe, why did he think the crosses had appeared in his church?

'I don't have the answer to it, but I can say that God's really blessed this church. Our offering's gone up from 15–20 dollars a week, to 150–200 dollars.' He paused. 'Now, some people are saying this is to do with a little baby that was killed round here in a car accident. This was in November, right before the crosses came; a tractor and trailer ran over a car and killed the little baby. She's buried right out here in the churchyard. Now right after the baby was buried, some people said they saw a little child sitting in the windows, and then some fingerprints appeared on the glass and stayed there for two months. Then they transferred over to this window.' Joe stood up and walked across to the window. 'You can see them there.' I studied the window closely. There, near the bottom of the frame, were three quite distinct, child-sized fingerprints. I rubbed them with my finger, to no avail.

'They're real small, ain't they? We keep a bottle of Windex and napkins up here for people who wants to try and wash them off. You can't do it. We wash those winders four times a week, and they will not come off. That's the mystery of it all. Now, if you look through this winder here . . .' Joe walked to the next window, gesturing for me to follow him, 'they say you can see the name of Jesus appear, J-E-S-U-, but with the E turned around backwards. 'Course, you can't see it now because it's the daytime, but if you look out at night you'll see it. I seen that. Now sometimes through these winders you get a picture of a face. Some people say it's Jesus, but I don't know about that. And many times you get a stair-step going up to the cross. Many people have seen that. And if you look here we got pictures of angels around the cross – dozens of them.'

On a table beside the lectern was a photograph album, containing pictures of the crosses taken from each window. One picture showed a cross obscured behind a cloud of dense white light, spotted with winged shapes, like a child's drawing of birds in flight.

'Those there are angels,' said Joe matter-of-factly.

Interleaved in the photograph album were letters of testimony. An Emily Cooper of Serviceville, Tennessee had written how she had seen 'a gold cross with a light-blue robe draped over it'. Another letter, scrawled on lined paper in a child-like hand, read:

I'd been having problems with fluid in my right ear. Two years ago I had tubes put in to drain them. It was all right until three months ago, when it came back again. Medicine wouldn't heal it, and the doctor wanted to put in more tubes. On my way home

I wanted to stop by the church and see the crosses and sign my name to the prayer-list, and God healed me – the fluid is gone. Thank you, Jesus. Glenda.'

'I just wanted to share those with ya,' said Joe, closing the book. He walked me to the door of the church, switched off the lights. The rain was still falling outside. 'Come back tonight,' Joe said, 'and you'll see the crosses. You'll see them for sure.'

The sky was darkening when I returned to the church that evening. The street-lights were illuminated on either side of the church. Joe's Cadillac was parked outside, and he and his wife Mildred were standing in the vestibule, waiting to receive visitors. A visitors' book was open on a table, with a collection plate beside it. I stepped into the church, and immediately caught sight of a cross, looming in the window nearest to me. I moved closer. It filled the glass, golden in colour, shaped not like the crucifix of biblical legend but like the cross of the crusaders. It looked 20 to 30 feet high, as if suspended in the air on the other side of the glass. I moved from window to window. Crosses shone brightly in each of them, the shapes irregular but unmistakable, some gold, some almost white. In one window several smaller crosses flickered around the main one.

I stepped out and walked around to the side of the church, looking for sources of light. Insects skittered in the tungsten glow of the street-light; that, it was clear, accounted for the large cross in each window. Small squares of light shone from a house set on a hill, perhaps 200 yards away. That, I thought, would cause the smaller crosses. I stepped back into the church. Surely the crosses were simply refractions of light. It was true, they seemed larger, more vivid, more *spectacular*, than a mere refraction of light would suggest; and whatever had caused them, they were undeniably beautiful. But surely they were no miracle.

I was looking out of the window when Joe Bullard came up beside me. 'Mrs Anderson from Kokomo came after all,' he said. He gestured towards a middle-aged woman, dressed in jeans and a pastel-coloured anorak, standing by the door with two friends.

Joan Anderson immediately struck me as a sober-minded, intelligent woman. We sat in one of the pews, and, quietly and methodically, she told me her story. She was fifty-five years old and she worked in quality-control at a General Motors plant in

Indiana. Fourteen months ago, she said, she had started to suffer from excrutiating headaches, sometimes up to six days in duration. CAT scans had failed to diagnose the problem, but eventually an MRI scan had discovered that she was suffering from a brain tumour. The neuro-surgeon had told her that because of the delicate position of the tumour he did not wish to operate straight away.

In the time since the pains had started, she said, she had become a different person, reclusive, unsociable. 'The pain was almost driving me out my mind. At three different times I thought about taking my life, because the pain was just unbearable. There was nothing I could do to stop it.' The weekend after the diagnosis she had arranged to drive down with friends to visit a friend in Knoxville. 'I really didn't want to go because I felt so bad, but they insisted I come.' During their visit, they had been told of the Crosses of Light; out of nothing more than curiosity, on their way home they stopped at the church to see them.

'We got here about two-thirty in the morning. We drove up and the church wasn't open. So we stood back about 5 feet from the window – there were five of us – and looked in through the church, and there, in the window on the other side, we could see a cross. I said a prayer right there, and when we pulled out of the driveway I could feel the hair on my arms standing up. And one of the ladies told the two teenage boys with us that we had just witnessed a miracle . . .

'We got home, and the next day was a public holiday, so I got up and cleaned the house. It really didn't dawn on me that I was doing something different; I just felt good. The day after, I got up and went to work, and I felt like my old self again – I was laughing and talking. I hadn't felt like myself for fourteen months; I felt like I was almost somebody else, a real strange feeling. And people at work were turning and giving me a second look. And by the time I got home I knew something had happened in my life.

'So I called the church here and told them I'd been there two days before and what I'd seen. And I said, I only have one question for you; have there been any healings? And the man said, oh my, yes. And I said, well, you can add someone else to the list, because I knew right then my tumour was gone. And I have not had the headaches since.

'I went back to the doctor a couple of weeks later and he showed me the X-rays and said the tumour was still in a very precarious position in my brain and he didn't want to operate right now. And I said, it's OK, you don't have to – I don't have the headaches any more. I said, I'm fine; I've had a miracle happen. And I guess God sent me this doctor too, because he was very accepting of what I said.'

'And you think the tumour has gone?' I said.

'It's gone.' Joan's voice carried not one iota of doubt. 'It's not there. I no longer have the pain. No one can question that of me. I'm 100 per cent convinced that viewing this cross that God put here is what healed me. I've been here three times since then, and I know these crosses are a miracle, a sign sent by God.'

By the time Joan had finished her story I had no doubt that she was telling me the truth. Or rather, I had no doubt that she believed implicitly in what she was saying. Her two friends had sat down beside us and were listening intently to our conversation.

A sceptic, I said, would look at the crosses in the windows and look at the lights shining outside and conclude that the one was simply a refraction of the other. Something in me felt dutybound to point this out, and I felt like the devil even as I said it.

But Joan simply smiled. 'I know what happened to me,' she said. She had a nice smile, and the most wonderful air of untroubled tranquillity about her. This is what happens, I thought, when people are confirmed in their faith.

'I've seen angels here too,' said Joan.

Angels?

'Yes, angels. We were looking out of this middle window,' she gestured towards the window on her left, 'and we could see these angelic shapes, maybe 3 feet tall. They were outside, dancing around the cross. They were working; they were real busy. Judy here said, I didn't think you had to work that hard when you were an angel.' Joan laughed. I looked at Judy, seated beside us. She was laughing too, nodding her head in confirmation.

'But they were happy,' said Joan. 'One even came up and looked right in the window. There was a man with us, looking out, and this angel just came and looked at him.'

'You've got to accept it and just go with it,' said Judy. 'You try and analyse it and you'll just come up with more questions. You can't explain these things and put them in little boxes. They don't fit.'

I walked back to the windows, thinking about this. The large cross stared back at me, but I couldn't see angels, no matter how hard I tried. Cars were turning into the parking-lot; I could see their headlights flaring in the window, forming smaller crosses which seemed to shimmy and dance in the glass. It was obvious to me that the crosses were refractions of light. Why couldn't anyone else see it? I tried to think it through logically. The street-lights formed the largest, most impressive crosses; but even before the street-lights were erected, crosses would have been visible in the window, formed by the light from the neighbouring houses, and by the lights of cars turning into the parking-lot. Surely someone would have noticed them in the twenty-seven years the windows had been in the church? But evidently nobody had.

The church was beginning to fill now; families and couples, some local people, and some who had apparently driven from miles away. They pressed their noses against the windows, whistled and took pictures. Some simply drifted in, looked at the crosses for a few minutes and then drifted out again, scepticism etched on their faces. Others settled in the pews and talked among themselves, as if this were a picnic or social gathering. 'Lookahere,' a man called his wife to the glass. 'Can you see a face in the light there? You can see the eyes there above the cross. It's Jesus, praise the Lord.'

A fat man in glasses said, 'It gives you strength, it really do. I work in insurance. I took this back to my office and told some people there, gave witness, and they were just moved in the power of the Lord.'

A tall, bearded man, his body joggling like plates of jelly in a tight red track suit, moved excitedly from window to window, joining in with conversations. 'It's the Lord's work, yes it is. The Bible said that signs and wonders will come to those who believe, and I do believe we're in the last days. The Lord be praised.' His eyes gleamed behind wire-rimmed spectacles, as if he was in the grip of some deep agitation. I thought of engaging him in conversation, then decided against it. 'Ah believe you can see Jesus anywhere and everywhere, in the clouds and the trees.' He was addressing the room at large. 'The Lord Jesus Christ just healed me from cancer, and he healed my wife from cancer too . . .'

Somebody else told a story about a woman from Alabama who was going blind, and came to the church and was healed.

I asked, did you meet her?

'No, sir, but I heard the story and I swear it's the truth.'

The room seemed to be filled with angels and crosses and signs of the miraculous, or the need of them; the fruits of divine apparition, or the human imagination, in full bloom. A family had gathered at the window from which Joe Bullard had told me you could see the name of Jesus – J-E-S-U. 'I can see it,' said the woman. I looked over her shoulder, at an angle, towards a blur of refracted light. Perhaps it did spell J-E-S-U; it was hard to say.

I stepped outside, walked around to the window I had just been looking through, and looked in the direction where the light source should be. A line of four lights from a house and its outbuildings glimmered on the hill.

A man stood on the steps of the church, smoking a cigarette, watching me. 'What you're witnessing right here is a miracle,' he said. I said nothing. His name was Bernie, he said, and he was a member of the church.

'I heard angels singing, like the church was filled full of them. This was at eleven o'clock at night. I don't explain anything. It's just what I hear, what God shown me himself. I've been sat right outside here on this step, and I've seen a cross up on that hill over there.' He shifted from foot to foot and tossed his cigarette aside in a shower of sparks. He gave me a shrewd look; as if he'd just made me an offer on a second-hand automobile and was waiting for me to call him on it.

'You get what you ask for in that church there,' he said. 'It's what you feel. If you feel nothing, you get nothing. If you're close to the Lord he'll give you a good blessing. But if you're just coming up here sightseeing, you'll see nothing. If you take one step towards him, he'll open his arms for you. But if you step in cold, you'll step outside cold. It's sad, but where there's Christ, there's the devil too. He'll fight, oh yes, he'll move in hard. When he makes this earth crumble, there'll be a lot of crying then.'

More cars arrived; people wandered in and out of the church, loitering in the parking-lot, as if reluctant to leave. To the side of the church, a handful of people had gathered around a tall man, with an aureole of curly hair, which made him look like a guitarist from some forgotten Seventies rock group – an enduring sartorial style in the South. He was pointing up to a tree, overhanging the rear of the parking-lot. 'You see that up there? There's a face up there in the tree. It's the face of Christ.' The thick branches of the tree were dappled in light and shade from the nearby street-lamp.

'I can see it,' said a woman standing beside me.

I couldn't see it. Bernie stood off to one side, watching the commotion with that same, shrewd look on his face and saying nothing.

The man with the curly hair said his name was Don Goodpaster. 'You one of those New Agers?' he asked, eyeing me suspiciously, although I had said nothing to suggest that I was. 'Cos if you are, whatever you say gonna go in one ear and out the other. That's why I bought my Bible here, to argue with you every word.' He was an author of children's books, he said, which he sold from a concession in Dollywood, the theme park devoted to the life and work of Dolly Parton, the buxom Country and Western singer, at Pigeon Forge, some sixty miles away. He was a regular visitor to the crosses. He had seen things, he said – miraculous things. 'I want to share them with you.'

It was past ten, and Joe Bullard was locking up the church. I offered to buy Don Goodpaster coffee. A group of people who had driven from Kingsport said they would join us. We drove up the road for a mile or two, to a coffee shop with strip-neon lighting and hard plastic seats.

Don Goodpaster placed his Bible on the table beside a styrofoam cup of diet Coke. He talked about being 'called' when he was eleven years old, and deciding that writing children's books was his way of 'serving the Lord'; he talked about encountering an angel while he was in hospital, following stress-related exhaustion. 'I was on my way to the operating theatre, and a man was lying on a gurney in the corridor; he rose up and said, I know you're anxious about this operation, but don't be; it's a piece of cake. I asked afterwards, and they said there was no one in the corridor.'

The other people at the table shook their heads and murmured their approval at this story.

Don turned to his Bible, and quoted the Book of Revelations, Chapter 2, verse 19. '"Write the things which thou hast seen,"' he read, '"and the things which are, and the things which shall be hereafter."'

I realised that he was talking to me. Now Don reached into his attaché case, and pulled out a colour photocopy of a photograph taken at the church, the same picture that Joe Bullard had shown me earlier, of the cloud of bright light obscuring a cross, the bird-wing shapes hovering to the side.

'Y'see here we have the picture of the angels,' said Don, making an unequivocal leap from the highly questionable to the irrefutable. He paused, to ensure he had the attention of his audience, then turned to me. 'Can you spell incredulous? Because that's what I was when I realised what I'm about to tell you. I'm fifty years old and I've never seen anything like this before.'

He placed his hand over the picture, as if he was about to do a conjuring trick. 'Now look at this picture here.' He removed his hand and started tracing shapes with his finger through the cloud. 'Are you seeing what I'm seeing?' We leaned closer. 'Are you seeing *a lion* in there?' There was a murmur around the table. 'Now if you look here . . .' His finger moved across the picture, tracing shapes and outlines. 'There's the mane; that there's the nose, and the eyes . . . That's the Lion of Judah.'

We had been joined by the waitress and her boyfriend, a pimple-faced youth in his late teens with a prominent Adam's apple. 'I see it,' said the boy.

I crinkled up my eyes. Maybe you could see the Lion of Judah in there. You could see almost anything.

'When I saw that,' said Don, 'I knew that I was seeing a miracle.'

We walked into the parking-lot and the people from Kingsport said goodbye. Don lingered by my car, as if he was not quite ready to leave, as if he could sense my scepticism about the whole affair, and felt I needed convincing. I opened the door to my car and swung inside. Don slid in beside me on the passenger side. A fine drizzle sparkled on the windshield, illuminated by the lights of the parking-lot; stars, not crosses. I was beginning to wonder how I'd ever get rid of Don. He told me about his books, about his business at Dollywood, about his rackety life which had caused him to turn his back on God. He told me how he had first come to see the Crosses of Light a month before and how he had been 'born again'. The first time he visited the church, he said, he had taken a photograph of one of the crosses and he had gone for a drive. He had driven up a hill. 'The Bible says, go up to the hill and find the wood to build.' He had placed the photograph of the cross on the dashboard of the car. 'And I asked God, if this is not true then burn the photo, and burn me up with it.'

He had fallen asleep then, and woken to see a hawk, a bluebird and a butterfly flying in a straight line past the window of his car. Then another car drove by, with a personalised number-plate reading 'John'. Don took this as a sign. He looked in his Bible, in the book of John, and his eyes fell on the words: 'Now do ye believe . . .' He fell silent, clearly expecting me to say something. I wanted to ask if he had been taking drugs, but thought better of it. He told me he was saved, for sure. Then he told me that with his books he was going to be the next Dr Seuss, and he was going to be rich.

I went back to my motel room feeling curiously deflated. The room seemed chill and forlorn – the cheap, gimcrack furnishings; the rattle of the air-conditioner, the television flickering silently in the corner. I was exhausted by the events of the day, exhausted by these people and their endless talk of miracles, faith and deliverance. I thought about the desire to believe; about the peculiar quirks of chance and hope that linked a small, rural church in Tennessee to an erstwhile TV comedian, the self-styled 'cross-chaser' of California, to Mr Creme in his comfortable house in North London, with his talk of miracles and masters. You could follow the chain back, through Mr Creme, to Alice Bailey, to Madame Blavatsky, to Himalayan masters, to . . . what?

I thought: You could go crazy looking for the meanings in things. Looking for meaning is one of the most urgent, compulsive and potentially hazardous human impulses. But sometimes things don't have meaning. They just are. The people I had encountered in the church that evening were looking for meaning, for confirmation, but also for mystery. It was what everyone wanted. The painter Dante Gabriel Rossetti once said that he believed in angels, because the more science tried to explain the world, the more important their existence became. And the more science appears to demystify the world, the greater the craving for mystery seems to become. Mystery itself seems to answer this craving: with visions of Mary, alien abductions, angelic visitations – a panoply of the imagined, the fraudulent and the genuinely inexplicable. And yet I was aware that in Joan Anderson's story I had experienced something in the church that was more than wish-fulfilment or opportunism; I had experienced some manifest evidence of faith in practice.

I wondered if I was asking the right questions. There was a simple scientific explanation for the crosses. But perhaps that wasn't the point. Sure, someone had said to me in the church, the street-lights are reflecting in the windows; any idiot could see that. But it's the *shape* that's important; it's the fact that they're crosses that gives the light meaning. It occurred to me, if the point of a miracle was to draw people closer to God, if it was God making His presence felt, then why not use the available materials, the street-lights and the rippled glass? The effect was exactly the same.

Ever since I'd heard about the crosses I had felt the tides of millennial expectation lapping around my ankles. For Buddy Piper and Mr Creme they were another sign of the coming of Maitreya, the realisation of the great myth of the golden age of love and sharing. For Joe Bullard, an old-fashioned Baptist, uncomplicated by esoteric theory, they were a sign of the last days. End Time.

Sitting in the pew of the church earlier that day, Joe had expounded on the nine signs of the coming of Christ. 'Book of Matthew, verse 24 ... One of the signs is to turn nation against nation, and this is happening. There'll be wars and rumours of wars. There'll be pestilence – and look at Aids. I'm a pre-millennialist. I believe that Jesus can come at any time.'

A sorrowful look had come over his face. 'All the signs of the world – things are getting worse. I believe they are. I believe we're in the end of time, I do. I'm not a date-setter, but between you and me, if I were setting a date I would say that the year 2,000 would wind it up. So I feel Christ can come back any time he wants to. He could come back tomorrow.'

I sat in my room, the air-conditioner rattling, wondering about this. Tomorrow was Sunday.

The next morning I telephoned Horace Gray. He confirmed that he had put the windows in the church twenty-seven years before: 'New doors and new winders. Me and one of the boys ... That glass is just a plain glass like they put in a church house. Ain't no difference in it. I don't know where the winders come from, but they didn't have crosses in them when I put them in. I've been in that church many times since then and I've never seen anything like that. This thing we're seeing up there is not like an old rugged cross like Jesus was hanging on, but it's a beautiful thing.'

What did he think caused the crosses?

Horace Gray's voice crackled down the line. 'I believe the Lord put them there. Where that church is at there's a whole lot of sinful people up there that needs to make it right with the Lord. They tell me, and I've seen a lot of people get convicted up there in the Lord.'

That evening I took the road back to the church in good time for the evening service. It had hardly stopped raining since I arrived in Tennessee. The plastic flags flapped in the wind above the car-dealers' lots; the charmless countryside was shrouded in grey mist. One of America's largest manufacturers of mobile homes is located near Knoxville, and a large proportion of the local population seemed to favour the dwelling – low buildings, like outhouses, dotted the hillsides, with asphalt drives and the inevitable pick-up truck parked outside. In the rain, everything looked tired, used up.

Joe was standing in his place at the door of the church when I arrived, wearing a worried expression. He took me to one side. There was something I should know, he said. There were members of the church who did not like the crosses and the changes they'd brought to the church. There had been Presbyterians, Methodists, Catholics, people who didn't even believe in Christ coming through the doors to witness the crosses, and some people didn't like that. That day, said Joe, he had received a letter notifying him that an attorney would soon be serving papers, removing him as pastor.

It was hard to get to the bottom of this, but the name of Buddy Piper seemed to have something to do with it. 'They say I'm not carrying the Christian message when I'm with Buddy Piper on the radio,' said Joe. 'Now I don't believe everything Buddy believes, but we're friends, and we agree on a lot of things. I believe everybody in the world should be fed; I believe in everybody helping each other. These are Christian values that I believe in. What's wrong with that?

'I don't ever ask a man what faith or religion he is. Hey, we're all God's children, no matter what you believe. We've had all sorts in here since these crosses came. We even had Buddhists in here, dressed like you see in the movies. Somebody said, you better get those boys out of here, but I wasn't going to move them. That's one reason I've got so much opposition. I've got people here believing nobody's going to heaven except Baptists (*bab-dists*). I don't believe it. How could anyone believe it?'

We were joined by Joe's two sons. David was a rotund man in his forties with an Abe Lincoln beard, wearing a battered felt hat. He told me he had been a boy preacher, preaching in revival tents throughout the South, then become an auctioneer. His brother Jack was a bearded giant of a man in his thirties who clasped my hand in a vice-like grip. Evidently, he had not felt the family calling; he used to be a night-club bouncer, he said, and now he worked in the salvage business.

David had a preacher's loquaciousness and easy charm. No sooner had we been introduced than he was telling me that he played piano, mandolin and guitar; that he had been married four times, and had ten children; and that he suffered from a heart condition and doctors had told him he had only six months to live. Twenty years ago, he said, when he was working as an auctioneer, he started experiencing black-outs. 'I went into hospital and they wanted to give me a test. They had me strapped on the table, and I could feel that wire going up in me. They said they were going to shoot the dye in it. It felt like I was on fire. They diagnosed I had a brain tumour. I said, Dr Galleon, do it again, because the Lord is going to heal me. So he said, OK, I'll try it again. He shot that dye in, and soon as he got through he walked over and looked at me, tears running down his face, and he said, I don't know what happened, but the tumour's gone. You can go home.' David watched me for my reaction.

I wasn't sure about the medical diagnosis, but I was becoming accustomed to talk of miracles.

'They telling me now I need a heart transplant; it's all that can save me. But I'm trusting to the Lord.'

Did David think the crosses were a miracle?

He smiled at me. 'I don't know what to think. We can't judge the way the Lord works. But these people here think it's a miracle.'

The church had begun to fill now, perhaps forty people, dressed in their Sunday best. The crosses shone in the windows like stage-props. The service seemed completely unstructured; a word of welcome from Joe Bullard, an announcement about a forthcoming marriage. People were invited to sing a song, or offer a testimony if they felt like it. Joe's son, David, sang a hymn, accompanying himself on the guitar, in a way which reminded me of Woody Guthrie. An elderly woman testified about a rainbow appearing in the sky on the day her son died, and sang an a cappella version of 'It's Me, Oh Lord' in a quavering falsetto. Then she went to the piano, and the congregation sang 'Oh, They Tell Me of a Home' and 'Jesus Calls Us O'er the Tumult'. There didn't seem to be a hymn sung that was less than 100 years old.

A guest preacher, whom Joe Bullard introduced as 'Brother Teffeteller', stood up to preach the sermon. He was a short, stockily built man; his left eye was made of glass and his battered appearance and pugilist's stance lent him the appearance less of a man of God than of a bar-room brawler. He took off his suit jacket, and threw it to his wife sitting in the front row, then rolled up his shirt-sleeves, as if he was looking for a fight. 'Look at these here crosses.' He gestured to the windows. 'We're in the middle of the miracle here and don't you doubt it.'

He preached like a train, pulling slowly out of the station, gathering pace, swooping up and down gradients, his voice dipping and swaying, plotting a course through biblical reference, personal anecdote, warnings of damnation and exhortations of salvation, so fervent and so discursive that I found it hard to follow. The meaning, I concluded, was perhaps less important than the conviction.

'I believe in the old ship of Zion, I seen it ride, I rode that thing out, and I've been called everything but a white man, Amen; I've been accused of everything you can think of and probably a whole lot you can't think of; I bin accused of everything but taking little black babies and painting them white, and I expect that's the next rumour coming, Amen, *Thank God*. He said I'll never leave yer, and I'll never forsake yer, and I'll go all the way with yer, even to the end of the day, glory to God I'm in that old ship of Zion . . .'

As he stalked the front of the church, gesticulating wildly, perspiration poured from his forehead, and damp patches grew under the armpits on his shirt. The man in the red track suit whom I had seen in the church the previous evening was here again, punctuating each turn in the preacher's tale with a shouted 'Amen', and 'I hear you, Lord'.

'Nature itself obeys God, the wind obeys God, the *devil* obeys God, the only thing that doesn't obey God is man . . .' Brother Teffeteller threw a challenging look at the congregation, and his voice dripped with sarcasm. 'We think we've arrived; we used to buy our suits down at the 5 and 10 and now we buy them at J.C. Penney. We used to drive Fords and now we drive Cadillacs. I mean, we've really arrived, Amen. We've got so educated we don't need God no more. We've got books written by people that know nothing, know no more about God than a billy-goat knows. I've got sixty-six books, that's all I need. This old country was established with a gun in one hand and a Bible in the other. And now they say you can't even pray in school . . .'

The sermon done with, he slumped, exhausted, in the front pew. I felt like applauding – it was a magnificent piece of theatre. But the congregation simply stirred in their seats and turned to the next hymn.

'He was a real fireballer,' said a man as we left the church.

A fireballer?

The man laughed. 'Yup, someone that comes in and burns like a fireball and then's gone again.' He looked at me intently. 'You believe in these crosses?'

I realised it was the first time anyone had asked me the question directly. 'I believe they're in the windows,' I said. 'But don't ask me if it's a miracle.'

'You oughta know what's going on here,' he said. 'This ain't no miracle, and I'll show you why.' I told him where I was staying, and he said he would call.

The fireballer, his wife and daughter were standing beside their car, saying their goodbyes. I complimented him on his sermon. He introduced himself as John Teffeteller. He and his wife ran a barber's shop, ten miles down the road, he said. But he preached wherever he was called – small churches, tent revivals, 'Wherever they want me. I tell you, fighting the devil's harder work than some of those bar fights I been in.'

I asked him, what did he think of the crosses?

'The Lord's sign, my friend. He's showing us that he's with us when we need Him.' He pointed to his daughter, an awkward-looking teenager, with pebble-glasses, standing uneasily by his car. 'The Lord looks over this girl, here. There's been many the day that we've thanked the Lord that Candy has seen morning. She has bad asthma and cystic fibro . . .' He turned to his daughter. 'What is it, darlin'? Fibrosis.' He laughed. 'I couldn't say peanut butter if my mouth was full of it, and I'm an educated man.'

I walked back into the church. There were two elderly women, who had arrived too late for the service, lingering by the windows, examining the crosses. They did not look like local people; they were not dressed for church, but bandaged in anoraks, hats and walking-boots. They introduced themselves as sisters, Anne and

Lillian. They had read Buddy Piper's account of the crosses in *Share International*, Benjamin Creme's magazine, and driven from Alabama to see them for themselves. This was interesting. So far, the only people I had met in the church were confirmed Christians. I did not need Don Goodpaster to tell me that Anne and Lillian were New Agers.

It was getting late and they had yet to find accommodation for the night. I led them back to the travellers' colony on the freeway, and we sat in Denny's, eating supper. Anne was dressed in a violent purple tie-dye top and an uncommonly jolly hat, and wore a large crystal on a chain around her neck. Lillian was no less distinctive. They looked like star-gazers, on their way to an astrology convention.

They were on a sort of pilgrimage, they said. Had I heard of the sighting of the Virgin Mary at Coniers in Georgia? I had not. 'Mary comes to a woman there and gives her messages there,' said Anne. 'On the 13th of the month, at noon. She was told to build a shrine, which she did, and water started coming out of a spring, which is supposed to be healing water. I drank some.'

And did you feel better, I asked.

She shrugged. 'I felt pretty good anyway.'

Anne held forth on her enthusiasm for Edgar Cayce and Alice Bailey, for clairvoyance and channelling and mediumship. She had been at Sedona in Arizona, she said. 'It's an energy vortex. And I asked God if I needed to be studying this stuff, I needed a sign. We were doing a meditation there – there was an Indian circle near by. And then, all of a sudden, I looked up and there, right in the middle of this dark cloud, a star came out. Except it didn't look so much like a star, more like a cookie-cutter.' She reached for my notebook and carefully drew a soft-contoured five-point star. 'This was at Cathedral Rock. It's on ley lines, you know. They see a lot of UFOs there too.'

The waitress brought the food and gave us a glance. We must have looked an odd picture: two elderly women and a long-haired Englishman, talking about UFOs and ley lines. We talked about Benjamin Creme, the crosses, and the other phenomena which Mr Creme claimed were signs of the coming of Maitreya – the visions of Mary, the healing waters of Mexico and Germany; the photograph of the mysterious visitor in Nairobi. Anne had seen the photograph in *Share International*. Once again, I was surprised by Mr Creme's apparent global ubiquity. Sitting in his North London home, listening to his tales of disembodied masters, I had come to think of him as a local story-teller, but he seemed to pop up everywhere. I remembered my conversations with the German man in Thalheim, and the Indian academic at Sai Baba's ashram in Puttaparthi. I had even seen a copy of *Share International* in the Tibetan library in Dharamsala. And here I was talking about him again in a coffee shop in Tennessee.

Anne regarded me querulously over her mashed potatoes and roast beef. 'Have you ever met Maitreya?'

I replied that I was sorry to say that I had not. Did she believe that he existed?

'I'm trying to work him into my belief system right now,' she said.

I thought this would not be too much of a problem. Once you believed in ley lines and cookie-cutter stars appearing in the clouds as signs of God, it was but a short step to believe that Maitreya was alive and well and waiting to reveal himself. Or was it? To believe in some things that seemed, to the layman, manifestly unbelievable did not mean that you had to believe in everything; but where did you draw the line? The scientific materialist would dismiss everything that could not be explained by empiricism or reason as fraud or delusion; but subjective experience constantly attested to the authenticity of the apparently inexplicable. I did not believe that the Crosses of Light were a miracle, but Joan Anderson did, and in some curious way they seemed to have been an agency in the healing of her brain tumour – and everything she had told me, the conviction with which she had told me, suggested that she had been healed.

What was a miracle anyway? A sign of the Divine, which, by definition, existed beyond the realm of scientific enquiry? Or, more simply, something that brought people comfort and succour and confirmed them in their faith? My mind went back to India, and to Sai Baba, and the claims made for his miraculous powers. I had only anecdotal evidence of his healings and materialisations. But the *vibhuti*, manifesting in the houses of Mr Patel and Mr Shah, that was real enough. I had seen it myself.

I asked Anne and Lillian, had they heard of Sai Baba?

'Of course,' said Anne. 'I've got some *vibhuti* in the car'. She was a constant fund of surprises.

She went to fetch it, and while she was gone, Lillian told me something of her life. She was married, she said, but things were not good with her husband. Undergoing past-life regression, she discovered that the root of her marital discord lay in a previous life. 'Apparently, we were connected in a previous life, and I sold his cows without his permission. But I think I may have been a man then, because a woman would never have done that, would she? A woman wouldn't have dared. And that's why he's so angry with me.' On the advice of her past-life regressionist, she had attempted to apologise to her husband for her previous-life transgression. 'But I'm not sure he's accepted my apology. I'm not sure he even believes me.'

I could see the problem, but I couldn't see a way around it. It seemed hard enough to convince your husband that you had been together in a previous life, let alone that you had stolen his cows; hard enough to convince someone they should accept an apology for a transgression committed in this life, let alone a previous one. I ate my food in silence, unsure what to advise.

Anne came back into the restaurant, clutching a small plastic bag, the kind used to store food in a freezer, or for illegal drugs. The waitress had given up any pretence of busying herself at the cash-till and was scrutinising us suspiciously. Anne opened the bag, took a dab of *vibhuti* on her fingertips, swallowed it, and passed the bag across the table. I did the same.

Thus sanctified, we said our goodbyes. There was a message waiting for me when I returned to my room: the man who had taken me to one side outside the church. We arranged to meet the next morning. I pulled the bedcovers over me, and drifted into sleep, the perfumed taste of the *vibhuti* fresh in my mouth, thoughts of miracles, real and imagined, coursing through my mind.

We met in Denny's. He was a heavily set man in his sixties, with a crinkled, pitted face, like a currant bun. He told me he had been a member of the Copper Ridge church for the past seven years; that he was ordained as a pastor himself. He came straight to the point. 'What's going on up there ain't right.'

He reached into a plastic bag and pulled out a piece of glass, identical to the glass in the windows of the church. 'I got this piece of glass out of Kentucky,' he said. 'If my information is correct it was made by Industrex in Kingsport, Tennessee. But you can get it in Alabama too. You can get this glass anywhere.'

I held my cigarette lighter behind it and a perfect cross flared in the glass, identical to the one Joe Bullard had made with my lighter in the window at Copper Ridge.

He smiled. 'If that's not an open and shut case in sheer con-artistry, I don't know what is. You hold that glass up to a street-light at night and you'll get exactly the same as you see in the church. This is no miracle. If it was a miracle you'd be seeing crosses with no light behind 'em.' But if it was a miracle you'd be seeing crosses with no light behind 'em. You wouldn't be seeing crosses in the winders, you'd be seeing them out there in the parking-lot. I don't have an axe to grind; all I want is the truth.'

He reached into his bag and pulled out a picture. It showed the outside of the church, with a cross hovering in the parking-lot. 'Now they been saying this proves the crosses are outside, but you can see it's a double-exposure.' And an amateurish one at that; a window frame was clearly visible, cutting across the bottom of the cross. 'Now people look at that picture and they believe it, because they *want* to believe it.' He sipped at his coffee. 'I went along with this programme for a while. You can say, look over there to the left and I can see an angel. You're playing on people's emotion. If you look out of the back to the right, you can see a little foggy, cloudy thing up there. Now I did this, and as God is my judge I had to repent on it, but I told people, you can see the name of Jesus up there – J-E-S-U, with the E backwards. It was just a reflection. And they said, oh yeah, I can see that. Well, I never saw it.'

I had seen it, I said. Or rather, I hadn't seen it.

'You see, people are looking for something. People are looking for a gospel, and Jesus said the gospel shall be preached unto all the world. If I told you there is a black sheep standing out in the parking-lot, you could believe it or not, until you get up and go see. Now Jesus said, my spirit will be with you. You can't touch it, but you can feel it. Jesus is spirit, and he said that those who worship me must worship me in spirit and in truth. But people aren't willing to accept that. They want something they can reach out and touch.'

But the odd thing, I said, was the effect this seemed to have had on people. It was one thing for the credulous to see what they wanted to see; but quite another for people to believe they had been healed. I recounted the conversation I had had with Joan Anderson.

'Well . . .' he swallowed his coffee. 'Let's get away from the glass for a moment. Jesus Christ said, as your faith be, so be it unto you. He said if you have the faith of a grain of mustard seed you can move a mountain. He's talking about a mountain of sin. Now when this woman talks about being healed, I can relate to that because I was healed. By all the laws of nature, I should be dead. I went to the doctor, and he told me he thought I had prostate cancer. I had all the signs. I smoked, I chewed, all of this good stuff.

'Now I believe sometimes God wants us to make bargains with him, if you will. And I said, God if you heal me of this, I'll never smoke and chew again. Well, I was going home, and the Lord spoke to me. He said, go to this church and let them anoint you with oil and pray over you. I didn't even know where the church was. But I knew their service started at seven – I had the radio on and I was listening to their programme. And this man said, I want to invite everybody out there to come to the church and we're gonna have a miracle – God just spoke to me and told me this. I thought: Yeah – I know what that is. So I found the church, I spoke to the pastor; they anointed me with oil and prayed over me. The next day I went to the doctor; they ran all kinds of tests on me and they couldn't find a thing.

'So I came away from the doctor, and I reached for a cigarette and something said, you'd better not. So I took my cigarettes and I took my chewing tobacco and I laid them on the altar of the church; and I've never touched either since.'

So, I said, miracles happen.

'Sure.' He considered me gravely. 'Miracles happen. But those crosses aren't miracles. If the crosses were of God they'd be there twenty-four hours a day. The pastor there is a con-artist extraordinary. He told me, if you keep your mouth shut we'll milk the public for all we can get out of this. I said, no way. The Bible says, for everything we do we're going to pay for.'

I said I had been told that there was bad feeling about the numbers of people coming to the church; the fact that it was drawing people of all denominations, and none.

He waved the argument aside. 'That's not the case. We had Catholic people, we had nuns and we always treated them nice. People have always welcomed anybody with open arms. The truth here is that they're playing on people's emotions. The crosses are getting to be a bad taste in people's mouths, and people don't like that.'

I felt that I had stumbled into a parochial row that I wanted no part in. Joe Bullard would leave the church, he told me; the members would see to that, and a new pastor would take his place.

And what then?

'I would say, if the new pastor is smart, the first thing he'd do is change the winders. Then maybe he would go so far as to change the name of the church. Then you would start a new foundation and start over. I would say, the best thing is to forget this whole thing ever happened.'

That evening, I drove up to the church for the last time. There were only a handful of visitors, lingering at the windows. The crosses were shining brightly – more brightly, it seemed, than I had ever seen them, as if to mock my disbelief. I wondered, are crosses shining all over America, in churches, bathrooms and cow-sheds, just waiting to be discovered?

I had been thinking all day about whether to tell Joe about my meeting with his dissenting parishioner, about the glass from Kingsport and the Cross of Light that had flared in Denny's cafeteria, but for some reason I didn't have the heart. I sensed that Joe Bullard knew perfectly well that he was presiding not over a miracle, but a quixotic trick of the light, but something told me that he recognised that the crosses had touched people in some way; that he knew that he had become the custodian of other people's faith. I'd grown to like him.

Joe shook me by the hand, and said, 'Hello, brother.'

I gestured towards the crosses. What thoughts do these inspire in you? I asked.

'It really helps me, because I've never seen nothing like it. I believe God believed in me; he entrusted me to open these doors to every individual, and that's why he put these crosses here. If I'd have seen this twenty years ago I'd have probably said I don't believe it; but we've seen them going on for a year; we've seen so many come through the doors, their lives changed; and we've seen a few of them get a little meaner too. But that's just natural.'

I walked back to the window. The cross shone brightly.

'It's something, ain't it?' said Joe.

I asked him again, what if somebody said the crosses were just a refraction of the light? What if somebody said they could prove it to you; would that change anything?

Joe looked at me, like he knew that I knew. 'No,' he said, 'that wouldn't change a thing.'

10

AN AUDIENCE
WITH THE GURU

In London, a journalist friend invited me to lunch, to meet her
mother, visiting from America. Francine was a born-again Christian,
the leader of her own church in Arkansas. She was a wiry woman
in her early sixties, bursting with energy, with a disarmingly direct
manner. No sooner had I sat down than she threw down the challenge:
what, she asked, do you believe? I liked her immediately, and just as
quickly knew that we would never agree on anything.

We ate rocket salad and soufflé, while Francine talked of the
turning point in her life. She had been born in France and raised,
in a rather desultory fashion, she suggested, as a Catholic. She
had married and given birth to a daughter – my journalist friend
– and then moved to London. But her marriage was unhappy. She
separated from her husband, her child grew. Francine found herself
alone and in a state of some confusion. Then, one day, on impulse,
she walked into a church close to Chelsea Embankment. She emerged
knowing that 'taking Christ into my heart was the only possibility of
salvation'. She had been 'born again'. It was a phrase that occasioned
a curious sinking feeling in my heart whenever I heard it.

It is an obligation on the born again to persuade others that they too
should be born again, and over lunch Francine turned the full force
of her evangelical persuasion on me. I felt flattered and assaulted.
She quoted scripture and creed; the Books of Jeremiah, Daniel and
Revelation. The End Time was upon us, she said. Love, kindness
and a good heart were not, in themselves, enough. Only those who
openly renewed their pledge to God and took Jesus into their heart
would be saved.

Where, I asked Francine, did this leave Mother Teresa – a Catholic
and not, to my knowledge, born again? Where did it leave the Dalai
Lama; where did it leave the untold millions who serve their own
god, or their fellow man, in their own way?

'If they are born again,' said Francine, 'they will be saved.'
And if not?

'They will go to hell.'

There was presently an evangelical revival occurring in a church in Pensacola, Florida, Francine said, which had been going on for the last two years without cessation, and which had drawn more than one million people to bear witness. I should go and see it, she said. 'And you can stay with my husband and me.'

'I wouldn't get out alive,' I joked.

'You're dead now,' she said. 'Only Jesus can make you alive.'

I received a package from Joan Anderson. She included a clipping from a newspaper in Virginia about more Crosses of Light appearing in a black Pentecostal church, the Tabernacle Church of God in Christ, in Norfolk. And there was news from Knoxville. A quorum of church members had voted out the Reverend Bullard, but he was refusing to leave the church. Meanwhile, his son David had visited a heart specialist and been told that he would not be needing the heart transplant after all. 'David,' Joan wrote, 'received the miracle he was praying for.' Joan herself had returned to her doctor for a final check on the condition of her tumour. The spot was still faintly visible on the MRI scan, but it was inactive. 'I feel really, really good,' she wrote. Buoyed by her recovery, Joan had been sending scores of people to the crosses in Knoxville. She had also started a correspondence with Jo Ann Noriega, the woman in whose house in California the first Cross of Light had appeared in 1988. Joan enclosed a copy of one of Jo Ann's letters. 'I want to share with you also that my husband Francisco in the past had a brain tumour just like yours,' Mrs Noriega wrote. 'He too was healed, Praise God!'

In *Share International* I read of new appearances by Maitreya, in Bogotá, Colombia; Iasi, Romania; and 'before 250 Catholic Christians' in Bolivia. 'Water,' the report read, 'was charged in the area beforehand.'

The message from Mr Creme's Master was customarily upbeat. 'Very soon, the world will see the Teacher ... Maitreya knows, already, those on whom He may count. Their numbers and their convictions are equal to the task. Within them shines the light of recognition and of hope, and their heart's ardour guarantees success.'

And Mr Creme had more news. 'A major American television network' had agreed to put their facilities at Maitreya's disposal whenever he saw fit. The light of expectation apparently burned on brightly.

I was commissioned to write a magazine article about a writer named Jini Fiennes, who died of cancer in 1993. A remarkable woman, she had overcome a childhood of parental indifference and abuse to shape a career as a writer. She had been born and raised as a Catholic, but in later life she had become a student of Tibetan Buddhism. Knowing that she was dying, she removed herself from her family – to prepare them and herself for her death – and spent the last year of her life living alone; at her bedside, *The Tibetan Book of Living and Dying* and a book of the teachings of Mother Meera. Not long before her death she embarked on a pilgrimage through France, to Santiago de Compostela in Spain, visiting Christian convents and shrines, but also a Tibetan Buddhist retreat. She wrote a book of her travels, *On Pilgrimage*, which is remarkable for its insight, its wisdom, her impatience with the soft-flab of self-pity, but above all for the way in which she goes beyond the architecture of religious belief, dogma and ritual, to find a unity and faith in the simple fact of love.

Bede Griffiths, the Benedictine monk who became a *sannyasin* and lived in a Hindu ashram in India, wrote: 'Ultimately a religion is tested by its capacity to awaken love in its followers, and, what is perhaps more difficult, to extend that love to all humanity.' One could go further. Ultimately the measure of every human being is their capacity to awaken the love in themselves and to extend it to their fellow man.

> In a loose, wide way [Jini Fiennes wrote in *On Pilgrimage*], I have never doubted love to be the central unifying force that in some mysterious way connects all nature, man and beast, insect and stone to the greater Cosmic good of God. Atman. Nirvana. Heaven. Some source of liberation. A sum of transposed live reality that is intelligent beyond intelligence and must remain a mystery.

At a dinner party given for her family and friends, I fell into conversation with a woman who had been at school with Jini. They had lost touch for almost thirty years, she said, but then made contact again, and discovered that their lives and interests had followed uncannily similar paths. She too had become interested in Buddhism, and she had read of Mother Meera, but she was actually a devotee of Sai Baba. She had read his teachings, felt drawn to him and persuaded her husband to go with her to India to take *darshan*. He too had become a follower. Neither had any doubts that Sai Baba was divine.

What, I asked, did Sai Baba mean in her life? I told her of my experiences at the ashram at Puttaparthi, and my reservations.

'You're too much the journalist,' she said. 'You should stop asking questions, and open your heart.'

It was what people kept telling me. I felt as I always did at such times, stranded between reason and a craving for faith, uncomfortable in the knowledge that while a spiritual belief may lead you to believe in anything, a materialist outlook on life will lead you to believe in nothing.

I received a package in the post, a number of slim booklets containing the teachings of an Indian swami named Mahaguru Yogi Arka – the Sun. The photographs showed a slim, handsome man in his early forties, with a dapper moustache and sleeked-back hair. I had never heard of him before, but the booklets suggested he travelled throughout Europe, Asia, Africa and North America, lecturing and teaching a form of meditation which he called Arka Dayan. The pamphlets provided contact addresses in Mysore, Harare, Ontario, London and Hong Kong.

One of the pamphlets listed 'A Few Assertions of Mahaguru Yogi Arka'.

> The highest philosophy of life is love and peace. At first man should believe and practise Humanism through which the truth of all religions can be comprehended . . . Suck up goodness from all angles and religions. Be kind to others. Discharge your duties sincerely and to the best of your belief and knowledge. Be not exhilarated in time of success and be not dejected in failures . . . If you have failed, do not feel that you have lost something. Please contemplate yourself and see, you have learnt something which will be a pillar for your success, and try again.

Shortly afterwards, I received a telephone call. Mahaguru was in England on a short lecture tour; would I like to meet him?

I was given the address of a private home where he was staying, in the North London suburb of Harrow. It was a short distance from the home of Mr Patel, where I had first seen the *vibhuti* appearing on the photographs of Sai Baba. Not far from the home of the other Mr Patel where, all those years ago, I had watched *King of Kings* and discussed prophecies. I rode the Metropolitan line for the umpteenth time wondering if there was a meaning in this. Perhaps the meaning was that I should move to North London.

It was another anonymous semi-detached house on a dreary side-street. I was shown into a room, where chairs had been arranged around the walls, and asked to wait. Books and cassettes were placed on a table. An Asian family came into the room – mother and father and two small children – nodded and smiled and took their seats.

At length, a woman popped her head around the door and beckoned me to follow her. She opened the door to a back room, silently waved me inside and closed the door behind me. The room was carpeted, but otherwise devoid of furnishings. The guru was seated on the floor, cross-legged, his eyes closed in meditation. Sitar music issued from a portable tape-recorder in the corner of the room. Incense perfumed the air. He did not appear to have noticed my entrance. I stood by the door unsure quite what to do. After some minutes he opened his eyes, and gestured to the space on the carpet in front of him. He closed his eyes again. I sat down in front of him. He wore an immaculate white silk robe, an ivory silk turban knotted around his head. His fingers were carefully manicured, and on his left hand he wore a glittering diamond ring. He opened his eyes, and they widened momentarily, as if he was surprised to see me sitting there. He smiled, revealing a set of brilliant, gleaming teeth. I said hello.

He nodded slightly. 'You have questions?'

I did have questions, but for a moment, they had completely deserted me. What do people usually ask of you? I said.

He thought about this. 'Imagine you are standing in front of an ocean,' he said. 'What do you want from the ocean?'

I answered, 'Peace.' It was the first thing that came into my mind.

He nodded. 'You see the ocean as something that can give you peace. Somebody else looks at the ocean and he wants fish to eat; another man thinks perhaps there is oil there that will make him rich. People want different things, and the ocean can give them everything. So you see, it depends what people want. If you want peace, then peace will come.'

He smiled. It really was a dazzling smile, ivory-white, almost sparkling, like a cartoon of dental maintenance.

I explained that I was writing a book; what advice could he give?

'You are like the moon. You must take the light from the sun and reflect it so that it is available for everyone.'

This struck me as an extremely politic, not to say poetic, answer. Then I remembered what 'Arka' meant. Did he mean I should be the moon to his sun? I was not sure I wanted that.

There are many gurus, I said; how does one know which guru to trust?

He smiled. 'I don't call it guru to begin with. Any spiritual person who imposes his teachings on someone, he is not reliable. Any spiritual person who makes any attempt to convert people and hold them, he is not a spiritual master. Any spiritual person who asks someone to trust him, he is not reliable. If any guru says, I am the only guru for you, then he is still ignorant. When you go to school, you want professors of chemistry, of zoology, of mathematics – they all contribute and then you graduate. There may be thousands of masters. Anyone who claims, I am the only one! The only representative of the higher consciousness – again, this is not right. How can he be the only one!

'If only one or two persons were going to be incarnations of the higher consciousness it means that consciousness is a politician. If that is the case I do not wish to follow the spiritual path; rather I become a sceptic, become voluptuous and just vegetate. The higher consciousness is like mother. We are all children from the same mother. Now children, when they are small, are very loving, very understanding. But as they grow they start fighting and they forget they are all from the same mother. But then some become aware. They start to ask, what is life? What is this mother that we all come from? And they wish to go back to her. And so they look very seriously, but they don't find answers, no matter how many books they read, no matter who they talk to. And so they walk and search, travel and search. But the spiritual truth can only be searched for internally and silently.

'Only a few can apply themselves to find the one answer to all the million burning ambiguous questions in their mind. And they close their eyes; they sit in one place and just watch the world, watch their mind, watch the activity of nature. Just watch, watch, watch. And so many great thoughts flash in their mind, and there is no confusion at all. Everything seems to be precise and in order, and is full of meaning in the manifestation of this cosmos. There are no complaints. There is only peace.' He closed his eyes and fell silent, as if offering an illustration of his point.

As a young man, he continued, he was profoundly inquisitive about life, 'And I wanted eternity – something that stays for ever.' He paused. 'Everything changes. First of all, our existence itself is changing; every day we grow older, and then one day we blindly depart the world without giving notice to anyone. Why is that? I wanted something perpetual, everlasting. And why is there so much greed and lust and covetousness? I wanted to know the law of constancy, so that ultimately you could get back to your own home, which is the heart.

'The heart and the mind; both have to co-operate to realise consciousness. So when the questioner realises that everything is in himself, answer is not necessary. And then, of course, there must be love.'

And how would he describe love? I asked.

'Love is the force of attraction. It is love that keeps the planets in place. Scientists call it gravity.'

He talked about the need for detachment; how we are prisoners of our desire, for material possessions, for power, prestige, for other people. 'Look at this ring. It is beautiful, no?' He slipped the diamond off his finger and threw it on to the carpet in front of him. 'If I want it, I have to reach and reach for it.' He stretched out his arm.

'But why not leave it there?' he said. 'Does it matter whether I have it? No, if someone wants it, if they really want it, they can have it. It's a beautiful ring, and its existence in the world is enough.' He scooped the ring into his hand and slipped it back on to his finger.

I shook his hand, and rose to leave.

'If ever you have a question to ask, just ask me. I will hear you,' he said. 'Sometime your urge to ask questions will stop.'

So, I said, if I want to find?

'Stop searching,' he said.

11

SAMMY DOESN'T LIVE HERE

The train from London to Carlisle was crowded with football supporters, returning home, jubilant in the wake of their team's victory in a cup competition, and I fell into conversation with a ruddy-faced man sitting opposite me, wearing a green baseball cap emblazoned with the legend 'Carlisle on the Road to Wembley' and nursing a can of lager. We talked about football, the price of beer in London versus the price of beer in Carlisle, the passing countryside.

I remembered that the chairman of Carlisle United had recently been in the newspapers, talking about having seen a UFO.

'Oh aye,' said the man, 'but he's put a lot of money into the club, I'll say that for him.'

It was a long journey. We talked about work, his sister who was a heroin addict, our respective destinations. I told him that I was on my way to Samye Ling, the Tibetan Buddhist centre, at Eskdalemuir. He knew it. He had helped to install a pipe system on the nearby road, he said, to prevent flooding.

What went on there, he wanted to know.

I told him what little I knew. It was a community of monks, nuns and lay people. There was a temple, which was said to be magnificent. It was quiet.

And what, he asked, do they believe in?

Reincarnation, I said.

'Oh aye?' He fell silent.

I told him of my visit to Sera monastery in India, and of Lama Osel, the eleven-year-old Spanish boy believed to be a reincarnation of Lama Yeshe.

He swallowed his lager. 'Well, if they believe that,' he said equably, 'it doesn't do any harm, does it?'

It was a reminder that most people would regard most of the

things that had been preoccupying me over the past eighteen months as at best slightly peculiar, and at worst insane.

'If it's peace and quiet you're after, you'll find it there,' said the taxi-driver who took me from Lockerbie. 'It's a mile and a half to the nearest pub. For years after they first moved in, I thought Samye Ling was the name of the man who ran it. "Is Sammy in today?"' He chuckled. 'He never was, of course.'

Samye Ling means 'place beyond thought'. It is named after Samye, the first Buddhist monastery established in Tibet, in the eighth century. Samye Ling was founded as a Tibetan Buddhist centre in 1968 by Chogyam Trungpa and Akong Tulku Rinpoche. When Trungpa left for America in the early Seventies, Akong Tulku Rinpoche took over the development of Samye Ling. He now spends much of his time abroad, and his brother Lama Yeshe Losal is now Abbot. In the past, despite the presence of some Tibetan monks, Samye Ling was primarily occupied by lay people. In recent years, however, Lama Yeshe has developed the centre's monastic life, and there are now some forty monks and nuns living there. Many of these have taken orders under a novel system of probation devised by Lama Yeshe, in response to the large numbers of young people expressing a desire for the monastic life. The probationary period lasts for a year. On average, a third drop out before the year's end; a third stay to the end of their probationary period and then leave; and the remaining third stay on.

Brightly coloured prayer-flags flutter in the trees lining the drive. There is a large, rambling, not particularly attractive stone house, which houses the offices, dormitories, dining room and kitchens. There are workshops, vegetable gardens, blocks to accommodate visitors, and a magnificent temple, three-tiered with a pagoda roof, its fascia picked out in dazzling blues, reds and yellows. A river runs through it. Peacocks strut across the courtyard. A sign at the gate announces that it is approved by the Scottish Tourist Board as a visitors' attraction.

From my room I can hear the cawing of the peacocks. The sky is slate grey and sullen with the threat of rain as I walk across the courtyard to the temple. The largest peacock is cawing from the temple roof, breast of lapis lazuli, stirring its feathers, as if a part of the temple decoration which has sprung to life. The Tibetan Buddhist aesthetic is not for puritanical or minimalist sensibilities. The ritual, the finery, the colours – the symbolism – all are intoxicating in their richness and vividness. It is the Buddhist equivalent of high church.

The temple walls are hung with embroidered *tankas* and paintings; blue-faced deities and dragon-protectors, haloed Buddhas and bodhisattvas floating on cushions against surreal landscapes of fields and mountains and clouds. Images of dragons and peacocks adorn the ceilings. The walls shimmer with colour. Inside an elaborate lacquered case, a prayer wheel spins endlessly.

On a shrine sits a 9-foot Buddha, of the deepest, most lustrous gold, serenely indifferent to the writhing serpent carvings on either side. The Buddha is flanked by gold cases, filling the height and breadth of the wall, containing images of the 1,000 Buddhas of this *kalpa*, or aeon of time – that is, Buddhas who will attain enlightenment without the benefit of tradition or teaching, but by their own endeavours, thereby perpetuating the teachings in times of darkness. Shakyamuni, or Guatama Buddha, was the fourth. Maitreya will be the fifth.

When, I asked a monk in passing, is Maitreya expected?

He glanced at his watch and smiled. 'Not yet . . .'

The genius of the Buddha was to recognise the basis of change and becoming. Through meditation he came to the great realisation: 'All is passing, all is sorrow, all is unreal.' Everything is impermanent, subject to change, decay and ultimate annihilation. There is no lasting satisfaction to be found in clinging to sensory pleasures, for they are bound to pass; they have no basis in reality. But he recognised too that behind this change there was something permanent, an unchanging reality that gives rise to all forms, all thoughts. This he called *nirvana*. In this state of enlightenment, the pangs of desire, of regret and sorrow dissolve, and the selfless qualities of kindness, compassion, love and serenity blossom forth. This was a profound psychological insight with a spiritual purpose, to come to understand, and to conquer, suffering; to make peace with the way things are. Thus, the Buddha is venerated not as a god, nor as an emissary of god, but as a man who has unlocked a fundamental truth of human existence, and in doing so given other men the teaching by which they can free themselves from suffering and unhappiness.

Once, in Bali, I struck up a conversation with a man working in the fields. The Balinese are extremely hospitable people; he invited me to his home, to meet his family. I followed him across the fields, along a path that led through a thicket of trees to emerge eventually at the gate of his house. It was a traditional Balinese dwelling, single-storey rooms arranged around an open courtyard, with an adjoining courtyard in which stood a number of religious shrines. Dogs and chickens scuttled between our feet; two young children sat rapt in front of a battered black-and-white television set, a Japanese cartoon-show barely discernible through the blizzard on the screen. My new friend made tea; we pantomimed a conversation, and then he said he had a gift for me. He vanished into one of the rooms, reappearing with a box of wooden carvings. They were made, he said, by his brother. He reached for a small carving of a turtle and passed it to me.

I thanked him. But I had nothing to give him in return; perhaps, I pantomimed, I might buy another carving? Yes, yes. He nodded happily. The Balinese are Hindu, but amongst the carvings was an exquisite Buddha, perhaps four inches high, in dark, polished wood, the finely carved face suggesting blissful serenity. I pulled out some notes and pressed them on my friend. His expression suggested it was far more than anyone in their right mind would pay. He reached back into the box and produced another turtle and pressed it on me.

In my hotel room, I took the gifts out of my bag and laid them randomly on the dressing table. The next morning I returned from breakfast to find that the houseboy had been in my room. Seeing my carvings he had rearranged them: the Buddha facing outwards, the two turtles turned towards him in positions of supplication. He had turned my gifts into a shrine.

Now I unpack the Buddha from my bag, and I too make a shrine, with fir cones and flat grey stones collected from the river bank, thinking as I do so: I would not have done this a year ago. I do not feel comfortable with pictures of living Hindu avatars, or images of a redeemer who died on the cross for my sins. But, for some reason, I feel comfortable with this small carving, symbolising purity of thought, and compassion.

Dawn is showing through the crack of the curtains. I fall out of bed, pull my pillow to the floor, sit cross-legged, and watch my breath. The last shadows of my waking dream recede. I take stock in my mind of where I am, what I am doing. I push the thought to one side and concentrate on my breath. Thoughts pop into my mind unbidden. Tea. Breakfast. Banality upon banality. Watch the breath. My legs begin to ache. A peacock cries outside. Some of the peacocks are white. You see white peacocks, somebody said yesterday, and you think you've been using John Major's lavatory. A reference to a writer who has admitted to smoking heroin in the loo on the ex-Prime Minister's campaign jet. He was fired by his newspaper, but was quickly snapped up by another one. Newspapers. My career. Where *is* my career right now? A twinge of anxiety, followed by a twinge of self-satisfaction – now *that* was a good piece – as my mind reaches quickly for an antidote. Watch the thought arise, see that it has no reality; it is only a thought. Let it pass. The thought comes that so much thought is merely memory, recycling the events and reflections of yesterday, and the day before yesterday. Reflecting on what is past, anticipating what is to come. Watch the breath. A train of thought, each thought coupled to the next; they appear from nowhere and go to nowhere. But what is the coupling? What is the rail? Now my legs are *really* aching. Don't think about it. Watch the breath. They're still aching.

> The body itself is not an obstacle when we accept it, understand and know it. Having been born, it grows up, gets old and dies. That's what it's supposed to do. It is the way it is.

Where have I read that? Ajahn Sumedho, an American Buddhist monk. He joined a community of forest monks in Thailand, then came to Britain to found a forest monastery. He lived with three other monks in a house in Hampstead, which is not a forest, but at least has a heath. Through a chance meeting with a jogger, the monks were given a forest in Sussex, where they established the first forest monastery in the West. If you are a forest monk, a forest will be provided.

Ajahn Sumedho also says this:

> Wisdom is something that's already there. It's not something you'll get, it's something you'll use. It's wrong to think you're going to become wise by meditating. Meditation is a way of learning how to use the wisdom that's already there . . . Wisdom is not something you don't have, but it's something that maybe you don't always use, or aren't always aware of.

Watch the breath. God, my legs hurt. I open my eyes. Twenty minutes. Is that all? I shave and it is time for breakfast.

We are, as I now remember Erica saying of Puttaparthi, a motley crew, but a different kind of motley crew. There are the monks and nuns. The lay residents, who stamp into the dining room in Wellington boots, muddy from the vegetable gardens or the building site that will be another visitors' block (it is a paradox that Buddhist centres and monasteries, ostensibly oases of peace and calm, should actually resound to the clatter of brick-laying and earth-movers – a symptom of the growing numbers in pursuit of peace and calm). There are students of Buddhism, people drifting through, a young boy with a wan, troubled face who speaks to no one; an elderly lady who has pitched her tent in an adjoining field.

For the first two days I have thought it cool, almost unfriendly; people have smiled, but nobody has introduced themselves or made any effort to show me the ropes; then, I realise, people are left alone; nothing is forced. If you want something, you have only to ask. By the end of my stay I will be aware of an incredible warmth. People have come to meditate, to *decompress*. Some seem troubled, or to have been troubled, but filled with resolve to be troubled no longer. Some talk of joining the community, of becoming monks and nuns themselves. A woman tells me she has come here intending to ask Lama Yeshe if she can take orders. She is in her mid-forties and has the appearance of life having treated her unkindly. She will see Lama Yeshe tomorrow, she says. She has been thinking about what she will tell him. 'I'll say, I want there to be one less harmful person in the world.'

In the dining room, some people look almost catatonic from contemplation, unable to muster so much as a wan smile, lost in their thoughts. Not the young monks and nuns, who chatter amiably among themselves by the toaster. I am astonished at how young most of these monks and nuns are; some look little more than teenagers, but their shaven heads, their bandages of maroon robes, sweaters and track-suit bottoms, their bright-eyed, alert expressions, obliterate any outward traces of personal history. It is impossible to surmise, to leap to the instant preconceptions we hold in the outside world: it's a punk, a hippie, a yuppie, rich, poor, working, unemployed. A couple, I notice, have tattoos on their hands and arms, shadows of some darker past life.

'I admire them,' says an older monk, seated next to me at lunch. 'You see their pals come up to see them – dreadlocks, dirty clothes, people you'd assume were smoking crack or dropping acid, and you can see where some of these kids have come from. It takes courage to do what they're doing and put all that behind 'em.'

His name is Nadan. He is around sixty, with tightly cropped greying hair, a puckish face, a glint of mischief in his eye. He has been at Samye Ling for more than twenty years, he says.

And before that? I ask.

'Chasing women, getting drunk . . .' He was once a croupier and casino manager, he said. In fact, he had the distinction of being the first person to open a gambling casino in Nepal.

In Nepal? His eyes glinted back at me. Was he pulling my leg?

'No, straight up. I was invited by the King to set it up.' It was a way, he said, of fleecing rich Indians. Ironically, perhaps, it had the effect of first introducing Nadan to Buddhism. Back in Britain, he visited Samye Ling. 'The Abbot gave me some advice about what to do with my life. I went away for a year and followed it. And it worked. So I came back . . .'

Nadan has recently emerged from a three-year retreat (actually, three years, three months and three days), taken by twenty-eight men and sixteen women.

How was it? I ask.

He thinks about this. 'Intense.'

It is obviously an impossible question to answer. I want to ask, what is the gain, suspecting, even as I say it, that 'gain' is the wrong word.

'No, no,' says Nadan. 'It's the right word. You could say "investment". If you believe that life does not end with death, it's an investment in your future.'

The retreat centre is now closed for refurbishment, but Nadan offers to show it to me. We drive the half-mile in a battered yellow van, paint tins rattling in the back, up a slip-road with a 'Private: No Entry' sign. The centre is comprised of two accommodation blocks, one for men, one for women. At the beginning of the retreat, the door to the outside world is locked. Men and women live in close, largely silent, community, the days spent almost entirely in solitary meditation. Much of this time is spent in a meditation box – a piece of wooden furniture half the length of a bed, with a small lectern to accommodate prayer sheets, in which the retreatant meditates and sleeps. Nadan clambers into the box to show me. With his robe and puckish face he looks like a puppet folded away for the night, ready to spring to life next morning.

Outside, huge, brightly coloured prayer flags flutter from the trees. There is a small garden, landscaped with rocks and gravel. In 1976, the XVIth Karmapa, the head of the Kagyu lineage, visited Samye Ling. (He is now dead; his reincarnation, the XVII, is living in Tibet.) The retreat centre was then at the planning stage, and the Karmapa offered his blessing, as he did so placing his foot against a huge piece of granite, about to be laid in the garden. It was only later that it was noticed that a footprint had appeared in the rock. It can be seen there now, distinct, unmistakable.

In the kitchen, beside the sink and draining board, stuck to the industrial-sized drying and sterilising unit, is a notice – in truth, a parable. There was a man looking for enlightenment, it reads; each day he waited for his teacher to arrive, to no avail. In the corridor was a mop and bucket. After some months he complained to his friend, 'Some person has left this here. It's never been put away in all the time I've been here.' Many years later, he was still waiting for his teacher to arrive, and still walking past his first teaching.

I have never seen so many people so ready to do the washing-up as I see here. On the door of the guest-block is a notice asking you to remove your shoes as you enter, but still the vestibule quickly accumulates dust and dirt. I think: There must be a cleaning rota. Someone else will do it. After two days I finally pick up the broom myself.

At breakfast I overhear two nuns at the next table. They are discussing the film, *The English Patient*. 'I'd love to see it,' says one. I wonder silently, is that allowed? I share the washing-up with a monk. He came here ten years ago, he says, on the advice of a lama. 'Because I was dying . . .'

Literally dying? I ask.

'Yup. I was given a year to live. I wasn't a monk then, but I became one.' He thought for a moment. 'Perhaps I was dying to be a monk.'

There is a small hill near by, with a copse of trees at the top of it, strung with prayer flags, visible from the road below. I hike up through the wet grass, and become aware of the sound of wind chimes, sounding in the branches above me. In the middle of the copse, a small shrine has been created. Around the Buddha, people have left offerings: shells, coins, candles, fir cones, bells, a china cat, a piece of coral, a phial of Body Shop perfume, a Star Wars badge. A child's windmill, made of silver paper, has been stuck in the earth beside the shrine and spins crazily in the wind.

I make friends with an elderly lady, Sally. We acknowledge each other one morning, walking along the river, and exchange passing conversation about the bird-life, about which, it transpires, neither of us knows anything at all.

We find ourselves seated together at lunch.

Is she a Buddhist? I ask.

'I suppose I am. But I don't like to think of myself as an "ist" at all.'

No clubs or labels, I say.

'Too much the stubborn individualist, I'm afraid.'

We talk about books, lamas, the Buddhist teachings, about the idea of non-attachment. 'I like what T.S Eliot said,' she says. 'Neither clutching nor clinging.' She spooned up some rice. 'I think it was Eliot anyway. It's just being in the moment, isn't it? Not clinging to the past, or clutching for something in the future. Just the moment.' She sighed. 'If only . . .'

How, I wonder, does one find faith?

She smiles. 'I think it becomes easier as one gets older. But I don't know if faith is the right word. It's more a recognition of the way things are and trusting to that, knowing that it's right.'

Acceptance, then?

'Hmmm. I don't much like the word acceptance. I agree with Dylan Thomas, "Rage against the dying of the light . . ." Acceptance sounds too supine to me, as if you're giving up. It's the wrong word. We'll have to find the right one.'

I see her the next day at lunch. 'Equanimity,' she says. 'That's the word I was looking for. Equanimity.' A good word.

Later that same day, I meet the elderly lady who lives in the tent, sitting on a log by the river, reading an Isaac Asimov novel. 'No, no, it's all right. You're not interrupting. I've read it four times already . . .'

She is a teacher by profession. Having spent many years teaching in schools in India, she has spent the past four years looking after her aged and infirm mother. 'They call it "care in the community . . ."' Now her mother is in a nursing home. 'I've come for some peace and quiet.'

I ask her too, are you a Buddhist?

'In a way . . . And a Christian, a Hindu, a Muslim, and a Pagan . . . Do you know the story of the three blind men and the elephant?' She tells it to me. Three blind men come upon an elephant in the forest. So this is an elephant, says one, grasping its tail – it's long and thin; no, says the second man, grasping its trunk – it's long, fat and open at the end. No, no, says the third man, grasping its leg – it's just like a tree trunk. 'You see?' she says with a chuckle. 'They were all right in a way, but all of them were seeing only part of the picture.'

We talk about Samye Ling. How peaceful, serene, friendly. 'You're falling under its spell,' she says. 'Have you been to Findhorn? Very different. All they talk about is fairies and goblins – flower fairies and vegetable fairies. They all believe in that. And we all have a Red Indian shaman protector – *apparently*.' She pauses to allow me to appreciate the sardonic note in her voice, but she is laughing. 'Oh, they're all right really. Hearts in the right place and so on. You mustn't mind me. I'm just a heretic at heart. But I do like the Dalai Lama, I'll say that. And he was very kind to me.'

She tells me the story. She was in Dharamsala, some years ago, and there was a party down in the valley, below the main temple and the Dalai Lama's residence. A hippie party: 'Lots of mushrooms in the omelette – if you get my meaning,' and bottles of bonded Scotch. 'Anyway, somewhat worse for wear, I drag myself back up the hill, and the snow is coming down; I find myself outside the temple, and I do the sensible thing, despite my condition, which is to find a doorway and curl up in it. And the next thing I know, the door is opened and I fall through it, and there are two Indian soldiers, pointing their bayonets at me. And standing behind them is a monk in a red robe, and I think: *I know you*. He's laughing fit to burst at the sight of this stoned old woman in his temple. And he reaches into the folds of his robe and produces some sweeties and a biscuit and gives them to me, with this wonderful smile on his face. That's what I'll always remember. That smile.' She pauses, lost in thought. 'I'd like to see the Pope do that.'

I walk along the river, stumbling over tufts and hillocks of grass, scrambling over the stones, lost in my thoughts. Two mallards swoop overhead, following the line of the river as if guided by radar. I have a book in my bag, the Portuguese poet, Pessoa.

> If only . . . if only I could be someone able to see all this as if he had no relation with it than that of seeing it, someone able to observe everything as if he were an adult traveller newly arrived today on the surface of life! If only one had not learned, from birth onwards, to give certain accepted meanings to everything, but instead was able to see the meaning inherent in each thing rather than that imposed on it from without. If only one could know the human reality of the woman selling fish and go beyond just labelling her a fishwife and the known fact that she exists and sells fish. If only one could see the policeman as God sees him. If only one could notice everything for the first time, not apocalyptically, as if they were revelations of a Mystery, but directly as flowerings of Reality.

A low-flying Phantom jet thunders overhead, making me jump. The sheep in the field on the other side of the river graze on, undisturbed.

I sit in my room, eyes closed, legs crossed, watching my breath. I wonder, what will the weather be like today? I'm hungry. I'm thirsty. Watch the cravings pass. Watch the breath. Flickerings of memory. Watch the breath. As the thoughts arise I try to glimpse between them to the very seat of thought – the light (this is how I imagine it) that illuminates the flickering images passing across my mind. But this too is only a thought.

But watching, I see how thoughts arise and fall away, how they have no permanence. So feelings come and go. So everything comes and goes. Negativity, self-pity, despair. We can choose to cling to them; or to let them go. We have choice. Watch the breath. These thoughts, they are flickering images, lines of type on a page which is the mind. But now my interior vision fragments in shards of light and shade; an image like a cell seen under a microscope begins to form, turning into a foetal shape, which in turn becomes a small patch of purple, as if seen through a tear in a cloth. The purple spreads, filling my interior vision until it is a plane of solid, vivid colour. I watch it for what seems like an age, lost in it. And as quickly as it came, it vanishes.

Watch the breath.

I have the most vivid dreams. A friend climbing into a car and driving away, with me scrambling to catch up, and being left standing there. I am standing at the top of a long, wide, sloping roof, like a ski slope, which ends at a drop of hundreds of feet: people are sliding down the roof, whooping with joy, then clambering back up to do it again. They call out to me to try it too, but I am terrified of losing control, of falling and plummeting to certain death. Eventually, I summon the nerve to do it. I slide down, feeling utterly exhilarated, and stop safely on the edge. I climb up to do it again.

Last night, I was talking to a young monk about India, gurus and swamis. He has friends, he tells me, who are followers of Sai Baba. 'They tell me amazing things, y'know? Sai Baba appeared to one of them in a house in Holland Park. It's kind of interesting . . .'

If you go to India, I say, perhaps you should go and see him.

'I don't think so.' He paused. 'I've found it, y'know?'

I realise, I have never dreamed of Sai Baba.

I am having trouble with the idea of non-attachment. I understand that by cultivating non-attachment one can ease the sting of pain and fear and anxiety, put them, as it were, at one remove, recognise them for the illusions they are. But isn't non-attachment equally a deterrent to pleasure? Isn't pain, or boredom, or dissatisfaction required to throw pleasure into relief – isn't much of what we regard as pleasure simply the cessation, however temporary, of pain or boredom or dissatisfaction? For example, today I was walking. After a mile, my legs began to grow tired and my feet to ache. I stopped to rest. And immediately just *sitting* and feeling the life flood back into my feet and legs was the most pleasurable thing I could imagine. But it was pleasure determined by the discomfort I was feeling moments earlier. And so I sat and basked in the feeling of relief, but a few minutes later I grew bored with just sitting, and wanted to walk again and so that in itself became pleasurable. Can there be such a thing as pleasure without its opposite? The things that we regard as pleasurable – good food, fine wine, enlivening conversation, time spent with family and friends – all lose their savour if we have too much of them. We need the sting of discomfort, of ennui, of loss, to appreciate them.

I suppose what I fear is that by cultivating detachment – by seeing everything with the same equanimity – I would lose the capacity to *feel*. I have an idea that it would somehow cut me off from the most vivid emotions of life. But then again, perhaps it would make those emotions even more vivid for being experienced directly and in the moment, neither clutching nor clinging.

If I changed, would I miss the person I was – the person I am, sometimes confused, sometimes happy, sometimes sad, angry, acquisitive, vain, always asking questions, and never finding the right answers? But this is only an idea, for, of course, I have not learned detachment. I have only the frustration of trying to formulate my thoughts, a pain at the top of my spine from sitting awkwardly, a sense of anticipation in the back of my mind that I will soon take a walk, which will be a pleasure.

On the walk, I think of the things that make life worthwhile. My family, my friends. My work. Words. Music. Bitter-sweet literature. Argument. Loving and being loved. Wise love. This is everything. I think: I do not believe in a Redeemer. We must save ourselves, and have faith in that belief. Do I believe in a Creator? I believe in the Creation. The great, un-nameable force, the Reality that lies behind that which we think of as reality, and which underpins all thought, all forms, all beings – and of which everything is a part. And this, surely, is love. It is the thing beyond self, for true love is selflessness. In this we are all mirrors of each other. One cannot be happy if others are unhappy. One may be indifferent, inured, preoccupied with the self. But never happy.

Happiness does not lie in separation from others, but in unity with them. Love is timeless and endless. Love goes on, and somehow, we go on as part of it, sometimes glimpsing it, sometimes blind to it, warm in its flame, cold and alone when we turn our backs to it. Ultimately, only love can conquer despair. Only love makes us whole.

There is soup and rice at six, and at seven Amitabha and Chenrezig prayers in the temple. I settle myself on the square solid velvet cushion, among a handful of people. The monks and nuns ranged along the sides of the temple on their raised platforms chant, their prayer sheets rustling on their lecterns. They are giving offerings to the Buddha and the protectors, praying to the *bodhisattvas* to maintain their vow to help all beings. The prayers are interspersed with the ringing of bells and cymbals, the thunder of drums.

The thousand and one Buddhas gaze down impassively. I close my eyes.

There is a Buddhist practice called the *metta bhavana*. *Metta* means 'friendliness'; *bhavana*, 'development'. Together, it means to develop strong feelings of goodwill towards everyone and everything we encounter. It is a meditation. Then you begin by dwelling upon the positive feelings you have for yourself, your positive qualities. You say inwardly: May I be happy, may I be well. You let the phrase resonate and uplift you. You single out a good friend. You let the flow of your inner friendliness embrace them – May you be happy, may you be well. Then a neutral person – someone you see at the newsagent's, or the bus stop. Then an enemy, someone with whom you strongly disagree, or feel antagonistic towards – May you be happy, may you be well. You bring all four people together in the same wish for happiness, then people in the vicinity, the town, the county, the country . . .

I try to focus on this, over and over – friends, work colleagues, ticket collectors, the people I love, the people I admire, the people I have hurt, deliberately or unthinkingly, those to whom I feel utterly indifferent, and those who I fear, who I feel have slighted me, whose talents or accomplishments I secretly envy. A procession through my mind, both shaming and warming. I open my eyes and find myself transfixed by the shining wall of Buddhas, seemingly dancing in the shimmering light. The prayers have stopped. There is only the barely perceptible sound of breath, rising and falling, a faint note of birdsong in the gathering dusk.

I leave the temple feeling heady, exhilarated. The light is fading. I find myself walking, effortlessly, as if my feet are hardly touching the ground. I strike out along the road, a fine drizzle blowing in my face. There is a turning where the woods fall away and I look down into a valley, flanked on either side by gently rising hills. In the distance, the river is a silver thread meandering between trees. Sheep, like cotton buds, graze on a green baize field. A crow tracks across the sky like a shadow passing over the billowing grey clouds. In the temple, the monks are praying for the world. I think: What is joy? Joy is non-attachment. Joy is not to be found in remembering the past, nor in anticipating the future. Joy is to be found only in the moment. And in that moment, I feel giddy with joy, knowing, even as I feel it, that this too will pass.

BIBLIOGRAPHY

Adilakshmi, *The Mother* (Dornburg-Thalheim, Mother Meera, 1995)

Aurobindo, Sri, *The Mother* (Pondicherry, Sri Aurobindo Society)

Batchelor, Stephen, *The Awakening of the West* (Berkeley, California, Parallax Press, 1994)

Bailey, Alice, *The Unfinished Autobiography* (New York, Lucis Publishing, 1951)

Beyerstein, Dale, *Sai Baba's Miracles: An Overview* (British Columbia Skeptics, Internet document)

Blavatsky, Madame Helena, *The Secret Doctrine* (London, Theosophical Publishing Co., 1888)

Bradley, Ian, ed., *The Penguin Book of Hymns* (London, Viking, 1989)

Butterfield, Stephen, *The Double Mirror* (Berkeley, California, North Atlantic Books, 1994)

Caldwell, Daniel, *K. Paul Johnson's House of Cards* (Tucson, privately published, 1986)

Cooper, John, *Did Madame Blavatsky Predict a World Teacher?* (Sydney, discussion document)

Connolly, Cyril, *Palinurus' The Unquiet Grave* (London, Horizon, 1947)

Cranston, Sylvia, *The Extraordinary Life and Influence of Helena Blavatsky: Founder of the Modern Theosophical Movement* (New York, Tarcher/Putnam, 1993)

Creme, Benjamin, *The Reappearance of the Christ and the Masters of Wisdom* (London, Tara Press, 1980)

Feuerstein, Georg, *Holy Madness* (London, Arkana Books, 1992)

H.H. Dalai Lama, *Awakening the Mind, Lightening the Heart* (London, Thorsons, 1997)

H.H. Dalai Lama, *Freedom in Exile* (London, Hodder & Stoughton, 1990)

Dowman, Keith, *The Sacred Life of Tibet* (London, Thorsons, 1997)

Harvey, Andrew, *The Return of the Mother* (Berkeley, California, Frog, 1995)

Harvey, Andrew, *Hidden Journey: A Spiritual Awakening* (London, Bloomsbury, 1991)

Huxley, Aldous, *The Perennial Philosophy* (London, Chatto & Windus, 1946)

Huxley, Aldous, *The Doors of Perception* (London, Chatto & Windus, 1954)

Gardner, E.L., *There Is No Religion Higher Than Truth: Developments in the Theosophical Society* (London, Theosophical Publishing House, 1963)

Greenfield, Robert, *The Spiritual Supermarket* (New York, Saturday Press, 1975)

Griffiths, Bede, *Universal Wisdom* (London, HarperCollins, 1994)

Godwin, Jocelyn, *The Hermetic Brotherhood of Luxor* (New York, Weiser, 1996)

Johnsen, Linda, *Daughters of the Goddess: The Women Saints of India* (St Paul, Minnesota, Yes International Publishers, 1994)

Johnson, K. Paul, *The Masters Revealed: Madame Blavatsky and the Myth of the Great White Lodge* (New York, State University of New York Press, 1994)

Journal of the Society for Psychical Research, April 1986, London

Indian Chelas on the Masters (Adyar, Adyar Lodge, The Theosophical Society,